MEDIA EFFECTS AND SOCIETY

Grounded in theoretical principle, *Media Effects and Society* helps students make the connection between mass media and the impact they have on society as a whole. The text also explores how the relationship individuals have with media is created, therefore helping them alleviate its harmful effects, and enhance the positive ones. The range of media effects addressed herein includes news diffusion, learning from the mass media, socialization of children and adolescents, influences on public opinion and voting, and violent and sexually explicit media content. The text examines the research done in these areas and discusses it in a thorough and accessible manner. It also presents a variety of theoretical approaches to understanding media effects, including psychological and content-based theories. In addition, it demonstrates how theories can guide future research into the effects of newer mass communication technologies.

New for the second edition are a new chapter on effects of entertainment, text boxes with examples in each chapter, discussion of new technology effects integrated throughout the chapters, expanded pedagogy, and updates to theory and research throughout. These features enhance the already in-depth analysis *Media Effects and Society* provides.

Elizabeth M. Perse (Ph.D., Kent State University, 1987) is Professor and Chair of the Department of Communication at the University of Delaware, Newark.

Jennifer L. Lambe (Ph.D., University of Minnesota, 2000) is an Associate Professor in the Communication Department, and a Senior Fellow of the Center for Political Communication at the University of Delaware.

Routledge Communication Series
Jennings Bryant/Dolf Zillmann, Series Editors

Selected titles include:

- Preiss et al.: *Mass Media Effects Research: Advances Through Meta-Analysis*
- Gayle et al.: *Classroom Communication and Instructional Processes: Advances Through Meta-Analysis*
- Allen et al.: *Interpersonal Communication Research: Advances Through Meta-Analysis*
- Burrell et al.: *Managing Interpersonal Communication: Advances Through Meta-Analysis*
- Knobloch-Westerwick: *Choice and Preference in Media Use*
- Ki et al.: *Public Relations As Relationship Management: A Relational Approach To the Study and Practice of Public Relations, 2nd Edition*
- Austin et al.: *Strategic Public Relations Management: Planning and Managing Effective Communication Campaigns, 3rd Edition*
- Hollifield et al.: *Media Management: A Casebook Approach, 5th Edition*

MEDIA EFFECTS AND SOCIETY

Elizabeth M. Perse
Jennifer L. Lambe

Routledge
Taylor & Francis Group

NEW YORK AND LONDON

Second Edition published 2017
by Routledge
711 Third Avenue, New York, NY 10017

and by Routledge
2 Park Square, Milton Park, Abingdon, Oxon, OX14 4RN

Routledge is an imprint of the Taylor & Francis Group, an informa business

First edition published by Routledge 2001

Library of Congress Cataloging-in-Publication Data
Names: Perse, Elizabeth M., author. | Lambe, Jennifer L., author.
Title: Media effects and society / Elizabeth M. Perse, Jennifer L. Lambe.
Description: Second edition. | New York : Routledge, 2017. | Series:
    Routledge communication series
Identifiers: LCCN 2016007993 | ISBN 9780415878197 (hardback) |
    ISBN 9780415885911 (pbk.) | ISBN 9780203854693 (ebk.)
Subjects: LCSH: Mass media—Influence. | Mass media—Social aspects.
Classification: LCC P94 .P384 2017 | DDC 302.23—dc23
LC record available at http://lccn.loc.gov/2016007993

ISBN: 978-0-415-87819-7 (hbk)
ISBN: 978-0-415-88591-1 (pbk)
ISBN: 978-0-203-85469-3 (ebk)

Typeset in Classical Garamond BT
by Apex CoVantage, LLC

MIX
Paper from
responsible sources
FSC
www.fsc.org   FSC® C013056

Printed and bound in Great Britain by
TJ International Ltd, Padstow, Cornwall

CONTENTS

PREFACE

Dramatic changes in the media environment since the first edition of this book was published have challenged traditional ways of looking at media effects. Our analyses of the media effects literature, presented in this volume, reinforce that our field's theories are still strong; they are broad enough in scope and flexible enough to encompass effects due to social media, user-produced content, and micro-targeted media. The changes in the media environment instead direct focus to different aspects of the media effects process. First, the notion of media exposure requires more conceptual clarity. Does multitasking mean that there is an additive effect of media exposure, or does the split of attention limit media effects? When people are always online, how can researchers quantify the amount of exposure? Perhaps effects become more contingent on attention than simple exposure.

Second, the changes in the media environment mean that selective exposure is more important than ever. There are nearly unlimited entertainment channels available through cable and streaming services. And people access news not only on traditional channels but through shared content on social media and use of aggregation services like BuzzFeed and theSkimm. The use of algorithms on social media leads to content that is individual and personalized, even without conscious choice. All these changes mean that researchers can no longer make assumptions about a common set of images to which everyone is exposed. The proliferation of different channels makes it even easier now to avoid dissonant information or new ideas. But, despite the fragmentation of media, there still remains a "water cooler effect" surrounding certain content like *Breaking Bad*, *The Bachelor*, *House of Cards*, World Cup Soccer, Super Bowl ads, and viral videos.

Changes in the economics of journalism coupled with the growth of Twitter and citizen journalism can affect news awareness and trust. Cell phone video from the scene of an event can add a sense of immediacy and realism that can increase awareness and engage the audience. On the other hand, unsubstantiated reports can be followed by disillusionment and distrust of media organizations.

This book focuses on the traditional areas of media effects, and on the impact of traditional media because these are reflective of the focus of our scholars. The impact of new media is incorporated throughout the second edition, with special focus in the crisis and politics and public opinion chapters (3 and 4 respectively). The technological characteristics and widespread use of smartphones coupled with a heightened need for information make them the perfect devices for seeking and sharing information during crises. Since the 2008 Presidential election, campaign managers have developed new strategies to engage and mobilize voters. Now social media is at the heart of political movements, for fundraising, connecting with constituencies, and mobilizing political action.

This book is the result of our years of teaching about media effects. It is based on the assumption that the mass media do have effects. Most communication scholars would be reluctant to argue that mass media are the sole or most substantial change agents in society, but it is clear that mass communication is an agent or catalyst to a variety of shifts and changes in people and institutions. It is certainly true that there was violence in society long before there was mass communication, but that does not mean that new media forms and content cannot serve as stimuli to violence. Certainly children were socialized before the development of television, but that does not mean that children's educational media cannot increase children's knowledge about the world.

The most commonly studied areas of media effects are well known, but it would be impossible to identify all the potential media effects. So, the goal of this text is not to identify the domain of the study of media effects; the breadth of the existing literature of the field illustrates the range of interests of the scholars of media effects. Instead, our goal is to focus on how media effects occur – to focus on theoretical explanations for media effects. It is our belief that these explanations can be tools in understanding message effectiveness. If we understand how media effects occur, then we can increase the likelihood of positive effects and lessen the chance of negative effects. The goal of this book is to enable students to understand how to enhance mass communication's prosocial effects and mitigate its negative effects.

This book was written for those who study and conduct research in media effects. We hope that our contribution serves some integrative function for the scholars of our field, those who produce our knowledge about media effects. The theoretical discussions of media effects are also designed to stimulate the intellectual inquiry of graduate students. We have not intended the chapters in this text to be comprehensive summaries of various areas of media effects; excellent overviews are available in other texts. Instead, we hope that the synthesis of different theories might increase graduate students' understanding of the process of media effects and stimulate their interest in new and creative approaches to research on media effects.

This book is also designed for undergraduate students, like those we teach at the University of Delaware – students with a background in mass communication and an interest in the products of our field. We have found that the study of media effects is a subject that is easy to make relevant to students. Every year salient events illustrate the power of mass communication to affect the audience. In recent years, we've seen the explosion of social media in

Presidential elections, social media's on-the-scene reports of the capture of the Boston Marathon bombers in 2013, concern about violent media motivating mass shooters like the Sandy Hook gunman in 2012, and ISIS' use of the Internet for recruitment and propaganda. In all of these and others, the mass media have played a critical role. The students of today were also raised in an increasingly media-rich environment. They can easily remember the impact of television programs such as *Blue's Clues* on their own early lives. They can recall how they might have been influenced by product advertisements and media celebrities as they were socialized into adulthood. The study of media effects can be a personal experience. Coupled with students' interest in producing effective media messages, we have found that our students become excited about the study of media effects.

This book is organized to serve two purposes. First, after the initial two introductory chapters, each chapter presents an abbreviated summary of some of the major areas of interest as well as some representative research findings. More important, each chapter presents a theoretical explanation to guide thought about that domain of study. That theoretical explanation guides the analysis of media effects and provides the explanation for understanding how those effects come about. Each chapter builds on previous chapters, so that the final chapters of the book use theoretical explanations presented in previous chapters.

The first chapter provides an overview to the study of media effects. In it, we present reasons for the importance of the area of study. We explain our presumption of media effects and spend some time discussing reasons that limit evidence for media effects. In general, there are good reasons to believe that the effects of the mass media might very well be stronger than social science concludes. The chapter ends with the first set of concepts that serve as tools to understanding media effects – ways to define and categorize media effects.

The second chapter begins with a brief history of the "received view" of the study of media effects. This commonly accepted history of the field can provide a context for the substance of the chapter – the four models of media effects. These four models – Direct Effects, Conditional Effects, Cumulative Effects, and Cognitive-Transactional Effects – are simplified explanations of the process of media effects. Each places different emphasis on different causes for media effects. These four models are the basis for the theoretical explanations in the following chapters.

Chapter 3 discusses media effects in crisis situations. Because crises are some of the most critical times in a society, different media functions become especially important. So, Wright's discussion of the functions of mass communication serves as the theoretical grounding of this chapter. The effects of dependency (Ball-Rokeach & DeFleur, 1976) help explain how media effects tend to be more direct and uniform during times of crisis.

The fourth chapter tackles a broad topic – media effects on public opinion. Effects of concern focus on politics and voting. A persuasion model, the elaboration likelihood model, serves as the theoretical grounding of this chapter. Media effects on public opinion are presented as conditional on the political expertise, interest, and involvement of the audience. This chapter includes discussions of agenda setting, news framing, the spiral of silence, effects of polling, how reporting affects voter turnout, and concerns about the impact of media on national elections.

Chapter 5 is another broad chapter. Its focus is learning from the mass media. Two general theoretical orientations to learning serve as the theoretical introduction. Learning is presented as either an active process, in which the audience invests interest and mental effort into cognitively processing media messages, or as a passive process, in which passive audiences absorb effectively created media messages. Specific issues of media effects include a discussion of when it is that children are old enough to learn from and be affected by media content, how media affects academic achievement, and knowledge gaps. This chapter provides important information for subsequent chapters that focus on the effects of learning prosocial and antisocial media content.

The sixth chapter covers one of the topics of media effects that has been of consistent concern to parents, educators, and scholars – the socialization effects of mass communication. Mass communication is certainly functional for society, but there are consistent concerns that entertainment programming instills in children and adolescents inaccurate, unhealthy, and potentially harmful beliefs, values, and behaviors. The main focus of this chapter is the acquisition of stereotypical schemas and the social learning of inappropriate and/or unhealthy behaviors.

Concerns about the effects of violent media content emerge regularly as a result of particularly salient violent events in society. The seventh chapter builds on theories and models of earlier chapters to describe how it is that media violence and sexually violent content translate into behavioral, cognitive, and affective effects. The theories are organized into those that provide primarily cognitive explanations (e.g., social learning theory, information-processing, priming), those with physiological explanations based on audience arousal reactions, and those that hold that media violence is not the cause of aggressive behavior.

The final chapter is an overview of various effects of entertainment. Uses and gratifications is the theoretical perspective that underlies media effects that result from seeking enjoyment from media content. This chapter covers such effects as mood regulation, learning from "fake news," parasocial interaction, body satisfaction, and media addiction.

ACKNOWLEDGMENTS

This book grew out of our teaching of a senior-level class on media effects. Our thoughts on this topic have evolved, to a large extent, as a result of our students. While we may not remember which students gave us which ideas, we appreciate their insights into the topics and (probably too extensive) readings we've assigned.

Special thanks to the staff at Routledge/Taylor & Francis, especially Linda Bathgate, who made this book a pleasant project. Thanks to our reviewers who offered specific suggestions and insights that we've included in this second edition.

Personal thanks to our families, who have supported us and, when necessary, distracted us while writing this edition. Thanks to our children and grandchildren who humor us when we comment on what they're doing on all their various screens.

NOTES ON THE AUTHORS

Elizabeth M. Perse (Ph.D., Kent State University, 1987) is Professor and Chair of the Department of Communication at the University of Delaware, Newark. She is currently researching and teaching mass communication theory and the uses of newer communication technologies. She has been identified as a prolific researcher in communication, having published one scholarly book, two textbooks, and more than 50 journal articles and book chapters. Her research has been published in such journals as *Journal of Broadcasting & Electronic Media, Communication Research, Journal of Communication, Human Communication Research, Communication Quarterly, Communication Research Reports, Journalism Quarterly*, and *Health Communication*. She serves on several editorial boards and is a past Chair of the Mass Communication Division of NCA.

Jennifer L. Lambe (Ph.D., University of Minnesota, 2000) is an associate professor in the Communication Department, and a senior fellow of the Center for Political Communication at the University of Delaware. Her research focuses on media policy, freedom of expression, audience attitudes about censorship and the role of audience perceptions of media effects in shaping those attitudes. She has published more than 20 journal articles and book chapters, as well as a number of encyclopedia entries and book reviews. Her work on censorship attitude measurement has been recognized by both academics and practitioners, and reprinted in a communication measures sourcebook. Her research has been published in such journals as *Journal of Communication, Communication Law & Policy, First Amendment Studies, Journalism & Mass Communication Quarterly, Journal of Broadcasting & Electronic Media*, and *Mass Communication & Society*. Professor Lambe teaches courses on media law and ethics, media effects, children and media, and media theory.

1 INTRODUCTION: DO MEDIA HAVE EFFECTS?

One of the primary focuses of the study of mass communication has been the social, cultural, and psychological effects of media content and use. Despite Berelson's warning in 1959 that our field was withering away, the study of effects has remained active and robust. Much of the empirical research published in the major mass communication journals concerns the effects of the mass media. There is no longer discussion in that literature about whether the media have effects or not; nor is our field as interested in identifying the different effects that media do have. Instead, most current research attempts to improve our understanding of media effects by refining our theoretical explanations of the processes by which media effects occur.

This chapter is an initial critical analysis of the effects of the mass media. It begins by presenting the domain of the study of effects, but then notes the limitations inherent in focusing on the media as a prime mover or cause for effects. Despite these limitations, though, it is important to focus our study on how media effects occur so that we can mitigate harmful effects and enhance positive ones.

What Kind of Effects do the Mass Media Have?

Media effects research focuses on the manifestations of the influence that the mass media have on people, institutions, society, and culture. Mass media have been hypothesized to have effects across a broad range of contexts. A quarter of a century ago, W. J. McGuire (1986) noted several of the most commonly mentioned intended media effects: (a) the effects of advertising on purchasing, (b) the effects of political campaigns on voting, (c) the effects of public service announcements (PSAs) on personal behavior and social improvement, (d) the effects of propaganda on ideology, and (e) the effects of media ritual on social control. He also pointed out the most commonly mentioned unintended media effects: (a) the effect of media violence on aggressive behavior, (b) the impact of media images on the social construction of reality, (c) the effects of media bias on stereotyping, (d) the effects of erotic and sexual material on attitudes and objectionable behaviors, and (e) how media forms affect cognitive activity and style.

More recent compilations of media effects research highlight other areas of media effects: (a) knowledge gain from educational television, (b) diffusion of innovations, (c) socialization to societal norms, (d) institution and industry changes to new technology, (e) the impact of perceived media influence, (f) stimulation of fear and other emotional reactions, and (g) effects on body image (Bryant & Oliver, 2009; Nabi & Oliver, 2009; Preiss, Gayle, Burrell, Allen, & Bryant, 2007). McQuail (2010) summarized the range of negative and positive effects on children, such as: (a) reduced time for play and exercise, (b) premature sexual knowledge and experimentation, (c) reduction of time spent on schoolwork, (d) learning prosocial attitudes and behaviors, (e) learning about the world beyond their direct experience, and (f) providing a basis for social connections with others.

There are other, less obvious and less studied possible media effects. Teachers and parents have been concerned that television viewing by children will take the place of reading, leading to lower reading skills and educational achievement (e.g., Ennemoser & Schneider, 2007). Even popular youth novels, such as the Harry Potter series, might not offset the appeal of television and video games (Rich, 2007). Scholars have found that exposure to television action programs was linked to adolescents' risky driving (Beullens, Roe, & Van den Bulck, 2011; Buellens & Van den Bulck, 2013). Pediatricians have been concerned that the promotion of high-fat, high-sugar food in television advertising contributes to childhood obesity (Chou, Rashad, & Grossman, 2008). In response to these concerns, a few television networks (e.g., NBC and Telemundo) have reduced the number of ads for unhealthy food in educational children's programming (Eggerton, 2007). Although there are few positive images of smoking on television programming now, smoking is still fairly common in movies. In *Avatar*, for example, Sigourney Weaver's character climbs out of her suspended animation pod craving a cigarette. There is evidence that early exposure to smoking in G, PG, and PG-13 movies is linked to adolescent smoking (Titus-Ernstoff, Dalton, Adachi-Mejia, Longacre, & Beach, 2008). Legal scholars struggle with the industry's responsibilities in instigating criminal behavior in particularly susceptible radio listeners, television and movie viewers, and listeners to popular music who imitate antisocial media actions (Cooper, 2007). Athletes are claiming to have learned tricks and techniques from playing video games (e.g., Suellentrop, 2010). NBC is starting to engage in "behavior placement," attempts to "sway viewers to adopt actions they see modeled in their favorite shows" (Chozick, 2010). This past year, these placements highlighted environmental issues in "green-themed" programming.

A number of recent studies reveal a growing interest in other health effects of media use. A startling recent Australian longitudinal study links television viewing to early death (Dunstan et al., 2010). The sedentary nature of television viewing was associated with increased risk of cardiovascular disease and cancer. Dermatologists are concerned that reality program viewing leads to indoor and outdoor tanning (Fogel & Krausz, 2013). Cosmetic surgery makeover shows have been connected to young adults' desires to undergo cosmetic surgery (Nabi, 2009). College students who watch reality television sexual relationship shows were more likely to engage in "one-night stands" (Fogel & Kovalenko, 2013). While there is evidence that television medical dramas can increase the audience's knowledge about healthy behaviors (e.g., T. K. Lee & Taylor, 2014; Valente, Murphy, Huang, Gusek, Greene, & Beck, 2007), these medical dramas build plots around deviations from the norms of professional ethics and bioethics (Czarny, Faden, & Sugarman, 2010). Exposure to critical newspaper reports about clinical trials has been associated with lowered intention to participate in medical studies (Len-Rios & Qiu, 2007). Some physicians are seeing what they call a "*House* effect." Patients self-diagnose rare conditions that they have seen on *House* and expect that their physician will run the same complex tests that House and his team routinely run (Persch, 2009).

The House *Effect*

Gregory House is the Sherlock Holmes of medical drama. Drug addicted, unable to form close personal relationships, he is interested in his patients only as diagnostic puzzles to be solved. He bends hospital rules and lies to his patients and his colleagues. He violates medical ethics regularly – failing to get informed consent before treatment or brazenly lying to patients and families to get them to sign consent forms. Thank goodness that most medical professionals are nothing like Dr. Gregory House. But, patients seem to be learning something about diagnosis from the program. Some doctors have identified a "*House* effect." It seems that viewers of medical programs, like *House*, are becoming more familiar with medical technology and procedures. When they see House and his team routinely use uncommon techniques and tests to diagnose rare conditions and diseases, they expect their own doctors to also order costly and complex tests. Some even arrive at their doctor's office convinced they have the same disease they've seen on the program. They are certain that their own symptoms match the rare diseases, allergies, and obscure forms of cancer that are the focus of the plots.

In real life, it can take years to diagnose an illness, simply because diagnoses are not always simple and absolute; there can be a lot of misdirection and uncertainty. Symptoms can be nonspecific (e.g., headache) and symptoms might not fit the "classic" or typical presentation of the disease. House and team, however, solve the puzzle within an hour. Real-life patients can become impatient and anxious and expect and demand more and more tests (just like on *House*).

Although there isn't (yet) any research evidence of a *House* effect, it is clear that television can affect people's beliefs about medicine. A plot on *ER*, for example, told the story about an African American teen who was diagnosed with hypertension (high blood pressure). The doctors counseled her to eat more fruits and vegetables and get more exercise. After watching the program, regular viewers of the program reported to follow those directions themselves (Valente et al., 2007). Medical shows like *House* (which will run in syndication for years) certainly will affect patient beliefs and expectations.

Scholars are uncovering the effectiveness of entertainment-education programming in bringing about prosocial effects. The appealing characters and dramatic narratives can foster parasocial relationships (e.g., feelings of friendships with characters, A.M. Rubin, Perse, & Powell, 1985), lead to involvement in the drama, and reduce resistance to persuasive messages and lead viewers to be more accepting of messages about such topics as teen pregnancy (Moyer-Gusé & Nabi, 2010), breast cancer (Hether, Huang, Becky, Murphy, & Valente, 2008), and HIV (Lapinski & Nwulu, 2008).

Political effects of the mass media continue to interest media scholars. There are concerns that the politicalization of the Supreme Court confirmation hearings can damage the institution of the Supreme Court. After analyses of surveys before, during, and after the Alito nomination hearings, J.L. Gibson and Caldeira (2009) located significant decreases in perceptions about the legitimacy of the Supreme Court. The increasing use of blogs and social networking sites for political campaigns (e.g., Plouffe, 2009), offer new directions for media effects on voting decisions. Scholars are still sorting out how news coverage affects solidarity and consensus during crises (D.M. McLeod, Eveland, & Signorielli, 1994), perceptions about political protest (Jha, 2007; D.M. McLeod, 1995), and on narcotization (Lazarsfeld & Merton, 1948). Writers are asking whether the contentious and sometimes violent political discourse popularized on the 24-hour news stations stoked the 2011 shooting of Arizona Representative Gabrielle Giffords and 19 others (e.g., Steinhauer, 2011).[1]

In general, media effects are usually described as cognitive, affective, or behavioral (Ball-Rokeach & DeFleur, 1976; Bryant & Zillmann, 2009; Chaffee, 1977). Cognitive effects are those that concern the acquisition of information: what people learn, how beliefs are structured (or restructured) in the mind, how needs for information are satisfied or not. These effects include concerns about what is learned as well as how much is learned. Whereas news and public affairs information is often the focus of cognitive effects, the cognitive impact of entertainment is also an important area of study. Affective effects involve the formation of attitudes, or positive or negative evaluations about something. Other areas of affective effects concern emotional reactions to media content, such as fright or amusement, or the development of feelings toward other objects as a result of media exposure, such as the generation of fear in society as a result of watching violent television programming. Behavioral effects are observable actions that are linked to media exposure. The most studied kinds of behavioral effects focus on anti- or prosocial behavior.

Media Effects Research is Thriving

Some of the first formal media effects studies were conducted in the 1920s when psychologists who were financed by the Payne Fund studied the effects of the movies (a new mass medium back then) on children. Since those earliest studies, scholars have published over 4,000 studies about the impact of the mass communication. To get some insight into the scope of that research, Potter and Riddle (2007) examined issues of 16 mass communication journals from a sample of issues over the years 1993–2005. They found that 962 articles reporting various media effects were published over that 12-year period – about a third of all the articles published in those journals. Not surprisingly, television was the focus of most of the studies (40.7%). Print media concerned 19.0% of the studies. Even in those early years, 12.5% of the studies examined the effects of the Internet. Cognitive (27.6%), behavioral (24.3%), and attitudinal effects (21.0%) were the most common focus of media effects research.

Media effects research is a theoretically rich field. Potter and Riddle (2007) identified 144 different theories featured prominently in the articles. *Cultivation* (our Chapters 6 and 7) was the most widely used theory. Other prominent theories include *Third Person Effects* (Chapter 4), *Agenda Setting* (Chapter 4), and *Uses and Gratifications* (Chapter 8). A summer 2012 update found these theories remain important to the study of media effects. A search of academic journal articles published in mass communication journals from 2006 through 2012 found that *Cultivation* was in the title or abstract of 39% of them; *Third Person Effects* was in the title or abstract of 31; *Agenda Setting* in the title or abstract of 87; *Uses and Gratifications* was in the title or abstract of 33. A Google Scholar search at that same time found many more mentions of these theories in that database. *Cultivation Research* was mentioned about 1,980 times, *Third Person Effects* was mentioned about 685 times, *Agenda Setting* was mentioned about 19,000 times, and *Uses and Gratifications* was mentioned about 5,960 times.

The Presumption of Media Effects

One of the first and most important assumptions of the study of mass communication has been the presumption that media and their content have significant and substantial effects. In 1922, Lippmann argued that mass communication could become the basis for people's view of the world. About the same time, Lasswell (1927) considered mass communication as a tool for manipulation and social control. This focus on media effects continued throughout the middle part of the twentieth century with the applied (and theoretical) research of Lazarsfeld's Office of Radio Research (later the Bureau of Applied Social Research). Concern about the negative impacts on children has been the basis of a "legacy of fear" (DeFleur & Dennis, 1994) and numerous government investigations and hearings that accompanied the introduction of each mass medium – movies, radio, comic books, and television (Rowland, 1983; Wartella & Reeves, 1985). Most recently, there has been a renewed political spotlight on television as a cause of violence in society, concerns that the Web is a source for premature sexual knowledge for children (because of indecent, sexually oriented content), and fears that the Internet supports terrorist activity (to recruit followers, coordinate activities, and as a repository for information about terrorist actions).

This presumption of media effects is easy to understand. It makes common sense that anything that consumes so much money ($882.6 billion in 2009, Welly 2009) and time (about 23% of the time we are awake, according to the U.S. Bureau of Labor Statistics, 2009) must have some impact on our lives. Daily household television watching time is just over 5 hours a day (Nielsen, 2009) and the average person listens to the radio about 15 hours per week (Arbitron, 2009). Americans are watching more video online and on their mobile devices (Nielsen, 2009). We know from personal experience that movies can frighten us or make us cry, that children learn their letters and numbers from *Sesame Street*, integrate ideas and characters from movies and television programs into their play, and that much of the world seems to revolve around U.S. football during Super Bowl week. Even media conglomerates acquire a variety of media outlets to create synergy, or cross-media spinoffs and promotions of products and personalities (e.g., music produced from television programs *American Idol* and *Glee*, Disney's presence in film, television, and retail).

It is important to realize, though, that there is a good deal of self-interest in promoting a belief in strong media effects. Media companies derive profit by promising that they are effective vehicles for advertisements or product placements, messages designed to persuade consumers to purchase. Although consumers rarely see them, advertising-supported media regularly promote themselves in trade publications as being able to "deliver" valuable demographic groups to advertisers. This notion of potent advertising effects is reinforced by the advertising business itself, which profits from advertising production and placement. Although advertisers are often reluctant to take credit for product trial (as in the case of underage alcohol or tobacco use), they do maintain that advertising leads to brand switching and/or reinforcement.

Some politicians, who use the media for reelection and to gain support for their political goals, seem to accept without question a view of strong media impact. During the 1980s, for example, Jesse Helms, a powerful Republican Senator from North Carolina, was interested in taking over CBS so that he could shape its news coverage (presumably to eliminate a liberal bias as well as to promote a more conservative agenda). During the 1992 Presidential campaign, Vice President Dan Quayle attempted to bring the issue of "family values" to the media and public agenda. One of his strategies was to show how the media legitimize unwed motherhood by depicting respected professional women, like the fictional television character Murphy Brown, becoming pregnant outside of marriage. The 1996 Republican candidate, Robert Dole, decried the violence in films (with Arnold Schwarzenegger standing at his side) and congratulated producers of films that promote wholesome values, such as *Independence Day*'s celebration of patriotism. In 2000, the Federal Communications Commission (FCC) investigated complaints that the U.S. Office of National Drug Control Policy offered television networks advertising in exchange for embedding anti-drug messages in television programming.

Although some politicians are motivated to promote public interest and media responsibility, others see media as convenient and easily understood scapegoats for social problems. Although there certainly are reasons to be concerned about the level of violence in our society, it is clearly simplistic and misleading to hold that violent themes in popular music, movies, comic books, or television might be the major cause for delinquency and the violent crime rate. But opposition to media violence is a less politically charged position than advocating dealing with other roots of crime, such as poverty, drug and alcohol use, dysfunctional home life, substandard or inadequate educational facilities, and easy access to weapons.

Even academic scholars have strong vested interests in holding that media have substantial effects. As McGuire (1986) wrote, "It would hardly enhance the self-esteem or status of academic researchers . . . to find that mass media effects studied by many in their discipline are trivial" (p. 174). The study of media effects is based on empiricism and rewards results. We cannot "prove" the null hypothesis and nonsignificant findings are typically not publishable. Most academics enter their fields hoping "to make a difference" in the real world. The contribution of communication research to the development and success of *Sesame Street* (Ball & Bogatz, 1970) illustrates how much our field has to offer. So, for academics, the assumption of effects offers practical value (and funding opportunities) to improving media effectiveness (along with the possibility of consulting) and the opportunity to influence government policy.[2]

The Strength of Media Impact

The question of whether media effects are strong or substantial has certainly not been settled; some of this disagreement is definitional. There is consensus, for the most part, among scholars that media do have some impact on various dimensions of social life and structure. But, as McGuire (1986) suggested, the effects seem quite small, given the amount of time, money, and energy devoted to producing and consuming media content. Meta-analysis, a statistical technique that combines the quantitative results of a body of research to examine effects and to estimate effect sizes, attests to the modest effects of media content on some commonly examined areas of media effects.

Hearold (1986) conducted a large meta-analysis of a variety of television effects. She found that television's impact on antisocial effects (e.g., aggression, materialism, use of drugs, cultivation perceptions, stereotyping) was $d = .30$.[3] For prosocial effects (e.g., altruism, counterstereotyping, activism, imaginative play), television's effect size was somewhat stronger, $d = .63$. Paik and Comstock's (1994) update of Hearold's (1986) analysis found that television violence had an overall effect size of $d = .65$, $r = .31$, $r^2 = .10$. Television's negative impact, though, was higher in experiments $d = .80$, $r = .37$, $r^2 = .14$ than for surveys $d = .38$, $r = .19$, $r^2 = .03$. Although the study of the negative effects of violent video games has been marked by inconsistent results, Sherry (2007) found an overall effect of $r = .15$ of game playing aggression.

W. Wood, Wong, and Chachere (1991) sought to uncover the effect size of media violence in studies that were ecologically valid. They focused on 28 studies of experimental exposure to film or television violence that used as their dependent variable aggressive behavior in naturally occurring social situations (free play for child samples or unconstrained social interaction for adult samples). In 16 studies, the experimental group was more aggressive ($d = .27$ for weighted analyses, $d = .40$ in unweighted analyses). An updated analysis of that study found effects to be a bit stronger: $d = .35$ for weighted analyses, $d = .48$ for the unweighted analyses (Christensen & Wood, 2007).

Television's effects on sex-role perceptions have also been isolated: $r = .101$, $r^2 = .01$, for nonexperimental studies, and $r = .207$, $r^2 = .04$, for experimental studies (Herrett-Skjellum & Allen, 1996). Media exposure has been found to affect sex-role stereotyping ($r = .117$ for nonexperimental studies, $r = .235$ for experimental studies) and stereotypical behaviors ($r = .235$) (Oppliger, 2007).

There is evidence of media's impact on political effects. Meta-analyses show that political advertising is linked to learning the issues of a campaign ($r = .21$), learning about the candidates' characters ($r = .19$), and affecting vote choice ($r = .19$, Benoit, Leshner, & Chattopadhyay, 2007). Similarly, watching political debates increases knowledge of the candidates' issue positions ($r = .256$), perceptions of the candidates' characters ($r = .266$), and voting preference ($r = .149$, Benoit, Hansen, & Verser, 2003).

These analyses demonstrate that, although media's impact is significant, it is not very substantial.[4] Variance accounted for by media exposure is quite small. But are these effects trivial? Hearold (1986) gives a context for interpreting these effect sizes. Meta-analyses have found these other effect sizes: gender on height, $d = 1.20$, one year of elementary school on reading, $d = 1.00$, psychotherapy, $d = .85$, tutoring on mathematic skills, $d = .60$, drug therapy on psychotics, $d = .40$, and computer-based instruction on mathematic skills, $d = .40$. Bushman and Anderson (2001) contextualized the effects of media violence by comparing the size of that relationship to other well-researched topics. Among the lists they compiled, the impact of media violence on aggression is the second largest. Only the impact of smoking on lung cancer was larger (see Bushman & Anderson, 2001). The effect of media violence was greater than the effects of condom use and sexually transmitted HIV and homework and academic achievement.

According to J. Cohen's (1988) classification of effects size, most media effects would be considered small ($r = .10$, $d = .20$), or moderate ($r = .30$, $d = .50$), but rarely large ($r = .50$, $d = .80$). But there is another way to consider effects size. Rosenthal and Rubin (1982) developed a way to translate these effects sizes into terms that can be understood by those not trained in statistics. The binomial effect size display (BESD) suggests that r be interpreted as a measure of difference between control and experimental groups. So that, if we could find a group of people who had never been exposed to television, and show them violent television programming, they should be 37% more aggressive (using Paik & Comstock's 1994 estimate) than a comparable group that did not view the programming.[5] Using this same method, Hogben (1998) estimated that eliminating television violence would reduce viewer aggression by 10%. Herrett-Skjellum and Allen (1996) also pointed out that media effects may be especially strong for the heaviest media users. Using their television sex-stereotyping effect size estimates for nonexperimental studies, they argue that television's heaviest viewers, compared to the lightest viewers, are almost twice as likely to hold sexist attitudes.

Some Problems in Interpreting Evidence of Media Effects

Despite the bias of the presumption of effects and the evidence drawn from meta-analyses, not all scholars agree that media have effects in all areas. There has, for example, been little consistent evidence that television affects academic achievement (Fisch, 2009; N. Shin, 2004) or children's cognitive development (D.R. Anderson & Collins, 1988). Analysis of the results of "naturalistic" studies of television violence observed that in 7 of the 23 studies in which direction of effect (30.4%) could be determined, the control group was more aggressive (W. Wood et al., 1991). Studies of the introduction of television found that children in a town without television were not significantly less aggressive than children in towns with television (Joy, Kimball, & Zabrack, 1986). The connection between availability of pornography and sex crimes is not well supported (Brannigan & Kapardis, 1986). Despite the enthusiastic adoption and use of violent video games, findings connecting game play and aggression are contradictory (Sherry, 2007). And, despite the stereotypical and segregated portrayals of African Americans on television, television exposure is linked to more positive attitudes and higher self-concepts among African American children (Graves, 1993; Stroman, 1986).

Moreover, media's impact does not seem to be consistent across cultures. There is a good deal of open and available sexual content in Japanese media, for example, but a much lower incidence of sexual crime (M. Diamond & Uchiyama, 1999). Similarly, media violence is common in Japan, but Japan is a less violent society than the United States (Faiola, 2004). Cultivation effects, commonly identified in the United States (Morgan, Shanahan, & Signorielli, 2009), have not been observed with heavy British television viewers (Wober, 1978) and Israeli teenagers (J. Cohen & Weimann, 2000).

Some scholars argue that there is a "publication bias," in which effects are more likely to be inferred because studies that do not find effects are less likely to be published (R. R. Levine, Asada, & Carpenter, 2009). Paik and Comstock (1994) found no evidence, though, that stronger effects were found in published studies. However, they drew these conclusions based on examining unpublished studies that were readily available as dissertations, theses, conference papers, and ERIC documents. There may be many other studies with null findings, though, that never become even that available (cf. Rosenthal, 1979).

It is clear that the most substantial media effects are located in laboratory settings. There is a good deal of value in conducting research in the tightly controlled setting of the laboratory (Kerlinger & Lee, 2000). Laboratory experiments allow a high level of control over conditions, subjects, and extraneous variables, so specific effects can be isolated and error variance minimized. Because treatments can be manipulated and time order can be controlled, causation can be determined. But there should be some caution interpreting effects from laboratory experiments. The control that is a strength of laboratory settings is also one of its greatest weaknesses. Laboratories are artificial; they do not account for the possibility of selective exposure available to people in the real world. For example, some subjects greatly affected by pornography in a laboratory might never choose to expose themselves to it voluntarily. Dependent measures (such as hitting a Bobo doll or pushing a button) limit the possible range of realistic responses to the stimulus (Brannigan & Goldenberg, 1987) and may not be valid or realistic measures of the study's construct (Freedman, 1984). The laboratory also lacks the normal social constraints on behavior. Studies have found, for example, that children are more likely to act aggressively when the experimenter leaves them alone than when an adult is present (Stein & Friedrich, 1975).

Experimenter effects may also account for some of the effects found in laboratory research. When a researcher presents media content to subjects, the subjects may presume that the experimenter approves of it, even if it is violent or pornographic. And when subjects are given the opportunity to act in what might be otherwise considered inappropriate or undesirable ways, they may be more likely to do so in the laboratory setting. Subjects may believe that they have the permission of the experimenter to act. Rosenthal (1979) estimated that these "experimenter effects," or the influence of the experimenter and the hypotheses on the results, range from $d = .23$ to $d = 1.78$. So, experimenter effects alone might account for the media effects located in experimental settings.

The major concern with evidence of media effects is inferring a causal relationship between media exposure and various effects. Meta-analyses demonstrate that there is some relationship between media exposure and some media effects. The relationship, though, does not necessarily reflect that media content leads to effects. There are two other possible explanations for that relationship. It is possible that certain predispositions may lead people to seek out certain types of media content. For example, people who hold more traditional sex-role beliefs may choose to watch television programs that reinforce those views. Or, cultivation effects might reflect that people who are more fearful may prefer to spend time safely in their own homes, watching television. A correlation between two variables may be spurious, or due to similar influence of a third variable on both. So, the strong correlation between the number of churches and bars in a community certainly does not indicate that as people drink and carouse more, they find the need to pray more. The relationship might be more easily explained by population size. As the number of people in a town increases, so does the number of churches, bars, stores, sidewalks, automobiles, schools, and so on.

Why aren't Media Effects Stronger?

If the mass media do have effects on individuals and society, why doesn't research find evidence of strong and substantial media effects? Of course, it is possible that the media do have effects, but they are slight, compared to the influences in the environment. But, there are several reasons to believe that the strength of media effects may be underestimated by research.

For ethical reasons, many studies limit dependent variables to those that do not harm subjects. For example, researchers studying the effects of pornography are more likely to measure attitudinal effects, rather than behavioral effects that might lead subjects to commit crimes or act in ways that would lessen their self-esteem. So, Malamuth, Haber, and Feshbach (1980) asked male subjects if they would act like the rapists in a rape scenario rather than providing the subjects an opportunity to act sexually aggressive. Josephson (1987) gave boys the chance to play a game of floor hockey after exposure to media content and used the number of fouls committed as a measure of aggression, rather than let the boys have a chance to act in a less socially sanctioned aggressive way. These "diluted" measures may not be very accurate ways of assessing effects of media exposure.

Measures of media exposure in natural settings are often imprecise and subject to a good deal of random error (e.g., Fishbein & Hornik, 2008; Webster & Wakshlag, 1985). Use of music and television are typically inattentive and fragmented now with widespread media multitasking (e.g., Crenshaw, 2008; Jordan, Trentacoste, Henderson, Manganello, & Fishbein, 2007). Newspaper exposure is usually operationalized as time spent reading or attention to different parts of the newspaper (e.g., D. M. McLeod & Perse, 1994), although people's reading speeds and interests vary. This error in measuring exposure can increase the amount of error variance in the study and reduce the relationship among the variables (Kerlinger & Lee, 2000), so media effects may seem less substantial.

Most experimental research is also based on the assumption that effects occur immediately after exposure to media content. Persuasion research has noted that some persuasive effects don't emerge for weeks. According to the "sleeper effect" (Hovland, Lumsdaine, & Sheffield, 1949), people who receive persuasive messages with a "discounting cue" (e.g., from a less credible source) are unlikely to be persuaded immediately. But, after a while, their attitudes change when the discounting cue has been forgotten. Some research, for example, suggests that cultivation effects might be due to a similar process; television viewers "forget" that the facts that they have learned refer to the television world (e.g., Shrum, Wyer, & O'Guinn, 1998). The delay hypothesis (Jensen, Bernat, Wilson, & Goonewardene, 2011) holds that the "full impact of fictional narratives may be felt over time" (p. 509). These delayed effects might emerge "as bits and fragments of the message are disconnected and then activated out of their original context" (pp. 509–510). Experiments are likely to be unable to observe these delayed effects.

For the most part, research designs tend to assume that media effects develop linearly. That is, as more media content is consumed, the greater the likelihood of effects. Our field depends on statistical techniques that are based on linear relationships, such as correlation, regression, and analysis of variance. If the media effects process is not a direct, linear one, our techniques may underestimate effects (e.g., Eveland, 1997). Persuasion research, for example, has found that the relationship between repetition and message impact is curvilinear. That is, as messages are repeated, not only does impact diminish, but, after a point, repetition may lead to less persuasion (e.g., Cacioppo & Petty, 1979). McGuire (1986) pointed out that there are models of advertising effects that are based on a threshold model (e.g., Bemmaor, 1984). That is, media content may have no impact until a certain level, or threshold, of exposure is reached. On the other hand, some media effects may have "ceilings," or points of diminishing returns.

B.S. Greenberg (1988) suggested that media content may have "drench" effects. According to the drench hypothesis, the media effects process is not a linear and cumulative "drip, drip" one. Instead, some media personalities, programs, and portrayals may be so potent that, although most images are ignored, these command attention and account for a good deal of media impact. An epidemiological approach to analyzing media effects would suggest that the media effects process may be very subtle and effects not noticed until media cause an imbalance in the social system. Then, media impact increases dramatically (e.g., Centerwall, 1989a, 1989b). If scholars are searching for linear media effects, then nonlinear ones will be less likely to be identified.

Media effects may appear to be less substantial because of conflicting processes. Television's heaviest viewers – young children and older women – are less likely to be aggressive, so television's effects may not be noticed. The cultivation hypothesis holds that heavy television viewers are more likely to believe that the real world is as violent as television's fictional programming (Morgan et al., 2009). So, these heavy viewers are more fearful and less likely to venture outside at night. Other theories maintain that high levels of media violence lead people to act more aggressively (e.g., C.A. Anderson & Bushman, 2002b; Bandura, 2009). These two processes, though, may serve to cancel each other out. If heavier viewers are more likely to stay indoors out of fear, they may be less likely to encounter situations where they may act aggressively.

Some writers argue that the thin performers and models in the media contribute to the prevalence of eating disorders among young women (M. P. Levine & Harrison, 2009). Adolescent girls are unable to attain the hyper-thin look of these media portrayals, so they become anorexic or bulimic. Yet, most research shows that reading and viewing media are inactive pastimes, associated with obesity and lack of exercise (Gortmaker, Must, Sobol, Peterson, Colditz, & Dietz, 1996). So media's influence on thinness may be offset by media's displacement effects. Other theoretical processes may hide the effects of media violence. If movie and television viewers become desensitized to violence because of heavy exposure to it, they may be less likely to be subject to arousal or priming effects (Roskos-Ewoldsen, Roskos-Ewoldsen, & Carpentier, 2009; Zillmann, 1982).

Some media may be so pervasive and so consistent in their effects that their impact is not noticeable. After all, it is almost impossible to find someone who doesn't watch television in industrialized societies. And those light viewers associate regularly with others who do watch television. Morgan (1986) suggested that "the longer we live with television, the smaller television's observable impact may become" (p. 135). Similarly, media's pervasiveness means that people are often exposed to conflicting messages. In the case of political advertising, for example, effects of ads for one candidate may be canceled out by ads for the opposition. The net media effect, then, may not be noticeable in situations where there are many contradictory media messages (Zaller, 1996).

The main reason that media's impact is not more substantial is that other aspects of life have stronger influence on people. As early as the Payne Fund studies (Jowett, Jarvie, & Fuller, 1996) of the 1920s and 1930s researchers were aware that the movies' impacts on children were dependent on age and cognitive abilities (Wartella & Reeves, 1985). Lazarsfeld, Berelson, and Gaudet (1968) observed that people's voting decisions were influenced more by the social groups (family, friends, and coworkers) than by media information and political advertising. When people are deciding whether to adopt an innovation (new idea, product, or way of doing something), mass media's impact is usually secondary to personal trial and social influence (Rogers, 2003a). Public affairs knowledge gain associated with news use declines dramatically when the influence of demographics (gender, age, education, income, and religion) is removed (J. P. Robinson & Levy, 1996). Knowledge gap research demonstrates that learning information from the media is highly dependent on socioeconomic status, education and income, (Tichenor, Donohue, &

Olien, 1970). Declining credibility of the news media may cause some people to discount their information (Pew Research Center for the People & the Press, 2008). Adolescents' decisions to drink beer and wine are more strongly linked to peer group influence than to exposure to alcohol advertising (Atkin, Hocking, & Block, 1984; Grube & Wallack, 1994). Cultivation effects have been explained better by a variety of other demographic and life-situation variables, such as the neighborhood in which people live or their personal experience with crime (e.g., Doob & Macdonald, 1979; J. Weaver & Wakshlag, 1986). Pornography is viewed as only one aspect of a range of individual conditions and social forces that influence the development of antisocial attitudes and behaviors toward women (Malamuth & Briere, 1986). The family communication climate may block some of the harmful effects of sexual media content on adolescents' moral development (Bryant & Rockwell, 1994).

It is clear that media impact is often diminished because many messages are avoided by those who might be the most affected by them. Selective exposure research has noted that many people seek messages that confirm their beliefs and feelings and avoid those that are discrepant (e.g., Cotton, 1985). So smokers may be more likely to avoid public service announcements (PSAs) that urge them to give up tobacco and pay attention to those messages that deny harmful effects of tobacco (e.g., Brock & Balloun, 1967). One of the primary uses of remote control devices is to avoid objectionable television content, such as commercials and political messages (J. R. Walker & Bellamy, 1991). Even when people do encounter messages that might affect them, they tend to reinterpret the messages to reinforce their preexisting beliefs and attitudes. Selective perception has been noted by communication scholars for decades in some classic studies in our field. Football fans of different teams see different numbers of fouls (Hastorf & Cantril, 1954), and political candidate supporters are more likely to believe that their candidate was the "winner" in Presidential debates (Jamieson & Birdsell, 1988). When Norman Lear created the ground-breaking situation comedy *All in the Family* in the early 1970s, he hoped to make people aware of their prejudices and reduce bigotry. Vidmar and Rokeach (1974) found, however, that both high- and low-prejudiced viewers used the arguments between Archie and his son-in-law, Michael, to bolster their own beliefs. More recent research has found that conservatives who watched *The Colbert Report*, a satirical "news" program formerly on *Comedy Central* that satirizes conservative talk show hosts, believe that Stephen Colbert supports, rather than mocks, conservative viewpoints (LaMarre, Landreville, & Beam, 2009). So, selective perception leads people to interpret media content in accordance with their own beliefs. Finally, many people tend to select media content to maintain or achieve equilibrium. That is, people chose media content that brings them to emotional and arousal states that make them feel comfortable (e.g., R. Kubey & Csikszentmihalyi, 1990). Bored people seek media content that is exciting whereas anxious people seek relaxing content (Bryant & Zillmann, 1984; Zillmann, Hezel, & Medoff, 1980). The search for equilibrium may make media effects harder to notice.

These explanations suggest that media effects might be obscured by meth-odological imprecision, theoretical forces, and many personal, social, and sit-uational constraints. Clearly, the probe for media effects demands continued efforts, refined theories and methods, and the integration of a wide range of intervening variables into research designs.

Criticism of Media Effects Approaches

Scholars who hold critical and cultural studies perspectives argue that the study of media effects is limited and the results of those studies obscured because of faulty assumptions. Gitlin (1978) explained that the dominant paradigm in the study of media effects is a behaviorist approach that directs scholars to be concerned with a very narrow definition of "effects." Because behaviorism focuses on outcomes that can be observed, much research has been limited to short-term manifestations of "effects" that can be easily meas-ured in laboratories or in surveys. Effects have been defined in most studies as attitude change or in specific, discrete behaviors. This means that, for the most part, research has not considered the effects of long-term, cumulative media exposure.

Gitlin (1978) also pointed out that most media effects research is grounded in "administrative" modes of research, which yield data to marketing or policy decision makers so that they can predict the impact of media campaigns. Admin-istrative research, then, also places value on short-term media impact that can be identified in pretests designed to help prepare campaigns or in postcampaign evaluations. Moreover, administrative media effects research is typically inter-ested in variables in the campaign that can be manipulated or controlled, such as media production variables or frequency of exposure. Systemic variables, such as media ownership and organization, are not relevant because they are part of the assumptions and administrative structure driving the research. So, structural variables, which may shape media production and content, are rarely studied in connection with media effects, so their impact is rarely considered.

Because media effects research has its roots in the United States (Rogers, 1994), it has been grounded in the assumptions of capitalism and democracy. Central to both is the value in "freedom of choice." There are two problems with the notion of choice. First, reinforcement, or rejection of media attempts to change one's choice, is viewed as evidence of limitations on media power (Klapper, 1960). But, the maintenance of the status quo is often a powerful, though less noticed, effect. Second, believing in freedom of choice assumes that various alternatives are indeed real choices. Different people might select different network news programs for different reasons (e.g., Palmgreen, Wen-ner, & Rayburn, 1980), for example, but are the programs sufficiently dif-ferent to lead to different effects? Morgan, Shanahan, and Signorielli (2009) argue that because television content, even that seen on cable and satellite networks, pay-per-view, and DVDs, is created, for the most part, by the same producers with the same end goals, so it will all share common themes and patterns of images. So, freedom of choice may be an illusion that leads scholars to hold beliefs about limited media power.

For these reasons, then, critical and cultural studies scholars are not surprised that only "limited" or modest media effects have been identified. Because of the assumptions and methods of the "dominant paradigm" (Gitlin, 1978), more powerful, yet subtle effects, such as social control, manufacturing of consent, and reluctance to challenge the status quo, are unable to be studied; so they are ignored.

Other scholars have criticized media effects approaches, suggesting that media effects are substantially weaker than the research shows.[6] Many of those criticisms are based on methodological issues, such as drawing casual connections from correlational studies, lack of control groups in natural experiments, and invalid measurement (e.g., Brannigan, 1987). Gauntlett (2005), for example, argues that media research, especially that focusing on violent media content, takes a narrowly individualistic approach. He points out that this approach allows a very limited conclusion: that a "particular individual at certain times in specific circumstances may be negatively affected by one bit of the media" (para. 7).

Fowles (1992) sees a political basis in acceptance of media effects assumptions. He suggests that religious groups often use attacks on sexual and violent media content as a way to capture media attention and uphold their position as guardians of traditional values. He also argues that media effects research is based on class issues. Researchers and academics are generally upper-middle class and value "high culture" more and don't consume much of the mass culture. Media research, then, can be seen as an attack on popular culture, which is often violent and "rowdy."

Ball-Rokeach (2001) notes weaknesses in media effects inquiries.[7] She finds, for example, "The near-exclusive focus on entertainment programming that continues to characterize social science inquiry is less and less defensible given the blurring of the distinction between entertainment and news genres" (p. 15). Ball-Rokeach (2001) and Gauntlett (2005) both point out that media effects research is based on the assumption that children and young men are "deficit" audiences and need special protections from the media. As Ball-Rokeach (2001) summarizes, "as long as it assumed that children and 'deficit males' are most at risk of media effects, the paternalistic social control perspective will continue to rule out of consideration what may be even more important effects concerns" (p. 16). These researchers hint that media effects research might be driven by third person effects beliefs (e.g., R.M. Perloff, 2009). People like researchers are less likely to be affected by media content. Instead, content is more likely to affect "deficit" audience members.

Why is it Important to Study Media Effects?

With all these questions about the existence and substance of media effects, why is it important to continue to study them? Students in introductory mass communication courses are often reminded that mass communication is functional in society (C.R. Wright, 1986) and an important field of study because of its role as a major societal institution.

Mass communication is an important economic force in the United States. In 2008, newspaper advertising revenues were $37.8 billion, digital music downloads were $3.8 billion, and U.S. video game revenues were $13.0 billion (Plunkett, 2009). In 2009, U.S. box office revenues were almost $10.6 billion (Box Office Mojo, 2010). In 2009, national cable advertising equaled $19.1 billion with broadcast network advertising adding another $20.3 billion (Nielsen, 2010).

Mass communication is also an important political force, acting as a watchdog over official actions and as the platform for political information and activity. The Watergate scandal, for example, was brought to light by the *Washington Post* and the Pentagon papers were first published by the *New York Times*. The Clarence Thomas Supreme Court hearings captivated the television audience in 1991. President Clinton's impeachment played out on television between late 1998 and early 1999. The world stopped on September 11, 2001 as the nation was gripped by coverage of the terrorist attacks on the New York World Trade Center. Then October 8, 2008, Vice Presidential debate between Joe Biden and Sarah Palin drew the largest audience for a political debate since 1992: 69.9 million viewers, the largest audience ever for Vice Presidential candidates.

Political campaigns are now built around television. In the 2008 presidential election, by October 6th, the Obama and McCain campaigns spent over $225 million on political advertising on television (Politicalmaps.org, 2008). Talk shows and news program coverage are crucial to campaigns. Our political leaders contact the public primarily through the mass media – press conferences, political talks. Ronald Reagan noticed that there was little political news that was made during the weekends, so he (a former radio announcer) began to make radio addresses about various issues on Saturday mornings. These addresses got so much news coverage (Martin, 1984), in part because there was so little else happening, that Saturday morning radio talks are still a current Presidential practice.

At the same time, mass media are a major source of entertainment and the main source for news for most people. In 2009, a majority of people in the United States turned to media for news: 73% watched local television news, 73% watched network news on broadcast or cable networks, and 67% read a local or national daily newspaper. In addition, 54% listened to radio news at home or in the car and 61% get some kind of news online (Purcell, Rainie, Mitchell, Rosenstiel, & Olmsted, 2010). Clearly, the media environment is changing. Online media use is growing, but it is important to remember that much of the news content on the most widely used sites is drawn from wire services or aggregated from legacy media.

Beyond the importance of mass communication in society, there are two main reasons for continuing to study media effects. The first reason is theoretical. Although most scholars acknowledge that mass media effects can occur, we still don't know the magnitude and inevitability of the effects. That is, we don't know how powerful the media are among the range of other forces in society. And, we don't know all the conditions that enhance or mitigate various effects. Most importantly, we don't understand all the processes by which mass communication can lead to various effects. Research in media effects must continue to add to our knowledge.

A second reason for studying media effects is practical and policy oriented. If we can elaborate the conditions and understand the various processes of media effects – how media effects occur – we can use that knowledge. At a practical level, understanding the processes of media effects will allow media practitioners to create effective messages to achieve political, advertising, and public relations oriented goals. Additionally, agencies will be able to formulate media campaigns to promote prosocial aims and benefit society as a whole. That is, understanding the processes of media effects will allow media practitioners to increase the likelihood of prosocial media effects. Most importantly, understanding how media effects occur will give parents, educators, and public officials other tools to fight negative media effects. If we understand the processes of media effects, we will also understand how to mitigate negative effects. No longer will changing or restricting media content be the only methods to stop media effects. We will be able to mitigate negative media effects by also targeting aspects of the process of impact.

Ways to Conceptualize Media Effects: Dimensions of Media Effects

Over the years, scholars have suggested that it is useful to analyze media effects along specific dimensions (J. M. Anderson & Meyer, 1988; Bryant & Zillmann, 2009; Chaffee, 1977; W. J. McGuire, 1986; J. M. McLeod, Kosicki, & Pan, 1991; J. M. McLeod & Reeves, 1980). Some of the dimensions delineate the type of effect; other dimensions elaborate the conditions of media impact.

Cognitive–Affective–Behavioral Dimension

Media effects are commonly described along a cognitive–affective–behavioral dimension, which marks a distinction between acquisition of knowledge about an action and performance of the action. Mass communication scholars have been greatly influenced by persuasion models that see human action as logical and driven by cognition (e.g., A. J. McGuire, 1985; D. J. O'Keefe, 2009). This dimension is important in keeping scholars from assuming that knowledge and attitudes translate directly into action. Persuasion research during World War II, for example, found that although media content may be quite effective at teaching information, it had less influence on attitude formation and motivation to act (Hovland, Lumsdaine, & Sheffield, 1949). The Theory of Reasoned Action (Fishbein & Ajzen, 1975) posits that, although knowledge and attitudes have some impact on behavior, their influence is mediated (or eliminated) by social constraints.

Micro- Versus Macro-level

Another dimension that describes the type of effect is one that focuses on the level of media influence: micro- versus macro-level. Most concern about media effects focuses on impressionable audiences and has been grounded in psychological approaches. So, there is a wealth of research on media effects at the individual, or micro-level. It is a fallacy, however, to assume that all media effects are accumulations of individual-level effects. Scholars recognize that a focus solely on individual-level media effects can obscure more subtle societal-level effects. Research on the effects of *Sesame Street*, for example, showed that children of all socioeconomic status (SES) classes learned from the program. But, that learning led to another, unintended effect: a widening gap in knowledge between higher and lower SES groups. Although all children learned from the program, children from higher SES families learned at a faster rate (T. D. Cook, Appleton, Conner, Shaffer, Tamkin, & Weber, 1975). So, individual knowledge gain may lead to greater inequities in society.

Another area in which an accumulation of individual-level effects might conceal more macro-level effects is news learning. Although many researchers have uncovered various media-related influences on public affairs knowledge (e.g., J. P. Robinson & Levy, 1986, 1996), these studies cannot assess the completeness, accuracy, or objectivity of media's presentations about public affairs. Several scholars argue that larger influences on news gathering and reporting may make individual-level knowledge effects inconsequential, because news sources and practices present only limited public affairs information to the public (e.g., Gitlin, 1980; Herman & Chomsky, 1988; G. Tuchman, 1978). So, knowledge gain by individuals may not necessarily be functional for society.

Several important effects of mass media may be at the societal, institutional, or cultural level. Over the years, for example, the expanding telecommunications revolution has changed, and no doubt will continue to affect, how political campaigns and the workings of government are conducted. Clearly, scholars need to consider various levels of media impact.

Intentional Versus Unintentional

Another dimension of media effects directs scholars to consider whether the effects are intended versus unintended – planned for or accidental. Although this dimension is a descriptive one, it also offers some insights in the processes of media impact. For example, the development of knowledge gaps between higher and lower SES children who watched *Sesame Street* is generally considered an unintended effect of the flow of media information. So, scholars and media policymakers study ways to close accidental knowledge gaps by increasing access to a variety of sources of information, by making information more relevant to lower SES groups, or by increasing the motivation of lower SES audience members to seek additional information. The identification of these knowledge-gap effects as accidental, then, has led scholars to focus on how knowledge is carried by the mass media, how audiences access that knowledge, and how people use media-delivered information.

Another example of the relevance of the intended versus unintended dimension is one effect of television violence. The cultivation hypothesis suggests that one, often overlooked, effect of television violence is that it affects social perceptions of heavy viewers and leads those groups who are victimized in television drama to feel fearful, alienated from society, and distrusting of others (Gerbner & Gross, 1976; Morgan et al., 2009). If scholars believe that these effects are unintentional due to the conventions of television drama production, they might advocate certain remedies to help mitigate these effects, such as television program ratings to help fearful people avoid certain programs or to help parents screen what their children watch. If, on the other hand, scholars believe that cultivation is an intentional effect designed to reinforce the existing power structure in society by structuring reality for women and minorities so that they avoid involvement in political affairs, possible solutions would be quite different. Those scholars (at the very least) would be less trusting of television program ratings affixed by television producers and probably not advocate that sort of solution to cultivation effects.

Studying unintended effects can be a way of increasing media effectiveness. Dramatic story lines in soap operas and telenovelas have been found not only to captivate their audiences but also to bring about knowledge gain and some prosocial attitudinal effects (e.g., Singhal & Rogers, 1989). These unintended effects have stimulated research into entertainment-education media effects (Singhal, Cody, Rogers, & Sabido, 2004). So this dimension of media effects directs scholars to search for a range of effects, beyond those planned for the media producers.

Content-Dependent Versus Content-Irrelevant

The content-dependent versus content-irrelevant distinction reflects the impact of specific classes of media content as opposed to the impact of media use itself. The most visible media effects research has focused on the effects of specific media content, such as stereotypes, violence, and pornography. This research assumes that specific content is linked to specific effects. As J. M. McLeod and Reeves (1980) paraphrase the nutritional analogy, "We are what we eat." We are what we watch. So, one way to reduce aggressive behavior in children would be to reduce the amount of violent media content that they read or watch. Or, one way to reduce sexual aggression against women would be to reduce access to media content that depicts violence against women. Although there is a good deal of evidence of the effects of specific media content, scholars should also be aware that some effects are due less to specific media content, and more to the form of the content or the act of media use.

Displacement effects are a commonly identified content-irrelevant effect. Lazarsfeld and Merton (1948) suggested that political involvement could suffer if people become politically "narcotized." That is, public affairs media use might replace real political action and some people might be informed, but politically apathetic. Watching television has been attributed with lower academic achievement because children are replacing homework and study with television watching (G. B. Armstrong & Greenberg, 1990; Borzekowski, & Robinson, 2005).

Other content-irrelevant effects may be due to the form of the media presentation. Tavris (1988) is one writer who has suggested that television's regular commercial interruptions has led to shorter attention spans. Scholars investigating how information theory (Shannon & Weaver, 1949) is relevant to media effects have found that the randomness of television's formal features are connected to aggressive responses (Watt & Krull, 1977). Kozma (1991) speculated how the form and use of different media lead to different learning styles and outcomes. And there is a good deal of evidence that arousing media content, whether it is violent, pornographic, or suspenseful, can lead to similar excitation effects (Zillmann, 1980, 1982). In order to understand how media effects occur, we need to uncover, first, if they are content-relevant or content-irrelevant.

Short-Term Versus Long-Term

Media effects can be long or short term. This dimension is not only a descriptive one, but also helps describe the process of media effects. When we examine media effects, we need to question how long the effect is theoretically expected to last. Some effects, such as increased arousal (or relaxation), are relatively short term, and disappear quickly. Others, such as agenda setting, may last somewhat longer, but may disappear as the media agenda changes. Still other effects, such as the social learning of aggressive behavior, are expected to be fairly enduring, especially if the aggressive behavior, once performed, is rewarded.

Some theories do not specify the persistence of their effects. Do the stereotypes that children learn from television persist even as children watch less and less television as they get older? How long do the effects of televised political ads (and their associated voting intentions) last? What are the possibilities that new ads (and new information) will change voting intentions?

And what are the implications of differing periods of influence? Clearly, short-term effects can have a profound impact. If, for example, a short-term arousal effect of a violent film leads someone to get involved in a fight, permanent injury could result. But, if agenda-setting effects last only as long as an issue stays near the top of the media agenda, what long-lasting impacts can result? Media effects scholars should be clear in specifying the duration of the effects that they study.

Reinforcement Versus Change

A final dimension of media effects is that of reinforcement versus change. Does media exposure alter or stabilize? The most visible media effects studies focus on how media content or exposure changes the audience (or society or culture). For example, we are concerned how placid children might be changed into aggressive ones by watching violent cartoons. Or that respectful men will change into uncaring desensitized oafs through exposure to pornography. Or that voters might have their political values adjusted through exposure to political ads. Or that ignorant citizens will become knowledgeable through exposure to public affairs news. And so on.

There is evidence, though, that communication's strongest effect, overall, is reinforcement and stabilization. Selective exposure leads people to prefer media messages that reinforce their preexisting views. Selective perception points out that people interpret media content to reinforce their attitudes. Because it is often easier to observe change than reinforcement, we often neglect media's power to stabilize. Advertisements that keep supporters active in a political campaign and keep them from wavering in support yield important effects. Media content that reinforces the already existing aggressive tendencies of a young boy may be an even more important influence than prosocial messages that have little impact. We must be careful not to equate reinforcement effects with null effects.

Summary

The study of media effects is grounded in the belief that mass communication has noticeable effects on individuals, society, and culture. Evidence for these effects, though, is problematic. On one hand, despite consistent findings of effects, the variance accounted for is typically small. Moreover, the strongest effects are usually relegated to laboratory settings, which are highly artificial. There are, however, several reasons to expect that research underestimates media effects. Our models, theories, and methods are still imprecise; we still cannot offer complete explanations for media effects. The study of media effects remains important so that we can increase understanding of the role mass communication plays in shaping our lives. Awareness of the process of media effects will allow us to use mass communication effectively to maximize desirable outcomes and minimize negative effects.

Notes

1 Islamic terrorist groups and both Democrats and Republicans have been accused of using aggressive political rhetoric and imagery. Democratic Senator Joe Manchin aired a television commercial that included video of him firing a rifle into a copy of the cap-and-trade energy bill that was pinned like a target to a tree. The most commonly mentioned instances, though, come from Sarah Palin's use of rifle-sighting cross hairs to mark the Congressional districts of 20 political opponents

during the 2010 election, her tweet after the passage of the health care reform bill "Don't Retreat, Instead RELOAD," and former Nevada Senate candidate Sharron Angle's hints that "Second Amendment remedies" might be necessary to combat the Democrats. It was this political discourse that was partial motivation for Jon Stewart's 2010 "Rally to Restore Sanity."

2 Simpson (1994) suggested that one reason for communication scholars' involvement in study of psychological warfare during the Cold War era was that they believed that it was an enlightened way to achieve world peace.

3 The effect size is based on standardizing different measurement scales so that they can be compared. It is computed much like a Z score – the difference between the means of the experimental and control groups divided by the standard deviation (Rosenthal, 1984). It is usually interpreted to indicate the size of the difference, in terms of standard deviations, between the exposure and control groups. An effect size of .30, then, indicates that the groups differ by .30 of a standard deviation.

4 Agenda-setting effects are an exception, however. Wanta and Ghanem (2007) found moderately strong effects (for our field) of media influence on the audience's agenda: $r = .529$.

5 The binomial effect size display may make some more sense when applied to medical settings. In 1981, for example, a drug study was prematurely discontinued because researchers decided that the effects were so significant and substantial it would be unethical to deny treatment to the control group. The effects size for this study was $r = .02$, $r^2 = .004$ (Rosenthal, 1984). Clearly, a success rate of 2% can be quite meaningful.

6 One argument: Although violent content remains widely available in the media (e.g., Signorielli, 2003), crime rates have dropped over the past 15–20 years. Given that evidence, some find it difficult to argue for strong media impact on societal aggression.

7 Professor Ball-Rokeach (2001) summarized her thoughts about the political basis for violence research based on her long career in media scholarship and her early work with the 1968 Violence Commission, set up by President Johnson after the assassinations of Martin Luther King and Robert Kennedy.

2 MODELS OF MEDIA EFFECTS

This chapter begins with an overview of the chronicle of the study of media effects. Although there is some disagreement about the progression of theory about and study of media effects, throughout the history of our field there have been bodies of research that emphasize different forces as the impetus for media effects. Those beliefs can be summarized by four basic models of media impact. This chapter presents these four models that will be the structure for the following chapters. Because this book focuses on understanding how media effects occur, these four models highlight aspects of media content and the audience that serve as the basis for influence so that we can understand the process of media effects.

The "Received View" of the Study of Media Effects

Many of the textbooks of our field (e.g., Baran & Davis, 2009; DeFleur & Ball-Rokeach, 1989; McQuail, 2010) describe the study of media effects as a series of "phases" marked by paradigm shifts – shifts in theoretical assumptions, the ways the scholars look at problems, and the ways that they interpret empirical results. According to this received view (i.e., generally accepted history of the field), there are three basic phases to the study of media effects.

The first phase covered the early twentieth century through the 1930s. Its focus on media effects was based on the stimulus-response model drawn from psychology and grounded in mass society theory drawn from sociology. The "magic bullet"[1] or "hypodermic needle" model held that the media were so powerful that the audience was powerless to resist their influence. This model was based on observations that the technological improvements in public communication and mass production of popular culture had created a mass audience attending to the same messages (Curran, Gurevitch, & Woollacott, 1982). The emphasis on instinct and stimulus-response learning drawn from psychology reinforced the notion that powerful stimuli, such as effective media messages, could induce people to respond mechanically, immediately, and relatively uniformly, consistent with the intentions of the creators of the messages.

At the same time, sociologists believed that the Industrial Revolution had led to a fragmentation of the social bonds in society, so that people no longer felt part of social communities but instead isolated and disconnected from others. A society based on the personal bonds of kinship and friendship, Gemeinschaft, was replaced by a society marked by personal distance and contractual obligations, Gesellschaft (see DeFleur & Ball-Rokeach, 1989, pp. 153–154, for a discussion of Tönnies, 1957). The social and psychological isolation brought on by the Industrial Revolution created a mass society in which people were aimless and disconnected from others. These masses, then, were especially susceptible to the influence of powerful, persuasive forces in society, such as mass communication.

This phase reflected the views of scholars of the era and found some support in some of the published research. Lasswell's (1927) analysis of propaganda, for example, was based on the assumption that the effective messages of World War I could teach scholars how to create messages to manipulate the masses. Studies of war bond drives of World War II (Merton, 1946) focused on the appeal of Kate Smith, a down-to-earth singer whose sincerity impressed radio listeners so much that they pledged millions of dollars to the war effort. Her appeal, according to Merton, grew out of listeners' desire for Gemeinschaft in the mass society. And, although the Princeton study of the audience response to the "War of the Worlds" radio broadcast (Cantril, Gaudet, & Herzog, 1940) showed that the impact of the program was limited by a variety of audience factors, news coverage and anecdotal accounts reinforced beliefs that mass communication could instill extreme emotions and reactions in the audience.

The War of the Worlds

On Sunday night, October 30, 1938, Orson Welles was already a bit of a prodigy in New York theater. By the age of 21, he was directing New York plays as part of the Federal Theatre Project (part of the Depressions' Works Progress Administration). He moved to radio drama and became Mutual Radio's Lamont Cranston – *The Shadow*. In 1938, CBS brought his troupe to the *Mercury Theatre on the Air*, which presented hour-long radio dramas on Sunday nights at 8:00. Welles and the Mercury Theatre had become famous because of their broadcast of *The War of the Worlds*. To media researchers, it showed that mass communication could have profound effects on its audience.

The show was put together quickly, but creatively. Welles decided to tell the classic tale in a series of news bulletins. It was a creative idea, but had some unexpected consequences. A report after the broadcast estimated that over a million people (just on the East Coast of the U.S.) were frightened and believed that aliens had really landed in Grover's

Mill, New Jersey (Cantril et al., 1940). The *New York Times* placed the story about the "panic" on their front page; newspapers printed stories well into November. And, the program became the basis for an early research project by Lazarsfeld's Radio Project at Princeton (Cantril et al., 1940).

There were many good reasons why so many of the audience members were frightened by the broadcast. First, it was an excellent retelling of the classic tale. (In fact, after the broadcast, Welles was wooed by Hollywood and was hired by RKO pictures with a contract that gave him an incredible amount of artistic control over his films.) But, it was probably the structure of the story and just plain coincidence that stimulated fear in the audience.

The *Mercury Theatre on the Air* was unsponsored. So, there were no commercial interruptions until 30 minutes into the drama when there was a required station identification. When people tuned in after the program began (and most who heard the broadcast did tune in late), had no signs that the show was drama – not a series of news bulletins reporting an alien invasion. The *Mercury Theatre on the Air* ran on Sunday nights opposite the most popular radio program of the era – *The Chase and Sandborn Hour*, with Edgar Bergen and Charlie McCarthy (a popular ventriloquist and his dummy). While Orson Welles was introducing his radio drama on CBS, a huge audience was listening to Edgar Bergen and Charlie McCarthy perform their comic routine. (Think about how odd it is that a ventriloquist was so popular on the radio.) It wasn't until a "past his prime" singer, Nelson Eddy, began to sing that the audience began to switch channels – and catch the news bulletins about the invasion. By the time the station identification aired, those who were frightened had gone into the streets, called their loved ones, or even gone to church to prepare for the end of the world.

The second phase of media effects research is often called the era of limited effects. This phase is marked by regarding media as having only minimal influence on the audience. Klapper (1960) expressed the limits on media effects: "Mass communication ordinarily does not serve as a necessary and sufficient cause of audience effects, but rather functions among and through a nexus of mediating factors and influences" (p. 8). Klapper elaborated two conditions under which mass communication could influence the audience: if normal barriers to effects are not operating or if mediating factors are congruent with media's influence. But his statements about the minimal effects of mass communication were supported by pages of evidence that filled most of his book. His generalization about the conditions of media influence received a good deal less attention in his work and the subsequent research of the era.

The reason for media's limited effects was the power of the audience to selectively choose and use media content. In other words, people controlled media and their content through various selectivity processes: (a) selective exposure, or control over what they watched, listened to, or read in the media; (b) selective attention, or control over which elements of media messages people would pay attention to; (c) selective perception, or control over how messages were interpreted; and (d) selective recall, or control over how and what was learned from the media.

This view of the power of the audience grew out of persuasion and election research that found that media's impact was limited by the social connections among people, the influence of people in the flow of information from mass media (E. Katz & Lazarsfeld, 1955; Lazarsfeld, Berelson, & Gaudet, 1968), and by a host of personal experiences and attributes (e.g., Hovland, Lumsdaine, & Sheffield, 1949). Social connections drew people together and led to shared interpretations of media messages. People's personal characteristics led them to seek out media content that reinforced their beliefs and preexisting attitudes. So, media's impact was seen as quite limited in this era. Social and personal characteristics of people influenced their selective approach to mass communication so much that media's main and most common impact was believed to be reinforcement.

This phase lasted until the 1960s and led several scholars to question the value of continuing to study media effects (e.g., Berelson, 1959). There seemed to be little justification to studying media effects, if media's influence was so minimal. The introduction and widespread adoption of television, though, brought scholars to a new phase of effects research.

Television was quickly embraced by the public. In 1950, only 9% of U.S. homes owned a television. By 1955, 64.5% of U.S. homes owned a television; by 1965, the percentage had increased to 92.6% (Television Information Office, 1985). Television became the dominant medium as people replaced radio listening and movie going with television viewing. By 1963, the typical household was watching television for more than 5½ hours a day (Comstock, Chaffee, Katzman, McCombs, & Roberts, 1978). And by 1961, television replaced newspapers as the most believable medium (Roper Starch Worldwide, 1995). Scholars began to question whether selective exposure was feasible in such a television-saturated media environment. During this period, several studies began to show that it was possible for the mass media to overcome the tendencies of the audience toward a selective approach to using mass communication. In fact, this era is often referred to as "the return to the concept of powerful mass media" (Noelle-Neumann, 1973, p. 68).

McClure and Patterson (1974) noted that television had the possibility to overcome some selectivity processes. During elections, political advertisements on television were so prevalent during prime time that people could not avoid them. Although people might selectively avoid news programs, it was much more difficult to avoid political ads interspersed during entertainment programming. McClure and Patterson found that people learned about the candidates from the many political ads on television, even if they weren't particularly interested in the election.

Other studies found strong media effects; that is, consistent reiteration of important news items led people to adopt the media's agenda as their own (M. E. McCombs & Shaw, 1972). Agenda setting marked the ability of the mass media to tell people "what to think about." Gerbner and Gross (1976) found that the heaviest viewers of television were the most likely to be "culti-vated" by its patterns of images and accept the television world view as their vision of reality. These heavy viewers, of course, were relatively unselective in what they watched on television.

Notice that these studies did not focus on obvious, behavioral media effects. McClure and Patterson (1974) did not argue that exposure to political ads led people to change their voting behavior, but that these ads had a "dramatic and direct" (p. 3) impact on people's beliefs about candidates. McCombs and Shaw (1972) did not argue that media were powerful in telling people what to think, but what to think about. And Gerbner and Gross (1976) did not argue that the violence on television made people act aggressively, only that watch-ing large amounts of television violence made people feel afraid. So, this era of media effects focused on media's power to bring about subtle, yet direct media effects.

An Appraisal of the Received View

Although the received view sees a progression of ways of looking at media effects, it is probably a simplistic report of the development of the study of media effects. Moreover, several scholars have argued that it is not a realistic account of the full range of media effects study. Wartella and Reeves (1985) suggested that the received view reflects an emphasis on the study of public opinion, voting, and marketing decisions, and ignores other areas of interest. The received view particularly does not describe the progress of research on the child audience. The Payne Fund studies, some of the earliest studies of the impact of movies on children, were conducted from 1929 to 1932, during the era of "direct effects." Yet, the various studies focused on a broad range of influences that mediated harmful effects of the movies, including age, gen-der, parental influence, family and social environment, predispositions, and experiences – the same kinds of influences considered in studies of the effects of television decades later. The effects of the movies were hardly considered direct by the Payne Fund researchers.

Others have argued that the "limited effects" phase of study is a misrepre-sentation of the research findings of the era. Chaffee and Hochheimer (1982) pointed out that effects identified during that period only seemed limited because of the marketing orientation of Lazarsfeld's research bureau. In the Erie County voting study (Lazarsfeld et al., 1968), voting was conceptualized as a marketing decision – a one-time choice at the polls. So the research-ers were concerned only with voting intention and ignored other possible political effects (see also Gitlin, 1978). Other effects, such as knowledge gain, or participation in political parties and other political activities were ignored, even though these might have greater impact on the political process as a whole.

Moreover, Lazarsfeld and his colleagues may have understated the impact of the media and overstated the role of personal influence. The data do not support a heavy reliance on interpersonal communication over mass media as a source of influence. When the Erie County panelists were asked to name the sources of information that influenced their voting decision, 56% of the men and 52% of the women made no mention of a personal contact as "influential." Three-quarters of the panelists made no mention of a personal contact as "most influential" (Lazarsfeld et al., 1968, p. 171). On the other hand, 68% found radio "helpful" in their voting decision; 66% reported that newspapers were "helpful." Of all the information sources, radio was found to be the "most important" source by 38% and 23% named newspapers (Lazarsfeld et al., 1968, p. 127). The media's role in voting was clearly strong and one that was important to the panelists.

Pooley (2008) presents a "new history" of mass communication research that summarizes the strong involvement of communication scholars in government- and privately funded research in the 1940s and 1950s. Communication scholars were central to programs that aimed to design and test psychological warfare, counter Nazi World War II (and later, Soviet) propaganda, develop effective educational radio broadcasting, and establish U.S. government propaganda/information services (i.e., Voice of America). In fact, Pooley presents evidence that U.S. government funds made up more than 75% of the support for Lazarsfeld's bureau, Cantril's Institute at Princeton, and Ithiel de Sola Pool's Center at MIT, three important centers for mass communication research at that time. This less publicized research certainly contradicts a belief in "limited effects."

The assertion of limited media effects also needs to be placed in the context of media industry connections to academic research. During that era, much research was funded by media industries[2] and academia provided the training for several notable names in the business.[3] Because the era of limited effects held that media served mainly to reinforce, rather than bring about change, the research of this era served as evidence that fears about media effects were groundless. Klapper's (1960) book, one of the most influential works of this era, was used politically by the television networks to argue against regulation. Klapper not only worked as a graduate student with Lazarsfeld's research bureaus, but was Director of Social Research at CBS when his book was published (Rowland, 1983).

Four Models of Media Effects

Although the received view is not a completely accurate depiction of the full range of the study of media effects, it illustrates that different emphases were placed on different contexts and different explanations for media effects. This section of the chapter presents four different models of media effects. These models depict four different processes of media effects, drawn from the various bodies of research of our field. These models differ because each places emphasis on different aspects of media content or the audience as the primary force driving media effects. It is important to remember that these four models are designed to focus explanations. So, they are simplified. Because each model focuses on only one part of the cause of media impact, no single model can be a complete explanation for media effects. But these models are valuable because they can direct study of the processes of media effects.

Direct Effects

The direct effects model focuses on media content as the most important explanation for media influence. Effects are seen as immediate (occurring fairly shortly after exposure), relatively uniform (similar across all audience members), and consistent with the goals of the media producer. Moreover, effects within this model are observable ones. The emphasis of this model is on effects that represent change, not reinforcement. Effects are either behavioral, cognitive, or affective effects that lead directly to noticeable actions. For example, the direct effects model is applicable in understanding how political ads might lead to voting for a specific candidate (a behavioral effect), or knowledge gain that would lead to a voting decision (a cognitive effect), or attitude acquisition that influences voting choice (an affective effect). The direct effects model, however, would not be useful in explaining how political campaigns would lead to feelings of political disenfranchisement.

The direct effects model ignores the role of the audience in the media effects process. People are assumed to be incapable of countering media's impact. They may lack the mental capacity to analyze media messages. So young children may be the targets of direct effects. Or people may have little background knowledge or context about certain events and issues and be reliant solely on media content. In these situations, effects may be direct. Most commonly, however, people are seen as reacting involuntarily and automatically to certain aspects of media content. Although people may have the mental abilities to evaluate content, the direct effects model holds that they are unable to resist the attentional "pull" of some of the features of presentation. Within this model, then, skilled media producers can create media content that is likely to invoke fairly predictable and uniform reactions from large parts of the audience.

Important Variables In The Model

Variables associated with media content are the most important to understanding direct effects. Most central are aspects of media content that (a) are perceived more automatically by people – such as those that attract orienting responses (involuntary attention) or unconscious responses, (b) are associated with increases in arousal, and (c) are depicted realistically.

Structural and Content Features. Structural and content media features, such as commercial breaks, cuts and edits, and camera and lens movement, are associated with the orienting response. The orienting response is involuntary and automatic attention that is unrelated to the meaning of the media stimulus (e.g., A. Lang, 1990). These structural features' demand on attention is usually explained by the natural need to detect movement so one can control and understand one's immediate environment (Reeves, Thorson, & Schleuder, 1986). Welch and Watt (1982), for example, hypothesized that children's attention to educational programs was a necessary antecedent to learning effects. The researchers found that shifts in scenes in television programs were associated with children's visual attention to the screen. Negative media images may attract the orienting response out of a survival instinct (Reeves, Newhagen, Mailbach, Basil, & Kurz, 1991). So people may remember negative news stories better because of that attention.

Some features of media content (such as certain musical themes or the presence of certain types of characters) may attract less conscious attention because people have learned to associate pleasure with those features. Levin and Anderson (1976), for example, speculated that children focused visual attention on the television screen when female adults, other children, and familiar animals were on because these were familiar sources of enjoyment. In contrast, media depictions of dangerous people, animals, and situations may evoke fear reactions because of stimulus generalization (Cantor, 2009). That is, some stimuli invoke conditioned or unconditioned fear responses. Realistic media representations may elicit those same automatic reactions. Features such as camera angles and distance influence how people perceive images. Low camera angles, for example, make objects seem bigger. Camera angles have been found to influence perceptions of the credibility of political candidates (Giessner, Ryan, Schubert, & Quaquebeke, 2011; McCain, Chilberg, & Wakshlag, 1977), impressions and recall of characters in pictures (Kraft, 1987), and product evaluations and descriptions (Meyers-Levy & Peracchio, 1992). Shots that mimic interpersonal distance are hypothesized to lead to more personal reactions to media personalities (e.g., Meyrowitz, 1982). All of us realize how "spooky" below-key lighting is (such as shining a flashlight up at our face from below our chin). Zettl (1973) suggested that "we affix this outer distortion to an inner disorientation. The face appears unusual, ghostly, brutal" (p. 32).

While interactive television is still in its infancy, several production techniques have been adapted to change the viewing experience. Sports productions, in particular, have begun to use subjective camera techniques, which "invite" the viewer to become involved in the onscreen action (Zettl, 2008). Examples are overhead cameras in sporting events and cameras mounted to players' helmets and NASCAR dashboards. The greater sense of participation in the action as a result of these techniques might heighten viewer involvement and increase the likelihood of media effects (e.g., Cummins, 2009; Cummins, Keene, & Nutting, 2012). And, most of us have "ducked" when an object in a 3-D movie came toward us. The growing availability of 3-D films and television programs has implications for media effects. Other research shows that personalization and customization of websites affects users' evaluations of the content (Sundar & Marathe, 2010). This suggests that customized and interactive media content is likely to impact effects.

Arousal. Media content variables may be important to media effects because they increase arousal. Arousal is an automatic, nonspecific physiological response that is conceptualized as an activator or energizer. Arousal is usually not under the control of an individual; it is stimulated by the environment. But, interpretation or labeling of what the arousal is due to is controlled by the individual (Zillmann, 1991b). Arousal is important to understanding media effects because it is associated with greater attention (Eysenck, 1993), so arousal can be associated with cognitive effects. As an activator, arousal has also been linked to increased affective and behavioral responses (e.g., Zillmann & Bryant, 1974). Arousal is increased by some structural features of media presentations, such as larger television screens (Reeves, Lang, Kim, & Tatar, 1999). Detenber and Reeves (1996) speculated that larger images are "compelling and significant stimuli" (p. 77) and humans have adapted to be "wary of big things." Arousal is also a common result of exciting media content, such as violence and erotica (Zillmann, 1991b). Comstock et al. (1978) considered the salience of a television act as an important antecedent to explaining media effects (see Fig. 2.1). Salience involves the arousal inherent in the depiction as well as the vividness of the image. Certain types of musical passages, such as those marked by increases in volume, expansion in high or low registers, harmonic ambiguity and tension, are associated with "chill" responses, that is, goose bumps, tingles, and arousal (Guhn, Hamm, & Zenter, 2007).[4]

Realism. When media content more closely resembles real-world counterparts, various theories hold that it is more likely to have an effect. Cultivation, for example, is based in part on the realism of television content, so that heavy viewers are more likely to accept television's distorted depictions as reality (Gerbner & Gross, 1976). Social learning theory holds that people are more likely to learn behaviors that are presented more realistically (Bandura, 2009; Comstock et al., 1978). And more realistic media content is more likely to activate mental images (e.g., Busselle, 2001). Research on video games, for example, found that when the game controller simulated the action of the game (in this case, boxing), there was more immersion in the game and more cognitive aggression (McGloin, Farrar, & Krcmar, 2013).

The vividness of media content, or the details of the imagery (Riddle, 2013) can have an impact on media effects. Because vivid content is easier to understand, viewers need fewer cognitive resources to pay more attention to and comprehend the images. Some research has found that, compared to more pallid content, vivid images of media violence are associated with greater

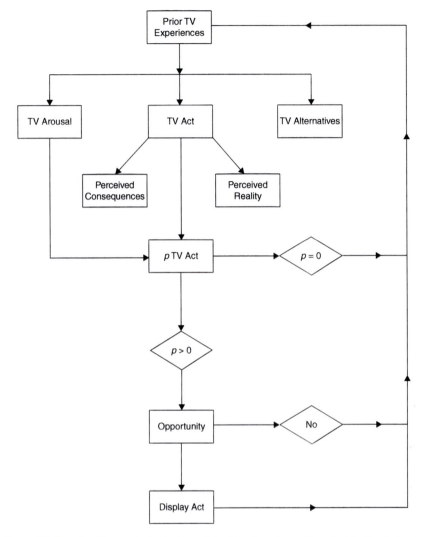

Figure 2.1 Comstock's psychological model. Adapted from Comstock's Psychological model of Television's Behavioral Effects. From Comstock, G., Chaffee, S., Katzman, N., McCombs, M., & Roberts, D. (1978). *Television and human behavior.* New York: Columbia University Press, p. 400.

attention to the program, more intense emotional reactions to the story, and greater transportation, or involvement, with the story (Riddle, 2013).

A related concept, presence, can also be relevant to this model. Presence is the extent to which audience members sense being in an actual environment while using a medium (K.M. Lee, 2004). Although there is a perceptual component to feelings of presence, several media attributes increase its likelihood. Larger screens and finer picture quality are linked to increased presence (Bracken, 2005; Lombard, Reich, Grabe, Bracken, & Ditton, 2000). Other research gives indications that presence might be increased by the enhanced image quality of high definition TV (HDTV, Bracken, 2006). Research has found that increased presence is linked to stronger perceptions about the dangers of hurricanes after watching news about storms (Westerman, Spence, & Lachlan, 2009) and to memory for product demonstrations (T. Kim & Biocca, 1997).

Summary

The direct effects model holds that media content invokes fairly predictable and uniform reactions from large parts of the audience. This model may appear to bear some resemblance to the outdated, early conceptions of the "propaganda," "magic bullet," and "hypodermic needle" models. Certainly, few mass communication scholars still accept the viability of these models, although the notion of a passive audience helplessly manipulated by enticing media images still invades the writings of popular authors. But the value of the direct effects model should not be dismissed. There are certain conditions when this model may be useful in understanding how media effects occur: (a) when the audience is incapable or unable to analyze and/or evaluate media messages or (b) when media content stimulates people to react unconsciously or automatically. Central to this model is the impact of media content variables to arouse and command attention. For this reason, most direct effects are relatively short term. This model and media content features may be an especially fruitful area of media effects research as new technology brings media content closer to reality (e.g., filmic special effects, high definition television (HDTV), large television screens and computer monitors, and virtual reality).

Conditional Effects

This model is drawn from the limited effects model described by the received view. Like the limited effects model, the conditional model places emphasis on the audience and is based on notions of selectivity (selective exposure, attention, perception, and recall) and social influence. The limited effects model downplays the possibility of most media effects beyond reinforcement, whereas the conditional model recognizes that media effects can occur and offers explanations for those effects. This model is called the conditional model, because media effects are conditional on the audience member. This model recognizes that all media exposure is not bound to result in media effects. The audience has the power to avoid exposure and reject influence. And, when media effects occur, they are certainly not uniform. Different people may be affected quite differently by the same media content.

To give a simple example: Certainly not everyone is going to cry at the end of a sad movie (such as *Titanic*). Some may never watch the movie because they dislike the actors or the story device. Even some of those who watch the movie will dislike it, and some may go to a movie they don't expect to like, just to accompany someone. And even those who like the movie may not cry. Different people have different feelings about expressing emotions in public places. Still others may be profoundly affected by the movie and find themselves sobbing at certain scenes. So, the conditional model holds that the explanation of the effects of the movie rests with the individual audience member.

Effects, according to the conditional model, can be cognitive, affective, or behavioral. The effects can occur immediately after exposure or require repeated exposure to similar messages. And the effects may be short term or long term. The conditional model, because it focuses mainly on the individual audience member, can be used to explain almost any media effect at an individual level.

The individual is the focus of media effects because of the individual's power to be selective. The audience member is central to the conditional model (and media content is ignored, for the most part) because of selectivity processes that act as barriers to intended media effects. People selectively expose themselves to media content. Mainly, they choose media content that is consistent with their interests, personal experiences, and their own needs and desires. Even when they are using media content, people pay attention quite selectively. For example, people often listen to what's happening on television while they do something else. They turn their complete attention to the set only when something interesting is happening. Finally, when they watch, read, or hear media messages, people selectively perceive those messages and interpret them within the framework of those interests, experiences, and needs. Selective exposure, attention, and perception, then, are barriers to effects that lead people to reject messages unless they fit into preexisting knowledge or interests.

But media effects often go beyond reinforcement. Change as a result of media exposure is likely. When change effects happen, they are conditional on some attribute of the audience. Although selectivity is generally seen as a barrier to effects, audience characteristics may act as lenses, and focus media's influence. Audience characteristics are conditions of influence.

This model is called conditional because when effects do occur, they are conditional on some attribute of the audience. For example, learning from the news might be conditional on the reasons the viewer is watching. Or cultivation effects from watching prime-time television might be conditional on whether the viewer has had personal experience with crime. Or, the effects of political messages about changes in Medicare funding might be conditional on the age of the audience member.

So, this model focuses discussion and explanation on the audience member. And audience variables are important – especially variables that deal with the social connections of people and those variables that concern how the audience interprets messages.

Important Variables In The Model

There are three classes of audience variables that can intervene in the process of media effects according to the conditional model: social categories, social relationships, and individual differences. These three classes of variables can act either as a barrier to media effects or as a lens to enhance the likelihood of media effects.

Social Categories. Social categories variables are aspects of people that are fairly easy to observe or uncover. They may be demographic characteristics of people, such as gender, age, socioeconomic status (SES), ethnicity, educational level, and geographic location of their home. Social categories may also reflect common self-designations such as religion, political party membership, and occupation. Social categories variables are often the variables measured by the U.S. census. Social categories are ways to separate people into broad groups. These variables are meaningful because we assume that, for the most part, everyone in one category is alike, and that people in one category are different from those in another category. For example, television programmers know that they can target certain types of television programs at women, because, for the most part, most women will prefer certain program genres. But, as a whole, women will prefer different types of television programs than men. So, gender is a meaningful social category for explaining television program preference. Another social category is age. Young children (ages 3 to 5) may be more likely to be frightened by television programs that do not frighten older children. So, a child's age is a meaningful way to explain some of the fright effects of the mass media.

Social categories variables provide explanations for media effects because the categories represent the common frames of reference of different groups of people. These frames of reference are reflected in shared interests, experiences, and abilities that affect selective exposure, attention, perception, and recall. So, social categories are really shorthand explanations for media effects.

The reason that young children are more likely to be frightened by some television programs is not solely because they are young. Age is really shorthand for levels of cognitive development. Young children's minds process environmental information quite simply (Flavell, 1963). They rely on superficial, physical features of a stimulus. Because of that reliance, they cannot understand the psychological motivation underlying action. So, Sparks and Cantor (1986) showed that younger children were more frightened by David Banner's transformation into the Incredible Hulk than older children, because younger children were not cognitively able to understand that the Hulk was really a good character. They saw the Hulk acting aggressively, and saw no connection between the Hulk and Banner. Similarly, Mares and Sun (2010) argued that age differences in program preferences are based on emotional preferences associated with different life stages. So, age marks the different personal goals of different life stages, such as achievement (in the young) and stability and meaningfulness (in the older). And, as people age, a biological decline in physiological systems might diminish older adults' emotional responses to negative films (e.g., Kunzmann & Gruhn, 2005).

Malamuth (1996) argued that gender is an important social category in understanding the effects of pornography for two reasons. First, evolution has favored males who have many, fertile sexual partners (echoing the content of much pornography). Second, males and females are socialized about sex differently in most societies and receive different messages about the rewards and dangers inherent in sexual activity.

Knowledge-gap research hypothesizes that SES is an important social category in understanding knowledge gain from the mass media. Higher SES groups (reflecting higher education and/or income) typically learn more and gain knowledge more quickly than lower SES groups. Socioeconomic status is such a powerful explanation because it represents many other individual factors, including greater access to more sophisticated information sources, better communication skills, political interest, and greater social utility for public affairs knowledge (D. M. McLeod & Perse, 1994; Tichenor et al., 1970). So higher SES groups are more likely to selectively expose themselves to news and selectively remember information that is useful to them.

Harwood (1999) proposed that social identity is a central variable in understanding why people select some media content and avoid others. This approach is based on uses and gratifications and sees group membership as a motivator in media selection. According to this approach, people who identify with certain groups are likely to select media content that features positive depictions of those groups and avoid media content that either ignores those groups or depicts them unfavorably. So, Abrams and Giles (2007, 2009) found that African Americans' social identity predicts avoidance of programs with stereotypical images of African Americans and that Hispanic viewers' social identity is linked to watching television that celebrates their ethnicity.

Social Relationships. Social relationships variables represent the social connections and interpersonal interactions among people that mediate media effects. This set of variables gained importance in communication research with the Erie County voting study (Lazarsfeld et al., 1968). Subsequent studies noted that people play a role in the flow of mass communication. The two-step flow holds that interested people pay attention to specialized media and pass along that information to others to whom they are socially connected. Researchers found that media messages flowed from opinion leaders to family members, friends, and even more casual coworkers. The two-step flow has several implications for media effects. First, people might become aware of and be influenced by media messages that they have not directly encountered. Second, the information passed along by opinion leaders is not necessarily isomorphic with that delivered by the media. As individuals, opinion leaders are affected by selectivity processes of selective exposure, attention, perception, and recall. Third, the personal influence represented by the two-step flow can be an especially powerful barrier to, or enhancement of, media effects (Rogers, 2003a).

Social relationships variables are also represented in the mediating impact of the social context of media exposure. Whether it is going to the movies, watching videos, or just sharing time in front of the television, group exposure to mass communication is quite common. The social facilitation hypothesis suggests that people should enjoy media content more in group settings than when alone. Often comedians seem funnier when we're watching their routines with friends than watching a cable special alone. Television producers have recognized the impact of an audience on enjoyment and routinely add studio audience applause and laugh tracks to programs (see Neuendorf & Fennell, 1988; Platow et al., 2005). These elements may increase enjoyment because they help reduce uncertainty about whether something is supposed to be funny, reinforce ingroup cohesion, or they may increase the arousal inherent in the viewing or listening experience. The arousal inherent in group viewing of sporting contests can also increase the pleasure of sports viewing (Zillmann, Bryant, & Sapolsky, 1989).

Who is in the audience with us can also influence our responses to media content. College men who watched a horror film with women enjoyed the experience more than men who did not watch the film with women (Zillmann, Weaver, Mundorf, & Aust, 1986). There are some possible explanations for this sort of effect. First, comforting a frightened companion might provide an excuse for bodily contact. Or the increased arousal offered by the frightened partner might be "transferred" into pleasurable feelings by the young man.

Children frequently watch television with their parents or other children (e.g., Alexander, Ryan, & Munoz, 1984; Nathanson, 2001; A.M. Rubin, 1986). Group viewing is a powerful mediator of television's effects on children. Even when children are watching with other children, they discuss the programs (Alexander et al., 1984). These discussions can increase awareness, attention, understanding, and knowledge. Nathanson (2001) points out that during adolescence, peers become potent sources of mediation, having stronger effects than parents. But, where parental mediation attempts to limit the impact of antisocial content, peer mediation encourages acceptance of antisocial messages.

Parents have many opportunities to influence how their children are affected by television. Scholars (e.g., Austin, Bolls, Fujioka, & Engelbertson, 1999; Messaris, 1986) point out that parents can mold their children's interpretation of television through discussion while viewing. Parents can help children learn about the conventions of the medium and distinguish fact from fantasy. They can highlight characters' motivations, provide background for unfamiliar content, and add explanations for confusing action. Most important, parents can emphasize positive aspects of programs and evaluate and criticize antisocial actions and characters.

Chaffee, J.M. McLeod, and Atkin (1971) initiated research on family communication patterns (FCP). These patterns represent the general orientation of parent–child interaction. According to their measures, family communication can be oriented toward maintaining harmony (sociooriented) or oriented toward exploring issues and ideas (concept oriented). These orientations are important to understanding children's media use and effects. Concept-oriented families encourage more news and public affairs media use;

sociooriented families are likely to comment more about imitating television characters (Chaffee, J.M. McLeod, & Wackman, 1973; Messaris & Kerr, 1983). Concept oriented mothers have more conversations about advertising with their children (Mukherji, 2005).

Individual Differences. Individual difference variables are those aspects that differentiate one person from another. These are characteristics that are unique to an individual. Unlike social categories variables, which are characteristics of groups of people that make them similar to others, individual difference variables are characteristics of people that make them different from other people – even from others in the same social category. So, although, as a whole, boys are more likely to act more aggressively than girls after watching a violent television program, boys are not equally aggressive. Several individual differences can explain why some boys are more or less aggressive than others (e.g., C.A. Anderson & Bushman, 2002b). Individual difference variables not only explain how people differ from one another, but also can explain how each individual's response to mass communication can be different at different times. For example, someone might typically be calm and not riled up by radio talk shows. But after a rough day at work (with many pressures from a demanding boss), that same person might get angry and aroused by the same talk show host. So individual difference variables are those characteristics that make people unique.

Avatars can Prime: The Proteus Effect

The use of avatars, or an on-screen representation of a user in a digital environment, is becoming more common. They were used with some instant messaging programs and chat rooms in the early years of the Internet. Now they are common aspects of video games, online worlds (e.g., Second Life), and popular fiction (e.g., *Avatar* the 2009 film). Researchers have discovered the Proteus Effect, which holds that users' behavior conforms to their digital self-presentation (Yee & Bailenson, 2007). (The term comes from the Greek god Proteus, who can shift his appearance at will.) Research using avatars created in the context of the game *Jedi Knight II: Jedi Outcast*, found that when people were assigned attractive and tall avatars, they acted more cordially in the online environment (Yee & Bailenson, 2007). Other researchers explained that the Proteus Effect was due to priming (Peña, Hancock, & Merola, 2009). According to priming, the situational cues of the avatar's appearance stimulate related thoughts and actions.

The researchers conducted an experiment that assigned college students to different avatars: black or white cloaks. Consistent with evidence that black clothes indicate villains, those with black cloaked avatars reported more aggressive intentions in an online environment. A second study assigned college students to one of three avatars: a doctor, a Ku Klux Klansman, and transparent (the control condition). They found evidence that the appearance of the avatar primes thoughts. When they created stories about ambiguous images, the Klansmen told more aggressive stories – evidence that the appearance of the avatar can prime cognitions.

There are as many individual difference variables as there are differences among people. Some of the most commonly researched individual differences are: personality, prior experiences, preexisting attitudes, physical and mental states, attitudes toward the media, and gratifications sought from the media.

Personality is usually conceptualized as the set of beliefs, values, and preferences that predispose people to act, think, feel, and behave in consistent ways. Personality is a trait; it is a fairly stable part of a person. Each individual's personality makes him or her unique and different from others. Research has shown that personality traits can be intervening variables in the media effects process, primarily because they affect selective exposure and attention. Neurotics (people who tend to be more anxious and socially isolated) avoid television comedy but prefer news programs (J.B. Weaver, 1991b). People who score higher on a psychoticism scale (those who have a lack of constraint and tend to reject rules and regulations) seem to prefer horror and/or slasher films (J.B. Weaver, Brosius, & Mundorf, 1993). Need for cognition, or a personality trait to mark preference for complex mental activity, is linked to attention to public affairs information in local news reports (Perse, 1990e). Sensation seeking, a personality trait that predisposes people to engage in highly arousing activities (see Zuckerman, 1994), is related to selective exposure to more stimulating media content, such as horror films (Edwards, 1991), pornography (Hirschman, 1987), and violent movies, videos, computer games, and websites (Slater, 2003). People low in sensation seeking avoid sexual and violent media content (Zuckerman & Litle, 1986) and prefer more "bland" music (Litle & Zuckerman, 1986).

People's own unique experiences are important in the conditional model. Several scholars hold that exposure to media content can shape perceptions of reality through cultivation (e.g., Gerbner & Gross, 1976). So, heavy media users are more likely to perceive a world that is like that depicted in the media. But media content is merely a source of vicarious experience. The real experiences that people have in their day-to-day lives are likely to have a mediating impact on the effects of media content. The kind of neighborhood in which someone lives, for example, has a greater impact on people's perceptions about how susceptible they are to crime than how much television they view (Doob & Macdonald, 1979). Weaver and Wakshlag

(1986) found that cultivation effects were mediated by people's direct, personal experience with crime.

The attitudes that people hold are potent individual difference variables that influence selectivity processes as well as media effects. A classic study conducted about *All in the Family* illustrates how racial prejudice affected perceptions about the television program. Critics of the program raised concerns that the show provided a platform for the bigoted views of the main character, Archie Bunker, a middle-age blue-collar worker who lived with his wife, daughter, and liberal son-in-law, Mike. Norman Lear, the show's creator, argued that the program's humor would be an effective weapon against prejudice because Archie's outrageous and inaccurate attitudes would be rebutted in arguments with Mike. Lear, however, did not anticipate the impact of selectivity. Brigham and Giesbrecht (1976) found that southern White viewers who expressed racial prejudices were more likely to like and agree with Archie Bunker and see his racial views as valid. Vidmar and Rokeach (1974) found similar connections between racial prejudice and perceptions about the program; those with more prejudicial attitudes were more likely to identify with Archie and believe that he made more sense in arguments with his more liberal son-in-law, Mike.

Baumgartner and Morris (2008) found similar effects more recently examining exposure to *The Colbert Report*, a mock conservative talk show, where the host, Stephen Colbert, parodies the style, tone, and language of a popular Fox news commentator, Bill O'Reilly (whom Colbert calls "Papa Bear"). Colbert's attempts to lampoon conservative news, however, seemed to backfire. The researchers found that when college students are exposed to the program, they become supportive of conservative Republican leaders and policies. As Baumgartner and Morris conclude: "Ironically, Colbert's attempts to poke fun at conservative commentators may be helping those same commentators spread their message" (p. 622).

Mental and physical states are variables that are important in the conditional model because of their impact on selective exposure and perception. We all know how our moods can affect our choice of media content. We all know what kind of music people prefer when they have just broken off a relationship: sad songs. It is clear that we use the mass media to help us manage our moods (e.g., Zillmann & Bryant, 1985). If we are bored, we might seek out exciting movies or television programs; if we are stressed, we might listen to calming music. We select media content that helps us feel better. Knobloch and Zillmann (2002) found that people in bad moods listened to joyful energetic popular music longer than people in good moods. We might also select media content that helps us forget about or escape from aversive, or bad moods. McIlwraith and Schallow (1983), for example, suggested that some people selected highly arousing media content to "block" hostile and negative mental preoccupations. Similarly, physical states can influence selective exposure to media content. Some interesting research has suggested that hormonal changes can affect women's television program preferences throughout pregnancy (Helregel & Weaver, 1989) and the menstrual cycle (Meadow-croft & Zillmann, 1987).

The attitudes that people hold toward media and their content can be a barrier to effects or a condition that enhances effects. Media credibility, for example, or how trustworthy one believes the media to be, may influence whether audience members accept what they hear, see, or read, or whether they reject or ignore the messages (Gaziano & McGrath, 1986; J. Kim & Rubin, 1997). Perceived realism, or how realistic one believes media content to be, is another attitude that intervenes in media effects (Potter, 1988). Perceptions of television realism are linked to greater television influence on perceptions of social reality, or cultivation effects (Perse, 1986), parasocial interaction, or pseudofriendships with television characters (J. Cohen, 2009; A.M. Rubin, Perse, & Powell, 1985), and social learning from television (e.g., Bandura, 2009). And, perceptions about how difficult it is to learn from different media (amount of invested mental effort, AIME), affect how children mentally process media information and the effects of that information-processing (Salomon & Leigh, 1984).

Another set of individual differences variables that intervenes in media effects is drawn from the uses and gratifications perspective. This perspective holds that the reasons that people use mass communication (or the gratifications that they seek from media use) influence the effects from that use (A.M. Rubin, 2009). Different media use motives lead to selective exposure to specific media and content, as well as to selective attention to different aspects of the message. In addition, different reasons for using mass media influence how involved (or uninvolved) people are with the content. So, media use motives are conditions of media impact. Media use reasons that lead to greater attention to and involvement with the content generally facilitate effects (Kim & Rubin, 1997). Media use reasons that lead to less attention to content may inhibit effects.

Research has shown, for example, that watching television to gain information for use in one's daily life leads to watching news and magazine programs on television (e.g., A.M. Rubin, 1981a). In contrast, watching television just to pass time leads to inattentive channel surfing (Perse, 1990a). The reasons that people have for watching television enhance certain media effects. Watching news for information is linked to greater knowledge gain (Gantz, 1978; Perse, 1990d). Watching news and soap operas for entertainment explains cultivation effects of local news and soap operas (Carveth & Alexander, 1985; Perse, 1990b). Perse (1994) uncovered four main reasons that college students have for using erotica: sexual enhancement (for information and foreplay), diversion (entertainment and relaxation), sexual release (solitary fantasy), and substitution (to replace a partner). Of these reasons, three were directly or indirectly related to greater acceptance of rape myths, or lack of sympathy toward rape victims. The other, sexual release, was a barrier to accepting rape myths. Clearly, it is important to understand why people use media in order to understand the effects of that use.

Summary

The conditional model, then, is an audience-centered model of media effects. It holds that media effects are conditional on the audience because people have the power to selectively expose themselves to messages, pay attention only to those aspects of the content that interest them, selectively interpret the content along with needs, interests, and experiences, and recall messages within their own individualized mental frameworks. Like the limited effects model of the received view, the conditional model recognizes the power of the audience to reject media influence. But, unlike the limited effects model, the conditional model holds that reinforcement effects are not the only effects. Change effects are also quite likely, but conditional on the audience. Audience variables provide important explanations for media effects, especially social categories, social relationships, and individual differences. This model is especially valuable when the focus is on individual-level effects and when individuals are able to select from among a range of media content, assumed to be mentally active and aware, and mentally process and interpret media content.

Valkenburg and Peter (2013) have developed a model of media effects called "the differential susceptibility model." They build on the conditional model to explain that audience members are differentially susceptible to media effects based on dispositions (e.g., gender, personality, moods, motivations), development (e.g., cognitive, emotional, and social development), and social susceptibility (e.g., family, peers, institutional and cultural norms). They explain that these conditions affect media influence directly and indirectly (through their influence on selectivity and cognitive processes). This model falls clearly within the conditional effects model.

Some theorists believe that the study of political communication is entering a new era of "minimal effects" that reinforce the importance of selectivity processes in media effects (e.g., Bennett & Iyengar, 2008). The increased number of cable and online outlets has led to a fragmented audience (cf., Webster & Phalen, 1997) who are increasingly able to engage in selective exposure to messages that reinforce their views. Consistent with the conditional model, however, Holbert, Garrett, and Gleason (2010) remind us that reinforcement effects are important effects.

Cumulative Effects

The cumulative effects model is drawn from the "return to powerful effects" era of the received view of media effects history. The main emphasis of this model is the ubiquitous nature of certain media content that overrides any potential of the audience to limit exposure to certain messages. This model focuses on the consonance and repetition of themes and messages across media content. The explanation for media effects, then, rests in media content – its consistent makeup and depiction. The audience is not relevant to this model because it is not within their power to avoid certain media messages. Some media content is so pervasive that selective exposure is impossible, so everyone is affected in ways that are consistent with media messages. So, amount of media exposure (as a measure of audience immersion in media content) and content analyses (as a measure of the nature of media's messages) are essential components to explaining media effects.

Unlike the direct effects model, this model explains that media effects are a result of cumulative exposure, not due to a single event. Through repeated exposure to similar content across channels, people are moved. The effects of this model are generally reality-construction effects. That is, through cumulative exposure, people begin to adopt the media's framing as their own representation of reality. Effects, according to the cumulative model, are limited to cognitions (belief and attitude acquisition) and affect (emotional reactions). This model, then, focuses on more subtle effects. Although behaviors may be linked to how people think and feel, behaviors are not seen as a direct result of media exposure. Effects are assumed to be fairly enduring because media content tends to be fairly consistent across time. If content changes, then effects might diminish.

Agenda setting can be viewed as a cumulative effect (e.g., M. McCombs & Reynolds, 2009; M. E. McCombs & Shaw, 1972). Agenda setting is conceptualized as the power of the news media to direct our concerns toward certain issues. The effect is a fairly limited cognitive one: the news media don't tell us what to think, but what to think about (B. Cohen, 1963). Agenda setting is based on observations that news content tends to be fairly consonant across news channels. Broadcasting, cable, and print news media highlight the same types of stories, issues, events, and people. Moreover, the processes of news-gathering and production enhance the similarity of news across channels. In the past, news wires have been prime sources for national and international news. Now, concentration of ownership and economy of scale have lead to proliferations of different news channels drawing from the same resources (e.g., CNN and CNN Headline News; NBC, CNBC, and MSNBC). Observations have noted that news organizations tend to be influenced by the same prestige news sources (e.g., G. H. Stempel & Windhauser, 1989).

In most societies, almost everyone sees some type of news. News is presented regularly on the radio, television, and cable networks. It's regularly available on the Web. Newsbreaks pepper network television. Newspaper headlines are displayed for sale in newsstands and boxes on street corners. People receive news updates on their smartphones via email, text, and Twitter updates. Even if people don't seek news out, it is almost impossible not to become aware of the top stories. Selective exposure is not a realistic option. Over time, people accept those issues on the media agenda as important issues.

Traditional cultivation research is another example of a limited effect (Gerbner & Gross, 1976; Morgan, et al., 2009). Through repeated, heavy exposure to television, viewers begin to believe that the real world is similar to the television world. The most researched area of cultivation effects is that of fear of crime. Heavy television viewers become more fearful. The cultivation effect is both cognitive (developing a world view based on television content) and affective (fear). Behavioral effects are rarely the domain of this approach.

Cultivation is based on the results of content analyses that reveal that violence of some kind and patterns of group victimization cut across all prime-time television content (e.g., Signorielli, 2003). Because most people watch television during those hours, they see those patterns of violence and images; selective exposure is not relevant. Because patterns of television viewing are fairly stable, cultivation researchers imply that effects are fairly enduring.

Important Variables in the Model

Media content is central to the cumulative effects model. The nature of the images and issues in the news media are important because they define what the effects are. The specific issues of the media agenda translate to the audience agenda. The patterns of victimization in prime-time dramatic programs (who aggresses against whom) translate into fear for those groups who are represented as victims.

More important, though, is the consonance of media content, or its consistency across channels. Because this model holds that selective exposure is not possible, media messages need to be fairly consistent across a range of readily accessible media outlets. The cumulative effects model is less applicable for specialized, or one-shot media messages, presented on a limited range of channels. The changes in the media environment may threaten the validity of the cumulative effects model. As the Internet becomes an important and widely used news source, personalized news services and menu-based news selection could undermine agenda-setting effects. R. Coleman and McCombs (2007), for example, found that agenda-setting effects, while still significant, were reduced among heavy Internet users. Some scholars have argued that the specialized nature of some cable channels may reduce cultivation's effects because viewers can avoid traditional television programming (e.g., Perse, Ferguson, & D.M. McLeod, 1994). Other scholars, though, point out that most television content is still programming created by the same producers (e.g., Morgan et al., 2009).

Summary

The cumulative effects model focuses on media content as the prime explanation for media effects. This model finds that the audience is not important to understanding media effects because some media content is so pervasive that it is impossible for people to ignore it. So, this model is appropriate when the focus is the effects of media content that are readily accessible and fairly consistent across media channels and context. According to this model, people are affected in fairly predictable ways by cumulative exposure to similar kinds of content. So, this model is not useful for considering one-shot media exposure. This model assumes that because media exposure patterns are fairly stable, effects are fairly enduring.

Cognitive-Transactional Model

This model is drawn from cognitive psychology. It applies the notion of schematic processing to the media context. Several theorists have explained that how humans mentally process environmental stimuli affects how we interpret and learn new information (e.g., Fiske & Taylor, 1991). The key to this model is the schema. Knowledge, according to this approach, does not exist as isolated chunks in our brains. Instead, all knowledge is organized into schemas. A schema is a mental structure that represents knowledge about a concept. Schemas contain the attributes of the concept and the connections among those attributes. Schemas have a hierarchical structure, so that some elements are more central than others. Schemas may exist independently or they may be interrelated through commonly shared elements. When we think of Ryan Seacrest, for example, we might also think about Simon Cowell, because of the common element *American Idol*.

There is a good deal of scholarly as well as common-sense evidence to support the existence of schemas. Word association tests support the notion that some concepts are linked more closely than others. Which is easier to remember: blue bird or blue frame? We all have experienced how some environmental stimuli bring to mind a whole host of other concepts. A certain song might bring to mind pleasant memories or wistful thoughts about a past relationship. The smell of turkey roasting certainly arouses memories of past Thanksgivings.

Some of the earliest scholarly evidence for the existence of schemas comes from F. A. Bartlett (1932). He observed that when people retold stories that took place in other cultures, they altered the details so that they were consistent with their own culture. Bartlett suggested that people had mental patterns that described the stories of their cultures.

Schemas exist for all domains: (a) role schemas (e.g., what a college professor is like), (b) person schemas (our understanding of others we know), (c) self-schemas (how we think about ourselves), (d) group schemas (e.g., males vs. females), and (e) event schemas (e.g., scripts). All of these are mental representations of our knowledge about various people, events, and issues. It is clear that schemas are also relevant in the mass communication context. We not only apply our schemas to interpreting mass media content (e.g., group schema and how women on television ought to act or person schema to help us anticipate how a favorite talk show host will deal with guests), but we also have schemas that help us understand mass media content specifically. We know, for example, that when we see a teenage girl begin to undress in an empty house in a horror film, mayhem is almost sure to follow.

Schemas not only organize knowledge, but they also serve several other functions that influence media effects. First, they direct selective exposure, perception, attention, and recall. The schema that is in use directs attention to certain aspects of the environment that are relevant to that schema. Second, because they organize knowledge, schemas control how new information is integrated with prior knowledge. How a news story is framed (with head-lines, graphics, or introduction) influences which schema is used to interpret the information and which schema any new knowledge is associated with. Third, schemas allow people to make inferences about new situations and help reduce uncertainty about what to think or how to act. When we attend the first class in a semester, for example, we have a fairly good idea of what will happen during that meeting, even if we've never been in one of that pro-fessor's classes. Fourth, schemas allow us to go beyond the stimuli and make inferences about things that are not shown. Most soap opera viewers, for example, know what is happening in the "fade to black" that ends a romantic sex scene.

There are two ways that schemas operate: through controlled or through automatic processing (Bargh, 1988). Controlled processing is individual-controlled mental activity. It usually involves goal-directed, thoughtful mental action. When students are studying for a test, for example, they very con-sciously look for links among the course concepts and try to connect class readings with lecture materials. Or, when well-educated, politically involved people read the newspaper, they may concentrate and try to integrate the new material with prior beliefs about political issues. In controlled processing, the individual chooses and self-activates the schema that they believe is relevant to the task. In a sense, controlled processing involves a good deal of selectivity. When one is goal-directed, he or she may focus only on those media messages that have relevance for the task.

Much media use, however, is not controlled. People are often more auto-matic in their approach to mass media consumption. Much television view-ing grows out of entertainment or relaxation motives, for example, that lead viewers to be more automatic in their viewing. When people are relaxed or distracted, they may react more automatically to the environment. Automatic processing is an effortless, low-involved mental processing of environmental stimuli. In this case, environmental stimuli (media content) may prime or acti-vate schemas. When a schema is primed, it is, in a sense, energized and moves to the top of the mind. As long as it is top of mind, that schema will be used to interpret stimuli; that schema will influence selective exposure, attention, perception, and recall. Priming is an unconscious, relatively short-term effect; a schema rarely is top of mind for more than a few hours. But, once a schema has been primed, it retains some of its energy, and is easier to bring to top of mind again. One way to think about priming is to think about computer files. When a schema is primed, it is pulled from the mental "hard drive." As other schemas are subsequently primed, that first schema gets "buried." But, it is easy to find and reactivate if few other schemas have been used, because it remains a "recent" file.

The cognitive-transactional model has a number of implications for media effects. In the case of controlled processing, media effects are influenced, to a large degree, by the goals of the individual and the schemas that he or she uses to interpret media content. With highly controlled processing, effects are likely to be cognitive, conscious, and fairly long term. But the kinds of effects depend on the schema that is self-activated. For example, when people seek out political information, they may use one of several schemas to evaluate candidates (e.g., Lau, 1986): (a) party identification (looking for consistencies or inconsistencies on political party stands), (b) issues (stands on relevant political issues), or (c) a personality schema (the kind of person the politician is). What people get from their media use, then, is influenced by their goals and the schema that they use.

In the case of automatic processing, media content can be an especially potent prime. Effective media messages can activate certain schemas that direct attention and influence the interpretation of and reaction to the stimuli. Advertisers know, for example, that putting a kitten or a baby in a commercial for toilet paper can associate a schema that includes the attribute "soft," which then might be associated with the product (see also, Baran & Blasko, 1984). Beliefs in the acceptability of rape and interpersonal violence can be primed through observations of violent sexual films (Malamuth & Check, 1981) and aggressive behavior can be primed by watching violent movies (Bushman, 1995). Media content can also prime sex-stereotyped schemas. Women who viewed gender-stereotyped television commercials are more likely to deemphasize achievement and emphasize homemaking in their personal goals (Geis, Brown, Walstedt, & Porter, 1984) than women who viewed commercials with women in nontraditional roles. And adolescent girls who view cosmetic commercials are more likely to rate physical appearance as more important than do girls who view neutral commercials (A. S. Tan, 1979).

And, once primed, schemas are more readily accessible, so a primed schema can also influence the interpretation of and reaction to subsequent stimuli. Researchers have observed that overhearing pro- versus antisocial news stories on a radio affected research participants' reactions in games, as well as judgments about the decency of the average person (Holloway, Tucker, & Hornstein, 1977; Hornstein, LaKind, Frankel, & Manne, 1975). Hansen (1989) observed that participants who watched sex-stereotyped music videos followed by a supposedly unconnected video of a male–female interaction evaluated the woman in the interaction more favorably when she acted more compliantly. Peffley, Shields, and Williams (1996) found that racial stereotypes can be activated by local news that features visual images of African American suspects. Some media content, then, can prime schemas that affect how we evaluate other stimuli that we encounter shortly after exposure.

Important Variables in the Model

The cognitive-transactional model is called transactional because both media content and audience factors are important to understanding media effects. Media content is important in its ability to prime. The audience members are important because schemas can be quite individualized.

Media Content. The salience of visual cues is important to understanding what can prime. When objects in the environment stand out, people pay attention to them (Kahneman, 1973). We notice quite easily, for example, the flashing lights and sirens of police and emergency vehicles. So, aspects of content that attract involuntary attention are more likely to prime. Sexual and violent content may be especially potent primes. Other characteristics of media content may increase salience. Berlyne (1970), for example, observed that people pay more attention to bright, complex, and colored stimuli. Studies have found that subjects paid more visual attention to people on television with more brightly colored clothing and hair (McArthur & Post, 1977; McArthur & Solomon, 1978).

Other content attributes are likely to facilitate priming. Berkowitz and Rogers (1986) pointed out that aggressive ideas are more likely to be activated when content is realistic. Subjects who believed they had watched violent documentaries were more likely to display aggressive behaviors than subjects who believed they had watched fiction (Berkowitz & Alioto, 1973; Feshbach, 1972).

Character identification may also increase priming effects because people might imagine themselves imitating the actions of characters with whom they identify (Dorr, 1986). Turner and Berkowitz (1972), for example, found that subjects who were instructed to imagine themselves as a boxer acted more aggressively after viewing a prize fight. Identification may increase the salience of the actor and stimulate more thoughts related to the observed action.

Audience Variables. The audience is also important to the cognitive model because the schemas that direct selectivity can be individualized. So media content that has the ability to prime may prime different kinds of schemas in different types of people. For example, a story about a vampire might prime thoughts of a dangerous monster (e.g., Dracula) for some people or thoughts of a romantic gallant man (e.g., Edward from the *Twilight* series) for others, depending on the elements of one's schema. Research suggests that political sophistication is reflected in the kinds of schemas that people use to evaluate political candidates (Lau & Sears, 1986). People who know relatively little about politics may make voting decisions based on more general, person schemas (is the candidate a good person?). Those who are politically knowledgeable may make decisions based on a candidate's public records on certain important issues. Social categories, social relationships, and individual difference variables are relevant to explaining the content of audience schemas.

The individual goals that people have when they approach media exposure influences controlled processing. More goal-directed media use is more selective (A.M. Rubin, 1984), so people may reject media messages that do not help them achieve their goals. To use an earlier example, if a politically sophisticated person is seeking information about political candidates, he or she may reject talk shows that focus on candidates' personal lives and habits.

People's moods can also affect the schemas that are more easily brought to mind. As Fiske and Taylor (1991) summarized: "All else being equal, people in a good mood are more likely to see the good sides of other people, and sometimes people in bad moods see others' bad sides" (p. 146).

Finally, individual differences can have an impact on schema activation because they can represent the kinds of schemas that might be chronically top of mind. Bushman (1995), for example, found that priming effects of aggressive media content were enhanced with individuals who were higher in trait aggressiveness. Bushman (1995) explains that "high trait aggressive individuals are more susceptible to the effects of violent media than are low trait aggressive individuals because they possess a relatively large network of aggressive associations that can be activated by violent cues" (p. 959). Similarly, Malamuth and Huppin (2005) argue that pornography's largest priming effects occur when there are other "risk factors," such as hyper-masculinity (a "script" that represents callous sexual attitudes, beliefs that violence is "manly," and perceptions that violence is exciting, Mosher & Tomkins, 1988).

Summary

The cognitive-transactional model is one that has a dual focus. It holds that media impact grows from cognitive reactions to media content. So, the model focuses on the mental organization of knowledge – the schema. Schematic

Table 2.1 Comparing and Contrasting the Four Models of Media Effects

	Models of Media Effects		
	Nature of Effects	Media Content Variables	Audience Variables
Direct	Immediate, uniform, observable Short-term Emphasis on change	Salience, arousal, and realism	Not relevant
Conditional	Individualized Reinforcement as well as change Cognitive, affective, and behavioral Long- or short-term	Not relevant	Social categories Social relationships Individual differences
Cumulative	Based on cumulative exposure Cognitive or affective Rarely behavioral Enduring	Consonance across channels Repetition	Not relevant
Cognitive-Transactional	Immediate and short-term Based on a single exposure Cognitive and affective Behavioral effects possible	Salience of visual cues	Schema makeup Mood Goals Individual differences

processing is seen as the basis for selective attention, perception, and recall as well as subsequent media effects due to that processing. Schematic processing, though, can be automatic or controlled. When processing is automatic, the audience is considered to be less active and the focus turns to media content. Some aspects of media content are salient and prime schemas. When schemas are primed, they direct attention, perception, recall, and other reactions to environmental cues. Variables that affect the salience of media content are important to understanding automatic processing.

When processing is controlled, schemas are self-activated. People are goal directed and channel their thoughts toward their goals. They select the schemas that they believe will help them achieve their goals. Media content is interpreted, then, according to the individual audience member's goals and schemas.

This model sees effects as a result of cognitive reactions to media content, in the case of automatic processing, or as a result of conscious mental effort, in the case of controlled processing. Effects are cognitive and affective, though reactions to the environment can also have behavioral aspects. The cognitive-transactional model accounts for short-term effects as a result of priming. But long-term effects can emerge as a result of controlled processing.

Some Notes of Caution about the Four Models

These four models depict ways to conceptualize the process of media effects. There are a few limitations to these models that represent different ways to think about media effects. The four models focus on content-dependent effects – effects that are based on the content of the mass media (see Chapter 1). Certainly, media effects can result from the use of the mass media, regardless of the content. For example, television viewing by children might take up time they should be spending on homework, leading to lower grades. Or, people might spend so much time online that they neglect their interpersonal relationships. Other theories and models explain the processes underlying displacement and other content-independent effects.

These models also have a social-scientific orientation. They are based on hypothesis testing and social-scientific research methods. Some critics of media effects research (e.g., Gitlin, 1980) argue that these sorts of models make it difficult to assess subtle, long-term effects at the societal level, especially the reinforcement of the status quo (E. Katz, 1987). Meyrowitz (1985), for example, argues that television can have profound effects, such as merging public and private spheres of society, a shifting expectation of Presidential leadership, and the "end of childhood" (p. 226). Although the four models of media effects can explain some aspects of these sorts of effects, they are limited in their ability to explain shifts in societal perceptions and norms.

These four models are simplified depictions of explanations for media effects. They are designed to focus attention on specific explanations for media effects. No single model is complete. It is, of course, unrealistic to ignore entirely the nature of media content as contributing to media effects as the conditional model does. It is just as unrealistic to ignore the possibility that different individuals will react differently to media content, as the direct effects model does. The most complete explanations for media effects are those that combine explanations from each model. For example, the most complete explanations for cultivation effects are those that combine aspects of the conditional and cumulative models. That is, when cumulative exposure to prime-time television drama is combined with certain aspects of the audience (e.g., educational level, gender, neighborhood of residence), more variance in fear of crime is accounted for. The value of each model, though, is in its ability to focus on the most important explanation for media effects.

Notes

1 Chaffee and Hochheimer (1982) pointed out that the term "magic bullet" may actually be a misnomer. In the medical literature, a magic bullet is a "specific medication, which hits only those few in the population who are diseased; it is 'magic' because it passes through all the others without any effect" (p. 286). In the context of media effects, a magic bullet would have specific effects on only a limited portion of the audience.

2 *The People's Choice* (Lazarsfeld et al., 1968) received some funding from *Life* magazine for rights to the story. Merton's (1949) study of opinion leadership in "Rovere" was funded by *Time*. MacFadden Publishing provided $30,000 to underwrite *Personal Influence* (E. Katz & Lazarsfeld, 1955; see Rogers, 1994, p. 296).

3 Frank Stanton, president of CBS, for example, had worked with Lazarsfeld at the bureau. He was the first Ph.D. in the broadcast industry (Rogers, 1994).

4 Another type of musical passage that evokes arousal is appoggiatura, notes that "clash" with the melody and sound a bit dissonant. One example of music that induces emotional responses is Adele's "Someone Like You," which seems to be a favorite when people "need a good cry." *Saturday Night Live* ran a skit in 2011 that illustrated the "power" of this song to bring people to tears.

3 MEDIA EFFECTS AND CRISIS

Graber (1989) defined crises as "natural or manmade events that pose an immediate and serious threat to the lives and property or to the peace of mind of many" (p. 305).[1] Crises emerge suddenly and arise from attacks on political leaders, such as the assassination of John F. Kennedy (1963) and the attempted assassination of Ronald Reagan (1981); from attacks by and threats from external forces, such as the attack on the New York city World Trade Center (2001), the terrorist bombings of London public transportation (2005), the hostage situation in Iran (1979 to 1981), and the Persian Gulf War (1991); from natural disasters such as Hurricanes Katrina (2005) and Sandy (2012), the Indian Ocean tsunami (2004), the devastating earthquake in Haiti (2010), the super tornados in the southern U.S. (2011), and the earthquake and tsunami in Japan (2011); from technical disasters such as the nuclear accidents at Three Mile Island (1979) and Chernobyl (1986), the BP oil spill in the Gulf of Mexico (2010), and the Columbia space shuttle explosion (2003); from health threats such as the H1N1 influenza outbreak (2009); from unexpected political unrest such as the Arab Spring (2011); from internal conflicts such as the National Guard shooting of nine students at Kent State (1970), the shootings at Virginia Tech (2007), the Beltway sniper (2002), the Columbine school massacre (1999), and the Los Angeles riots following the first Rodney King verdict (1992); and from terrorist activity, such as the bombings at the Oklahoma Federal Building (1995) and the anthrax attacks (2001). Crises affect large numbers of people and are marked by sudden onset, uncertainty, and lack of control, emotional reactions, and threats to lives and property.

No matter what the cause, times of crisis are extraordinary periods that are marked by instability, uncertainty, stress, and emotional significance because of fear of undesirable outcomes. Normal activities cease. When President Reagan was shot in 1981, for example, Congress recessed in the midst of debate, the New York and American stock exchanges halted trading, and the Oscar presentations, scheduled for that evening, were postponed. Both Presidential candidates suspended their campaigns less than 2 weeks before the election when Hurricane/Super Storm Sandy hit the east coast in October 2012. Immediately after the terrorist attacks of September 11, 2001, the stock market closed until September 17, its longest closure in almost three-quarters of a century. International flights were suspended, schools were closed, and events were cancelled. People gathered to watch the rescue efforts unfold. Times of crisis heighten the importance of the role of the mass media in providing information and explanation. Because of their resources and unique access to government agencies and officials, society relies on the media to collect information and guide public response.

Theoretical Focus: The Functions of Mass Communication

One approach to analyzing the relationship of mass media to society is structural functionalism. Functionalism is based on a biological analogy. Society is viewed as a complex system of interrelated parts – all of which perform specific activities that are designed to maintain society's even and steady functioning. These activities are termed functions. Functions are repetitive activities that are designed to ensure harmony and stability in society. If there is a disruption in society, various aspects of society act to ensure a return to a state of equilibrium (Merton, 1968).

C.R. Wright (1986) summarized much of the writing about the functions of mass communication and notes that mass media serve both latent (hidden) and manifest (obvious) functions for society, individuals, societal subgroups, and culture. Based on Lasswell (1948), Wright points out that mass communication serves four major functions for society: surveillance, correlation, socialization, and entertainment. He also notes that these activities of the media may not only be functional, or positive, but they may also be dysfunctional and have negative consequences.

Surveillance is the information function of mass communication. As a society grows and becomes more complex, it becomes important to have a sentry or watch dog monitor the environment so that other groups in society can devote themselves to other functional activities. Complex societies rely on mass communication for surveillance most typically through news reports. The mass media collect, summarize, and report the information that various groups need to conduct their own work (e.g., stock market reports, weather, or summaries of legislative activity). We also rely on mass communication as an advance warning system to alert society in times of danger and crisis.

As a result of its surveillance activity, mass communication performs other functions for society. Surveillance can increase perceptions of equality in society. Because many forms of mass communication are publically accessible, information can be available to all members of society and everyone has a chance to benefit from that information. Through ethicizing, surveillance allows society to maintain social control by pointing out deviant behavior and holding it up to ridicule. And coverage by the mass media also raises awareness of the social standing of those issues, events, and people that they cover through the status conferral function (Lazarsfeld & Merton, 1948).

Surveillance, though, can also be dysfunctional. "War nerves" is a phenomenon that emerges during crises in which people become stressed and anxious because of information overload. Some alerts may also lead to overreaction and panics or paralysis through fear. One latent dysfunction is narcotization. Lazarsfeld and Merton (1948) feared that media surveillance could begin to replace political activity in society. That is, as people try to keep up with news and public affairs information, they actually become more apathetic toward societal issues. The sheer amount of time spent with the media may displace political action. Or, the intellectual analysis of political information misleads people into thinking they are actually involved in the political process, when they are not. Media use for surveillance, in this case, replaces political activity. As Lazarsfeld and Merton (1948) said, people may "mistake *knowing* about problems of the day for *doing* something about them" (p. 106).

Correlation is the editorial and explanation function of mass communication. Information is often complex. Through correlation, mass media clarify and explain the relevance of information. If through surveillance the mass media tell us what is happening, through correlation the mass media relay what it means to us. Correlation is a correction of some of the dysfunctions of surveillance. Information overload, for example, can be reduced through synthesizing and digesting information to highlight the most important bits of news. Correlation is common in the mass media. Editorial pages in newspapers present opinion and suggestions about public affairs. One simple example of correlation is the typical weather forecast. Through surveillance, the weathercaster displays maps that mark cold and warm fronts, jet stream movement, and isobars. Unless we're familiar with climatology, these markings often make no sense. But, the weather forecaster explains these to the viewers and relays what we can expect the weather to be, based on those data.

Correlation can be dysfunctional for society. If people rely too heavily on mass media's interpretation of news, they may lose their own critical abilities to evaluate information on their own. Or, media organizations may be hesitant to criticize and editorialize against powerful institutions and people in society out of fear of retaliation. Media organizations rely heavily on government sources, for example, and might be reluctant to lose access to those sources (e.g., Herman & Chomsky, 2002).

Socialization is the function of mass communication that deals with the transmission of social values and cultural heritage. A society is marked by commonly shared cultural norms, values, and experiences. Mass communication serves to display and reinforce those values and experiences. Mass communication can also integrate new members of a society, children and immigrants, by teaching and relaying those norms, values, and experiences. Through socialization, mass communication promotes societal integration and cohesion.

An emphasis on cohesion, however, can be dysfunctional. If mass communication ignores subgroups in society, regional and ethnic differences may be diminished, reducing cultural and intellectual diversity in society. Mass media content often is not a multifaceted presentation of societal norms and values. Unfortunately, because of demands of the marketplace, media content is often simplified, stereotyped, and representative of the values of the dominant social class. Those images may lead to improper socialization and learning inaccurate, slanted representations of societal values.

The entertainment function serves as a source of rest, respite, and diversion. The strong work ethic in our society led to mass media entertainment being considered dysfunctional for many years. Some writers were concerned that popular culture would debase people and might even displace more intellectual pursuits (see Mendelsohn, 1966). But, it is clear that amusement and relaxation are functional. Individually, people need to rest and regroup. For society, entertainment provides shared experiences, like media events such as the Olympics (e.g., Rothenbuhler, 1988), and a source for social cohesion. But, entertainment can also be dysfunctional. Mass media entertainment can displace other more worthwhile activities. And, much of the concern about antisocial effects focuses on violent or sensational media content.

Functionalist approaches to understanding mass communication have been criticized (e.g., Elliott, 1974). Some argue that the approach is tautological; that is, it is based on the assumption that if something exists, it must serve some purpose, so it is functional. Existence, then, is equated with function. Moreover, functionalism's emphasis on stability means that it is unable to provide an explanation for change in society. Despite these limitations, understanding society's and individuals' expectations about mass communication may help in understanding the role that it plays and the effects that can emerge in times of societal upheaval.

Functions of Mass Communication during Crises

Graber (2010) explains that crises have several stages. The first stage is the discovery of the crisis or threat of disaster. At this phase, uncertainty is the highest and the threat least understood (Olsson, 2010). Mass media organizations react by sending resources to the scene and contacting officials, agencies, and experts who can explain what is happening.[2] The broadcast media react rapidly and interrupt or suspend regular programming to cover the crisis. It is radio and television that become primary sources for information – even for those involved in the crisis. During the initial hours of the Persian Gulf War, for example, world leaders followed CNN's news coverage of the bombing of Baghdad. Even the Federal Emergency Management Agency (FEMA) monitors ABC, CBS, NBC, and CNN during natural disasters (Goldman & Reilly, 1992).[3] News anchors typically become conduits for disconnected reports from those on the scene – professionals, experts, eyewitnesses, and onlookers. The news is viewed as a "command post" that coordinates and disseminates pertinent news information (Quarantelli, 1981). These bulletins are often unedited and unverified. Crises almost eliminate gatekeeping (Waxman, 1973). Rumor and disinformation are passed on alongside accurate reports (Dynes, 1970). During coverage of the 9/11 attack, news organizations formatted television screens to be able to display a maximum amount of information. Split screens were common to accommodate two video feeds;

updates crawled across the bottom of the screen. "Unedited" video was common; video of the collapse of the towers was played and replayed.

Coverage of a crisis can consume media. As the most immediate and most relied upon medium, television devotes extraordinary resources to crisis coverage. Television news responded to the attacks on the World Trade Center towers by dropping regular programming and carrying all news for the next three days. Even stations with no regular news shifted to all-news programming from other stations. The fall television season premier was delayed; the Emmy awards program was postponed. Most of the nation's radio stations shifted to all-news, many carrying news from the major radio news organizations. News was available almost everywhere. Televisions were turned on; radio news replaced music in public places.

September 11, 2001 was the first test of the Internet's ability to be a major news source. News web sites quickly became strained as people sought information (Spence, Westerman, Skalski, Seeger, Sellnow, & Ulmer, 2006). News sites conserved bandwidth by forgoing photos and graphics (Carey, 2003). Some news organizations borrowed server capacity from other nonnews parts of their corporations: ABC.com, for example, used server space from ESPN.com (Carey, 2003).

The media planned coverage of Hurricane Katrina, as the "monster" storm moved toward New Orleans. Journalists and satellite trucks were positioned to wait out the storm and report on the aftermath. Brian Williams and an NBC crew settled in to report from the Superdome. As we soon learned, the aftermath of the storm was far worse than the storm itself. Although television coverage of Katrina did not displace regular programming, the audience saw expanded news reports from the Superdome, from national reporters situated in the city's central locations, and from local reporters, informed by their knowledge of local topography, reporting from around the city (Daniels & Loggins, 2007; Izard, 2010; G. H. Stempel, 2010).

Media coverage has always been central during crises. For 4 days in November, 1963, television reported without interruption on the assassination and funeral of President John F. Kennedy. The 1986 launch of the Challenger space shuttle was initially minor news, covered live only by CNN. But immediately after the explosion that killed the seven astronauts, including teacher Christa McAuliffe, all three networks turned to live, continuous coverage. Media focus continued throughout the evening, especially when President Reagan canceled his State of the Union address. ABC was the only network to have a reporter in Tehran during the first week of the 1979 Iranian hostage crisis and was the clear champion in media coverage. Expanded news reports filled late evening, after the local news. These reports proved to be so popular that the program was continued as *Nightline*, even after the crisis passed. The 1991 Persian Gulf War is a good case study of increased news coverage. The National Media Index, which tracked the news in the three major networks, five major newspapers, and the three major news magazines, reported that during January 21, 1991, through February 3, 1991 (the weeks following the air strike on Baghdad), news increased to 130% of its normal volume; almost 93% of all news was Gulf War related (Dennis et al., 1991).

During times of crises, the mass media's functional importance dramatically increases. Schramm (1965) noted that crises heighten society's needs for information, interpretation, and consolation. Intense uncertainty coupled with fear of danger lead people to rely on the only central source that has access to news sources and information. During the 1973 Yom Kippur War, "the media had become central to people's lives" (Peled & Katz, 1974, p. 52) for information about family members at the front. Because the blackout required everyone to stay indoors, 53% of the Israeli respondents wanted television to devote most of its time to surveillance and correlation. Another one-third expected tension release and solidarity building from television. During the Persian Gulf War, respondents believed that television's most important function was providing information ($M = 6.09$, on a 7-point scale), followed by explanation ($M = 5.76$), building solidarity ($M = 5.52$), and reducing tension ($M = 4.95$). Just as the U.S. was beginning the War on Terrorism by invading Afghanistan a year after September 11, Delaware residents saw the functional importance of the media. They reported that the media should provide ($M = 5.85$, on a 7-point scale) and explain information ($M = 5.77$) and report news that builds solidarity ($M = 5.78$; Perse et al., 2002).

The functional importance of the media to provide surveillance and correlation is reflected in increased news use during crises. On hearing startling news, people often turn to the media, usually television, for confirmation and details (e.g., Carey, 2003; B. Greenberg, 1965; Riffe & Stovall, 1989). News ratings can be extraordinarily high during times of crisis. On hearing of President Kennedy's assassination, five out of six people who could, abandoned their daily routine and turned to television for further information (Sheatsley & Feldman, 1965). President Kennedy's funeral a few days later attracted 81% of the television audience. George Bush's address on the evening of 17 January, 1991, about the air strike on Baghdad was seen by 79% of all U.S. households (Record-Breaking TV Audience, 1991). During the first week of the 1973 Yom Kippur War, almost all Israelis were listening to radio and television; 68% listened to the radio all day long and 55% even reported that they listened to the radio while they were watching television (Peled & Katz, 1974). Thirst for news was so great that people stayed up late listening to the radio and wanted the daily television news expanded. After hearing of the attempt on President Reagan's life, 90% of Gantz's (1983) respondents watched television or listened to the radio; 28% continued to follow the news after 11:00 p.m.

The most watched news story of the century (Pew Research Center for People & the Press, 2010) was the September 11 terrorist attacks, followed closely by 78% of the population. Carey (2003) notes that some people "dropped their everyday routines" (p. 2) to watch television all day. Althaus (2002) reports

> The tragedies of 9/11 had the immediate effect of more than doubling
> the size of the evening news audience, from 13% of American adults in

the week of September 3–9 to more than 26% in the week of September 10–16. Nielsen Media Research later estimated that 79.5 million viewers were tuning into any of 11 broadcast or cable networks showing news coverage on the night of 9/11.

(p. 518)

The radio news audience increased during the first stage of coverage of 9/11. National Public Radio saw a 20% increase in their news audience (Carey, 2003). Many reported listening to international radio, such as BBC, to get an international perspective on the events (Carey, 2003).

Traffic to Internet news sites increased during the first stage of the 9/11 crisis. Between 9:00 and 10:00 a.m., traffic to MSNBC.com increased 500%; traffic to CNN.com increased almost 450% (Rappoport & Alleman, 2003). Fully 29% of Internet users sought news about the attacks online (Rappoport & Alleman, 2003). This focus on news resulted in fewer visits to non-news web sites; traffic to eBay and Amazon both declined on September 11 (Rappoport & Alleman, 2003). The authors also saw increased traffic to Internet news sites on November 12, 2001, with the crash of Flight 587, and in early October, 2001, with the discovery of anthrax-laced letters.

Natural disasters are also marked by a heightened need for information and increased news use. On the day of the eruption of Mount St. Helens in 1981, 85.4% of respondents living in eastern Washington turned to television for information; 81.8% used the radio. Information seeking remained high the following day; 89.1% turned to television for news and 86.6% also listened to the radio (Hirschburg, Dillman, & Ball-Rokeach, 1986). The researchers concluded that uncertainty increased the importance of the media and people's reliance on them for news.

Surveys of residents of Galveston, Texas, who had experienced the 1983 devastation of Hurricane Alicia further point to the importance of the media. Researchers interviewed these residents about their reactions to the 1985 warning for Hurricane Danny (it bypassed Galveston and struck the Louisiana coast [Ledingham & Walters, 1989]). About half of the residents reported that media sources were the most important for information about what to do during Danny's warnings but only 15.8% spent more time watching television. Over three-quarters of the residents (77.7%), however, watched television specifically to monitor the storm's progress or to watch the weather forecasts. Although time with the media did not increase for many, storm-related news may have displaced entertainment viewing.

Even those not directly affected by hurricanes turn to television for information. Hurricane Katrina was the top news story of 2005 (Pew Research Center for the People & the Press, 2011). About 70% of people said that they followed the hurricane coverage "closely." Fully 89% of their respondents relied on television for news about the disaster. Another 35% turned to newspapers; 21% to Internet news. The public not only were interested in following the disaster, but gave the news media "generally good marks" for their coverage (Pew Research Center for the People & the Press, 2005, p. 2).

Hurricane Sandy in 2012 showed the strength of online and mobile media. FEMA, the Red Cross, and local government and disaster agencies turned to social media to spread information and alerts. Early reports were that The Weather Channel (weather.com) saw record numbers of page views on their web site and mobile streaming. The October 29 views (298 million) were almost triple the number on August 26, 2011 – when Hurricane Irene was threatening the same coast (Winslow, 2012). Early reports after the storm were that there were over 20 million tweets about the hurricane, although this is likely an underestimate (Tibken, 2012).

Hyping Hurricane Irene

Hurricane Irene was due to arrive the weekend of August 28, 2011, about the same date that Katrina arrived in New Orleans in 2005. The storm wasn't the largest one, but it was going to be the first hurricane to make landfall on New York City since 1893. The media were ready. Cable news channels and The Weather Channel reported on Irene's progress almost around the clock. The Weather Channel sent spotters and reporters along the path to be sure to capture the first images of the howling winds and crashing waves. Hurricane reports so consumed the news that few other news events got attention – even the announcement that the U.S. had killed the No. 2 leader of al-Qaeda.

Some praise the media for such intense coverage. Some believe it saved lives. The media coverage prepared the population in Irene's path, prevented injuries, and limited damage. Others, however, severely criticized this carnival of coverage. They believe that the media coverage was designed to create ratings and media hype. One of The Weather Channel's advertisers reminded viewers that The Home Depot was there for poststorm repairs. Lise King, a fellow at the Harvard's Carr Center for Human Rights Policy, pointed out that media coverage of hurricanes is driven by two contradictory goals – information and entertainment: "The two agendas cannot co-exist, as one serves to lead citizens into calm action and the other is meant, by nature, to drum up emotional responses in order to keep the viewer tuning in" (Bauder, 2011, D3). Federal Emergency Management Agency (FEMA) personnel were concerned that people would remember the hype. The next time they are cautioned to prepare and evacuate, they might not. They might think it's just another case of media-manufactured hysteria.

The unpredictability of weather, it turned out, shifted Irene's course. She degraded to a tropical storm and spared the major cities of the region, but hit other areas hard. The storm caused almost $16 billion damage, making it the sixth costliest U.S. hurricane.

Surveillance and correlation are the most apparent functions of the mass media during crises, but the mass media also serve solidarity-building and tension-reduction functions. During the days following the assassination of President Kennedy, television coverage provided emotional support to help viewers deal with their shock and grief (Mindak & Hursh, 1965; Schramm, 1965). Although surveillance and correlation were most important, about one-third of Israelis expected television to reduce tension and build solidarity during the Yom Kippur War (Peled & Katz, 1974). Dramatic programming, such as action adventure and movies, were linked to tension reduction. Peled and Katz (1974) suggested that these programs distracted viewers from their war fears. Even news reports helped to reduce tension and build solidarity. The authors note that these effects might have been due to morale-bolstering approaches to news reporting. During natural disasters, emergency relief workers encourage media coverage for two reasons: to expedite the flow of emergency information to victims (surveillance and correlation) and to build public sympathy to encourage donations and aid (Sood, Stockdale, & Rogers, 1987).

Media coverage is often geared to tension reduction and solidarity building. During the 1991 Persian Gulf War, news stories built on the "yellow ribbon" theme. Kaid, Harville, Ballotti, and Wawrzyniak's (1993) content analysis of newspaper coverage of the Gulf War, for example, concluded that the U.S. involvement in the war was portrayed negatively in only 3% of the stories. Newhagen (1994) found that network television news was also mainly more supportive and less critical of U.S. involvement in the war. Dennis and his colleagues (1991) reported that 3 weeks prior to the air strike, stories focusing on the controversy about entering the war outnumbered stories about supporting the war by 45 to 8. In the following weeks during the air and ground wars, "yellow ribbon" stories outnumbered "controversy" stories 36 to 19.

More recent crises have also illustrated the tension-reduction and solidarity functions of mass communication. Although undergraduate students turned to coverage of the 9/11 terrorist attacks more for surveillance reasons, they also sought reassurance from the news coverage (C. Hoffner, Fujioka, Ye, & Ibrahim, 2009). They reported watching for reassurance that everything would be OK, for reassurance that the U.S. was safe, and in order to feel a sense of community. They sought out news stories that highlighted the generosity of people, survivors being reunited with loved ones, and stories of donations of time and money (C. Hoffner et al., 2009). In 2012, a content analysis of tweets during Superstorm Sandy found that over 42% with #sandy were not informational, but focused on emotional reactions to the storm (Lachlan, Spence, Lin, & Del Greco, 2014).

Hutcheson and his colleagues (2004) analyzed the rhetorical themes used by U.S. government and military leaders in news stories dealing with the aftermath of the September 11 strike published in news magazines for the first 5 weeks after the attacks. They found that these reports served to foster and maintain solidarity by reinforcing a collective U.S. identity (Hutcheson,

Domke, Billeaudeaux, & Garland, 2004). This collective identity is created and maintained by:

- affirmation of American values and ideals that drew upon the U.S. "mythology" of individualism, liberty, and equality;
- affirmation of U.S. international power and dominance, thereby tapping into the nation's long-established self-image as a world super-power;
- emphasis on unification among Americans along ideological and racial lines, which paralleled a pattern in Presidential inaugural rhetoric of emphasizing national unity within diversity;
- shifting of blame for the September 11 attacks away from the United States and portrayal of the international community as united behind a U.S. campaign against terrorism, both of which positioned the United States as a moral leader among nations;
- and, finally, demonization of the "enemy," which followed a familiar good-versus-evil discourse employed effectively during the Cold War and the Gulf War (p. 30).

The media often serve tension-reduction functions during crises. Coverage of extreme weather events, such as Katrina, is often framed as entertainment (Daniels & Loggins, 2007). The approaches of storms are tracked like races. Weather forecasters present probabilities of "direct hits." Storm chasers and reporters are positioned in the path of the storms. Reports focus on excitement and anticipation. Videos recount the strength of winds and waves by showing the collapse of bridges and docks and the flooding of city streets. After the 2012 Japanese earthquake, cameras around the Pacific coast were poised to capture the images of tsunamis rising from the sea. Shafer (2012) wrote about the appeal of "disaster porn," or the voyeuristic search for images that follow disasters. After Hurricane Sandy, for example, images of flooded streets, ruined amusement park rides, and upturned trees were the popular content of tweets, emails, and YouTube videos.

The media served tension-reduction functions immediately after the September 11 terrorist attacks. Some thought news coverage resembled a "terror spectacle" that mirrored Hollywood blockbusters like *Independence Day* and *The Towering Inferno* (Kellner, 2003). Other analyses found that coverage of attacks included more features of crime stories than political stories (e.g., a focus on the "crime," reports of eyewitnesses, and efforts to identify and apprehend the criminals, McDonald & Lawrence, 2004). Spigel (2004) chronicled how entertainment television responded to the atmosphere of fear and apprehension. Networks not carrying wall-to-wall news replaced programs and movies that might contribute to the fear with other more distracting programs. USA network, for example, canceled its run of *The Siege*, a program dealing with Arab terrorists. TBS replaced violent movies like *Lethal Weapon* with comedies like *Look Who's Talking*. Audiences, however, seem to find some solace in violent films. Video outlets reported heightened sales of movies with terrorist plots (Spigel, 2004). When television returned to regular programming, this move was seen as a patriotic act: a return to normalcy and a "public service" (Spigel, 2004, p. 237).

Crisis Coverage as a Media Event and Disaster Marathon

Even as society becomes complex, it is still important for social rituals and events to reinforce shared values and traditions. Symbols represented in social rituals, such as parades celebrating patriotic holidays, bond individuals to each other and to society (Durkheim, 1964).

More recently, though, a society's social rituals are displayed and experienced through television. E. Katz (1980) conceptualized these media events as the coronations (parades, weddings, and funerals), contests (in which superpowers compete), and conquests (the stories of heroes) that reinforce the shared traditions and values of a society (Dayan & Katz, 1992). According to Katz (1980), media events (a) are broadcast live so that the coverage allows viewers to feel as though they are experiencing the event as it happens; (b) are planned to ease access to and coverage by television; (c) are dramatic and contain emotional and symbolic content; (d) compel viewing as participation in history; (e) are suspenseful (although the event may be planned, the ultimate outcome is unknown); (f) are framed to capture and hold the audience's attention; and (g) focus on the people involved as symbols.

E. Katz and Liebes (2007) point out that *media events* focus on media coverage of occurrences that are designed to serve integrative functions in society. These sorts of stories, they argue, are now upstaged by a media focus on disruptive events, disaster, war, and terror – the *disaster marathon*. When the media focus their coverage on events such as natural disasters and acts of terrorism, they attract an anxious and fearful audience, not a festive one. Another key distinction between media events and disaster marathons according to Katz and Liebes (2007) is preplanning. Although there are journalistic routines for covering crises, these events are not preplanned. Reporters need to race to the location, anchors are called to the studio, graphics and video are hastily prepared.

Many crises are covered by the media as media events and disaster marathons. As soon as news of a crisis is released, intense television coverage transports the audience to the locale – New Orleans, New York City, Baghdad, Oklahoma City, Cape Canaveral. Although the crises themselves are rarely planned, the media have policies and plans and devote resources immediately to coverage of the crisis. The coverage focuses on the dramatic and is framed as a contest (will the United States be able to secure the release of the hostages in the embassy?), as a conquest (Schwarzkopf's "How we won the war" speech after the 1991 Persian Gulf ground war), or as a coronation (G. W. Bush's "Mission Accomplished" visit to the USS aircraft carrier *Abraham Lincoln* in 2003). Personalities become central to the coverage: the bravery of Jacqueline Kennedy; the firefighter carrying the rescued youngster from the bombed-out Oklahoma federal building; Christa McAuliffe. And symbols represent the crises: the yellow ribbons of the 1991 Gulf War; the single rose standing in the surf after the memorial service for those who died on TWA flight 800; the skeleton of the fallen World Trade Center tower.

The framing of crises as media events can fulfill surveillance and correlation functions by providing coverage of the incidents, but mainly they serve to socialize and entertain. A prime function of media events is to facilitate and reinforce societal cohesion. The live coverage by television, accessible to all, gives viewers a sense of connection to others who are sharing a common experience. The symbols that dominate the coverage give rise to common emotional reactions. The media coverage of crises endows a shared memory. Most baby boomers will always remember the Kennedy assassination. Their children will remember the Challenger explosion. Most everyone will remember where they were when the World Trade Center towers fell. Media events also serve an entertainment function; the coverage of the Persian Gulf War especially illustrates its framing, in part, as entertainment. CNN gave its war coverage a title ("A Line in the Sand") and a theme song (rhythmic drum roll). The glorification of the success of U.S. military equipment was reminiscent of video games (e.g., smart bombs) and sporting events (the Patriots vs. the Scuds). Coverage of September 11 had elements of entertainment. The collapse of the towers and the images of the firefighters covered with gray ash all were elements of a terrible horror film. The heroism of the passengers of Flight 93 has become one of the amazing tales of that day.

Do the Media Fulfill Their Functions?

The functions of mass communication become particularly apparent during times of emergency. The press devotes resources to fulfilling the public's needs for information, explanation, socialization, solidarity, and tension release. The effects of mass communication during times of crises can be understood within this framework. Through their surveillance and correlation roles, media may increase awareness of threats through news diffusion and contribute to other cognitive and/or learning effects. Through solidarity-building and tension-reduction roles, media may contribute to rally effects and the formation of other attitudes.

Diffusion of News

One of the most researched effects of mass communication during crisis situations is news diffusion. This area of study focuses on the information role of mass communication. News diffusion research examines the means through which people learn about news events and how rapidly news of an event is spread throughout a system. The study of the diffusion of news events not only has theoretical importance for understanding the role of mass communication in the spread of information, but it also has real practical value. Officials need to know the most rapid and effective way to alert the public about impending disasters and subsequent relief efforts. DeFleur (1987) reported that the first quantitative news diffusion study considered how people found out about the death of President Franklin D. Roosevelt in 1945. Since the 1940s, many other studies suggest the following conclusions about diffusion of news.

The more important an event, the higher the rate and amount of diffusion.

The prime determinant of how quickly and completely news of an event spreads is the importance of the event. News of life-threatening hazards can diffuse quite rapidly; in 1982, 80% of a Chicago sample had been alerted about the cyanide-contaminated Tylenol capsules within 24 hours (Carrocci, 1985). The assassination of a leader is perhaps one of the greatest crises a society can experience. The news of the assassination of President Kennedy spread rapidly: 42% of people heard of the shooting within 15 minutes (B. Greenberg, 1965); by 60 minutes, 90% of the country had heard; within 3 hours of the shooting, almost everyone had been informed. The spread of the news of the attempted assassination of President Reagan was not quite so rapid (Weaver-Lariscy, Sweeney, & Steinfatt, 1984): within 1 hour, 64% knew; this percentage increased to 81% within another 30 minutes.

The 2011 terrorist attacks on the World Trade Center towers diffused extremely rapidly. A sample of East Lansing, Michigan, respondents reported that by 9:00 a.m. (15 minutes after the first plane crashed into the North Tower), 22% knew of the attacks; by 10:00 a.m., 82% were aware; by 11:00 a.m. (after U.S. airspace was shut down, the two towers collapsed, the plane crashed into the Pentagon, and Flight 93 crashed in rural Somerset County, Pennsylvania), 94% were aware of the attacks (B. S. Greenberg, Hofschire, & Lachlan, 2002). Within 30 minutes, 52% of a sample of college students on a southeastern U.S. campus was aware of the strike; 73% had heard within an hour (C. Hoffner, Fujioka, Ibrahim, & Ye, 2002). Fully 99% were aware within 2.5 hours. Reflecting the global importance of the attack, news diffused quickly internationally: 70% of a German sample was aware of the attack within an hour (E. M. Rogers, 2003b). More than 99% of a sample of residents of Albuquerque, New Mexico, were aware of the attack less than 3 hours after the first plane struck the North Tower (E. M. Rogers, 2003).

News of the disintegration of the space shuttle Columbia on February 1, 2003 (at the end of its 28th mission), on the other hand, diffused more slowly. The shuttle tragedy occurred at 8:00 a.m. EST. By 9:30, only 17.6% of a sample of college students located in the southeast U.S. reported hearing of it. Two-thirds of the sample had heard by noon (4 hours after the event); 85.6% had been informed by the end of the day (Ibrahim, Ye, & Hoffner, 2008).

The 1986 assassination of Sweden's Prime minister, Olof Palme, provided the context for a large-scale international comparative study of news diffusion. Researchers from 11 different countries conducted studies of the spread of news of the event (Rosengren, McQuail, & Blumler, 1987). The results of these studies confirm the role of news importance in amount of news diffusion. In the five Nordic countries (Sweden, Iceland, Norway, Denmark, and Finland), almost 100% of the population was aware of Palme's death within 12 hours. In the United States, however, after 48 hours, only 72% of the public was aware (Gantz & Tokinoya, 1987). These differences reflect the distance and importance of Swedish influence in Europe and the United States.

Comparisons of the diffusion of different news events reinforces that the impact of the event determines the rate and level of awareness. In 1960, researchers (Budd, MacLean, & Barnes, 1966) compared news diffusion of two events that occurred within a day of each other: the ousting of the Soviet Premier Nikita Khrushchev (a major event during the Cold War era) and the arrest of a Presidential assistant, Walter Jenkins, on a morals charge (a more minor event). The researchers concluded that "in less than one and a half hours, a higher percentage of persons were aware of the Khrushchev incident than knew of Jenkins after 15½ hours" (p. 225). The first hour after the announcement of each event, 30% were aware of Khrushchev but only 13% were aware of Jenkins. After 8 hours, almost everyone (93%) was aware of Khrushchev; only 50% were aware of Jenkins. Clearly, diffusion is determined by the impact of the news.

The time of day that the news is released determines both the communication channel that is the first source of news as well as the rapidity of diffusion. Life's daily rhythms determine the primary initial source of news.

As Mayer, Gudykunst, Perrill, and Merrill (1990) concluded after their analysis of awareness of the Challenger explosion: "*where* one is affects *how* one discovers the occurrence of a major news event . . . *how* one discovers the event then affects *how quickly* one hears of the event" (p. 121).

B. S. Greenberg (1965) reported that interpersonal contact was quite important to the spread of the news of the Kennedy assassination for his sample of San Jose, California, residents. Of those who first heard of the shooting in the first 15 minutes after it happened, about 38% learned from someone else. Of those who learned within the next 15 minutes, 55% learned from interpersonal contact; 57% of those who learned in the next 15 minutes cited interpersonal channels as their source. Kennedy was shot at 10:30 a.m. Pacific time, a time when many people were at work or busy with errands. At a time with fewer televisions and fewer television stations, television would be less important as an initial source. Mendelsohn (1964), however, in his sample of teens and adults in Colorado, found that radio was an important first source for news of Kennedy's shooting: 39% cited radio as their source. Media habits of the teens, who had radio as a typical accompaniment to daily activities, may explain its importance in that study.

A study of diffusion of the news of the 1991 air strike on Baghdad illustrates how time of day influences the channel of first information. B. S. Greenberg and his colleagues (Greenberg, Cohen, & Lee, 1993) collected data across all four time zones of the United States. The bombing first occurred at 6:30 p.m. EST, when many were watching the evening news to see the U.S. reaction to Iraq's failure to withdraw troops from Kuwait by the January 15 deadline. In the Eastern time zone, television was the first source of information for 68% of the respondents. Television's role grew smaller for respondents in earlier time zones: 53% and 50% first heard via television in the Mountain and Pacific time zones respectively. Interpersonal sources were more likely sources earlier in the day: 16% of respondents learned from interpersonal channels, 21% and 29% relied on those sources in the Mountain and Pacific time zones. The researchers concluded that earlier in the day people are more likely to be outside the home, working or running errands, and more likely to hear news from interpersonal sources. Those at home were more likely to hear the news from television, a home-centered medium. These findings confirm Gantz's (1983) conclusions about channel use and news diffusion. How people find out about an event is due mainly to where people are when the news is released – at work or at home. For those at home, radio or television are usually the first source of news; for those at work, where media are less likely to be readily available, interpersonal communication is usually the first source.

The timing of a fraternity house fire on the Indiana University campus that resulted in one death and several injuries illustrates the impact of people's routines on awareness (Gantz, Krendl, & Robertson, 1986). The fire occurred early on a Sunday morning. Because there were no classes scheduled that day, most students were off campus. Although this was an important event to the student community and news of the fire diffused fairly rapidly throughout the day (by 6:00 p.m., 78% of students were aware of the fire), fewer than one in five of the respondents named any mass media channel as their source of awareness. Instead, over 80% heard the news from interpersonal sources. This finding may be due to the lack of media coverage or availability to students living on and off campus.

The time of day also influences news diffusion because of journalists' routines. Diffusion of news about Palme's assassination was slower to take off in some Nordic countries than in Japan or Iceland. Part of the explanation is due to time zone differences. Palme's death (which occurred around midnight Swedish time) was announced about 8:00 a.m. Saturday morning in Japan and at 12:30 a.m. in Iceland. But the slow initial rate of diffusion in Sweden was also due to journalist and government routines. At that hour, Swedish news desks were closed for the evening. Moreover, the intense importance of the assassination required confirmation before it could be publically announced. Swedish broadcasting was handicapped by the late hour because of personnel shortages and because it was difficult to reach government officials to confirm the event. So, the first announcement of the tragedy wasn't until 1:10 a.m. (Rosengren, 1987).

Comparison of the different studies of news diffusion of the September 11 attacks reinforces the importance of time of day on the speed of diffusion and the channel of first knowledge. As Rogers (2003b) notes:

> The local time of day when the terrorist attacks occurred (8:45 A.M. eastern standard time in New York and Washington) was an important factor in the relative speed of diffusion. In Albuquerque, New Mexico, this event occurred at 6:45 A.M., a time when many people were still asleep or were awakening and traveling to work. . . . In Germany, the first terrorist attack was at 2:45 P.M., when most people were at work or at home. (p. 22)

Because of the time of the day on a workday, most people in the northeast and Midwest learned about the attack from the mass media (see Rogers, 2003b, for a summary of seven news diffusion studies conducted after September 11). Radio featured heavily in diffusion (from 15% to 27% across the seven studies); perhaps people were listening while getting ready for work or traveling to work or school. The earliest to find out about the strike reported to learn from television or radio (W. J. Brown, Bocarnea, & Basil, 2002). The importance of interpersonal communication in the diffusion process increased as time passed (Kanihan & Gale, 2005; Rogers, 2003b). Rogers (2003b) suggests that this event was so important that people passed the information along to strangers, similar to the diffusion of Kennedy's assassination (B. S. Greenberg, 1965). Although the Internet was widely used for news and email, few learned of the news from the Internet: less than 1% (Brown et al., 2002; Jones & Rainie, 2002).[4]

The almost universal use of smartphones and social media suggests that time of day might become less important in describing news diffusion. Clearly, interpersonal connections become more important to the spread of news, as individuals who witness an important event can share news immediately to friends and followers on social media. News organizations encourage their audiences to alert them to breaking news via social media. And, because people use their smartphones just about everywhere, there are fewer time-of-day limitations to the spread of news. Herrmann and his colleagues (Herrmann, Rand, Schein, & Vodopivec, 2013) analyzed Twitter feeds during four "urgent events": the death of Bin Laden, election night 2012, Hurricane Sandy, and Hurricane Irene. They found time-of-day effects in flow of tweets for some events (reflecting the diurnal pattern in Twitter, Naaman, Zhang, Brody, & Lotan, 2012). They also found differences in the number of tweets based on type of event; diffusion curves of hurricanes were somewhat different than the diffusion of the other events, which suggests that type of event might still affect diffusion in an environment of almost instantaneous communication by social media.

Social Media in Crises

Analysis of Twitter messages during the summer 2012 Virginia earthquake showed that the first Twitter reports sent from the epicenter reached New York City before the shockwaves – and before the National Geological Survey's alert (which can take 2 to 20 minutes to digest data and generate alerts). According to SocialFlow, a company that analyzes social media messages, Twitter messages flowed at about 5,500 per second (Hotz, 2011). Facebook reported that "earthquake" was posted in the status updates of about 3 million users within 4 minutes of the quake. Wikipedia had an article about the earthquake within 12 minutes.

In March 2012, the American Red Cross established its Digital Operations Center, the first social media based operation devoted to aid during emergency situations. Communication infrastructure is often damaged or overloaded during crises and disasters. The 9/11 explosions destroyed radio and cell phone antennas. Hurricanes damage landline phone infrastructure. Cell phone voice calls were overloaded after the Virginia earthquake. The Red Cross and other disaster workers recommend that people communicate by text or email – text messages use less bandwidth and are more likely to get through and save bandwidth for communication among emergency and rescue workers.

Recent natural disasters have shown that social media are not only the first source of news about a disaster, but also they are valued because they provide current hyperlocal information – useful to a targeted and well-defined community. After the July 2011 marketplace bombing in Mumbai, India, for example, Twitter users created spreadsheets to organize the locations of those who had volunteered refuge to those lost and injured. A software engineer used Ushahdi, an open-source Web and mobile application, and Twitter posts to create a color-coded map to report alerts and updates, such as traffic, deaths, and hospital contacts. During the 2011 Mississippi River flooding, the Army Corps of Engineers used Facebook to deliver hyperlocal information about rebuilding and insurance to those in the affected regions. Phone lines were overloaded during the 2008 Mumbai coordinated terrorist attacks, but guests of the Taj Mahal Tower and Palace Hotel were able to send text messages about the siege.

A 2011 Red Cross survey found that social media play an important role in crises. People feel that the Internet is the third most useful channel for information – after television and local radio. Facebook is the most widely used social medium. In the survey, 91% of respondents said that they have used Facebook for information during natural disasters; 25% said they used Twitter. About 25% said that they would also use social media to let their family and loved ones know they are safe.

The more important the event, the smaller the role of audience characteristics in its diffusion.

A Swedish diffusion study of the assassination of Olof Palme found one minor difference in time of awareness among people: Men got the news a bit earlier than women (Weibull, Lindahl, & Rosengren, 1987). All other differences could be explained by people's daily routines. Younger people tended to stay out later on Fridays, so they were more likely to learn about the event earlier; older people learned the next morning. Similarly, R. J. Hill and Bonjean (1964) concluded that any differences between males and females in awareness of news events in diffusion studies of that era were due to daily routine. If an event occurs on a workday, there are differences in routines for males and females. In those days, because more males worked outside the home than females, gender influenced the source of knowledge through its link to where the individual was.

Other studies have supported the limited role of demographics in the diffusion process. Awareness of the death of ex-President Eisenhower in 1969 was not related to age or education (M. T. O'Keefe & Kissel, 1971). Although older Americans might find the news of his death more relevant because of his importance as a leader of World War II military forces and as President during the 1950s, personal relevance did not influence how quickly someone became aware of the death; nearly everyone was informed of Eisenhower's death. Studies of diffusion of the news of the September 11 terrorist attack also found few differences based on gender or ethnicity (Ruggiero & Glascock, 2002).

There has been some conflicting evidence about the role of emotional response to news and diffusion. There are theoretical reasons to expect that those who are more upset when they hear of a major news event would seek out others for comfort. College students who were upset about the Challenger explosion were more likely to inform others of the tragedy (R. W. Kubey & Peluso, 1990). But, although adults who were more upset by the space shuttle explosion ultimately were more likely to talk to others about it, they were not more likely to pass along the news immediately (Riffe & Stovall, 1989). Some studies of news diffusion of the terrorist attacks of September 11 found that emotional reactions had no impact on sharing the news with others (e.g., W. J. Brown et al., 2002). Other researchers found that feeling upset, sad, fearful, and angry were all related to contacting more people to share the news (C. Hoffner et al., 2002). Similarly, people who felt more sadness (but not anger) when they learned of the destruction of the space shuttle Columbia were more likely to pass the news along to others that they knew (Ibrahim et al., 2008).

Characteristics of the critical news event, then, appear to influence the rate and amount of diffusion. Certain audience variables, especially certain social categories, have an impact on rate of diffusion and communication source of first knowledge through their impact on daily routines.

Effects of Surveillance and Correlation Media Content

Do the Mass Media Provide Surveillance and Correlation?

By their very nature, crises erupt suddenly. Threats of natural, technological, or political disturbances stress the public, but strain the resources of news-reporting agencies. Organizations have general plans and policies for covering crises and disasters (e.g., Kueneman & Wright, 1975), but in the midst of the situation, journalists' normal routines are upset (G. Tuchman, 1978). News organizations have many goals in mobilizing their coverage of crises. The need for profit and ratings demands speedy coverage and the "scoop," but coverage also is driven by public service. News agencies try to alert the public, calm fears, provide an official channel for information, and create public sympathy to increase humanitarian aid efforts (Kueneman & Wright, 1975; A. F. Simon, 1997; Sood et al., 1987). Although their goals are noble, news organizations often fail to fulfill the public's need for information.

Crises can disrupt normal newsgathering and reporting. All too often, natural disasters create havoc: electricity is lost, travel is dangerous or impossible, and communication links are cut. When Hurricane Andrew hit south Florida early Monday morning on August 24, 1992, the nation's news media were focused on the Louisiana coast. It wasn't until almost 24 hours later that we had any notion of the devastation the winds and rain had wreaked on the area. Hurricane Andrew devastated local media (Goldman & Reilly, 1992). The CBS-owned station, WCIX, was off the air for most of Monday. Andrew's winds toppled the microwave tower linking ABC with its affiliate. CNN could not contact its two affiliates and its Miami satellite truck had been damaged in the storm; reporters could not transmit video of the damage. The only video out of South Florida early on Monday were shots of Miami's mayor in largely undamaged downtown Miami. Obstacles to media reporting led initial reports of the damage to be greatly underestimated and relief efforts delayed.[5]

The intense need for information after the September 11 attacks overwhelmed the Internet. It was impossible to access any of the major news sites (Rappoport & Allerman, 2003). The destruction of cell phone and telephone networks in attacks caused great problems to rescue workers by limiting their abilities to communicate (Carey, 2003). The attacks knocked eight television stations off the air (Carey, 2003). But, as so many television viewers rely on cable, the impact was far less than the 1993 attack on the same building.

During disasters and crises, those who are in positions to answer questions and provide explanations are often those who are too busy to talk to the news media. Firefighters and police officials are in the midst of rescue efforts; medical personnel are treating patients; government and military leaders are planning strategy. The public was largely uninformed about President Reagan's true medical condition for quite a while after the assassination attempt. But, we should be grateful that the medical personnel spent their time with the President rather than with reporters.

During the first stage of crisis coverage, news organizations struggle with demands for immediate information and the need for accuracy in reporting. The public's demand for information is so great at these times that radio and television usually interrupt normal programming and devote all their resources to coverage of the crisis. But because of strains on newsgathering, there is often a shortage of news, and the need for news outstrips the information available. Experts and commentators rush to the television studios. And television stations play every bit of video that they have; but there may be long minutes when there is nothing new to release. Reports and speculation are repeated. As a television station manager said when interviewed after the Kennedy assassination, "Every bit of wire news was aired, re-aired, broadcast again and again" (Nestvold, 1964). What little video is available is played over and over. Most Americans surely have the image of the World Trade Center towers collapsing burned in their memories forever.

Normal gatekeeping is abandoned and almost all information passes through the gates – whether it has been verified or not (Waxman, 1973). Home video is aired (often with the caption "unedited video"). News anchors take telephone calls on the air from bystanders. Reports may be incomplete, inaccurate, and conflicting. Early reports after the attempted assassination on President Reagan's life, for example, announced that James Brady had been killed. Immediately after the 1989 San Francisco earthquake, all four news networks initially underestimated the strength of the earthquake. Although all eventually reported the accurate Richter reading (7.1), first estimates hovered between 6.2 and 6.5 (McKenzie, 1993). In the confusion following the Oklahoma federal building bombing, news organizations reported speculations about a Middle Eastern connection that were later found to be false. Some of the international news coverage of the 2011 Japanese earthquake and tsunami was so inaccurate that Japanese journalists created a "wall of shame" with almost 70 entries (E. Johnston, 2011). Fox News, for example, showed a map of Japanese nuclear power stations that included "Shibuya Eggman," which is a concert hall in Tokyo. Britain's top-selling tabloid, the *Sun*, warned people to "Get Out of Tokyo Now!" when there was little risk of radiation or tsunami in the city. After the Summer 2013 crash of Asiana flight 214 in San Francisco, the midday anchor for San Francisco's KTVU mistakenly aired bogus and racist names for the flight crew (Peralta, 2013).

Reporters rely on information drawn from police scanners, which are often uncertain and unreliable. In 2009, for example, reports on CNN and Fox News led to the temporary shutdown of Washington's Reagan Airport with their inaccurate reports of an exchange of gunfire between coast guards and another boat on the Potomac River during President Obama's commemoration of the anniversary of the September 11 attacks on the Pentagon. This report, based on Coast Guard scanner transmissions, was false. Dave Statter, an emergency services reporter, believes that mainstream media's need to compete with social media has led to a "standard operation procedure has become report first, confirm second, and correct third" (Fahri, 2013).

There is evidence that misinformation can now spread instantaneously. During Hurricane Sandy in 2012, social media helped spread dramatic, but fabricated photos of storm surge crashing into the Statue of Liberty, flooding in the New York Stock Exchange, and sharks swimming through flood waters in New Jersey. At least one person, @ComfortablySmug, tweeted misinformation that the New York Stock Exchange was "flooded under more than 3 feet of water" and that New York Governor Andrew Cuomo was "trapped in Manhattan" and "taken to a secure shelter."[6] The tweet about the Stock Exchange was reported by other journalists, including some from the *Wall Street Journal* (Palazzolo, 2012). News coverage following the 2013 bombing at the finish line of the Boston Marathon was peppered with errors. Various news outlets reported that the suspect was a "dark-skinned male," that a "Saudi national" injured in the bombing was a suspect, that there were five unexploded devices, and that an arrest had taken place early in the investigation. All this misinformation was tweeted and retweeted almost instantaneously (Chertoff & Lawrence, 2013; Starbird, Maddock, Orand, Achterman, & Mason, 2014).

At the early stages of coverage, rumors abound. The 9/11 terrorist attacks saw the Internet as a disseminator of erroneous reports. Lasorsa (2003) summarized about a dozen of these rumors, including that someone rode a piece of the building to safety, that Jews working in the towers were warned ahead of attack, that Flight 93 was shot down by U.S. planes, and that five firefighters in an SUV were rescued after two days buried in the rubble. Stempel and his colleagues (C. Stempel, Hargrove, & Stempel, 2007) examined belief in three "conspiracy theories" about the 9/11 attacks: that the government either assisted or looked the other way because they wanted a war in the Middle East, that the Pentagon was struck by a cruise missile rather than an airplane, and the collapse of the Twin Towers was helped by secretly planted explosives. They found that beliefs in these conspiracies were predicted by use of "less legitimate" media, such as blogs and supermarket tabloids. Those who use "legitimate media," such as daily newspapers and network TV news, were less likely to believe.

Given the incomplete and misinformation provided during the first stage of crisis coverage, it is clear that media do not fulfill their surveillance and correlation functions well. There is evidence that media coverage may not only fail to inform, but it may misinform. Graber (2010) pointed out that the initial report of the 9/11 attack described the crash as an "aviation accident." NPR initially reported that a Palestinian group had claimed responsibility for the attack.[7]

Disaster researchers recognize the existence of various, inaccurate "disaster myths." The most common element of these myths is the belief that humans act and engage in irrational and exploitive behavior in times of crisis. Disaster myths suggest that (a) panic is a common reaction, (b) most victims are in shock and unable to care for themselves, (c) those who are not disabled loot, and (d) most people leave their homes for relief shelters (Goltz, 1984; Wenger, 1980). These myths may be perpetuated by media coverage of disasters that exaggerates evacuation efforts, interviews the most easily available "victims" (those in relief shelters), and reports "nonevents" (e.g., "there were few reports of looting") as well as popular culture, such as disaster films (Mitchell, Thomas, Hill, & Cutter, 2000).

Disaster myths became a common part of media coverage of the aftermath of Hurricane Katrina. Media reported widespread looting, rapes, and shooting at rescue helicopters (Campbell, 2010). As Campbell recounts, it seemed that New Orleans became the post-apocalyptic world of *Mad Max* or the lawless and leaderless society of *Lord of the Flies*. These reports were based on hearsay and rumor and likely untrue. Tierney and her colleagues (Tierney, Bevc, & Kuligowski, 2006) point out how harmful these disaster myths can be. These myths are not only wrong, but they can influence governmental and public responses during disasters. In New Orleans, for example, the false assumptions about looting and social breakdown led officials and responders to misallocate resources from rescue to law enforcement functions.

Graber (2010) suggested that surveillance and correlation may not be fulfilled until the second stage of crisis coverage, well after the initial emergency. By this time, facts have emerged and been verified and the full impact of the crisis has been assessed. At this stage, though, print media can do a more complete job of integrating and synthesizing the material and are able to provide more complete explanations.

Other Effects of Surveillance and Correlation

There are several other potential media effects due to media coverage of crises. Some crises may become part of the media agenda long enough that agenda setting occurs. That is, the audience may accept the issue as an important one facing society. The intense coverage of the Persian Gulf War, for example, led it to the top of the audience agenda during the early months of 1991 (Iyengar & Simon, 1993). Larson (1980) suggested that media coverage of some disasters, such as plane crashes and droughts, have been followed and associated with limited agenda-setting effects. There have been few studies, though, that focused specifically on the agenda-setting effects of crisis coverage; this may be due to the short duration of stage-one crisis coverage. One study of Missouri media and respondents 2 months following the September 11 attacks found evidence of agenda setting about terrorism. There was a strong rank-order correlation ($r = .71, p < .05$) between media coverage of terrorist themes and the public's concern with certain themes: future terrorist attacks, effect on the economy, Israel–Palestine conflict, biological threats, air travel safety, war protests, and Afghan civilian deaths (Craft & Wanta, 2004).

Another study reported that the anthrax letters post-9/11 brought the topic of bioterrorism to the media agenda (Montani, 2006). Prior to 9/11, bioterrorism was barely covered in major newspapers and science magazines. After 9/11, there was a steep increase in stories, which then leveled off, but to a higher level than before the attacks.

More research has focused on the effects of media coverage of terrorism. Scholars suggest that this coverage can result in knowledge gain, status conferral, media frame shifting, and contagion effects. Due to the pressures of crisis coverage (need for speed and access to information), media coverage of terrorist acts is often incomplete. That is, terrorist acts and goals are often reported and interpreted by authorities who are opposed to the terrorists (Picard, 1993); therefore, terrorists' objectives are rarely discussed. Coverage mainly focuses on the tactics the terrorists employ and the resulting harm to victims; still, some limited learning may result. Weimann (1987) pointed out that terrorist acts have led to awareness of the plight of Palestinian refugees, Lebanese prisoners, and other politically disenfranchised groups. And the intense coverage of terrorist crises can provide a window for citizens to observe how well their government officials perform under pressure.

Other scholars are concerned that media coverage might confer status on terrorist groups. Status conferral is one outcome of surveillance (Lazarsfeld & Merton, 1948). Because media coverage signals importance, coverage of terrorist acts might serve to legitimize the instigators' cause and, further, to gain sympathy for their cause (Weimann & Winn, 1994). It seems reprehensible to many that terrorists might benefit from their actions; an empirical test supports the notion that media coverage leads to status conferral (Weimann, 1983). Experimental groups of college students either read or watched television news reports of two specific terrorist acts. Control groups read or watched the news without reports of those acts. Pre-and posttest responses indicated that exposure to media coverage led to a significant increase in beliefs that the problem driving the terrorist act was important, should be covered by the media, and should be solved by international organizations. Comparisons between experimental and control groups reinforced this effect.

Ross and Bantimaroudis (2006) found that media were so influenced by the 9/11 terrorist attacks that terrorism moved to the center of media coverage of other international events and issues. They found that "the unambiguous and virtually uncontested government message that the Middle East was a hotbed of terrorism was adopted by the media to frame terrorism as the leading 'enemy' of the United States" (Ross & Bantimaroudis, 2006, p. 95). This led, they argue, to a shift in media framing to contexts outside the original terrorist attack. Their content analysis showed that whether Yasser Arafat and Ariel Sharon were "friends or foes" of the U.S. became a part of the media frame in editorials and news coverage of the leaders of Israel and the Palestine territories.

Another concern about media coverage of terrorism is fear of contagion, or fear that the publicity given to the terrorist acts will lead to imitation by others.[8] Although media coverage is certainly not the direct cause of terrorist acts, several aspects of its coverage may spawn imitation (Dobkin, 1992). There are concerns that media coverage may present information about terrorist methods, strategies, and techniques. As Dobkin (1992) summarized, reports of terrorist acts may serve as triggers to other groups, may increase the morale of other terrorist groups, or encourage common criminals to adopt terrorist techniques. There is evidence to support the contagion effect. Media coverage of Irish Republican Army actions has been linked to subsequent terrorism (Z. C. W. Tan, 1988). Weimann and Winn's (1994) comprehensive analysis of contagion effects of terrorist acts reported or not reported on television found that terrorist acts reported on U.S. network televisions are more frequently and more rapidly replicated than those acts not reported. They found that reported acts are likely to be replicated in 16.7 days (compared to 25.4 days for unreported acts). And, within 60 days, a reported act is likely to be imitated 25.7 times (compared to 12.0 times for unreported acts).

Concerns about the effects of media coverage of terrorism lead to policy concerns. Media coverage of terrorist acts can be functional; coverage can stop rumors from developing and help inform the public about dangers in the area. Because media coverage is a tool to gain publicity and sympathy for terrorist causes, some advocate that terrorists be denied media coverage. Press coverage has several dysfunctional outcomes beyond status conferral for terrorist groups and their causes (Bassiouni, 1982). Media coverage can also inform the terrorists about law enforcement location and activity. Media activity in the area can impede negotiations and tie up phone lines. And, the need for information may lead the press to distract officials and negotiators with requests for interviews.

C. R. Wright (1986) pointed out that one of the dysfunctions of surveillance could be "war nerves" or stressful emotional reactions to news coverage. There is a good deal of evidence that watching disaster coverage on television results in emotional responses, such as depression and even posttraumatic stress symptoms. Scholars report that people exhibit symptoms of post-traumatic stress from indirect exposure – news exposure. Some children and adolescents who watched news reports of the Oklahoma City bombing showed stress symptoms (Houston, Pfefferbaum, & Reyes, 2008). Some people who read newspaper accounts, listened to radio news, and watched television coverage of the September 11 attacks were unable to sleep, had difficulty concentrating, and felt depressed (Dutta-Bergman, 2005). Houston's (2009) meta-analysis of the connection between media use and post-traumatic stress found a modest, though significant relationship: an effect size of $r = .152$. The effect of media exposure was stronger on youth ($r = .207$) than adults ($r = .124$). The effect size for exposure to television ($r = .146$) was smaller than the effect size for studies that measured exposure to a variety of different media ($r = .220$). Although these effect sizes are small, Houston (2009) points out that they are comparable to the effects of media violence.

Terror Management Theory

Terror management theory (J. Greenberg, Pyszczynski, & Solomon, 1986) holds that people control the "terror" associated with their awareness of their own mortality by investing in beliefs and actions that give their lives meaning.

When confronted with awareness of death, people's cultural world views (socially shared systems of beliefs and values) become more salient and more important. Media coverage of crises reminds people of death and mortality. This media coverage, then, can stimulate thoughts of death, reinforce support for one's own culture, and lead to altruistic actions that support one's culture (Yum & Schenck-Hamlin, 2005). Hundreds of studies have shown that mortality salience (reminders of death) is related to more positive evaluations of those who share cultural, religious, and political beliefs and is more punitive toward those who violate those beliefs and values (F. Cohen, Oglilvie, Solomon, Greenberg, & Pyszczynski, 2005). One interesting study used terror management theory to explain the lower divorce rate after the 1995 Oklahoma City bombing (Nakonezny, Reddick, & Rodgers, 2004).

The September 11 attacks were the first on the U.S. mainland. The round-the-clock media coverage reinforced the terror of the attacks as well as the uncertainty about their cause. There were certainly concerns of additional attacks, especially with the anthrax scare coming so soon after 9/11. Researchers found that anxiety and thoughts of mortality and death were common in the aftermath of 9/11 (e.g., Dunkel, 2002; Yum & Schenck-Hamlin, 2005). People engaged in altruistic and culture-affirming acts, such as donating blood or attending religious and memorial services (Metz & Youniss, 2003; Yum & Schenck-Hamlin, 2005). There were other effects, due to people's need to reinforce their cultural beliefs. Experiments found that reminding people of the 9/11 attacks heightened support for George W. Bush (e.g., F. Cohen et al., 2005; Landau et al., 2004) and prejudice against Arabs and Muslims (Das, Bushman, Bezemer, Kerkhof, & Vermeulen, 2009). As Das and her colleagues summarize, "individuals will exhibit higher levels of prejudice against outgroups to the extent that they are more terrified after watching terrorism news" (Das et al., 2009, p. 458).

Effects of Solidarity-Building Media Content

In times of crisis, the media react to society's need for surveillance and information by devoting massive time and energy to coverage of the crisis. All too often, though, it is difficult to gather information. Yet, it would be dysfunctional for media coverage to cease until information can be collected and verified. In order to reduce tension in society, media devote a good deal of coverage to media content intended to comfort their audience. Solidarity building is functional for society in times of crisis. Media highlight the wisdom of leaders and the bravery of rescue workers or soldiers to reassure society that "we are all in this together" and that everything possible is being done for survival. During coverage of the 9/11 attacks, CNN's logo was draped in red, white, and blue. Fox News anchors wore patriotic label ribbons. Dan Rather (the CBS news anchor) and Tom Brokaw (the NBC news anchor) both were openly emotional as they reported the news. So, although the media may be unable to fulfill surveillance and correlation needs, they are able to offer assurance and tension reduction. Some of the effects of this content are rally effects and willingness to accept censorship.

Rally Effects

Rally effects are relatively rapid increases in Presidential approval ratings during and just after times of crisis.[9] These solidarity effects are termed rally effects because they signal a patriotic solidarity – a sort of "rallying around the flag." Coser (1956) wrote that conflict with forces external to a society (such as wars and terrorist attacks) leads society to ignore within-group disagreements and to mobilize against the source of the external threat. The more dramatic and sudden the threat, the more likely rally effects are (Mueller, 1970). Because most intense conflicts involve the President taking some visible and decisive action, the President benefits from expressions of patriotism and solidarity.

Rally effects result from Presidential action against intimidations from other governments, such as Kennedy's war stance during the 1962 Cuban missile crisis and Reagan's 1983 invasion of Grenada. George H. Bush enjoyed incredible approval ratings during the 1991 Persian Gulf War, reaching up to 93% of the country approving of his handling of the conflict. Clinton's order to attack the Iraqi intelligence headquarters in 1993 was also followed by about an 11% surge in his popularity. Rally effects have followed direct violent attacks on the President. Ronald Reagan's initial popularity following his 1980 landslide election over incumbent Jimmy Carter was beginning to fade. Two months after he took his oath of office, Reagan's approval rating stood at only 59% and there was a good deal of opposition to his legislative agenda. John Hinckley's bullet, however, changed that.

Rally effects emerge during or after Presidential reactions to terrorist threats, such as Reagan's responses to the hijacking of the cruise ship, *Achille Lauro*, in 1985. Jimmy Carter even enjoyed a brief surge in popularity in 1980 after the aborted attempt to rescue the Iranian hostages. George W. Bush's approval ratings were slightly below average for first-term presidents.[10] The September 11 attacks led to an increase in his approval ratings from 51% to 91% (D. Moore, 2001).

Rally effects are relatively short term and fade relatively rapidly after the crisis has been resolved (Bowen, 1989). George H. Bush's popularity as the leader during the Persian Gulf War, for example, did not last long enough to ensure reelection in 1992. His son's approval ratings reached 25% three times in 2008. But, these short-term effects have some long-term implications such as heightened support for the President in areas unrelated to the crisis (Bowen, 1989). President Johnson, for example, enjoyed a relatively long "honeymoon" period following the assassination of his predecessor due to the support given to him by a grieving public. This support translated into legislative action; Johnson was able to guide civil rights legislation through Congress where Kennedy had failed. Before the attempt on his life, Reagan was facing a good deal of opposition to his proposals to cut taxes and the budget; after he regained his health, his proposals were adopted by Congress. As Nacos (1990) wrote, "In a sense, the crisis triggered by the shots on T Street resulted in a renewed honeymoon for the President and his policy" (p. 156).

Rally effects reflect the solidarity that emerges when society is threatened (Coser, 1956). Need for information and explanation are certainly strong during crises (D. M. McLeod, Perse, Signorielli, & Courtright, 1993; Peled & Katz, 1974). But the need for solidarity building is heightened. A panel of Delaware residents was asked during the Persian Gulf War and 1 year later about the importance of the four media roles: providing information, explanation, solidarity building, and tension reduction. Endorsement of the solidarity-building media role was significantly higher during the war; endorsement of the surveillance role was stronger 1 year later than during the war (McLeod et al., 1993). In fact, McLeod and his colleagues found that respondents were less likely to endorse restrictive attitudes toward the media a year after the conflict than during the war. During crises, the public may be looking to media to act more as a cheerleader than a watchdog. After 9/11, the media learned that "Professional neutrality was often suspected as disloyal, if not even treacherous. Alternatively, media learned that patriotism, appropriately displayed, was professionally rewarding for the journalists and institutionally lucrative for the media" (Wong, 2006, pp. 123–124).

The mass media contribute to rally effects in two ways. First, because of their resources and direct access to those in authority, media are the primary conduit of information for the public. Second, during crises, when solidarity building is important, the media take a less critical stance toward government policies; they rarely challenge Presidential action. Coupled with increased media use during crises, media content is likely to contribute to rally effects.

Prior to the 1962 Cuban missile crisis, there was a good deal of national concern about the buildup of Soviet offensive weapons 90 miles off the coast of Florida, but there was certainly not widespread support for Kennedy's Cuban policies. In the month preceding the blockade, Republicans, some conservative Democrats, and anti-Castro Cuban exiles demanded government action against Castro. The Kennedy administration, however, advocated caution and rejected a military intervention. At that time, press coverage of Kennedy's position was divided in support: around 40% of coverage in the *New York Times*, *Washington Post*, and *Chicago Tribune* was favorable to Kennedy's stand (from 37.3% of the stories in the *Tribune* to 43.8% of the stories in the *Times*) while between 25.2% and 46.4% was unfavorable (Nacos, 1990). Of the sources cited in news stories in those three papers, almost half were in favor of the administration's position (from 42.6% in the Tribune to 49.3% in the Post); from 14.3% to 43.7% were against the position (Nacos, 1990). When Kennedy announced the Cuban blockade (which is, technically, an act of war) on October 22, 1962, news coverage became more supportive. Of the stories in the three newspapers about the Cuban crisis, from 56.8% to 67.8% were supportive and only 13.4% to 16.1% were against Kennedy's actions.

Moreover, the sources cited in the articles were more supportive (from 62.5% to 82%) and far fewer against the administration's actions (from 1.8% to 6.0%; Nacos, 1990).

During the 1991 Persian Gulf War, media content was also marked by a lack of critical discussion of the administration's actions (Kellner, 1993). Dennis et al. (1991) noted that Bush used a strategy that attempted to "unite the country under the umbrella of support for the troops rather than seeking to win over skeptics to his approach" (p. 48). The media embraced the yellow ribbon theme. According to content analyses, during the first 3 weeks of the war, newspapers devoted less than 3% of their space to antiwar activities; television news granted peace protests less than 1% of news air time.

The post-9/11 coverage was marked by focus on "patriotic journalism principles" (Wong, 2006). These principles include a loyalty to the state, reporting from the government's perspective, reporting to mobilize but to discourage protest and dissent. Maureen Dowd, a *New York Times* columnist, noted that journalists didn't question the administration's curtailment of civil liberties because they truly believed that these extreme actions were necessary to fight terrorism (Kellner, 2003). Dan Rather explained that patriotism prevented U.S. journalists from asking "tough" questions about the war on terrorism (Kellner, 2003). A content analysis of news on ABC, CBS, NBC, CNN, Fox, and PBS between March 20 and April 3, 2003 (at the beginning of the Iraq War) found that nearly two-thirds of news sources could be categorized as prowar; only 10% could be categorized as antiwar (Johansen & Joslyn, 2008).

Willingness to Accept Censorship

Democratic nations are marked by few overt restrictions on press freedom. Yet, during crisis situations there are often more reasons for "press management." Local broadcast stations are concerned that coverage of civil disorder might lead to panic, draw crowds, and incite rioting (e.g., Graber, 2010; Kueneman & Wright, 1975). So, news reports may be edited to eliminate potentially damaging information. Surveillance may be sacrificed because of possible negative effects. During war, or military threats from external forces, these fears become especially important. The history of press coverage of military activity is marked by attempts to manage the information reported by the press (Pfau, Haigh, Gettle, Donnelly, Scott, Warr, & Wittenburg, 2004; Woodward, 1993). There are often essential reasons to limit front-line news reports. As early as the U.S. Civil War, news media were scrutinized for information about weapons location and troop movement (Griffith, 1986). Information is often restricted to prevent news that might reveal military strategy and tactics that could be used by the enemy. Press restrictions during war are justified to protect the lives and the security of the nation. The instantaneous delivery of news worldwide by international news sources (e.g., CNN) has fueled the military's resolve to manage news coverage of conflicts (e.g., Sharkey, 1991).

During wars, the public seems to accept these press restrictions. Typically, most people in the United States advocate press freedom. Immerwahr and Doble (1982) found that almost three-quarters of their respondents believed newspapers could print material, even if it was embarrassing to the President or the government. Fewer than 30% were willing to restrict communists from public access to television audiences. In times of military crisis, though, press censorship is more likely to be endorsed. Gaziano (1988) found that 69% of her respondents felt that the government should censor television news stories if there were threats to national security. During the Persian Gulf War, acceptance of news censorship was expressed by a majority of Delaware respondents (D. M. McLeod, Perse, Signorielli, & Courtright, 1999). Respondents seemed to prefer supportive information and sanitized coverage (e.g., no information provided by the Iraqi government, no coverage of antiwar protests, and no images of wounded or dead soldiers).

Ironically, restrictive attitudes toward the press may grow out of media coverage and people's expectations about the roles of the mass media. D. M. McLeod and his colleagues (1999) observed that television news viewing was associated with greater acceptance of government control over military coverage. The "yellow ribbon" coverage of television news (Dennis et al., 1991) as well as the human interest stories about soldiers at the front and the families they left at home may have fanned patriotic feelings and reduced scrutiny of government actions. The importance of the different functions of mass communication had significant impact on respondents' willingness to censor war coverage. Those who believed that it was less important for media to provide information were more likely to believe that the media were a threat to the war effort and want the media curtailed from showing enemy and POW videos. Those who believed that it was less important for the media to provide explanation wanted the media prohibited from showing pictures of battle and wounded soldiers and felt that the government should be trusted to know what kind of news the public should receive. Those who believed that it was important for the media to build solidarity were more likely to believe that the government should select the reporters who cover war news and also allow the media to show only supportive information. This antidemocratic turnaround by the public in times of military crisis is a dramatic, though short-term effect of media coverage and expectations about the functions of mass communication.

Research suggests that coverage of domestic terrorism leads viewers to support restriction of domestic civil liberties (e.g., Brinson & Stohl, 2012). Media use was also linked to support for censorship following 9/11. Television news viewing was positively linked to support for expansion of government powers and limits on privacy and freedom of expression (Scheufele, Nisbet, & Ostman, 2005). Newspaper reading was not. The authors hypothesized that these differences were due to media content. Newspapers presented information. Television coverage, however, focused on solidarity-building content marked by characterizing the U.S. as a "nation under siege." As Scheufele and his colleagues (2005) noted, media content served to marshal public support for policies that restricted personal freedoms:

> CNN covered "America's New War," MSNBC's banner at the bottom of the screen read "America on Alert," and on Fox News it was the "War on Terror." In addition to the beat of the war drums, episodes of civic religion, including flag-waving ceremonies, religious services, and celebrity telethons were prominently featured, feeding sentiments of nationalism and patriotism. (p. 214)

How Functional is Solidarity Building during Times of Crisis?

There are few doubts that solidarity building during times of crisis is functional. Television coverage following the Kennedy assassination helped people overcome fears about the stability of the country as well as their own personal grief (Mindak & Hursh, 1965; Schramm, 1965). Knowing that shock and grief are widespread provides comfort in times of upheaval. Disaster workers count on human interest stories to increase humanitarian aid in areas hit by natural calamities (A. F. Simon, 1997; Sood et al., 1987).

Some have raised concerns, though, about the mass media's abdication of their watchdog role during times of crisis. No responsible media organizations would want to endanger U.S. troops through irresponsible coverage. But it is difficult to justify some military restrictions. For example, Edward R. Murrow, during World War II, was initially denied permission to broadcast live during war raids by Britain's Ministry of Information (Woodward, 1993). The damage done by the German bombers was certainly visible to the pilots; few military secrets could be exposed by the broadcasts. Other details of World War II were kept out of the press by U.S. military censors. The public was not fully informed about the extent of the damage at Pearl Harbor; nor were they told about the kamikaze boat and plane attacks near the end of the war. Press restrictions have become even broader in recent conflicts. There was a total news blackout of the U.S. invasion of the small Caribbean island of Grenada and press restrictions during the Persian Gulf War have been called "unprecedented" (Sharkey, 1991). The Center for Public Integrity concluded that, increasingly, information about Defense Department activities is being restricted or manipulated not for national security purposes, but for political purposes – to protect the image and priorities of the Defense Department and its civilian leaders, including the President (Sharkey, 1991, p. 1).

Some writers have suggested long-term outcomes of acceptance of censorship. First, it is clear that military restrictions yield a sanitized and distorted image of warfare. A public that does not understand the horror of war might be more likely to endorse future military engagements and less likely to demand diplomatic solutions to international problems. There could even be a residual agenda-setting effect that leads the public to accept military issues as important along with increased support for military spending (perhaps at the expense of other spending).

Perhaps more important, though, is how the media's performance during military crises may affect the public's perceptions about the media's roles in society. Scholars have argued that the media have important responsibilities in democratic societies (Gurevitch & Blumler, 1990). The press should provide news to allow citizens to make informed decisions. They should encourage discussion of public affairs and be a platform for a wide variety of different viewpoints. The media should act as a watchdog, and approach official statements skeptically and critically. Finally, the media should fend off attempts to curtail their democratic role. During international crises, governments make decisions and take actions that can have serious long-ranging consequences. If media abdicate their responsibilities during those critical times, it may be difficult to regain their position in society – relative to those they are supposed to be watching and those to whom they owe a responsibility.

Explaining Media Effects in Times of Crisis

Which models of media effects can explain these effects during crisis? There is striking evidence that many of the initial and most noticeable effects are almost universal and uniform. During crises, people overwhelmingly turn to television (e.g., Dimock, Doherty, & Tyson, 2013; Gallup Organization, 1991; Gantz, 1983; Hirschburg et al., 1986; Peled & Katz, 1974; Sheatsley & Feldman, 1965). Diffusion of news is rapid and complete (e.g., B.S. Greenberg, 1965; Rosengren, 1987; Weaver-Lariscy et al., 1984). Rally effects reflect dramatic increases in Presidential popularity (e.g., D.M. McLeod et al., 1993; Nacos, 1990). Most people prefer solidarity building than information from the media (e.g., D.M. McLeod et al., 1999).

Audience variables seem to play little role in explaining these effects (Lowrey, 2004). The time an event happens interacts with people's daily routines to explain when and where news is heard (e.g., Gantz, 1983; Hill & Bonjean, 1964; Weibull et al., 1987). Preference for television as a news source may also be linked to lower educational levels (e.g., Peled & Katz, 1974). But, overall, the role of audience variables seems to be quite small (e.g., McLeod et al., 1993, 1999). Instead, the driving force for many of the effects of crisis media coverage seems to derive from the nature and content of the media coverage.

The direct effects model may provide a good explanation for these media effects. People respond almost immediately and uniformly to media messages about crises. When people overwhelmingly turn to the media, selective exposure is irrelevant. Moreover, their responses are determined, to a large degree, by the content of the media, rather than people's interpretations of that content. Many of the effects, though, seem to be relatively short term. After crises, people return to the concerns of their normal lives; typical media use patterns resume; rally effects dissipate. Of course, there may be other long-term implications and outcomes of crisis situations. But, the most commonly mentioned media effects may be best explained by the direct effects model. Why is the role of the audience in the media effects process reduced during times of crisis?

Dependency Model of Media Effects

Ball-Rokeach and DeFleur (1976) and DeFleur and Ball-Rokeach (1989) articulated a theoretical statement that explains the varying power of the role of mass media in the media effects process. According to their dependency model of media effects, how dependent the audience is on mass media to fill needs is a key variable in understanding media effects. Dependency is defined as "a relationship in which the satisfaction of needs or the attainment of goals by one party is contingent upon the resources of another party" (Ball-Rokeach & DeFleur, 1976, p. 16). Dependency on the mass media is likely to be higher under two conditions. In the first condition, as societies become more complex, mass media perform specialized and unique functions – especially gathering and disseminating news. A second condition that heightens audience dependence on the mass media is crisis, conflict, and change, which creates uncertainty in society and, in turn, increases the audience's needs for information, tension reduction, and solidarity. These needs can be supplied typically only by the mass media, because of their role in society and their superior resources. As Ball-Rokeach and DeFleur (1976) wrote:

> The potential for mass media messages to achieve a broad range of cognitive, affective, and behavioral effects will be increased when media systems serve many unique and central information functions. That potential will be further increased when there is a high degree of structural instability in the society due to conflict and change. (p. 7)

Crises are times of great conflict, potential change, or upheaval. Because of their resources and access, media have the unique abilities to gather information and make it available to the audience. Crises are times when the audience is highly dependent on the mass media. Mass media have the ability to control what news is reported and how it is framed. Mass media also take the responsibility to explain the significance of various bits of information. In crises, because there are few, if any, other sources of information, the media, to a large degree, are able to limit how information is interpreted. So, with standardized information comes fairly uniform interpretations. Times of heightened dependency, then, are marked by fairly uniform and universal media effects (Lowrey, 2004).

Ball-Rokeach and DeFleur (1976) noted that media dependency can intervene in several cognitive, affective, and behavioral effects, such as ambiguity reduction, attitude formation, agenda setting, belief acquisition, value clarification, emotional reactions, feelings of alienation or solidarity, and behavioral activation or deactivation. In times of crisis, increased dependency makes it more likely that media effects will be direct. But dependency may also be conceptualized as a variable – a condition of influence – that can intervene in the process of media effects even when society is not threatened. We consider later in this volume how other media effects can be heightened when people, for various reasons, might be more dependent on the mass media than on other sources of information.

Summary

Functional approaches to understanding the role of mass media in society point out that mass media serve society by providing surveillance, correlation, socialization, and entertainment. Although these functional activities are constant, during times of crisis, the functional nature of mass communication is especially apparent. Because of heightened uncertainty and fear, people rely on mass media for information, explanation, and solidarity. Mass communication is an important source for news diffusion, or alerting people to events and threats. But, because of constraints on newsgathering, the information function of the mass media is often quite limited during the acute phase of a crisis. Media's solidarity-building function, though, is valued by society and the audience. For short periods of time, media solidarity building can have effects on how the public perceives its leaders. Ironically, solidarity building may also be seen in public acceptance of limits on press freedom.

Many of the media effects during crises seem to be fairly uniform and universal; audience variables offer little explanation for these effects. Effects during crises can be explained by the direct effects model because of increased dependency on the mass media. Heightened needs brought on by conflict and uncertainty lead to greater reliance on the major source for information and explanation. This state of dependency reduces differences among people. The media's tight control of information limits selective exposure and perception, so effects are directed by the nature of media content. Many of these effects, however, although they are dramatic, are often short term. Research, though, needs to explore if and how these short-term effects might have long-term ramifications for people, the media system, and society.

Notes

1 Graber (2010) distinguished crises from "pseudo-crises." There are events that get "crisis-like" attention from the news media, but offer no real immediate threats to society. These events, such as the death of Michael Jackson (2009), the meltdown of Charlie Sheen, the rescue of the Chilean miners (2010), and the criminal trial of Casey Anthony, consume media and audience attention. Although some of these may focus on important issues, such as drug abuse and mine safety, their coverage is due more to the appeal of celebrity or interest in salacious details.

2 After the 1979 Three Mile Island nuclear accident, the *Philadelphia Inquirer* sent staff to copy the license plates of all vehicles in the parking lot, so that people on the scene of the accident could be interviewed. NBC flew a helicopter into Mount St. Helen's crater after its 1980 eruption to use the footage in coverage. KCNC-TV in Denver used every staff member to cover the 1999 Columbine school shootings (Scanlon, 2009).

3 A major criticism of FEMA's lack of response to the dreadful conditions in New Orleans in Katrina's aftermath was officials' (especially Michael D. Brown's) seeming lack of awareness of media coverage. CNN's Soledad O'Brien and ABC's Ted Koppel both reprimanded Director Brown for his lack of awareness of the conditions: "We were showing live pictures. . . . Don't you watch television?" (Campbell, 2010).

4 Clearly the Internet and smart phones are becoming a more important aspect of news diffusion. After the destruction of the space shuttle Columbia in 2003, 7.2% of a sample of college students enrolled at a southeastern U.S. university reported that they learned of the tragedy from a web site. Now Twitter, texts, and Facebook have been used to spread news of political unrest and natural disasters (American Red Cross, 2011; Guarino, 2011; Hotz, 2011; Howard & Hussain, 2011).

5 Not only was the American public generally unaware of the extent of the damage left by Hurricane Andrew, but FEMA also was uninformed. FEMA monitors and relies on the four major news networks (ABC, CBS, NBC, and CNN) for information from disaster fronts (Goldman & Reilly, 1992). So, federal relief efforts depend on news coverage.

6 @ComfortablySnug was later identified as a campaign manager for a Congressional candidate. At least one New York City councilman has called for the Manhattan district attorney to file charges against him for "falsely reporting an event." @ComfortablySnug has apologized, but some have argued that actions such as his during disasters are "the modern version of someone falsely screaming 'Fire!' in a crowded theater," which, according to Supreme Court Judge Oliver Wendell Holmes, is dangerous speech, not protected by the First Amendment (Palazzolo, 2012, p. B1; *Schenck v. United States*, 1919).

7 Media coverage of 9/11 and the aftermath might be linked to one of the largest signs of misinformation: that Saddam Hussein was involved in the 9/11 attack (Althaus & Largio, 2004).

8 Concerns about the imitation of violent and other antisocial acts portrayed in the media are common. In the case of air terrorism, for example, D.B. Cooper, the notorious hijacker who disappeared without a trace after parachuting with a bag of money, is believed to have spawned a rash of copycat hijackings.

9 Most research focuses on increases in Presidential approval ratings. But, it is reasonable to expect that other officials might also see their approval ratings rise in times of crisis. Chris Christie, governor of New Jersey during that catastrophic impact of Superstorm Sandy in 2012, saw high approval ratings as New Jersey voters approved of his strong presence and handling of the storm's approach and aftermath (Edwards-Levy, 2012). A *Saturday Night Live* skit attributed his popularity to the navy blue fleece he wore as he surveyed storm damage. Christie himself poked fun at his popularity and the fleece by claiming "It's basically fused to my skin at this point," and "I'm gonna die in this fleece" (C. Roberts, 2012). His office even released a comic video in which the fleece is lost, along with Christie's "power" (M. Yang, 2013).

10 George W. Bush's postinaugural approval ratings ranked third lowest among first-term elected Presidents since 1953. Kennedy had the highest approval ratings (72%), followed by Eisenhower and Obama (68%), Nixon (59%), Clinton (58%), George W. Bush (57%), and Reagan and George H. Bush (both 51%) (Jones, 2009).

4 POLITICAL COMMUNICATION AND PUBLIC OPINION

Every media effects study, at its core, begins with a conception of how the media *should* operate in society. Nowhere is this normative foundation more evident than in the realm of political communication. Gurevitch and Blumler (1990, p. 270) identified the eight functions that media ought to serve in a democracy. The common theme throughout these functions is that media ought to help identify the key issues of the day, provide a platform for rational, deliberative discussion of these issues, and allow for the formation of public opinion which will guide political decision making.

Gurevitch and Blumler's Functions of Media in a Democracy

1 Surveillance of the sociopolitical environment, reporting developments likely to impinge, positively or negatively, on the welfare of citizens

2 Meaningful agenda-setting, identifying the key issues of the day, including the forces that have formed and may resolve them

3 Platforms for an intelligible and illuminating advocacy by politicians and spokespersons of other causes and interest groups

4 Dialogue across a diverse range of views, as well as between power holders (actual and prospective) and mass public

5 Mechanisms for holding officials to account for how they have exercised power

6 Incentives for citizens to learn, choose, and become involved, rather than merely to follow and kibitz over the political process

7 A principled resistance to the efforts of forces outside the media to subvert their independence, integrity, and ability to serve the audience

8 A sense of respect for the audience member, as potentially concerned and able to make sense of his or her political environment.

From: Gurevitch, & Blumler (1990)

Public opinion is a concept that is difficult to define because it has roots in the concerns of a number of different disciplines (Price, 1992). What, for example, is a public? What counts as an opinion? Can a group of people hold a single opinion? The fields of sociology, psychology, political science, political philosophy, polling, and communication all consider different aspects of the phenomenon referred to as public opinion. Graber (1982), though, provided a definition that is serviceable for communication scholars: "Public opinion is group consensus about matters of political concern which has developed in the wake of informed discussion" (p. 556).

This definition illustrates that public opinion is something that is marked by being endorsed by a number of people (a group). Public opinion is not the expression of narrow views of political isolates. Public opinion focuses on matters of political concern. Sentiments that large groups of people share are not necessarily public opinion. Beliefs about how investment adviser Bernard Madoff (who was convicted of defrauding thousands of investors out of billions of dollars) should be punished are not a matter for public opinion. Expressions about the proper role of the federal government in oversight of the financial industry, though, might be the content of public opinion. Graber (1982) also stated that her definition of public opinion assumes that people are mentally active and involved in forming and supporting their opinions.

Scholars suggest that public opinion has several different roots. Ideally, active and knowledgeable public opinion should emerge from political ideology. Political ideology is a set of general principles about how society ought to function, usually described in terms such as "liberal" or "conservative." Ideology, though, explains only part of public opinion. Other sources for public opinion are self-interest, social group identification, opinion leadership, the expression of personal values, and interpretations of history and events (Kinder & Sears, 1985). For most people, politics is unobtrusive, experienced vicariously through the reports of the mass media. Through its surveillance function, mass communication watches, monitors, and reports on political matters. It is through the mass media that most people learn about political issues, assess which issues are important, and gauge which positions are endorsed by the majority. Mass communication, then, is the platform on which political matters are discussed and political events are played out.

The opinions that people express about matters of political concern, though, are not always thoughtfully derived. People may express views about issues that they know little about. Surveys of news awareness consistently demonstrate that many people are both uninformed and misinformed about current events (e.g., Kohut, Morin, & Ketter, 2007, 2011; J. P. Robinson & Levy, 1996). Even with high-profile international events, such as the building of the Berlin Wall (Converse, 1975) and the war in Iraq (Kull, Ramsay, & Lewis, 2004; Pew Research Center for the People & the Press, 2008), many people are mistaken about facts underlying those events. People may even express opinions without any basis. Schuman and Presser (1996) asked respondents about little known pieces of legislation — the Agricultural Trade Act of 1978, and the Monetary Control Bill of 1979. Nearly 30% of the public offered an opinion on the bills, despite their obscurity.[1]

It is clear, then, that public opinion has different meanings. For some, public opinion is well formed, grounded in solid knowledge, fairly stable, and predictive of political action. Others, though, hold pseudo public opinion, which is a more short-term reaction to political issues or politicians and candidates and not based on depth of prior knowledge. This chapter focuses on the role of mass communication in the formation and expression of public opinion. The effects of mass communication, though, are not uniform. The existence of real and pseudo public opinion suggests that media effects are conditional, based on the political involvement and abilities of people.

Theoretical Focus: Elaboration Likelihood Model

The elaboration likelihood model (ELM) was formulated by Cacioppo and Petty as a general theory of persuasion or attitude change. While much persuasion research has been conducted outside the field of mass communication, it is clear that persuasion is at the heart of understanding many media effects. Now, more than ever, media technologies are used to persuade people to support candidates or issues, to try products, to adopt healthy practices, and to support charitable causes (Petty, Briñol, & Priester, 2009). Upon introduction of the ELM Petty and Cacioppo (1986) noted that even though the study of persuasion had compiled a substantial set of theories and data, "there was surprisingly little agreement concerning if, when, and how the traditional source, message, recipient and channel variables affected attitude change" (p. 2). The ELM is a theoretical approach designed to make sense of the seemingly disparate findings of persuasion research.

The ELM is based on several assumptions (Petty & Cacioppo, 1986). The first is that people want to hold correct attitudes. Correct attitudes are those that have some underlying rationale. Correct attitudes are also ones that people believe will help them function in their daily lives. So, attitudes have some sort of basis that makes sense to those who hold them. Moreover, there is no single way or process in which these correct attitudes can be formed.

The second assumption is that, although people want to hold correct attitudes, people's capacity to process persuasive messages is limited. The ideal view of attitude formation is a mindful one, in which people pay attention to a message, learn its content, and yield to its suggestion (A. J. McGuire, 1985). There are times when issues are important to us and outcomes may affect us directly that we put a great deal of effort and energy into forming our attitudes. We may do our own extended research, discuss the issue with others, acquire a good deal of knowledge about the topic, and evaluate messages about the issue carefully against that knowledge. It is impossible for us, however, to carefully scrutinize and evaluate every persuasive message that we encounter. If we did, we would get very little else done because we would be spending so much time thinking about the many messages we encounter daily. And, intense analysis of persuasive messages would distract us from other more interesting and valuable aspects of our lives. So, we pay only fleeting attention to messages that aren't very relevant to us. Even if messages may be relevant, we might be forced to make snap decisions because we haven't the time to analyze and evaluate the arguments of the messages. Or, we may form attitudes based on the authority or expertise of the message source simply because we haven't the background knowledge to understand completely the complexities of the message's arguments.

Based on these two assumptions, Petty and Cacioppo (1986) proposed there are two general routes that characterize people's mental strategies when they encounter persuasive messages: central and peripheral routes. Attitude change is the result of either of two major influences: the content of the message or the characteristics of the situation (Stiff, 1986). Figure 4.1 illustrates the process of persuasion according to the ELM.

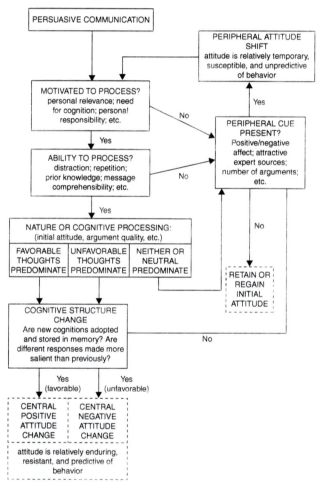

Figure 4.1 From: Petty, R.E., & Priester, J.R. (1994). Mass media attitudes change: Implications of the Elaboration Likelihood Model of Persuasion. In J. Bryant & D. Zillman (Eds.), *Media Effects: Advances in theory and research* (pp. 91–122). Hillsdale, NJ: Lawrence Erlbaum Associates, p. 99.

The central route is characterized by consideration of the issues and arguments in the message – elaboration on the central information in the message. This route reflects the ideal way that public opinion is formed. The recipient considers the information in a message, compares it to prior knowledge, and either integrates the new information or rejects it. Attitudes formed via the central route are more long term and fairly predictive of behavior.

The peripheral route is the route followed by recipients who are either not motivated to devote mental energy to considering the message, or are not able to totally understand the information (due to mental abilities or environmental context, such as distractions). Persuasive effects are still possible in the peripheral route, but they are based on peripheral cues, such as source attractiveness or credibility, or the number of arguments, and so on. Attitudes formed by the peripheral route are generally shorter term and not necessarily predictive of behavior.

Different variables are relevant to the ELM because of their impact on the likelihood of elaborating on messages. These variables are typically receiver variables, or variables that relate to the audience, and affect the motivation or ability to engage in central message processing. Message variables, or those that deal with message construction, are relevant because they describe peripheral cues related to attitude change (in the peripheral route) or substantive arguments in the message (in the central route).

Recipient Variables

In general, recipient variables can be classified as influencing either motivation or ability to engage in central message processing (Petty, Cacioppo, Strathman, & Priester, 2005). The "default" mode of processing is the peripheral route. Only when individuals possess the motivation *and* ability does central processing of a message occur (Eagly & Chaiken, 1993, p. 320). Motivation to process messages has been linked to personal relevance and personal characteristics (Petty & Cacioppo, 1986). One truism of persuasion research is that people react differently to messages that are personally relevant (Johnson & Eagly, 1990). Various approaches to persuasion have noted the importance of personal relevance or involvement: social judgment theory (C. W. Sherif, M. Sherif, & Nebergall, 1965), attributional approaches (S. E. Taylor, 1975), cognitive response approaches (Petty, Ostrom, & Brock, 1981), cognitive dissonance (Festinger, 1957), and functional approaches (D. Katz, 1960). When people hear messages that affect them in important ways, they pay more attention to the messages and put more mental energy into considering their content. So, for example, Rothschild and Ray (1974) found that people's recall of political ads depended, in part, on the importance of the election. They reasoned that the outcome of the Presidential elections was more personally relevant to people than the outcomes of local elections. In a set of three experiments, Braverman (2008) found highly involved individuals were more likely to be persuaded by the message content in informational health messages rather than by the peripheral aspects inherent in testimonials; low-involvement people were more persuaded by testimonials. So, greater involvement is linked to the central route to persuasion. When people are not involved with the message topic, they put less mental effort into message reception and follow the peripheral route.

There is evidence that some people are intrinsically motivated to follow the central route. Some people share a personality trait, need for cognition (NFC), which leads them to enjoy thinking and relish putting effort into cognitive activity. Those who score high on NFC measures prefer complex mental tasks as opposed to simple, repetitive activities. They enjoy puzzles. They are also more likely to be employed in jobs that require a lot of thinking (Cacioppo & Petty, 1982). High NFC individuals are more likely to consider product attribute information than low NFC people when asked to evaluate an unfamiliar product after viewing a brief advertisement (Haughtvedt, Petty, & Cacioppo, 1992). When they encounter arguments, those higher in NFC think about the messages more and are more likely to follow the central route, even with political messages (Braverman, 2008; Cacioppo, Petty, Kao, & Rodriquez, 1986).

Other recipient variables affect the ability to engage in message elaboration. Intelligence or educational level, for example, might be related to being able to understand messages better, which enables greater elaboration and thought about the implications of the arguments. For those with lower intelligence or less education, some arguments may be too complex, so the listener pays attention, instead, to easy-to-comprehend peripheral cues. Petty and Cacioppo (1986) pointed out that prior knowledge affects thinking about messages. Because prior knowledge is often reflected in schemas, prior knowledge may result in central, but biased, elaboration. So, schematic-based central processing may be colored by the nature of the prior knowledge.

An individual's social context may also affect the route of thinking. Distractions reduce the ability to think about a message. So, distractions reduce the likelihood of elaboration and disrupt central processing. Studies confirm the effects of distractions on processing and persuasion (Petty & Cacioppo, 1986). When messages are heard in distracting contexts, recipients are less able to generate positive thoughts about the message, so distraction reduces persuasion. But, distractions also keep recipients from generating negative thoughts, or counterarguments, resulting in lower likelihood of rejecting the message.

Multiple Roles For Recipient Variables

Individual variables can have an impact on persuasion in different ways, depending on the circumstances (Petty, Briñol, & Priester, 2009). For example, one's emotional state can have differential effects on the process of persuasion depending on the likelihood of elaboration. In low elaboration scenarios, people can sometimes misattribute their mood as a reaction to a message (Schwarz, 1990). Emotions can also impact one's motivation to process a message centrally. People may be less likely to actively engage in processing arguments when they are feeling happy, because they may be more confident in their existing views than when they are sad (Tiedens & Linton, 2001). Under high elaboration conditions, one's mood can shape the accessibility of certain thoughts that may bias reactions to particular arguments (Petty, Briñol, & Priester, 2009).

Message Variables

Message variables typically have their greatest impact on persuasion by acting as peripheral cues. Source credibility is perhaps one of the most researched persuasive techniques. Sources who are credible are ones with superior knowledge (expertise) that can be trusted to present material objectively (Hovland, Janis, & Kelley, 1953). Messages that are attributed to more credible sources will be associated with heightened attention and persuasion (A. J. McGuire, 1985). The ELM, however, points out that source credibility is more important to persuasion through the peripheral route, when arguments are not scrutinized (Petty, Cacioppo, & Goldman, 1981).

Source attractiveness is another message factor that is not directly related to central argument quality. This peripheral cue, though, has predictable impacts on persuasion. In general, more attractive sources are more persuasive (Chaiken, 1979).[2] There are several explanations offered for this effect: (a) attractive sources may also be perceived as credible; (b) they may serve as distractions from weak arguments; or (c) the positive feeling associated with attraction may enhance favorable thoughts toward the message.

Other message variables that serve as peripheral cues are the number of arguments in a message and the number of people endorsing a message. In general, the number of arguments used in a message increases persuasion because the position appears to be more strongly supported. But, this factor works only in the peripheral route, when recipients do not scrutinize whether the arguments are strong or valid (Petty & Cacioppo, 1984). Similarly, when a message contains endorsements, a greater number of endorsements acts as a peripheral cue ("If so many use this product, it must be good" Axsom, Yates, & Chaiken, 1987). This cue is very much the bandwagon effect of propaganda analysis (A. Lee & E. B. Lee, 1939).

There are, however, indications that some message techniques can increase the likelihood of central processing by motivating people to become more involved with the message. Unexpected or unusual newspaper headlines may surprise readers and lead them to scrutinize an article that they would normally only skim (Baker & Petty, 1994). Research has also shown that questions (compared to statements) and implied (rather than explicit) conclusions can draw people into thinking about messages more (e.g., Hovland & Mandell, 1952; D. J. Howard, 1990; Petty, Cacioppo, & Heesacker, 1981).

The channel of origin on which a message is carried can also affect the ability to process the message. In general, media with reception pacing controlled by the audience (e.g., print or Web) enable central processing (Holbert, Garrett, & Gleason, 2010; P. L. Wright, 1981). Newspaper readers, for example, can stop and think about ideas and issues whenever they like. Material accessed via the Internet is consumed at a time, place, and pace of the individual's choosing, conditions ripe for high motivation and an ability to concentrate (Holbert, Garrett, & Gleason, 2010). But other forms of media can be out of the audience's control. Traditional television and radio programming, for example, continue on, whether the audience wants to stop and think or not; so, these media lower the likelihood of elaboration. P. L. Wright (1981) also pointed out that the typical reception context of audiovisual media is a busy and distracted one. So, audiovisual media reception is likely to follow the peripheral route. Different media may also interact with peripheral cues. Visual media, for example, are more effective to deliver messages that use source attraction appeals.

Multiple Roles For Message Variables

Petty and Priester (1994) pointed out that it is impossible to classify any message variable as absolutely central or peripheral. Different variables can serve multiple roles; they can, at different times, serve as central or peripheral cues, depending on personal relevance. When a topic is particularly personally important, it is possible for source credibility to backfire. A message about the importance of hiring more police officers may include several strong arguments, including the need to reduce drug crime. But, if the source is the public safety official who stands to benefit from increased personnel, financial resources, and political power, highly involved and knowledgeable audience members might detect the bias in the advocacy of hiring more officers. And, source attraction might serve as a very central cue in messages that advocate diet, fitness, and beauty products. A trim, attractive model, for example, can illustrate the effectiveness of exercise equipment (e.g., Petty & Cacioppo, 1980).

Value Of The ELM For The Study Of Media Effects

The elaboration likelihood model offers some utility to understanding the process of media effects. It provides an explanation for a distinction between long-term and short-term effects of persuasive messages. It specifies the aspects of messages that might be more important in understanding media effects. It points to the characteristics of people that influence their reactions to media messages. It demonstrates the potential for variables in the persuasion process to have different effects depending on the interaction between the individual and message variables.

The elaboration likelihood model offers several connections to models of media effects. First, the ELM has some similarities to the cognitive-transactional model. Both suggest that individuals can engage in different types of thought. The central route is similar to controlled processing; the peripheral route is like automatic processing. Both central and controlled processing are intentional, individual controlled, and goal directed. Both peripheral and automatic processing are more passive and affected more by nonsubstantive characteristics of the message stimulus. Like the conditional model, selective exposure is important to the ELM. Both suggest that people process information relevant to their own situation.

The ELM has wide utility and broad scope; however, scholars have criticized it for lack of specificity and because it is difficult to disprove (Stiff & Boster, 1987). Because different variables have been described as having different effects depending on personal relevance, the ELM may be more descriptive than predictive. That is, it may be easier to describe what has happened, after the fact, rather than predict the specific effects of different variables. For that reason, any number of different effects of persuasive messages can be explained by the model.

Stiff (1986) advocated an alternate explanation for the processes delineated by the ELM. Based on his meta-analysis, Stiff found that highly involved individuals evaluate both central and peripheral cues, contrary to his characterization of the ELM's assertion that people process only central or peripheral cues. Stiff suggested that Kahneman's (1973) elastic capacity model presents a more ecological explanation of message processing. According to Kahneman, people can manage several cognitive tasks at the same time, depending on the amount of mental capacity the tasks require. Stiff's meta-analysis found that when message involvement is low, people process few central or peripheral cues; as involvement increases, processing of both central and peripheral cues both increase up to a point. When involvement is high, processing focuses on central cues. According to Stiff, the capacity model explains that at high involvement, cognitive capacity is focused on central information, so little capacity is left to consider peripheral cues.[3]

There may be some validity to persuasion scholars' concerns about the multiple, unspecified roles of different variables in the process. The conditional model, though, operates at the individual level and recognizes that effects are conditional on aspects of people. Clearly, different message aspects can affect different people in different ways. Petty, Wegener, Fabrigar, Priester, and Cacioppo (1993) also pointed out that, although most research on the ELM has used experimental analysis of variance (ANOVA) designs, the true process cannot be described as a dichotomy. In reality, people do not follow either a central or peripheral route. The likelihood of elaborating on messages is most likely a continuum. The ELM is particularly relevant when considering the effects of the mass media in the political realm because of the distinction between pseudo and true public opinion (Graber, 1982).

The Distinctions between Informed and
Pseudo Public Opinion

Noelle-Neumann's (1993) discussion of the evolution of the concept of public opinion highlights that a belief in rationality undergirds many definitions. As early as 1923, J. T. Young defined public opinion as the social judgment of a self-conscious community on a question of general import after rational, public discussion (pp. 577–578). Blumer (1946) saw public opinion as an aspect of social relations: People confront an issue of concern and explore different solutions to the issue through public discussion. This notion of a rational public engaging in public discourse about political matters is grounded in Libertarian philosophy – discussion eventually leads to knowledge of the truth (e.g., Mill, 1859; Milton, 1644). But scholars quickly realized that not all political opinions are based on rationality and public discussion. People may not be able to develop thoughtful opinions because they don't have the education, background knowledge, or resources to understand political matters, or they may be unmotivated to seek the information they need to make informed opinions (Price, 1992).

Graber (1982) built on these limits to the development of public opinion and the thoughtful, rationally based opinion formed after consideration and discussion with interested and informed others. Informed public opinion is held by political elites in society who are especially attentive to political matters. Public pseudo-opinions, on the other hand, are "opinions expressed by various publics which lack a sound information base and the honing that comes from dialogue and debate" (Graber, 1982, p. 556). Graber likens pseudo-opinion to snap judgments or top-of-mind reactions. These opinions may be based on impressions, moods, recollections of past opinions, or the parroting of opinion leaders' opinions. Pseudo-opinion is held by political non-elites, who pay only superficial attention to political matters, if they pay attention at all. Graber (1982) characterized such opinion as "ill-considered, fleeting, and unstable" (p. 556).

Role of the Mass Media in the Formation
of Informed and Pseudo-Opinion

Because political events and issues in modern societies typically take place in specialized locations, most citizens experience politics vicariously. So they rely on the surveillance function of the media to monitor and report on important events and issues. For most, then, media content is the symbolic input for public opinion – informed or pseudo. Graber (1982) argued that the role of the media in the development of public opinion differs for elites and non-elites. For elites, information from the media becomes just one of many sources of data. Because of their political involvement and interest and their vast base of prior knowledge, elites treat media coverage as foreground, or sources of new and/or specific information. Elites analyze new information from the media and compare it to prior background knowledge they have. As a result, new information may be integrated with prior knowledge to reinforce existing opinion, or it may lead to some changes in opinion, or it may be rejected entirely. Non-elites, on the other hand, are not so interested in politics and they have relatively little prior knowledge about political issues. For non-elites, media coverage is not only a source of new data, but their only source of information. For non-elites, media content is both foreground and background.

The Media Environment

The nature of the media environment has changed dramatically in the past decade. The spread of digital cable television, increasing access to high-speed Internet connections, the proliferation of mobile devices for accessing information, and the vast expansion of online content have coalesced to provide a wealth of choices for news, entertainment, advertising, and social interaction. Competition for an audience is fierce. It is easier than ever before for audience members to interact with, and even create their own, media content (Chaffee & Metzger, 2001). There is debate among scholars as to whether these changes in the media environment have positive or negative implications for democracy.

From the optimistic perspective, the Internet makes political information directly available to citizens through government, candidate, and other web sites, and allows new avenues for two-way communication with candidates and those in public office (Kenski & Stroud, 2006). Citizens can participate in new ways that cost less than traditional participation in terms of time and money, including donating online to a campaign, signing an electronic petition, or emailing their representative about policy preferences on an upcoming vote. Communication professors Stephen Coleman and Jay Blumler argue that "the Internet possesses a vulnerable potential to revitalize our flagging political communication arrangements by injecting some new and different elements into the relationship between representatives and represented" (2009, pp. 9–10).[4]

More skeptical about the transformative capacity of new media, other scholars point out that these technological changes have hastened the trends of fragmentation and polarization. Where media audiences once were truly a mass of many diverse people, today's audiences are much more fragmented because of the ease with which one can exercise selectivity in media exposure (Chaffee & Metzger, 2001; Bennett & Iyengar, 2008). In his book *Republic. com 2.0*, law professor Cass Sunstein (2007) addresses the normative concerns for democracy with an information environment where people can choose to only be exposed to those things with which they agree. Media activist Eli Pariser (2011) goes one step further in *The Filter Bubble*, detailing how algorithms used by web search engines like Google and Yahoo, by social networks like Facebook, and by online retailers like Amazon.com and Netflix, exercise selectivity on your behalf by showing you results that are tailored to your interests. The algorithms make use of past information about what you have searched, what web sites you have visited, what links you have clicked, and what you have purchased to sort through available data and present you with the program's informed guess as to what you would prefer to see. This means, for example, that a conservative and a liberal searching for information about "abortion" on Google will have two different sets of links appear on the first page of their results.

Furthermore, in today's media environment it is possible for some people to choose to largely avoid exposure to political communication altogether. In his book *Post-Broadcast Democracy*, political science professor Markus Prior (2007) details how people who prefer news are able to take advantage of the increased availability of political information to become more knowledgeable and to be more active in the political process. However, people who prefer entertainment can effectively avoid most political news, lowering their knowledge and participation levels. The percentage of people who avoid news altogether, though, has remained relatively steady at about 17% over the years (Pew Research Center for the People & the Press, 2010, p. 4).

A more personalized media environment also raises the concern that political discussions will become less deliberative and more polarized (e.g., Gurevitch, Coleman, & Blumler, 2009; Sunstein, 2007). In fact, in an era of fragmented audiences, news media may have an economic incentive to abandon the traditional journalistic ideal of objectivity and instead provide partisan perspectives on the issues of the day (Mullainathan & Shleifer, 2005). If people are primarily attending to content with which they agree, there is little hope of the type of substantive discussion that can lead to the formation of meaningful public opinion.

During election campaigns, the role of television continues to be criticized as well. One consequence of television has been to change the type of candidate that is likely to be successful; looking attractive on television and an ability to perform well on camera are crucial determinants in a candidate's electoral chances (Graber, 2009). The visual demands of television may lead to an emphasis on image over issues. Particularly during Presidential campaigns, the 30-second television ad continues to be an important part of the media environment. This short time-frame does not lend itself to substantive discussion of issues, although A. Johnston and Kaid (2002) find that contemporary political ads tend to blend "image and issue information, making it difficult to separate them into distinct genres" (p. 162).

Citizens United: Campaign Spending on Television Advertising

Several recent decisions by the United States Supreme Court have resulted in a massive increase in the amount of money spent on political advertising. The landmark 2010 decision in *Citizens United v. Federal*

Election Commission ruled that campaign spending limits put in place in 2002 violated the First Amendment to the U.S. Constitution by restricting campaign expenditures on the part of corporations, labor unions, and other associations. The decision was built on two ideas: that spending money on elections is a form of free speech, and that corporations, labor unions, and other associations have the same constitutional right to freedom of expression as individuals. The decision permitted the formation of super PACs (political action committees) that can raise and spend unlimited amounts of money on campaigns so long as they do not coordinate directly with a particular candidate's campaign. Such super PACs spent more than $62 million during the 2010 election cycle and almost ten times that during the 2012 election cycle (Center for Responsive Politics, 2014).

Not only has the total amount of money spent on advertising vastly increased, but the source of spending has shifted away from individual candidate campaigns and political parties to nonprofit organizations that are not required to disclose who their donors are. Election and tax laws now allow these anonymous contributions to social welfare nonprofit groups, and this "dark money" is not traceable. Additional court rulings in *SpeechNOW v. FEC* (2010) and *McCutcheon v. FEC* (2014) removed caps on the amounts that individual donors can contribute in an election cycle. Wealthy individuals can now essentially underwrite Presidential campaigns.

Television stations benefit tremendously from the new rules, as much of this increased spending ends up paying for advertising placements on their stations. Despite the proliferation of new media forms like social media and YouTube, in the 2013–2014 election cycle more than one billion dollars was spent on television ads (Kantar Media/CMAG, 2014). Almost 40% of that money came from "dark money" groups that are not required to disclose their donors.

For more information about campaign finance laws and the amounts of money spent on election campaigns:

Wesleyan Media Project Advertising Analysis
    http://mediaproject.wesleyan.edu/
OpenSecrets, a project of the Center for Responsive Politics
    http://www.opensecrets.org/
Consider the Source, a project of the Center for Public Integrity
    http://www.publicintegrity.org/politics/consider-source
National Institute on Money in State Politics
    http://www.followthemoney.org/

Another concern about television advertising during Presidential campaigns is the cost. Roughly two-thirds of the expenses for a Presidential campaign are in the form of advertising, most of that on television (Graber, 2009). This means that only well-funded candidates have a real chance of election. Because of this high cost, candidates have also shown a growing interest in using "free" media to campaign. Appearances on late-night talk shows and other entertainment venues have become common. Candidate web sites and social media presence are also increasingly important in campaigns.

Media Use by Elites and Non-Elites

According to a 2010 report by the Pew Research Center for the People and the Press there has been an overall increase in the time people spend with news, largely due to the rise of online platforms.[5] But this increased usage is not equally distributed among the audience; people who are highly educated are driving the trend. Elites and non-elites differ substantially on the amount of time spent with news, and on their sources for obtaining news.

According to the 2010 Pew report, those with postgraduate education spend approximately 96 minutes attending to news each day, while people with a high school diploma or less spend only 58 minutes a day on average. Those with a Bachelor's degree spent 80 minutes a day with news, and people with some college education 71 minutes per day (p. 3). Those who are highly educated are more likely to get their news from a combination of digital and traditional sources (newspaper, television, and radio). Nearly 69% of those with postgraduate education reported getting news from an online source when asked about their prior day's media use (p. 3). According to Pew, 36% of people find their news through a combination of online and traditional sources. That is still slightly less than the 39% of the population that uses *only* traditional sources. Rare is the individual who *only* relies on the Internet to the exclusion of traditional news outlets, though, with only 9% of the population recording such behavior (p. 2).

Among traditional media, newspapers continue to be the preferred source for elites. Regular readers of major national newspapers like the *New York Times* (65%) and the *Wall Street Journal* (71%) are more likely than not to have graduated from college (p. 72). Research on newspaper reading (Bogart, 1989) supported the conclusion that the newspaper is a preferred news source by politically active people. D. M. McLeod and Perse (1994) found significant links between newspaper use and both political interest and political involvement. Frequent newspaper readers are more likely to talk about politics and current events in daily conversations than infrequent readers. They are more likely to vote (75% compared to 55% of infrequent readers). More frequent newspaper readers (43%) consider newspapers important to them as citizens and voters, compared to only 19% of infrequent readers.

Despite consistent viewership declines, television remains the source of news for more people than any other medium (Kohut, Doherty, Dimock, &

Keeter, 2010, p. 17). On average, over 21.6 million people watch one of the three major network news programs each night (Pew Research Center for the People & the Press, 2011, p. 7). About 40% of the public regularly watch cable news, and half the audience regularly watches local television news programs (Kohut et al., 2010, p. 21). Television doesn't just attract *more people* than other media, but on average people spend more *time* with TV news than with other forms of news (p. 17). Television news use, as well as television viewing in general, though, is linked to lower levels of education (e.g., Pew Research Center for the People & the Press, 2010; Shoemaker, 1989). Viewers with less education tend to seek entertainment rather than news and information from television (e.g., A.M. Rubin, 1984) and other media (Prior, 2007). Rhee and Cappella (1997) found that political sophistication was negatively correlated with television news exposure.

The ELM, coupled with differential use of television, newspapers, and the Internet for news, can explain the development of pseudo and informed public opinion. First of all, newspapers, television, and the Internet differ dramatically in the amount and kind of information they present. Newspapers and online media, the preferred choices of those who are more likely to be public opinion elites, provide more in-depth central information; television presents more peripheral information. Limited central processing via television news has been explained by television news' information constraints because of space and time. Most television news compresses the stories to fit a limited time – 22 minutes for network national news, for example, after subtracting time spent on commercials. So, television covers far fewer stories than newspapers. Moreover, television news stories are far shorter and present fewer details than comparable newspaper stories (Eveland, Seo, & Marton, 2002; Graber, 1990). Although some argue that television's visuals add information a newspaper cannot furnish (e.g., Graber, 1990; Katz, Adoni, & Parness, 1977), most research confirms television's limited effectiveness in transmitting information (J. P. Robinson & Levy, 1986).

Television's mode of presentation is also less suited to imparting central information than other forms of media. Whether it is because of reliance on attention-grabbing visuals which can evoke strong emotional responses, or limited time and space, or a general orientation to infotainment, television frames news stories in ways that limit development of viewers' understanding.[6] Framing is defined by Entman (1993) as the highlighting of certain aspects of a topic to make them more noticeable. Framing works to subtly shape a particular interpretation of a news story. Public relations practitioners and news sources try to frame issues and events in ways that will lead to favorable media coverage of their point of view (Schaffner & Sellers, 2009). Journalists may or may not adopt those frames; news routines and commercial pressures also play a role in shaping media frames (Reese, 2010).

Most television news is framed episodically rather than thematically (Iyengar, 1991, 2010; Livingston, 2007; Postman, 1985). Episodic framing depicts "public issues in terms of concrete instances or specific events" (Iyengar &

Simon, 1993, p. 369), such as covering crime by covering criminal acts and their victims. Thematic framing "places public issues in some general or abstract context" (p. 369), such as discussing the causes of crime or reason for the changes in crime rates and occurrences. Episodic framing can limit in-depth understanding of public issues by personalizing and oversimplifying complex problems.

Differences in online, newspaper, and television's typical exposure situations suggest that television news viewing is more likely to follow the peripheral route. Because of the way that television news is presented, the audience is less likely to be able to follow the "central route." Because television's presentation and pacing are real time, audiences are not able to review or reflect on what they have seen or heard or to stop and ponder something they do not understand (P. L. Wright, 1981). Newspaper reading and online news viewing, on the other hand, is audience controlled. People can stop and think about stories at their own pace. Online, people can follow hyperlinks to find out more about a particular topic. Television news viewing is a more distracted activity, accompanied by daily routines (M. R. Levy & Windahl, 1984; A.M. Rubin & Perse, 1987a). People who access news via mobile devices may be more distracted, as well. So levels of attention to news stories fluctuate, and viewers may miss entirely some aspects of stories.

Finally, television news viewing, newspaper reading, and online news exposure are associated with different motives for use. Although information seeking motivates the use of news media (Perse & Courtright, 1993; Kohut et al., 2010; A.M. Rubin, 1981b), television news viewing typically includes a strong entertainment component (e.g., Palmgreen, Wenner, & Rayburn, 1981; Rayburn, Palmgreen, & Acker, 1984; Rubin et al., 1985). Frequent newspaper readers, however, are more oriented toward seeking information from print media. They read newspapers more for information than for entertainment (Kohut et al., 2010) and are also more likely to use other print media for information, such as news magazines (Bogart, 1989). Dimmick, Chen, and Li (2004) found that people using the Internet for news rated it higher than other media in terms of being helpful for such things as "getting the latest updates on news stories," "using my time wisely," and "for a variety of choices in news coverage" (p. 25).

Political Schemata of Elites and Non-elites

One axiom of news research is that education is a significant and substantial predictor of learning from the news (Berry, 1983; M. E. Grabe, Kamhawi, & Yegiyan, 2009; M. E. Grabe, Lang, Zhou, & Bolls, 2000; B. Gunter, 1987; Price & Czilli, 1996; J. P. Robinson & Levy, 1986; Tichenor et al., 1970). Education may have an impact because it signals sharper cognitive skills and abilities to process information. But, education's greatest impact may be due to its association with prior knowledge (Berry, 1983; Price & Czilli, 1996; J. P. Robinson & Levy, 1986). Greater prior knowledge may grow out of the use of superior information sources, higher cognitive ability, and greater interest in the news. Many scholars also explain that "people who possess large stores of information need well organized schemata to organize it, and these schemata aid in the acquisition of new information" (Price & Zaller, 1993, p. 138).

Public opinion elites may be seen as political sophisticates (Rhee & Cappella, 1997). Political sophistication is expertise in the political arena. It is marked by greater prior knowledge about political matters (Y.-K. Lee & Chang, 2010; Price & Zaller, 1993), more ideological stances on issues (Rhee & Cappella, 1997), and more analytic processing of political messages (Hsu & Price, 1993). Political experts have more complex and developed schemas about political matters than novices (Fiske & Kinder, 1991; Ha, 2011). Rhee and Cappella (1997), for example, found that political sophistication was related to higher argument quality and greater construct differentiation (i.e., number of distinct concepts) about the health care debate. Elites, then, not only have greater political knowledge as background, but have more complex political schemas.

Most of the research on political novices, or non-elites, focuses on their lack of elaborate political schemas. Non-elites, then, learn less from news and are not as analytical when encountering political messages. The ELM might suggest that non-elites follow a more peripheral route when encountering political information. There has been little speculation about what sorts of schemas non-elites use, however. An interesting finding drawn from news research suggests that non-elites might simply transfer accessible schemas from daily life to the political context. Price and Czilli (1996) found that human interest and personalized news stories are associated with greater learning, regardless of prior knowledge. Their least knowledgeable respondents (2 standard deviations below the mean) recalled 82% of news stories focusing on people in the news, but only 33% of nonpersonality stories. Graber (1988) suggested that human interest stories are remembered because they easily tap schemas that refer to people's own personal experiences. The episodic framing of most television news is easily adapted to such schemas.

Together, these findings illustrate that there are two general kinds of schema that may be reflected in pseudo and public opinion. When forming political opinions, elites may use schemas that have been developed specifically for political information processing and decision making. These schemas are ideologically based, and concern party or political stands or beliefs about political issues (Lau, 1986). Non-elites, on the other hand, may simply transfer schemas that they use every day to the political arena. These schemas most likely deal with political leaders and candidates as persons and as personalities.

Media Effects of Political Communication and the ELM

The elaboration likelihood model and Graber's concepts of public opinion elites and non-elites focus on the importance of two models to explain the effects of political communication. The conditional model suggests that effects will depend on whether audience members are elites or non-elites and whether they follow central or peripheral political information processing. The cognitive-transactional model suggests the schemas people use affect the effects of political messages. These two models will be applied to help understand a variety of traditional political media effects.

Agenda Setting

Agenda setting is a theory about the news media's power to structure the importance of political issues in the public's mind. Quite simply, agenda setting holds that, through gatekeeping, the news media select and highlight certain events, people, and issues. Through repetition and because of consistency across media, the public begins to adopt the news media's agenda and believes these same events, people, and issues are salient and important.

Even before the seminal Chapel Hill study of the role of the news media in establishing issue salience in undecided voters in the 1968 election (M. E. McCombs & Shaw, 1972), the notion of news media as the constructors of social reality was recognized by scholars. Lippmann (1922) speculated that people respond to the pictures of the world that they have in their heads, not to events in the real world. Lazarsfeld and Merton (1948) held that media performed a status conferral function for society by focusing attention on important people, events, and issues.

Researchers have found a good deal of support for agenda setting. The original 1972 study (M. E. McCombs & Shaw, 1972) found a substantial .98 rank-order correlation between amount of news coverage of issues and the rank ordering of those same issues by undecided voters. Since then, support for agenda setting mounted. Dearing and Rogers (1996) listed over 100 studies confirming the agenda-setting hypothesis. M. McCombs (2005) synthesizes more than three decades of related research. There is strong evidence of a causal connection between news prominence and public salience. Funkhouser (1973a, 1973b), MacKuen and Coombs (1981), and Lowry, Nio, and Leitner (2003) looked at agenda setting over long periods of time. These studies make it clear that media coverage of issues such as crime, urban unrest, the Vietnam War, and drug use does not always follow real-world indicators. In fact, at times, the news media highlight issues as they become less serious. And, most interesting, the public's beliefs in the importance of issues correspond more closely to news coverage than to real-world indicators (Lowry, Nio, & Leitner, 2003). Experimental manipulations of the evening news (Iyengar & Kinder, 1987; Iyengar, Peters, & Kinder, 1982) reinforced the connection between news coverage and issue salience. When participants watched news reports over the course of a week that highlighted stories about U.S. defense preparedness and pollution, they rated those issues more important than participants who had seen news reports providing only minimal coverage of those issues.

This conceptualization of agenda setting is an effect that can be described by the cumulative model of media effects.[7] Agenda setting is not an effect that occurs after a single exposure to the news. Instead, salience emerges in the public's mind because of consistent coverage of certain issues over a period of time.[8] And, selective exposure to specific newscasts is not relevant to agenda-setting research. There is remarkable consistency in the top stories across most news outlets (e.g., Dearing & Rogers, 1996; M. McCombs, 2005). Evidence suggests that even online, people tend to seek news from web versions of traditional media (J. Hamilton, 2004) and that those web sites tend to mirror each other and their offline counterparts in terms of issue agendas (Aikat & Yu, 2005; M. McCombs, 2005). Moreover, the agenda-setting effect is limited to certain cognitions. Agenda setting does not claim that the news media shape our opinions or direct our actions about an issue, only that they establish the issue's importance in the minds of the public.

Agenda Setting as a Peripheral Effect

Considering how central agenda-setting research has been in the study of mass communication effects, it may be interesting to note that it can be characterized as a peripheral effect. That is, issue salience does not depend on careful consideration of the content of news stories. Instead, it is signaled by peripheral cues inherent in news coverage. How is it that we know which stories are the most important in the news? Quite simply, journalists give simple signs to signal importance. The most important stories are those that are reported at the beginning of a newscast, are placed prominently on a web site's home page, take up the front page in the newspaper or the most time in a newscast. Frequently, journalists alert us to a story's importance by interrupting television programming or by even summarizing "today's top stories." These cues are noticeable and peripheral; they do not affect the information content of the news stories.

Agenda-setting scholars also based their analysis of the media agenda in an analysis of peripheral cues. Most studies determine the most important stories in the news through frequency; researchers simply count the number of stories about an issue as a measure of the media agenda (e.g., Brosius & Kepplinger, 1990; Funkhouser, 1973a, 1973b; Iyengar et al., 1982; Kiousis, 2004; M. E. McCombs & Shaw, 1972). Others may weigh a news story by its proportion of the total news (e.g., Wanta, 1997). W. Williams (1985) summarized other content analytic measures of news prominence: story placement, headlines, photos, column inches for print media, and video tape and static visuals for television news (see also Kiousis, 2004 and Watt, Mazza, & Snyder, 1993). All of these are peripheral signals, not central news content.

Additional evidence for agenda setting being a peripheral effect emerges from the study of the kinds of issues that are most easily transferred from the media agenda to the audience agenda. In general, issues can be characterized as obtrusive, that is, directly experienced, or unobtrusive, distant from one's daily experiences. Agenda setting seems to be stronger with unobtrusive issues than with obtrusive ones (e.g, Deemers, Craff, Choi, & Pessin, 1989; Iyengar et al., 1982; M. McCombs, 2004; Watt et al., 1993; D.H. Weaver, Graber, M.E. McCombs, & Eyal, 1981; Zucker, 1978). This is easily explained. When issues are obtrusive, or directly experienced, such as inflation, the public does not need the news media to alert them to their importance. But, the less direct experience that they have with an issue, the more they depend on the news media for awareness. So, agenda setting appears to be stronger for less personally involving issues.

There is also some limited indication that the politically involved may be less likely to adopt the media agenda (Iyengar et al., 1982; J.M. McLeod, Becker, & Byrnes, 1974; D.H. Weaver et al., 1981; but see M.E. McCombs & Weaver, 1985; Wanta, 1997). Just as Graber (1982) described public opinion elites, politically involved elites do not need to rely on the news media for information. Their involvement and interest leads them to use the mass media only as one source of foreground information. They have many other, more direct sources of information. Moreover, their political involvement leads them to establish issue priorities based on their own interests and knowledge. Wanta (1997) explained that the politically involved probably are more active and critical when using the news. The low involved are those who passively accept the media agenda.

One final bit of evidence suggests that agenda setting arises from the peripheral route: agenda-setting effects are relatively short term. Without reinforcement from the news, the public's memory about issues decays (Wanta, 1997; Watt et al., 1993). Agenda setting's endurance varies by medium (newspaper's impact seems to last longer, Wanta, 1997) and by issue. This, of course, makes common sense; issues drop from both the media and audience as news coverage brings new issues to prominence.

If agenda setting is a peripheral effect, relatively short term, with its greatest impact on non-elites and strongest for uninvolving issues, what makes it an important media effect? Is the power to structure political reality important for those who are least interested in politics? There are many answers to that question. First, the study of agenda setting alerts us to the power of the news media to highlight certain issues at the expense of coverage of other issues. During the period leading up to the passage of health care reform in 2010, a lot of coverage was given to tangential and sometimes misleading debates about provisions such as "death panels,"[9] and to fierce arguments at town hall meetings organized by members of Congress with their constituents. The actual provisions of the legislation, on a matter of great consequence, received relatively less coverage. As Dearing and Rogers (1996) suggested, the newsworthiness of issues (especially in terms of their conflict) affects media interest in those issues.

Dearing and Rogers (1996) and M. McCombs (2004) also pointed out that although the focus of most agenda-setting research is the causal connection between the media and audience agenda, there is evidence that the media and audience agenda can also have an impact on the policy agenda. That is, agenda setting may have an impact on the actions of legislators and govern-ment officials.

Equally important to the development of public opinion, agenda setting may ignite political interest and involvement, even in non-elites. When there are natural disasters, media coverage can help to galvanize the public to help. For example, after the 2010 earthquake in Haiti, visuals of people searching for their missing relatives, scenes of massive destruction and piles of dead bod-ies are tempered with stories of rescue and accompanied by information about how and where to donate money. Television in particular can provide power-fully evocative images that motivate people to take action (Stanley, 2010).

Petty and Priester (1994) pointed out that what is a peripheral cue for one might be a central cue for another. For non-elites, visuals can be powerful central cues that command their attention and stimulate intense affective reac-tions. Through agenda setting, then, the media may bring issues to public attention and activate elites and non-elites alike. Agenda setting might be a stimulus to bring non-elites to political activity.

Agenda Setting as a Cognitive-Transactional Effect

Since the 1980s, agenda setting has grown into a theoretical approach to media effects much broader than originally proposed. Scholars have expanded the concept of agenda setting to the cognitive-transactional model, terming it "second-level agenda setting." According to this model of agenda setting, the media agenda does not merely establish a set of issue priorities in the public; it also sets the criteria that the public use to judge the effectiveness of political leaders or the policies proposed to solve public issues.

The work of Iyengar and his colleagues (Iyengar & Kinder, 1987; Iyengar et al., 1982; Iyengar & Simon, 1993), for example, has demonstrated that when the news media focus on certain political issues, the public uses the Pres-ident's performance on those issues as the gauge to how well he is doing his job. For example, President George W. Bush's approval ratings from the time he took office in January 2001 ranged in the area of 50 to 60%. Immediately following the attacks of September 11, 2001, his approval ratings skyrocketed to 80 to 90% (D. Moore, 2001). The change was attributed to a shift from people focusing on Bush's domestic agenda to emphasizing his response to the terrorist attacks. Similarly, President Carter's approval rating was also affected by the media agenda, but in a negative direction. Iyengar et al. (1982) found that experimental manipulations that inserted stories about defense prepar-edness into network news coverage led to greater weight being attached to Carter's performance on defense.[10]

A cognitive-transactional model explanation of these effects suggests that when the news media highlight certain issues or events as important, these become salient issues and events to the public. The salience of these issues primes them in the minds of the public. Repeated news coverage repeatedly primes these issues. Moreover, when thoughts have been primed, they are more easily accessed. So, when people are asked to evaluate the President's performance, for example, greater weight is given to his performance on those recently primed issues and events. In a sense, the media agenda sets the criteria for judging the President.

The evidence of second-level agenda setting offers some interesting implications, both theoretical and practical. This notion of agenda setting might provide an explanation for rally effects, such as Presidential support during times of international crisis (see Chapter 3). Crises are characterized by intense media coverage. During crises, the media agenda may be consumed by stories about critical events. As that event is placed on the media agenda, it may become the primary criteria for judging how well the President is performing his job. Because much media coverage during times of crisis serves a solidarity-building function, it is most likely favorable to the government. Because the public is dependent on the news media for information about the crises, their sole source of information is favorable. Hence, an increase in the public's approval of the President – a rally effect.

Is second-level agenda setting a central or peripheral effect? It too might be characterized as a peripheral effect. Priming is a result of more automatic information processing that responds to environmental stimuli (or salient media content). Non-elites, or those who are less politically interested and knowledgeable, might be more likely to rely on salient media coverage as the basis for evaluating political leaders. Miller and Krosnick (2000) also found that people who are knowledgeable *and* have a lot of trust in the media also exhibit second-level agenda setting effects because these individuals have chosen to trust a particular media source and accept information they glean there without further analysis. The elites who are less trusting of media might be more likely to rely on their own background knowledge.

Does that mean second-level agenda setting is not important because it is a peripheral effect? As a conditional effect, the media's agenda-setting impact affects people only under certain conditions. The ELM suggests that one of those conditions is political interest and involvement. Although we cannot know the exact proportions, it is clear that the majority of U.S. citizens are not public opinion elites. For non-elites, almost all political issues might be non-obtrusive, so their perceptions about political issues might be easily affected by the media agenda. Moreover, with less interest in politics, non-elites might be easily primed by salient coverage of certain political issues. Also, for non-elites, impressions of political candidates might be based on evaluations drawn from criteria on the media agenda. During his campaign for President in 2004, George W. Bush's adviser, Karl Rove, is thought to have orchestrated gay marriage amendments in many states key to reelection (Reed, 2004) as a way to galvanize evangelical voters who had stayed home in prior elections. Rove assumed that voters who turned out to support amendments against gay marriage would also vote for Bush over the Democratic candidate John Kerry; he was correct. Political messages during elections might be looked at as attempts to control the media agenda, and, so, control the criteria that the large number of non-elites – and elites who are highly trusting of media – use to judge candidates. In an election, each vote counts the same. If media content can sway a large number of voters, this is certainly no meaningless effect.

Framing

Within the realm of politics and public opinion, second-level agenda setting theory posits that news media are not limited to merely establishing the salience of certain topics, but through the description of those topics also serve to make salient particular criteria by which political actors and issues will be evaluated. Framing research also holds that how the news is presented affects what people think about issues, people, and events. There is disagreement among scholars about the extent to which these concepts overlap. Some argue that framing is a subset of second-level agenda setting, and that frames are one way in which topics can be described (see, e.g., M. McCombs, 2004, pp. 86–97; M. McCombs & Ghanem, 2001). The prevailing view, however, seems to be that the concept of framing is broader than that (see, e.g., Maher, 2001; Nelson, 2011; Scheufele, 1999; D. Weaver, 2007). Framing research examines *why* and *how* frames appear in the news as well as the impact they have on people's political judgments. Framing researchers also examine aspects of issues or candidates that have been *excluded* from discussion.[11]

Framing involves selection and emphasis. Much as you must make choices about what to include and exclude when you are taking a photograph, journalists must make choices about what to include and exclude in their stories. In so doing, some aspects of a perceived reality are made more salient. As Entman (1993) summarized, frames can define problems, diagnose causes, make moral judgments, and suggest remedies (p. 52). Nelson (2011) distinguishes *issue* framing from *news* framing. Issue frames are specific to a particular topic and they usually "lay blame and favor particular solutions" (Nelson, 2011, p. 193). The "pro-choice" and "pro-life" frames in discussing abortion are a clear example of issue framing. News frames, on the other hand, are more generic templates that can be applied across many different stories – the *conflict* frame, for example, is a common news frame that presents a story as an argument between two or more competing groups. Political actors actively seek to influence issue frames (Schaffner & Sellers, 2009; Scheufle & Tewksbury, 2007). Journalists may or may not incorporate those issue frames in their stories. News frames originate from the journalists, as the practices and pressures of news production also play a role in determining the presentation of stories. Both types of framing are communicated to the audience through the use of different story introductions, word choices, the selection of interviewees (and which parts of their interviews to include in a story), and visual content, for example. News and issue frames, then, are media content attributes that can be identified through content analysis (e.g., Iyengar & Simon, 1993; W. R. Neuman, Just, & Crigler, 1992; Tankard, 2001).

Framing effects go beyond setting an agenda and establishing issue salience. Framing effects involve how people interpret the news, the connections they make between concepts, and the judgments they form after viewing or reading the news. Framing activates "some ideas, feelings, and values rather than others," and "can encourage particular trains of thought about political phenomena and lead audiences to arrive at more or less predictable conclusions" (Price, Tewksbury, & Powers, 1997, p. 483). Frames in news stories can affect political opinions.

There are some types of news frames that are used quite commonly (e.g., Iyengar, 1991, 2009; Iyengar & Simon, 1993; W. R. Neuman et al., 1992). Episodic framing involves a focus on the presentation of concrete examples. It relies on visuals and individual examples of a larger problem. Episodic framing of poverty, for example, might highlight the plights of individuals in poverty, what brought them there, how they live day to day, or how they use government aid. Thematic framing presents an issue in context. It does not focus on individual examples, but on collective experiences and conclusions. Thematic framing is not visually oriented and involves a more abstract presentation. Thematic framing of poverty might present statistics about the prevalence of poverty currently and over time; it might also explain causes of poverty. Other frames identified by researchers include the protest paradigm (D. M. McLeod & Hertog, 1992). The protest paradigm is more episodic than thematic. It frames protest stories as battles between police and protesters, and focuses on violence, conflict, and deviance, rather than an explanation of the issues driving the protest.

Framing effects can be explained by the cognitive-transactional model: Media content attributes can lead to relatively automatic and predictable responses in particular people (see e.g., Scheufele, 1999). Scheufele and Tewksbury (2007) argue that while agenda setting operates through increasing the *accessibility* of particular issues or aspects of issues, making them easier to recall when a judgment must be made, framing operates through a process of *applicability* (p. 15). Increasing the applicability of a concept means that, after reading or viewing a message, the audience member is more likely to draw a connection between two concepts (Nisbet, 2010; Price & Tewksbury, 1997; Scheufele & Tewksbury, 2007). So, for example, if a news article talks about extending tax cuts for the "job creators," some members of the public are likely to make a connection between tax cuts and unemployment levels. But if a news article discusses returning tax rates for the "wealthiest 1% of households" to their previous rate, then the link of tax rates with unemployment becomes less applicable. If something is accessible but not seen as applicable, it will not be used in making political judgments (Nelson et al., 1997).

There is support for the psychological nature of framing effects. Researchers using thought-listing techniques found that different news stories with different issue frames about education, crime, political and economic issues resulted in different kinds of thoughts about the issue (de Vreese, 2004; Price et al., 1997; Valkenburg, Semetko, & de Vreese, 1999). Different news frames activate different cognitive reactions. Episodic and thematic framing of news stories result in different attributions of the causes of social problems and the solutions to their problems (Iyengar, 1991, 2009). Episodic framing of poverty in America, for example, led viewers of news stories to hold the poor themselves responsible for their plight and see the cause for poverty as the individual's own kind of (or lack of) education and character.[12]

Framing has also been found to be related to the kinds of solutions to political problems that people endorse. After September 11, Edy and Meirick (2007) found that the frame people had adopted about the events of that day impacted their endorsement of military action in Afghanistan. D.M. McLeod and Detenber (1999) reported that differently framed news reports of the same political protest had different effects on viewers. Experimental participants viewed one of three news stories that differed in the tone and substance of their coverage of an anarchist protest that resulted in protester–police confrontation. Viewers of the "high status quo bias" story (a frame that presented protesters as a threat to police and to society as a whole) were less likely to support the protesters, less critical of the police, and less likely to attribute widespread support for the protesters' cause. Although research has not been able to link viewing of a single news story to changes in public opinion, there is concern that negative coverage of political protest might lead to accessible opinions that protest might be deviant, that protest should be contained, and that protest is not an effective method of changing society. This, of course, is troubling to those who see political protest as an expression of free speech, as one basis of our form of government, and as a way to introduce social change (e.g., Gitlin, 1980).

News framing research, then, posits that the structure and content of news stories have short-term effects that may have long-term implications. Directly after watching the news, framing effects are seen in the thoughts and impressions of the audience. These thoughts and impressions may become more accessible and applicable and affect more long-term impressions and political opinion.

Are Framing Effects Central or Peripheral?

Within the ELM, framing effects might be described as more peripheral effects. Price and his colleagues (1997) were able to stimulate different effects with the same news substance, framed simply by different introductory and closing paragraphs. Framing elements might be characterized as peripheral cues. Discussions of the protest paradigm, for example, suggest that news stories frequently marginalize protest because journalists do not allow the protesters to speak for themselves, show visuals primarily of deviant behavior, and do not explain the substantive reasons or ideology driving the protest; so, protest stories generally lack central information.

Studies also suggest that political ideology may lead people to resist framing effects. That is, framing seems to have its largest impact on those who are not political partisans (e.g., Iyengar, 1991) or politically involved (e.g., Kinder & Sanders, 1990). Democrats, for example, are more likely to attribute societal causes for poverty, even in the face of episodic news story framing (Iyengar, 1991). This may be explained by the fact that people with strongly held beliefs are less likely to be susceptible to framing effects (Chong & Druckman, 2007). News story framing effects are conditional, then, on the political ideology of the viewers; partisans with strong beliefs are less affected by framing. News framing effects might be characterized as peripheral effects, then, because they are more pronounced among the less partisan, less politically involved – the non-elites.

Spiral of Silence

The spiral of silence (Noelle-Neumann, 1991, 1993) is an approach that contends that the mass media are a powerful force, not only in establishing public opinion, but in reducing the number of divergent opinions in a society.[13] The spiral of silence is a theory about the expression of public opinion. This theory has two central elements that contribute to the public expression of political opinion: individuals' fear of isolation and the mass media. According to Noelle-Neumann (1991, 1993), people are essentially passive; one of their main goals is to avoid social isolation. One way to avoid social isolation is to avoid expressing opinions that might be rejected by the dominant groups in society.[14] So, before expressing any political opinion, people monitor the political views expressed in society. There are two main arenas in which people monitor political views. In the interpersonal arena, people are aware of the political views of those with whom they interact. If people see interpersonal support for their political views, they will express them. The second arena is the mass media. Noelle-Neumann (1991, 1993) saw the mass media as a powerful creator of social reality through their coverage of public opinion. The mass media project their construction of the political views in society (which may not be an accurate representation of the majority public opinion). Without interpersonal support for their views, people will not express opinions that diverge from the mainstream, as presented by the media. So, according to the spiral of silence, the mass media serve as the representation of the dominant views in society. And, without interpersonal support, people will not express political views that do not conform to media coverage. So, a spiral of silence grows; divergent opinions become less likely to be expressed. The mass media, then, can be quite powerful in shaping public opinion and maintaining social control. Noelle-Neumann's (1993) definition of public opinion reflects the power of social control: "Public opinions are attitudes or behaviors one *must* express in public if one is not to isolate oneself; in areas of controversy or change, public opinions are those attitudes one can express without running the danger of isolating oneself" (p. 178).

As conceived by Noelle-Neumann, the spiral of silence is an effect best explained by the cumulative effects model. In fact, the spiral of silence is one of the theories that initiated media scholars to "return to the concept of powerful mass media" (Noelle-Neumann, 1973, p. 68). As a cumulative effect, the spiral of silence focuses on the importance of consonant media content. Media coverage of the dominant opinion is assumed to be consistent across a range of media outlets. Because the approach assumes a passive audience, people's selective actions are not viewed as particularly important because people are not likely to seek out divergent media messages in alternative media. And, Noelle-Neumann (1993) assumed that a fear of isolation is fairly constant across people. So, the effects of the spiral of silence are thought to arise after cumulative exposure to consistent media depictions of the dominant public opinion.

Noelle-Neumann (1984) reported various polling results that suggest that the spiral of silence can lead to changes in public opinion. In the 1965 German election, for example, reports about voting intentions for one of the two parties were fairly similar over the course of the campaign. But, as the campaign progressed, polls found that an increasing proportion of the German public believed that the Christian Democratic Union (CDU) party would be the victor. The final days of the election saw a swing in voting intentions, as more people moved toward support of the CDU. Despite the neck-and-neck race, the CDU won the election. Polling about support for the death penalty (Noelle-Neumann, 1993) also suggested how *perceptions* about public opinion can lead to *changes* in public opinion. As perceived support for the death penalty (perceptions about what most people felt about the death penalty) declined in Germany, public opinion supporting the death penalty also declined.

The spiral of silence, however, deals more centrally with political discussion. The notion of public opinion growing out of the reasoned search for truth is grounded in valuing free and open discussion. Without discussion, the truth cannot be identified (e.g., Mill, 1859; Milton, 1644). Informed public opinion depends on discussion to crystallize ideas and identify faulty assumptions, data, and logic. Graber (1982) pointed out that informed public opinion can develop only in the "wake of informed discussion" (p. 556). The importance of political discussion is reinforced by news acquisition research that finds that interpersonal discussion about issues in the news is a potent predictor of knowledge about the news (J. P. Robinson & Levy, 1986). Knowledge gaps between groups develop, in part, because higher socioeconomic groups tend to have more social contacts for whom knowledge is relevant (Tichenor et al., 1970). The stifling of public expression of opinion is an important effect in democratic societies.

There is only limited research support for the spiral of silence. While there is a small but significant relationship between people's perceptions of the climate of opinion and their willingness to speak out about controversial issues, it does not appear that fear of isolation is the primary explanation (Glynn, Hayes, & Shanahan, 1997; Scheufele & Moy, 2000). Most of the research focused on Noelle-Neumann's concept of fear of isolation found that it is not substantially related to fear of opinion expression. Glynn and J. M. McLeod

(1985) tested Noelle-Neumann's assertion that public opinion "hard cores" (those most strongly involved in political issues) would be less affected by fear of isolation and be willing to express minority opinions. The researchers found no support for Noelle-Neumann's hypothesis. After a meta-analysis of over 100 studies that examined the relationship between fear of isolation and willingness to speak out, Glynn et al. (1997) found no overall support for this aspect of the spiral of silence. Moreover, Kennamer (1990) reminded us of the wealth of theory and research about selectivity processes (i.e., selective exposure, attention, perception, and retention) that argue against Noelle-Neumann's proposal. Through such processes as cognitive dissonance, egocentrism, and psychological projection, people tend to attribute their own opinions to others. That is, people avoid information that conflicts with their own attitudes. When confronted with contrary information, however, they tend to interpret that information in a way so that it does not contradict their own attitudes. So people should not be so swayed by media depictions of public opinion.

Researchers have identified a number of other individual difference variables that are related to opinion expression. Matthes, Morrison, and Schemer (2010) examined the role of attitude certainty, the level to which a person feels confident in an attitude that they hold about a particular issue or person. They found that people who were very confident about their position on an issue were not influenced by the perceived climate of opinion to speak out (or stay silent). However, people who were low or moderate in terms of their confidence about their attitude did evaluate the climate of opinion in deciding whether or not they would be willing to speak out. This does support Noelle-Neumann's concept of the "hard cores" being willing to speak out regardless of the opinion climate.

Willnat, Lee, and Detenber (2002) conducted a study in Singapore, and found that a general fear of speaking out publically – what they called "communication apprehension" – is also related to one's willingness to be publically outspoken about a controversial issue. They also included measures of how independent and interdependent people consider themselves to be. These individual-level measures were included to help account for differences between cultures in terms of the emphasis on the rights of the individual or the good of the collective. The study found no relationship between one's level of independence or interdependence and willingness to speak out.

Scheufele and Moy (2000) make a compelling argument, however, that researchers should pursue the role of cultural understandings of conflict resolution, and of how people should behave in interpersonal relationships, in influencing one's outspokenness. Cross-cultural research is made difficult by the fact that what may be considered a controversial issue in one country may not be so in another, so finding ways to measure outspokenness in a manner that can be compared can be challenging. It is further complicated by the fact that different cultures foster different kinds of personality traits that may be related to one's willingness to express an opinion (see Scheufele & Moy, 2000, p. 18).

It also may be that the spiral of silence varies by society as a result of different media systems (Glynn & J. M. McLeod, 1985; Salmon & Kline, 1985). The United States values free speech and dissent. The cultural commitment to freedom of expression, and the traditional notion of objective journalism, may marginalize fewer voices. This is not always the case, however. Eveland, D. M. McLeod, and Signorielli (1995) found that people tended to overestimate support for the first Gulf War. In their survey of Delaware respondents during the second and third weeks of the air war, only 46.9% of respondents supported the war. But, 81.4% believed that "most people in the United States support the war." The researchers suggest that the overwhelmingly supportive war coverage of the U.S. news media (see Dennis et al., 1991; Kaid et al., 1993; Newhagen, 1994) contributed to this "pluralistic ignorance."

González (1988) noted that the spiral of silence offers no explanation for the 1986 Philippine revolution that ousted the Marcos regime. The Philippine media under the Marcos regime were tightly controlled by allies of the government and presented a highly consonant and consistent view of government support. But, their ubiquity and power were not able to squelch rebellious factions of society. Moreover, there is evidence that people sought out the limited number of alternative newspapers that published alternate views. Different cultural values may limit the scope of the spiral of silence.

Changes in the media environment may also lessen the impact of the spiral of silence. The availability of social networking sites like Facebook and Twitter helped facilitate the Arab Spring even as regimes clamped down on traditional media and tried to block Internet access (J. Moore, 2011). With the vast array of opportunities to find like-minded people online, it may be less likely someone would feel isolated in their opinions and unwilling to express them – although they may be expressing them only to people who already agree with their position. McDevitt, Kiousis, and Wahl-Jorgensen (2003) examined the impact that the ability to be anonymous online had on willingness to express minority views. They found that participants who interacted in a computer-mediated forum were more likely to be viewed as moderate in their opinions than participants who interacted about the same topic in a face-to-face setting. This finding stood whether the computer-mediated participants held majority or minority opinions. In the computer-mediated condition, everyone tended to "adopt a communication strategy that allowed for participation without explicit opinion expression" (McDevitt et al., 2003, p. 466). This suggests there is something unique about online interactions that may alter the spiral of silence process.

Are Effects Central or Peripheral?

The spiral of silence might be characterized as a more peripheral effect. The effect seems to be explained less by the arguments that the media present to support a political view. Instead, the spiral grows out of a kind of "bandwagon" effect. Media coverage implies that a certain view is dominant in society, supported by the majority. So, it is the amount of support that is important to this effect more than the quality of the idea. This may be characterized as a peripheral cue.

There are other indications that the spiral of silence is a peripheral effect; it may have its greatest impact on those who hold pseudo public opinion. Although Noelle-Neumann (1993) argued that, for the most part, the effects of the spiral of silence are fairly uniform, she does recognize that there are some groups that fall outside its influence: the hard core and the avant garde. The hard core are the "minority that remains at the end of the spiral of silence process in defiance of the threats of isolation" (p. 171). The avant garde are those who do not fear isolation or are willing to pay the price of being isolated. These groups are the knowledgeable and politically involved who introduce new ideas to society or keep nondominant views alive. The spiral of silence, then, might have some aspects of the conditional model. Effects might be conditional on one's political involvement. The politically involved – the public opinion elites – might have a good deal of interpersonal resources, based on their political activity, that provide interpersonal support for their views, even if the media characterize those views as minority views. So, the social relationships of the elite might insulate them from the effects of the spiral of silence. Graber (1982) might recognize the hard core and avant garde as public opinion elites. Even without the support of interpersonal networks, these groups might have the inner strength to resist the pull of societal conformity. They too would be less affected by the spiral of silence.

Non-elites, on the other hand, hold only pseudo-opinions that are not well grounded in political discussion, social contact, or political activity. Because they use the mass media as both background and foreground information, they may be more likely to be affected by media reports of public opinion. Because their own political opinions are not particularly strong, they may be more likely to be pulled by the "bandwagon" of what the media depict as the dominant political view.

The Effects of Public Opinion Polls

Public opinion polls are a central feature of democracy today. Cable news channels and online news sites are endlessly in search of content to fill the 24/7 news cycle. Public opinion polls are a ready-made peg around which news stories and discussions can be built. Increasingly, news organizations conduct or commission their own polls as a form of marketing (Rosenstiel, 2005). Changes in technology have also made it easier and less expensive to conduct public opinion polls (Frankovic, 2005), which means the quality of some polls is questionable (Bennett, 2011). Historically, polls are intended to facilitate the democratic process by providing the means by which the electorate can communicate their opinions to politicians and legislators. But, it is clear that polls do more than communicate opinion; they may also shape it.

Several effects of polls have been proposed and researched. K. Lang and G.E. Lang (1984) summarized evidence that polls can have an energizing effect on voters. When people are asked their opinions by pollsters, they become more aware of and interested in an issue. There are also concerns that political elites manipulate the general public, through public opinion polling, to further their own ends (see, e.g., Bennett, 2011). Most research, though, has focused on three specific effects: bandwagon effects, underdog effects, and effects on voter turnout.[15]

Both bandwagon and underdog effects hold that public opinion polls lead to changes in public opinion. Bandwagon effects are shifts in public opinion toward the dominant opinion. That is, when people hear results of public opinion polls that show that the majority hold opinions contrary to their own, people tend to shift their opinion toward the majority. Underdog effects are the opposite of bandwagon effects. Underdog effects are shifts in public opinion toward the minority candidate or opinion. A necessary condition to both bandwagon and underdog effects is awareness of public opinion. With issues or elections that receive a good deal of media coverage, poll reports are widely reported in the media, so awareness of polls is typically quite high (e.g., Lavrakas, Holley, & Miller, 1991). Bandwagon effects are found more commonly (see Marsh, 1984, for a summary of that research; see also Diaz-Castillo, 2005). In fact, they were found by Lazarsfeld et al. (1968) in their Erie County (Ohio) voting study. Some undecided voters made their voting decision based on Franklin D. Roosevelt's dominance in the polls. But, there has been some evidence of underdog effects as well (e.g., Ceci & Kain, 1982). In fact, John Anderson's surprising third-party showing in the landslide 1980 election was attributed to underdog effects; people voted for him simply because they expected him not to win (Tannenbaum, 1986).

There are several theoretical explanations for both bandwagon and underdog effects.[16] The spiral of silence offers one explanation. It holds that bandwagon effects result because people want to avoid social isolation, so they adopt the majority opinion. A cognitive dissonance approach (e.g., Morwitz & Pluzinski, 1996) argued that bandwagon effects are the result of dissonance reduction by voters who support a candidate who is not supported by the majority. So, when people become aware of polls that report that their position is contrary to the majority, they are likely to change their opinion. But, there is an important distinction that differentiates this cognitive dissonance approach from the spiral of silence. There are two conditions that are necessary to produce dissonance. The first is exposure to and awareness of contrary poll information. The second is belief that the poll information is correct. Morwitz and Pluzinski (1996) found that people will not change their minds if they believe that their candidate will win, even in the face of contrary polling information. This approach differs from the spiral of silence because it recognizes the impact of selective perception of polls. Henshel and Johnston (1987) quite simply proposed that public opinion polls lead to bandwagon effects indirectly through their impact on campaign contributions, volunteerism, and endorsement. Large contributors, for example, might want to back a winner. Political activists may also monitor the polls to decide the candidate to which they will attach their own careers (also see Traugott, 1992).

Underdog effects have been explained by sympathy, where people vote for the loser because they feel sorry for the candidate. There is also a more rational explanation for underdog effects. Marsh (1984) suggested that underdog effects may be due to a desire to reduce the margin of victory for the winner. So voters may vote for the underdog to limit the confidence and political power of the victor because they fear what he or she might try to do once elected. Or, in parliamentary systems, voters may choose to vote for their second choice party so as to encourage a coalition with their chosen party (Donsbach, 2001).

In addition to the impact of poll information itself, students of mass communication effects should consider how the *framing* of stories about public opinion polls might also generate effects. Bennett (2011) argues that media reports about polls often oversimplify the nuances of public opinion and the limitations of the polling methodology so as to present a clearer story, focusing on public opinion as "news output rather than democratic input" (p. 256).

Over the past 10 years, tracking polls have become quite popular near the end of Presidential elections. Tracking polls are very brief daily public opinion measurements, either using a panel of respondents, or a cross section. Tracking polls contribute to "horse race" media coverage of elections because journalists analyze slight shifts in these daily poll reports as though they are of great significance when the changes may be quite trivial (Frankovic, 1998; Rosenstiel, 2005). Rosenstiel (2005) argues that regular coverage of tracking polls displaces other news stories, shifting the emphasis of news from understanding the election's issues to predicting its outcome (p. 711). It is important to remember that even though all reputable media report sampling error in polls, most analysts fail to take sampling error into account in their interpretations of the polls. So statistically nonsignificant shifts in opinion are frequently characterized as "real" shifts. How the news media frame poll reports might have an impact on the effects of those reports. Framing shifts in opinion or voter preference as the result of a candidate's "momentum" (Hickman, 1991), for example, might have a larger bandwagon effect than framing the results as due to other adjustments.

But, bandwagon and underdog effects are not found universally in research (see Diaz-Castillo, 2005). Hickman (1991) pointed out that the effects of public opinion polls on the audience are highly conditional on an individual's orientation, poll awareness, decision-making urgency, trust in polls, and political commitment. Individuals who have a higher orientation toward wanting to support the winner, who are aware of polls and find the information useful, who feel a need to make a decision quickly, place a good deal of credibility in the polls, and are not particularly committed to a candidate or a party are more likely to be affected by polling information. Conversely, those people who are less oriented toward wanting to support the winner (who may base their candidate selection on other criteria), who are not aware of or do not attach too much importance to polls, who make their decisions early in the election or at a more leisurely pace, attribute lower credibility to polls and media coverage of polls, and are politically committed, should be less affected by poll reports.

Concern about the impact of polls has generally focused on their effect on non-elites (Hardmeier, 2008). Ceci and Kain (1982), for example, observed that the greatest shifts in candidate preference (both bandwagon and underdog effects) among their experimental participants were among those participants who were not particularly committed to their candidate. Among those who felt strongly about a candidate, there was little shift after exposure to polls. Lavrakas et al. (1991) found both bandwagon and underdog effects in their analysis of the 1988 Presidential election. But, these effects occurred almost exclusively in the less-educated population. As we have seen, educational level is often a signal for political interest, knowledge, and relevant social contacts. It also signals being more able to follow the central route when considering political messages. The more educated might be more likely to be public opinion elites. Lavrakas et al. (1991) also observed that late deciders (those who made their voting decisions late in the election) were more likely to experience bandwagon and underdog effects. This finding might suggest that these effects are more common among the less knowledgeable and less politically involved – the non-elites. Shapiro and Jacobs (2011), however, report that the highly educated and engaged are "most vulnerable to perceptual biases – their prior theories and political attitudes determine how they seek out and evaluate new information rather than the other way around" (p. 725). The effects of public opinion polls on public opinion, then, might be characterized as a peripheral effect – the specifics of which are conditional on the political abilities and interest of the individual.

Effects of Media Reports of Polling on Voter Turnout

Since the advent of television and more sophisticated polling and projection methods, there have been concerns that reports of election returns on Presidential election days might have an impact on election-day voting. In the United States, this concern is magnified because the country covers three time zones (not to mention Alaska and Hawaii). So, television might begin to report election returns and projections while polls in the western part of the country are still open. Those western voters who wait until after work or dinner to vote have probably seen some reports of election returns or exit polls. In the 2000 election, news organizations began calling the state of Florida for Al Gore after polls in the eastern part of the state (and in the Eastern time zone) closed but before voters in Florida's panhandle (and in the Central time zone) had finished casting their ballots. After the panhandle votes were in, those predictions were changed for George W. Bush to take Florida's electoral votes, and then finally Florida was declared too close to call (Frankovic, 2005).

Although some people are concerned about the bandwagon and under-dog effects that might occur from voters seeing early results, most scholars and policy researchers are concerned about the impact of election returns on voter *turnout*. (In fact, Gartner, 1976, believed that bandwagon effects mainly affect turnout, rather than voting; the losing candidate's supporters are less likely to vote.) These writers are concerned that reporting early returns may disenfranchise voters in other time zones and lead them to stay away from the polling booths. Voter turnout is a concern in a democracy. Because our system of government is based on participation, citizen participation is valued. Voting is one of the most central and easiest ways to have a say in governance.

This problem was particularly notable in 1980. The election had appeared to be a close one up until the final day of the campaign. Early election returns, however, quickly revealed that Reagan would likely win in a landslide. The first television network named Reagan the winner by 8:15 p.m. EST, while voters in the western states were still voting. There is an indication that many western voters believed that their votes did not count and chose not to vote (Jackson, 1983). Although these votes may not have changed the outcome of the Presidential election, there were many other candidates for statewide and local offices, as well as local issues on the ballot. If voters did not vote, they did not participate in elections that touched them even more closely than national offices.

Sudman (1986) explained that people vote when the perceived benefits of voting outweigh the perceived costs. Benefits derive from (a) the impor-tance of the election (important elections provide more benefits for voting); (b) the closeness of the election (elections whose outcomes are more uncertain provide more benefit); and (c) belief in the importance of voting in general. Costs associated with voting include the time required (including travel time), interference with other activities, and inconvenience (e.g., having to stand in line). Television reports of early election returns, the results of exit polls, or election projections influence only the perceptions about the closeness of the election. So, media reports that suggest that an election is not close should decrease the benefits of voting and lead to lower turnout. On the other hand, if reports suggest that an election is closer than earlier thought, these reports can increase voter turnout. So, in only a few elections should there be a con-cern about election-night reporting affecting voter turnout.

Several suggestions have been offered over the years to reduce the effect of early election returns, reports of exit polls, and election projections (e.g., Tannenbaum, 1986). Some of the suggestions are based on changing the vot-ing day or the times that polls are open. For example, a uniform poll closing time, which would mean that east coast election polls would stay open until west coast polls close, would lead to later reports of election returns. Other proposals include establishing longer voting periods, from 24 to 48 hours, to diffuse the impact of election result reporting. Some have suggested that election results not be released to the media and the public until all polls are closed across the country. Still others advocate public boycotts of exit polls or voluntary restraint by the news media. All of these proposals have associated problems, and despite Congressional hearings in the 1980s and 2001, none have been adopted in the United States.[17]

It is important to remember that these effects are quite difficult to identify and, when found, are quite small. These effects too might be limited to less politically involved voters – the non-elites. K. Lang and G. E. Lang (1968) suggested that this is a reason for the small effects of election reporting and projections on voter behavior. Only a small number of voters are susceptible to influence. These effects are limited, not only limited to the portion of voters who wait to vote and watch television returns, but to those who are volatile or "floating" voters (Großer & Schram, 2010). Those whose votes change easily are typically less politically knowledgeable and involved. And, interestingly, less involved citizens are less likely to watch election returns, so they are less likely to be aware of election-night reporting. Lang and Lang (1968) further explained that election-night reporting is likely to affect only those who vote based on the utility of their vote in that election. But, voters who decide based on political ideology, dedication to a candidate's cause, or beliefs in the importance of the democratic system are less likely to be affected by television reports of election returns and projections. This effect, then, is a conditional effect; elites are less likely to be influenced by media coverage of election results. However, the desire to institute a remedy for these perceived effects stems, at least in part, from a belief that *other* people are impacted by hearing poll results – a third-person effect (Pan, Abisaid, Paek, Sun & Houden, 2006; Wei, Chia, & Lo, 2011).

Third-Person Effects

There is evidence that there is a good deal of pluralistic ignorance, or a general misperception of what others really think and feel (A. C. Gunther & Chia, 2001; Toch & Klofas, 1984). One implication of pluralistic ignorance is the spiral of silence; another is third-person effects (Davison, 1983). Third-person effects are based on perceptions that others will be more affected by negative media content than oneself.[18] So, people have a tendency to believe that media messages are persuasive and effects are common. But, they also believe that they are immune to this influence themselves. So, people overestimate media's influence on others and underestimate their influence on themselves.

There are two components to third-person effects: perceptual and behavioral. The perceptual component deals with beliefs that others are affected by negative media content. Support for the perceptual component of third-person effects is a robust research finding (Paul, Salwen, & Dupagne, 2000; R. M. Perloff, 2009). For example, people believe that others will be more affected by pornography (A. C. Gunther, 1995; Wu & Koo, 2001; Zhao & Cai, 2008), political ads (Cohen & Davis, 1991; Rucinski & Salmon, 1990), violent and misogynous rap music (D. M. McLeod, Eveland, & Nathanson, 1997), news coverage about the environment and about public opinion polls

(Jensen & Hurley, 2005; Pan, et al., 2006), neutral product advertising (A. G. Gunther & Thorson, 1992), product placement of alcohol in youth-oriented films (D. H. Shin & Kim, 2011), violent video games (Boyle, McLeod, & Rojas, 2008), and media images of slimness (David & Johnson, 1998).

The behavioral component of third-person effects is founded on the actions that people endorse, based on their biased perceptions of others. Davison (1983) gave one of the first examples of third-person behavioral effects. During World War II, one part of Japanese propaganda was directed toward African American soldiers, advocating that they desert. The U.S. military decided to withdraw African American troops, but not because the soldiers were persuaded by the propaganda. It was their White commanders' fears that the soldiers would be persuaded to do so by the propaganda that led to the troop withdrawal.

This behavioral component of third-person effects makes a good deal of conceptual sense and may account for some of the calls for laws and policy change (such as in the case of election-night reporting and exit polls) in situations where few effects have been firmly established. The behavioral component, however, has been less widely supported in research.[19] But, third-person effects have been linked to advocating censorship of, for example, rap music (D. M. McLeod et al., 1997), media violence and pornography (Rojas, Shah, & Faber, 1996), films with homosexual content (Ho, Detenber, Malik, & Neo, 2012), and advertising for gambling (Youn, Faber, & Shah, 2000).

Third-person effects may be linked to a sense of paternalism, or a desire to protect others from harm. Or, they may be due to some desire for self-protection. If, for example, others are more affected by media violence, reducing the amount of violence in the media might lessen the likelihood of becoming a crime victim. Some individual difference and social relationship variables have been examined as influencing the size of third-person effects. Expertise in a topic has been linked to larger third-person effects (Driscoll & Salwen, 1997; Lasorsa, 1989). Experts may believe that their superior knowledge protects them from influence. Ego involvement, or believing that a topic is personally important, has also been associated with increased third-person effects (R. M. Perloff, 2009). As ego involvement increases, one's latitude of acceptance decreases (C. W. Sherif et al., 1965). So, ego-involved people are more likely to perceive media coverage as biased. Their own knowledge and involvement, however, protect them from influence. But, they expect others to be affected by biased media content. From a social relationships perspective, social distance appears to magnify the third-person effect (Andsager & White, 2007; Perloff, 2009). That is, people who are more similar to the respondent were perceived to be less affected by media content than those who were less similar.

The third-person effect is an interesting way of looking at the effects of public opinion and media content. Third-person effects' impact on perceptions of political opinion and endorsement of political action suggest that it may be an important process in the development of political opinion. It is not clear, however, if third-person effects are best explained by the conditional effects model or the cognitive-transactional effects model. The conditional effects model is supported by the introduction of individual difference and social relationship variables as important contributors to understanding third-person effects. But the role of existing schemas about media effects and the stereotypes about different potential audiences suggests that an information-processing approach to exploring third-person effects might provide enhanced explanation for the effects.

Summary

The arena of effects of the mass media during elections is the one that first stimulated belief that media effects were limited (Lazarsfeld et al., 1968). But, the range of political effects extends far beyond elections. Public opinion is an important concept that ties together research on news, media coverage of political affairs, political cognitions, and political activity.

The ELM, coupled with Graber's (1982) conception of public opinion elites and non-elites, provide a framework that signals the importance of the conditional model in understanding media effects on public opinion. If we consider only the elites, who use the central route more often when confronted with political media, media effects might be limited only to knowledge gain and attitude reinforcement. But, change effects might be much more likely among the non-elites, who are more likely to rely on peripheral cues to help them navigate the political world. And, although media may be more likely to affect the less involved, the sheer numbers of less involved may make these effects meaningful and relevant.

Notes

1 Although when a "don't know" option was explicitly offered as part of the question, 90% of the respondents chose it (Schuman & Presser, 1996, p. 159). See also G. F. Bishop, Oldendick, Tuchfaber, and Bennett (1980) for similar findings about bogus legislation.

2 One of the most notable examples of the effect of source attraction is the outcome of the 1960 Presidential candidate debate between John F. Kennedy and Richard M. Nixon. One of the myths surrounding that first debate was that television viewers were captivated by Kennedy's youthful attraction and put off by Nixon's discomfort and sickly appearance. So, television viewers believed that Kennedy won the debate. Radio listeners, though, were impressed with Nixon's command of the facts and believed he won (e.g., E. Diamond & Bates, 1992; Jamieson & Birsdell, 1988). Others, though, questioned the factual basis of these reports (Vancil & Pendell, 1987). Kraus (1996) concluded, however, that there was evidence to support the popular myth. It is interesting to note, though, that even in 1960, the total television audience for the first debate was estimated to be 4.5 times larger than the radio audience (Kraus, 1996).

3 See Petty, Kasmer, Haugtvedt, and Cacioppo (1987) for a reply to Stiff's critique of the ELM. See Booth-Butterfield and Welbourne (2002) for a general review of this debate.

4 Coleman and Blumler consider the Internet's potential *vulnerable* because market forces are largely guiding its development, and are unlikely to shape it so as to maximize its democratic capacity. They argue that public policy must play an active role in order to fully realize what new technologies could provide in terms of democratic citizenship (2009, p. 11).

5 The Pew Research Center for the People and the Press conducts a comprehensive media consumption survey every two years. Reports can be found online at http://people-press.org/.

6 The use of mobile devices to access news, and the production processes to make that access available, may also generate an increase of episodic frames (Livingston, 2007).

7 There is a fair amount of research on agenda setting based on the conditional model. D. B. Hill (1985), for example, examined the impact of audience demographics (social categories) on agenda setting. M. E. McCombs and Weaver (1985) argued that agenda setting was based on an active audience and that people who were higher in "need for orientation" (an individual difference) were more likely to adopt the media agenda. This body of research has found that there are certain conditions that increase the likelihood of agenda setting (see Wanta, 1997). Including these conditions in research designs generally leads to greater variance explained (beyond the impact of news exposure) in agenda-setting effects.

8 There is no established length of time that it takes for agenda setting to occur. Researchers have found agenda-setting effects after time lags as short as 1 week to as long as 9 months (Wanta, 1997). M. McCombs (2004) reports that 1 to 2 months is the typical lag between media coverage of an issue and the public's identifying that issue as important (p. 44).

9 The actual legislation proposed requiring insurance providers to cover optional consultations between patients and their caregivers regarding hospice care and other end-of-life options, to create plans for themselves and their loved ones. Opponents to health care reform argued that the government would end up convening "death panels," making decisions about which patients were worthy to live (Rutenberg & Calmes, 2009).

10 These findings might also provide an explanation for Carter's defeat in the 1980 election. The hostage situation in the Iranian embassy was an important issue on the media's agenda at the end of Carter's term. His failure to achieve either a diplomatic or military end to the crisis probably led to his being evaluated quite unfavorably by the public.

11 The concept of framing as it is used in the communication literature originated from research in sociology (Goffman, 1974) and psychology (Kahneman & Tversky, 1984).

12 This finding directly contradicts the folk wisdom of American journalism (Chaffee, 1992). Journalists have traditionally used the examples of specific individuals to dramatize abstract stories, in the belief that individuals' plights would arouse public opinion. Iyengar's (1991) research pointed out that episodic framing leads people to absolve the government from blame for individuals' problems.

13 Questions about the influence of a scholar's own political beliefs on theory development and testing have been raised about Noelle-Neumann's (1984) spiral of silence (Kepplinger, 1997; Simpson, 1996, 1997).

14 Noelle-Neumann (1993) based her assertions that fear of isolation was a potent motivating force on research by Asch (1956) and Milgram (1974). In Asch's study, 76% of research participants yielded to group pressure to agree that lines were the same length when they obviously were not. Milgram's research focused on the willingness of research participants to inflict pain on someone at the urging of the

experimenter. About two-thirds of the participants yielded to the experimenter even in the presence of evidence that the other participant was in pain.

15 See Donsbach (2001) for a summary of eight possible effects of public opinion polls on voters: bandwagon, underdog, defeatist, lethargy, mobilization, guillotine, facilitating tactics, and preventative tactics (p. 22).

16 See Hardmeier (2008) and Diaz-Castillo (2005) for more detailed summaries of the theoretical explanations proposed to explain bandwagon and underdog effects.

17 Other countries have enacted policies forbidding the publication of public opinion results prior to elections. For a summary of those restrictions, see Donsbach and Hartung (2008).

18 The emphasis on harmful effects due to negative or undesirable media content is an important one. Some studies demonstrate that the third-person perception is attenuated for desirable messages, sometimes even reversed (Andsager & White, 2007; A.C. Gunther & Mundy, 1993; Henriksen & Flora, 1999; Perloff, 2009; White, 1997). This is referred to as a first-person effect. For a summary of the literature about first-person effects, see Golan & Day (2008).

19 Feng and Guo (2012) reported findings from a meta-analysis of third-person effect studies examining the relationship of third-person perceptions with support for censorship and found a weak effect size overall.

5 LEARNING FROM
THE MEDIA

Learning is the acquisition of knowledge about a domain. Learning increases understanding about that domain and may enhance the ability to perform a behavior related to that domain. Learning results in (a) cognitions, or increased knowledge; (b) affect, or feelings about a domain; and (c) behaviors, through the acquisition of skills or motivation to act. Learning from the mass media is at the heart of many media effects. Chapter 4 mentioned several political effects involving learning: information acquisition that influences political attitudes and voting decisions. The next chapter will focus on how children are socialized, including how they learn values and behaviors. Most considerations of media effects imply that, somehow, media content is learned and becomes the basis for knowledge, attitudes, and action.

Mass communication research has only recently begun to develop general theories that explain how people learn specifically from media. For basic theories about the learning process, we need to turn to cognitive psychology, because it is the field that most directly focuses on the mental operations that lead to learning. Mass communication research, though, has not ignored explanations for learning altogether. Because of our field's emphasis on different issues, mass communication has taken a different approach to understanding learning from the media. The focus on the functions and responsibilities of the media in democratic societies (e.g., Gurevitch & Blumler, 1990) has directed research on how much people learn from news and which medium is better for learning (e.g., Eveland & Dunwoody, 2001; Eveland, Seo, & Martin, 2002; M.E. Grabe, Kamhawi, & Yegiyan, 2009; J.P. Robinson & Levy, 1986). Concerns about the educational impact of television on children have directed research on children's attention to television (e.g., D.R. Anderson, Huston, Schmitt, Linebarger, Wright, & Larson, 2001; Levin & Anderson, 1976; Schmidt & Vandewater, 2008). Working parallel to cognitive psychology, mass communication researchers made important contributions to understanding how it is that the audience learns media content. More recently psychophysiological methods, which track physical reactions while people are being exposed to media content, have also helped to clarify how people process information.

This chapter begins with a discussion of various learning theories drawn from cognitive psychology and mass communication. There are two basic approaches to explaining learning: *active* and *passive* approaches. The active approach is drawn from cognitive psychology. These theories assume that the audience is active and engages in mental activities that result in learning. Active learning theories fall within two models of media effects: the conditional model or the cognitive-transactional model. The active approach holds that learning occurs because people are motivated to learn and mentally engaged in the acquisition of information. The passive approach finds evidence in mass communication research. This approach assumes that people are either unmotivated or unable to learn, so effective messages must be created to attract attention and instill information, without people realizing it. Because the audience is passive, media producers must take the initiative to create media content that attracts attention and can be easily remembered. So, the main focus of the passive approach is media content variables and they fall under the direct and cumulative effects models.

Of course, the reality of learning is a combination of these two approaches. We know that learning is an interaction of both the audience's mental activity and the media content. In the college classroom, for example, passive students who are asleep, distracted, or inattentive will not learn the material, no matter how gifted the instructor or how comprehensive the instructional materials. And the most active, talented, interested, and motivated students will find it difficult to learn from an instructor who is disorganized, inarticulate, and vague. Recent models attempt to explain how people can process information and learn through both active and passive routes simultaneously. It is useful first, however, to consider active and passive approaches separately, because the two approaches place different emphases on different aspects of the learning process.

Theory: Two Approaches to Learning

Active Models of Learning

Active models consider learning to be "an active, constructive process whereby the learner strategically manages the available cognitive resources to create new knowledge by extracting information from the environment and integrating it with information already stored in memory" (Kozma, 1991, pp. 179–180). There are three different, but related active learning approaches. The *structures* approach sees learning as the movement of information through mental "structures." The *process* approach describes learning as an active process. The *schematic* approach is based on the cognitive-transactional model and sees learning as a result of schematic processing.

The Structures Approach

The structures approach sees learning as the result of the movement of information through mental "structures" such as the sensory register, short-term memory, working memory, to long-term memory. These structures are sequential;

information must move through them in the order specified in the model. The most complete learning is the result of the movement of information through all the structures to long-term memory. But, all information is not automatically learned; not all information moves through the complete set of structures. Information that does not complete its trip through all the structures is not learned. This is an active approach because movement of information through the structures to long-term memory is due to motivation and ability (similar to the central route of the ELM). Figure 5.1 summarizes the structures approach to learning.

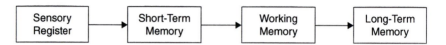

Figure 5.1 Structures model of learning.

Sensory Register. Information enters this system through the sensory register (Klatzky, 1980; also called the sensory store, Wyer & Srull, 1986). Information enters as sensory data from each of the five senses (sight, hearing, smell, taste, and touch). These data are held in the same form as they are received by the senses: Sounds are held in the sensory register as auditory patterns; sights are held as visual images. The sensory register is the entryway to the system; learning does not occur in this structure. In fact, humans are not necessarily consciously aware of data in the sensory register because it stores basic impressions of the environment. Data are held in the sensory structure typically for a very short time.

   The sensory data decay rapidly unless they move on to the next structure. Incoming data push out older data; in a sense, the sensory register has a self-erasing function. Note that, contrary to popular beliefs, humans do not retain an impression of everything they encounter. Hypnosis cannot resurrect data lost from the sensory register. Meaningful data in the sensory register is not left to decay; it is converted from its raw form as sense data and moved into the next structure, short-term memory (STM).

Short-Term Memory. Short-term memory is the state of current consciousness and awareness. Information in STM is what we are currently considering or thinking about. Short-term memory is fleeting; it decays in about 20 to 30 seconds (J. Brown, 1958). Short-term memory also has a very limited capacity. Humans can retain about 7 (plus or minus 2) bits, or discrete items, in STM (H. A. Simon, 1974).[1] As in the sensory register, new information crowds out the old. Humans have learned to compensate for the limits of STM. For example, students know that it is impossible to retain all the instructor's points in a class, so they take notes. In a sense, the notes are records of the information bits in STM. The information needs to be translated to a more permanent record before it decays or is replaced by a new point. If information is meaningful, and if the opportunity is there, the information moves to the next structure, working memory (WM).

Working Memory. Working memory was originally conceived of as a compo-nent of short-term memory, but now cognitive scholars believe there is a struc-ture, or work space, with two specific functions. First, WM is the structure where information is prepared for long-term memory (Wyer & Srull, 1986). The structures model does not specify the processes that occur, although "rehearsal" is most commonly mentioned as the mental action in WM (J.R. Anderson, 1995; Klatzky, 1980). Another function of WM is to use informa-tion retrieved from long-term memory (LTM) in dealing with current stimuli. Working memory holds material from LTM so that we can apply that material to our current situation. The mental activity in WM, then, is conscious, not automatic. And, while WM is also limited in capacity, the allocation of WM resources and space may be controlled by "the total information load and, in part, by the relevance of the information to immediate processing" (Wyer & Srull, 1986, p. 326). So, the displacement of information may be controlled by the individual, by deciding which information to consider. Or, displace-ment may be automatic, much like the "crowding out" of old information by new in the sensory register and STM. So, WM balances preparation of new information with the use of already learned information. Information can stay in WM indefinitely, as long as it is relevant to current goals. Information, though, can be displaced in working memory; if it has not been adequately prepared and transferred to LTM, it is not completely learned.

Long-Term Memory. Long-term memory is the structure that stores what is learned. Long-term memory is often conceptualized as an orderly storage space, with no known limit, filled with various bins that hold specific types of information (Wyer & Srull, 1986). Various bins might hold *episodic* material about specific events, objects, or people. Some bins may hold only *semantic* material, which is the more general material that we have learned that includes the rules about how language operates, or how concepts are interrelated. Infor-mation in LTM is learned, but it is not immutable. If it is recalled to WM, it might be changed or adjusted by new information. Episodic information, because it is about specific instances, is more likely to be changed than informa-tion stored in semantic memory, because semantic information is more general.

Long-term memory is usually conceived of as permanent; once something is placed in LTM it is considered to be learned. Forgetting is usually attributed to not being able to locate the correct "storage bin." Forgetting is similar to "losing" a computer file, when we have simply forgotten what "folder" we put it in. So, we might recognize the face of someone that we meet on the street, but not be able to place them, until they remind us that we met at a confer-ence in Chicago. That data cue us to the correct storage bin. So, our memory returns. Other scholars suggest that information can decay in LTM. Evidence that younger people have better episodic memories than older people suggests that these memories in older people have decayed over time (Squire & Slater, 1975). Decay, though, could be mistaken for forgetting due to interference effects (Klatzky, 1980). Multiple associations to the same stimuli are often confused. Psychologists have found that memory for a list of paired words can interfere with prior word-list memories, if the word lists share common elements (J.R. Anderson, 1995). For example, memory for the association "book, blue" could interfere with the prior memory of the association "book, black." Forgetting attributed to age might simply reflect the greater number of associated experiences that people have stored as they live longer. Note that forgetting affects episodic memory, not semantic memory.

The Process Approach

The process approach describes learning as an active process that involves (a) attention (devoting mental energy and effort to information tasks); (b) recognition or categorizing (identifying what the information relates to); and (c) elaboration (rehearsing information, relating it to prior knowledge). Once again, learning is a complicated process done by an active audience. This conceptualization of learning as a process is derived from Craik and Lockhart's (1972) proposal that greater learning is the result of greater "depth" of mental processing. Depth "implies a greater degree of semantic or cognitive analysis" (Craik & Lockhart, 1972, p. 675). Depth is characterized by progression through different "levels" of mental processing. Craik and Lockhart (1972) defined the levels of mental activity generally as sensory analysis, pattern recognition, and stimulus elaboration. Mental structures are not important to this model; mental activities, or processes, are.

Greenwald and Leavitt (1984) built on Craik and Lockhart's ideas to propose that audiences' cognitive responses to media content could be conceptualized as mental engagement with the content. Different levels of mental engagement are reflected as sequential cognitive processes that become progressively become more complex. These processes are voluntary attention, recognition, and elaboration (Greenwald & Leavitt, 1984; Perse, 1990c). This approach sees mental processing as an orderly sequence of different processes. Processing is sequentially ordered; the output from one process is the input of the next (Treisman, 1979). For information to be processed at a deeper stage, it must have been processed at all lower stages. The most complete learning occurs after information has been completely processed, after information has been attended to, recognized, and elaborated on.

Voluntary Attention. Voluntary attention is a mental and perceptual focus on a stimulus in the environment. It is the allocation of mental, conscious effort and cognitive capacity (Kahneman, 1973). It is a readiness to process information. Cognitive capacity is limited, so when we pay attention to something, we have to reduce or eliminate attention to other stimuli. Voluntary attention is the necessary first mental process that precedes learning. Voluntary attention is contrasted with involuntary or reflexive attention (also called the orienting response). Reflexive attention is involuntary or automatic attention. There are stimuli in our environment that attract attention because they are loud, intense, complex, novel, or threatening (Berlyne, 1960; Watt, 1979). Reflexive attention may lead to voluntary attention. For example, the siren and flashing lights of a police vehicle behind us on the freeway attract our attention involuntarily. If the vehicle seems to follow ours, we pay a lot of attention to it, and start to analyze why the police officer is following us. In this case, reflexive attention leads to voluntary attention. Reflexive attention, however, is not a necessary precursor to voluntary attention. Voluntary attention is controlled by the individual and originates with the individual's goals. *Voluntary attention* is willingness to direct attention to something that we are doing, not something that is happening to us. Once cognitive effort and capacity have been voluntarily applied in voluntary attention, the information is ready for the next cognitive process: recognition.

Recognition. After people have paid attention to something and set aside cognitive effort for mental processing, this stage begins information processing. As Greenwald and Leavitt (1984) suggested, recognition is the process that defines the identity of the information. Recognition answers the "What is this?" question. Recognition is a three-part process of analysis, comparison, and decision. Recognition involves separating the stimulus from its context and categorizing it, first, as familiar or unfamiliar. If it is familiar, it is compared to information drawn from long-term memory, to see what it resembles (Klatzky, 1980). It is identified, coded, or labeled, based on that comparison. If, after identification, the information is still relevant, the next stage of mental processing begins.

Elaboration. Elaboration is the most complex mental process. Elaboration is the integration of the new information into long-term memory; it is necessary for long-term learning. Elaboration involves several mental activities; it relates the new information to existing knowledge and images. The information can be mnemonically linked to similar information, placed in an organizational structure of information, or be associated with mental, affective, and behavioral responses. As elaboration continues, there are several possible outcomes. First, the information can be rejected if it contradicts prior knowledge or values. Second, the new information may be so consistent with prior beliefs and attitudes that it is absorbed without much change to what we already know and believe (a reinforcement effect). Novel information can also involve changes to existing knowledge.

Implications of Different Levels of Processing. This model, then, sees learning as a result of progressively deeper and more complex cognitive processes. Each process is preceded by a less complex process. And information must move through the less complex processes before it can be processed more deeply. Recognition must be preceded by voluntary attention; elaboration must be preceded by recognition. But more complex processes do not necessarily follow. All information is not learned; all information is not subjected to complex mental processing. Recognition does not necessarily follow voluntary attention and elaboration does not necessarily follow recognition. Once we have paid attention to something, we may be distracted by something else, and never get to recognize the information. Or, once we recognize something as familiar, we may see that it does not interest us, or help us achieve our goal, so we stop processing it.

The Schematic Approach

The schematic approach is drawn from schema theory and firmly based on the cognitive-transactional model of media effects. A schema is "a cognitive structure that represents knowledge about a concept or type of stimulus, including its attributes and the relations among those attributes" (Fiske & Taylor, 1991, p. 98). This approach to learning holds that schemas are at the heart of understanding information processing and learning. Two processes link schemas and learning: First, preexisting schemas influence what is learned; second, learning also involves the development of new schemas and the modification of existing ones.

The schemas that people already hold affect learning because they affect categorization, perception, and retention (S. E. Taylor & Crocker, 1981). Humans try to make sense of their world. When they encounter a stimulus in their environment, they search their minds for what they believe is the appropriate schema to characterize or match the stimulus. The schema that is selected, then, structures how the stimulus is interpreted. Imagine the differences in what we would notice in a friend's apartment, for example, if we visited it with the intent of subletting it instead of simply attending a party there. Schemas direct attention to schema-relevant aspects of the stimulus. Schema-irrelevant aspects tend to be ignored (Hastie, 1981). Schemas affect memory; it is fairly easy to remember schema-consistent information (S. E. Taylor & Crocker, 1981). New instances that relate to preexisting schema are easily integrated into that schema and learned. Learning, then, is the linkage of new information to preexisting schemas. Learning new information may alter a schema. As people gain more experience and learn more, their schemas about that domain become more elaborate. It is possible to learn schema-inconsistent information. Fiske and Taylor (1991) explained that memory for schema-inconsistent information can be the result of very thoughtful process, where people attempt to make sense of the inconsistencies. So, they try to think of explanations for the inconsistencies and link those explanations to preexisting schemas. Dealing effectively with inconsistent information, then, might be a sign of expertise in a domain of knowledge, along with larger, more complex schemas that are interlinked to other, related schemas.

This explanation of schematic learning assumes controlled mental processing. That is, the schemas that are activated are selected by the individual. Schematic processing may also be automatic; that is, the schema that is used to evaluate and learn new information may be cued or primed by the stimulus (in this case, a media message) itself. For example, imagine a student who has a research paper due at the end of the semester about the effects of alcohol advertising on underage drinking. When reading *Sports Illustrated* purely for recreation, the student comes across an article about the connections between alcohol advertising and sports promotion. The story most likely will cue the student to use a "research paper" schema to read that story because it seems relevant to an important task. Once a schema is cued, it operates similarly to those schemas that are selected consciously. Schematic mental processing and learning are based on the schema that is at top of mind.

An important implication of schematic learning is that it requires a tremendous amount of mental effort to learn information unless there is a schema with which to link it (Graber, 2001). Schemas develop through experience. The more experience that we have with a domain, the more developed the schema about that domain becomes. So, learning something new involves creating a new schema. Students who are taking a class in an entirely new subject recognize how difficult it can be to develop new schemas. Typically, it involves learning a new vocabulary and definitions for a new set of terms. Learning in a new domain often involves searching one's mind to find analogies, or similar examples – a search for a schematic link. A student learning about the properties of radio waves, for example, might look for their similarities to ocean waves. Schemas develop with experience; so as we pay attention, categorize new information, and attach it to developing schemas, we can say that we are learning more about that domain.

Learning, then, is application of schematic processing (see Figure 5.2). According to this model, what people learn is related to the schema that is activated (either self-activated or primed by the stimulus itself) during exposure. This model explains why learning might be incorrect (if an inappropriate schema is used to understand the information). This model also explains why learning is easier when there is prior knowledge – because it is easier to attach new information to existing schemas than to create a new schema.

These three approaches describe three different ways to conceptualize learning, but there are several connections among them. All three models recognize that learning is a result of a top-down or conceptually driven mental activity. Controlled schematic processing, for example, is quite clearly a top-down mental process. People pay attention to and notice aspects of the environment that are consistent with the schemas that they have selected. The structures approach holds that in WM, prior knowledge is selected from LTM for comparison and to aid pattern recognition. The process approach recognizes that the individual's goals direct mental activity (Wyer & Srull, 1986). There are, however, some distinctions between the three models. The structures and automatic schematic models, and the process model, to some extent, all describe learning as initially a bottom-up, or stimulus-driven mental process. That is, the mental activity is stimulated by what we perceive and how we mentally react to stimuli in our environment. So, the structures approach holds that information moves from the sensory register, to STM, to WM, to LTM. In automatic schematic processing, a salient stimuli in the environment cues a schema. In the process model, involuntary attention may lead to deeper mental processes if the stimuli are relevant to the individual.

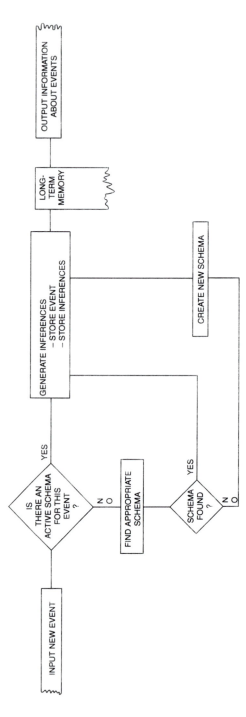

Figure 5.2 Schematic information processing. From: Hastie, R. (1981). Schematic principles in human memory. In E.T. Higgins, C. P. Herman, & M. P. Zanna (Eds.). *Social cognition: The Ontario Symposium* (Vol. 1, pp. 39–88). Hillsdale, NJ: Lawrence Erlbaum Associates, p. 45. Reprinted with permission.

Together, the three models give a fuller description of how learning occurs. Working memory may be the structure that represents the location for processes in the other approaches. Because WM involves retrieving information from LTM for comparison, it may be the location of schematic priming as well as recognition. Working memory may also be the location of elaboration and schematic learning. Readying information for LTM may involve elaboration, or linking the material to prior knowledge. That linkage may involve selecting the appropriate storage bin or schema.

Relevant Variables. Several audience variables can impact learning via the structures and process approaches. As an active and audience-centered process, learning depends on the amount of effort that the individual is willing and able to put forth to learn. Motivation is a key component of learning. Cognitive scientists have proposed that there is an additional structure that contains the goals that direct the mental processing (the goal specification box, Wyer & Srull, 1986; the executive planner, Kellerman, 1985). An individual's goals direct the flow of information through the structures and control the mental actions in the various structures (Wyer & Srull, 1986). So, greater motivation is associated with greater mental activity that leads to greater learning (Kellerman, 1985).

Another variable associated with motivation is the amount of invested mental effort (AIME; Salomon & Leigh, 1984). Salomon explains that AIME represents beliefs about how easy or difficult it is to learn from a particular medium. When people believe a medium is difficult, they invest more effort and tend to learn more (Salomon, 1983; Salomon & Leigh, 1984). Because AIME is conceptually defined as "the number of non-automatic mental elaborations applied to a unit of material" (Salomon, 1983, p. 42), when people believe that greater AIME is required to learn, they will invest more mental effort.

Variables associated with opportunity to process messages are also relevant to the structures approach. The pace of the presentation of the material can affect processing. If information is presented at a rapid pace, it may exceed the limited space available in STM and information may be lost. The context of information reception may also affect the opportunity to process. If one is in a distracting environment, or trying to pay attention to more than one information source at a time, effort may be divided and information learned incompletely. Television news, for example, is not learned very well by a large part of the audience (J. P. Robinson & Levy, 1986); one explanation may be the context of watching news in the household, surrounded by a variety of distracting activities (A.M. Rubin & Perse, 1987a).

Motivation is also key to the schematic approach to learning. As with the structures and process approaches, strength of motivation is also important. Controlled processing takes mental effort, so greater motivation is associated with that mental effort and learning. The schematic approach also recognizes the importance of the kind of goals or motives that direct mental processing. Garramone (1983), for example, found that different goals for watching televised political advertisements (to form an impression of the candidate or to learn about the candidate's stand on the issues) were related to attention to different aspects of the ads and recall of different information. Perse (1990c) observed that different reasons for watching local news were associated with attention to and elaboration of different types of stories. Researchers conclude that different goals or motives for processing information result in the use of different schemas during message reception; so what is learned is due to the schema that is used.

Because what is learned is dependent on the schema that is used, the schematic approach also recognizes the importance of aspects of the message as priming automatic processing. Certain message elements have priming potential, or salience. Salient message elements not only prime related schemas, but also may attract involuntary attention. The discussion of message elements as a source of involuntary attention is presented in depth in the next section that considers passive models of learning.

Implications of Active Approaches for Media Effects. Together, these three active approaches to learning point out that learning is not necessarily easy. Learning depends on the movement of information, elaborating on information, relating new information to prior knowledge, modifying existing schemas, and creating new schemas. Learning might also be related to following the central route of the elaboration likelihood model (ELM; Petty & Cacioppo, 1986). Learning requires motivation, effort, and opportunity. If any of those are absent, people might fail to learn, or they may learn new material incompletely or incorrectly.

The different approaches have other implications for media effects. First, focused attention is a necessary, but not sufficient condition for learning (Chaffee & Schleuder, 1986; Welch & Watt, 1982). Attention involves a visual (in the case of visual media), audio (in the case of audio and audiovisual media), and mental orientation to the information. Because attention is the entry point for the structures and process models, without attention, there is no possibility of learning. But, the active models all point out that attention is not sufficient for learning. It is merely an important first step that precedes more complex mental processes that result in the transference of information to LTM.

Second, selective attention can be conceptualized as a mental activity within the process model. The recognition stage involves categorizing information, answering the "What is this?" question. Once something has captured our attention, we compare it to previously encountered material, decide if it is relevant to our goals, and continue to process the information if it is relevant, or reject the information and stop processing it if it is not pertinent to our goals. *Attention* can be conceptualized as an intentional scanning for potentially relevant material (E. Katz, 1968). But recognition acts as the internal gatekeeper that admits or restricts content to further elaboration.

Third, motivation or processing goals are indirectly related to learning (Kellerman, 1985). Researchers who have explored how different motives for using media content are related to learning from the news typically have had only limited success (e.g., Gantz, 1978). These modest findings are due no doubt to ignoring that motivation has its more direct effect on mental processing. Studies have found that seeking surveillance is linked to attention to the news (J. M. McLeod & McDonald, 1985; Perse, 1990c, 1990d). Moreover, surveillance gratifications are also linked to elaborate mental processing of the news (e.g., Perse, 1990b; A.M. Rubin & Perse, 1987). Although the effects of increased and differential motivation might be reflected in greater learning, motivation's greatest effect is directly on effort, attention, and depth of elaboration.

The schematic model of learning explains why prior knowledge is associated with greater learning (e.g., A.M. Robinson & Levy, 1986). When people already have schemas about a particular news topic, they are more likely to pay attention to stories about that topic and remember information. Graber (1988) suggested that lack of relevant schemas is an explanation for low levels of news awareness about people and politics in third-world nations. Either people do not remember stories about these topics or their memory is inaccurate and based on simplistic, stereotypical schemas (e.g., African politics are primitive). Schemas facilitate learning from the mass media.

News teasers, or promotional previews for news features, increase memory for stories (Chang, 1998; Schleuder, White, & Cameron, 1993) because they act to prime appropriate schemas so they are ready to use. When news viewers have the appropriate schema already at the top of mind, they are ready to process the news story information. Schleuder and her colleagues (1993) suggested news directors could act in the public interest by "teasing" stories that have particular importance to ensure that viewers will learn vital information.

The kinds of mistakes that people make trying to remember news stories illustrate the impact of errors in schematic processing. Findahl and Höijer (1985) reported on three types of errors in Swedish news watchers' memory for news. News viewers confused the details of two news stories about demonstrations, a peaceful one in a Swedish town and another, more contentious confrontation between protestors and police in Paris. Confusions may grow out of using the same schema to interpret two different news stories, so the details from the stories are intermingled and confused. Swedish news viewers also confused the location of an oil tanker accident. There are two large islands off the Swedish coast, Gotland and Öland. Swedish school children usually learn about these islands as a unit. So, in trying to remember news stories, some viewers overgeneralized, and remembered (incorrectly) that the tanker accident had run aground on Öland, instead of Gotland. Still other news viewers incorrectly remembered that a government organization had granted loans to industry, when they had been granted by a private bank. The researchers suggest these mistakes were due to prior knowledge about the involvement of government institutions in granting loans.

Passive Model of Learning

The passive model is based on the assumption that audiences may be unable or unmotivated to acquire new information. So, learning is based on media content that will attract the attention of these inactive audience members. Children, for example, are often considered to be cognitively immature and not able to be self-motivated. So, the development of programs like *Sesame Street* built on research that identified media content elements that attracted the "passive" child audience (e.g., Levin & Anderson, 1976). Television viewing can be considered a passive pastime (e.g., Gerbner & Gross, 1976; Krugman, 1965) or an opportunity for relaxation (e.g., A.M. Rubin, 1983). So learning from television news might be due more to effective presentation of the news rather than audience self-motivation. This model, then, focuses on passive learning, or learning as result of attention that occurs relatively automatically, "without regard to the *meaning* of the content to the viewer" (D.R. Anderson & Burns, 1991, p. 19). The focus is on media content variables that attract the involuntary attention of the audience.

Formal Features of Television and Children's Attention to Television

Formal features of a medium are the production techniques and elements that are used to convey meaning. In newspapers, for example, formal features involve headline size and placement, photographs or other graphic elements, the use of quotations, and so on. In television, formal features involve visual elements, for the most part, especially the characters that are on screen, the pace of action and shots, the complexity of the screen images, camera angles, and transitions. But, the auditory aspects of television are also relevant because much television "viewing" involves listening to the television while focusing visually on another activity (D.R. Anderson & Burns, 1991). Research on the impact of formal features of television and children's learning from educational television programs focuses on identifying the program elements that are associated with children's visual attention – what they look at while they are in a room with the television on. This research is motivated by the assumption that attention is the necessary and crucial prerequisite to learning (Levin & Anderson, 1976; Welch & Watt, 1982). Although learning from television involves more than simply looking at the screen, without attention, learning cannot occur. Studies that have been conducted that vary formal features without varying the nature of the educational material find that program elements that stimulate children's attention lead to greater memory for the material (Bryant, Zillmann, & Brown, 1983; Welch & Watt, 1982).

Studies of the effects of various formal features on children's visual attention to television are based on observations of children while in a room with the television turned on. Children are usually provided toys with which to play, so that the television is not the only object of interest in the room. Then, researchers observe the children, note when their eyes are on the television, and connect visual attention to program elements to identify the formal features associated with visual attention (e.g., D. R. Anderson, Alwitt, Lorch, & Levin, 1979; D. R. Anderson & Levin, 1976; Diener et al., 2008; Huston & Wright, 1983; Huston et al., 1981; S. R. Levin & Anderson, 1976; Lorch, Anderson, & Levin, 1979). Children's visual attention to television is usually stimulated by the presence of females, other children, puppets, familiar animals, animation, "funny" voices, dancing, singing, rhyming, repetition, alliteration, sound effects, and the "fade to black."

Various explanations have been offered for the impact of several of these particular formal features on increased attention. Welch and Watt (1982) used information theory (Shannon & Weaver, 1949) as the basis for their study. They explained that simple, more predictable images on the screen are more interesting to children because the children were cognitively immature and unable to mentally process complex inputs. Condry (1989) offered several rationales for the impact of formal features on children's attention to television: (a) formal features may highlight significant aspects of the content; (b) formal features may convey information about setting and context; (c) they can cue the level of mental effort needed to process the material (e.g., Amount of Invested Mental Effort (AIME); Salomon & Leigh, 1984); or (d) they can signal the intended audience (e.g., boys vs. girls).

Program Attributes and Learning from the News

News awareness is especially important in a representative democracy. Citizens are expected to base their votes for elected officials on knowledge about political issues and candidates' views on those issues. And, people are expected to be aware of issues and to inform their elected representatives of their own views. Through their surveillance function and extensive newsgathering resources, the mass media are the conduit through which most people get their news. Research, however, paints a dismal picture of news awareness (Kohut et al., 2007; Pew Research Center for the People & the Press, 2011; J. P. Robinson & Levy, 1996). Memory for news is usually quite low. G. Gunter (1985) found that British people scored less than 50% on a test of news awareness. A U.S. sample understood the main point of only 4.6 out of 14 news stories (J. P. Robinson & Levy, 1986). More recently, Graber (2001) found that immediately after viewing a regular 30-minute newscast, people remembered fewer than 10% of the stories. These findings about news memory have stimulated research designed to ascertain the news production elements that will lead to greater memory for news.

This research offers several generalizations: Visuals can be used effectively to increase news recall. Compared to a "talking head" (visuals that focus on the news reader), including "interesting" video increases memory for the news (D. K. Davis & Robinson, 1986; Edwardson, Grooms, & Proudlove, 1981) because it is linked to excitement, interest, and curiosity. Visuals have the ability to trigger emotional reactions to a greater extent than nonvisual content (Graber, 2001). In her book *Processing Politics* (2001), Graber explains that emotional arousal causes a physical reaction which means those images "are more likely to be embedded in long-term memory and to be retained even when they are infrequently rehearsed" (p. 35; see also A. Lang, 2000). Even computer-generated graphics seem to increase memory (Edwardson, Kent, & McConnell, 1985), particularly animated graphics (Fox et al., 2003). But, not all visuals are effective. Redundancy between visuals and verbals in news increases news retention (Graber, 2001; Reese, 1984). But using nonredundant, or general file footage, does not aid recall (Brosius et al., 1996; Graber, 2001; Low & Sweller, 2005; Walma van der Molen & Van der Voort, 2000). It also matters what kind of visuals are used. For example, a negative news story is more likely to be remembered (Newhagen & Reeves, 1992), but people tend to forget the stories that precede it (A. Lang, Newhagen, & Reeves, 1996).

Another generalization drawn from this body of research is that people tend to remember stories about more familiar topics. It requires less cognitive effort to process stories that "fit" in an existing schema. For example, domestic news is remembered better than international news (D. K. Davis & Robinson, 1986; Graber, 2001; E. Katz et al., 1977).

Still other generalizations about news format effectiveness are drawn from classic persuasion research (e.g., Hovland et al., 1957). Story placement in the news affects recall; stories that are either first or last are more likely to be learned than those stories in the middle (D. K. Davis & Robinson, 1986). Longer stories are more likely to be remembered than shorter ones (D. K. Davis & Robinson, 1986; Graber 2001). Repetition (Graber, 2001; R. Perloff, Wartella, & Becker, 1982; Sweller, 2005) and recapping increases recall (Bernard & Coldevin, 1985).

Other studies of memory for non-news content add knowledge about other message elements associated with learning. Images with motion – either movement of the object in the image, movement of the camera, or the appearance of movement through editing – attract and retain higher levels of attention than static images (Ravaja, 2004). When a moving video camera is used, as opposed to using zooms, people recall more of the details of the image. Kipper (1986) commented that the moving camera provides viewers with more information about the image and a greater sense of the environment of the shot. People who are pictured with a camera angle looking down on them are judged to be less powerful than if the camera is looking up at them (e.g., Giessner et al., 2011). Memory for information on call-in radio programs is greater than memory for the same information in a structured interview format. Andreason (1985) explained that this effect is due to an orienting response to the novelty of hearing a variety of different voices. Researchers have begun to explore the structural elements of Web-based information that are associated with learning. Some theorists argue that because the Web provides users with the ability to set their own pace and order of learning through the use of hypertext links, it should increase the amount that is possible to learn from provided content (for a summary of this argument, see Eveland & Dunwoody, 2001). Others, however, argue that the free-flowing design of web sites may require a lot of cognitive effort to navigate, leaving less information-processing capacity for actual learning to occur (Bucy & Newhagen, 2004; Eveland & Dunwoody, 2000). Provision of a site map, which allows users to get a sense of how information on a web site is organized, can decrease the amount of cognitive effort to navigate a site, thereby increasing the potential for learning (Shapiro, 2005).

Theoretical Explanations for Passive Learning

Theoretical explanations for the effects of news content variables on learning are based on the impacts of the orienting response and arousal. The *orienting response* is an automatic response to stimuli in the environment that is associated with alertness, attention, and arousal. Orienting responses are involuntary, but they are associated with learning because of their association with attention and arousal. Certain media content features have the ability to stimulate this reaction.[2] Changing visual images, flashing lights, color, visual complexity, cuts between scenes, camera movement, and object movement on the screen have all been associated with orienting responses in television viewing (A. Lang, Potter, & Bolls, 2009; Reeves et al., 1986). *Arousal* is a physiological response that "intensifies motivated behavior" (Zillmann, 1991, p. 104). Arousal influences learning because it directs attentional capacity (Graber, 2007; Kahneman, 1973). So, media content associated with arousal (e.g., emotional content, negative video) should be learned better because of increased attention. But, if certain media content demands a lot of attentional capacity (negative news stories or difficult concepts), attention to surrounding content will be impeded and that content will be less likely to be learned (e.g., Newhagen & Reeves, 1992; Thorson & Lang, 1992). The limited capacity of attention explains why nonredundant words and video are associated with lower learning; the need to pay attention to two separate inputs can exceed viewers' ability to pay attention (A. Lang, 1995; Low & Sweller, 2005). Kozma (1991) built on the limited attentional capacity concept to explain why it may be easier to learn from different media, arguing that certain media facilitate the mental operations that are necessary to learning. Print and online media, for example, allow greater learning because readers control the pace that the material is presented (see also P. L. Wright, 1974). Television's fast pace crowds STM beyond its capacity. Graber (2001) debates this argument, however. She argues that the substance of much of what is on television is poor, but that the medium itself has tremendous potential for effective learning.

Another explanation for the effectiveness of media content variables is that attention is a learned response to certain features. The orienting response is a "primitive" response that occurs because of novelty, surprise, and threat (Lang, Potter, & Bolls, 2009; Shoemaker, 1996). But, certain media features may attract attention because people have learned to associate certain features with certain types of content (D. R. Anderson & Burns, 1991). When scary music begins to play while watching a movie, for example, audience members become aroused in part because we have been trained to associate the music with something frightening about to happen.

Krugman (2000) proposed that learning from television can be a passive process that involves overlearning repeated content, such as advertisements. Repetition moves familiar content from STM to LTM, which leads to subtle shifts in the relative importance of certain attributes of objects. This learning cannot be measured by asking people to recall factual information, because they are not consciously aware of having processed the information. This learning occurs without much awareness on the part of the audience and it is unique to visual media. Krugman argues that recognition tasks are a better measure of whether or not this kind of learning has occurred. Krugman's approach might derive a theoretical explanation from schema theory. Focusing on advertising specifically, Krugman argues that through automatic processing of visual content, certain schemas might be primed that then influence perceptions about consumer products.

Another style of learning that marks a more passive approach to media exposure is incidental learning. *Incidental learning* is learning that occurs incidental to another task. That is, incidental learning from television could occur when viewers are watching primarily for entertainment, not to pick up information (e.g., R. P. Hawkins & Pingree, 1982). Similarly, people can learn about current events while surfing the Internet for other purposes (Tewksbury, Weaver, & Maddex, 2001). Tian and Robinson (2009) found that incidental learning of health information can be an important aspect of media use. Most scholars believe, however, that incidental learning is not entirely a passive process (e.g., J. R. Anderson, 1995; Eysenck & Keane, 1992). Research that explored incidental learning of word lists revealed that the depth of intensity of mental processing predicted learning, regardless of whether research participants were trying to learn the words or not (Hyde & Jenkins, 1973). Researchers found that participants who were told to rate the words on their "pleasantness" remembered the same number of words as those who were told that their memory for the words would be tested. Participants who were supposed to count the number of "e"s and "g"s in the words, however, learned fewer words than the group who expected to be quizzed. Rating words for pleasantness required participants to consider the words' meaning and associations – a form of elaboration. Other research supports the more active nature of incidental learning. Older adults were more likely to incidentally learn details of a television program that were central to the story (Stokes & Pankowski, 1988). And, incidental learning is higher when the material is meaningful to the learner (McLaughlin, 1965; Tian & Robinson, 2009).

Models that Combine Active and Passive Elements

Increasingly, scholars are proposing general models of learning from media that encompass *both* active and passive elements (see, e.g., Bradley, 2007;

Fisch, 2000; Graber, 2001; Lang, 2000). These models aim to explore the characteristics of content that foster or hinder learning, while also accounting for the important role of audience variables in specifying media effects. These models adopt the schematic processing model's understanding of memory being a network of interconnected pieces of information. When a particular memory is recalled for use, the other things that are linked to that memory are easier to access than unrelated information. These models also emphasize the limited capability of the human brain to process media content. Lang's *Limited Capacity Model of Mediated Message Processing* (2000), for example, conceives of media messages as being received first by the senses, and being stored very briefly – from 300 milliseconds for visual information, to 4 or 5 seconds for auditory information. But the brain cannot process everything that is perceived, and so only a small percentage of those stimuli are brought into working memory. According to Lang, the process by which sensory information is transferred into working memory can be consciously or unconsciously directed by a person's goals, or it can be activated by some characteristic of the content itself (pp. 48–49).[3]

Fisch (2000) proposed the Capacity Model to understand how children learn information from educational television programming. He emphasizes three concepts: (a) the narrative content of a program, or its story; (b) the educational content of a program, or the actual material being taught; and (c) the *distance* between the two types of content, which is "the degree to which the educational content is integral to or tangential to the narrative" (p. 66). He argues that processing of narrative content will always trump processing of educational content. So, if the educational content is too distant from the narrative content, or if the narrative content is so complicated as to use up most of the resources of working memory, then children will be unable to process educational content well enough to learn. But, if a child has a lot of prior knowledge about the topic, or if they are particularly interested in the topic, they may be able to process information regardless of how interwoven the educational and narrative content are.

Children's Learning from Media

When are Children Old Enough to Learn from Media?

Chapter 6 of this book will focus on socialization effects of mass communication. Socialization, of course, is based on learning. But the ability to learn from media is not the same for all children. As children age, their interactions with and reactions to media change. Understanding what children learn from media continues to be an important question given the pervasiveness of media in today's culture. On average, children spend so much time with media that it is second only to sleep in terms of how their days are spent (Rideout, Foehr, & Roberts, 2010; D.F. Roberts & Foehr, 2008). Television continues to be the most used medium, but an increasing trend is that children are multitasking, using several forms of media simultaneously. This has led researchers to distinguish between the amount of media *use* versus the amount of media *exposure*. Media *use* is the total amount of time spent with media in a day, and for children ages 8–18, the average is 7 hours and 30 minutes. Media *exposure* is the sum of time spent with all media, which for the same age group is 10 hours and 45 minutes per day (Rideout, Foehr, & Roberts, 2010). That means for about 2 hours and 15 minutes a day, children are exposed to more than one medium at the same time. And the environment for media use can also make a difference in its impact (Endestad et al., 2011). As of 2004, 68% of 8–18 year-olds in the United States, and 33% of children from birth to age 6, had a television set in their bedroom (D. F. Roberts & Foehr, 2008). Among children birth to age 6, 23% also had a video player in their bedroom, 10% had a video game player, and 5% a personal computer (D. F. Roberts & Foehr, 2008). Not surprisingly, those percentages grow rapidly among older children. And the addition of mobile access to the Internet means that children with cell phones, tablets, or other portable devices can have access to media whenever, wherever they choose.

In answer to the important role of media in childhood, the American Academy of Pediatrics (AAP) has established a health initiative regarding media and children.[4] Among their recommendations is that children ages 2 and younger should not be exposed to television or other entertainment media at all. This recommendation, issued in 1999, came at the same time as an increase in television and video offerings designed specifically for children under age 2 (D. R. Anderson & Pempek, 2005; Diener et al., 2008; Wartella, Vandewater, & Rideout, 2005). Researchers studying this age group refer to such media, like the Baby Einstein videos, as foreground television. *Foreground* television is programming developed to attract and maintain the attention of a particular age group – in this case, those under 2. By contrast, *background* television is programming to which a child is exposed, but which is developed for other audiences and therefore does not command the same level of attention (D. R. Anderson & Pempek, 2005; Lemish, 2007). Earlier research, on programming like *Sesame Street* which is designed for slightly older children, showed that children under 2 attended to television programming about a third of the time it was on (D. R. Anderson et al., 1986). However, research examining foreground television for infants shows babies attend to videos targeted to them as much as 50 to 75% of the time (D. R. Anderson & Pempek, 2005).

Videos for Babies

The American Academy of Pediatrics discourages screen media use for children under 2 years of age. But studies show very few families follow this recommendation completely. In a 2013 survey "Zero to Eight," Common Sense Media found that kids aged 0–2 watch about an hour of media per day. The vast majority of their screen time is spent with television, DVDs, or streaming video.

Preschool children have become an important target market, with entire cable networks devoted to programming for this age group, including Nick Jr., Sprout, and Disney Jr. Streaming services such as Netflix also offer programming designated for "little kids." One very successful area has been educational videos designed for children under 2. LeapFrog has a series of videos that teach letters and numbers. The Preschool Prep Company offers a 10-disc series teaching letters, numbers, shapes, colors, and so on. Perhaps the best-known video series for babies was Baby Einstein.

Baby Einstein was founded in the late 1990s by Julie Aigner-Clark, a former teacher who was staying at home with her children. The videos combined music with visuals of children's toys, actual kids engaged in play, and shots of real-life animals. Each 30-minute video focused on a theme, such as water, the sky, poetry, and classical music. The series includes titles such as "Baby Mozart," "Baby Galileo," and "Baby Einstein: World Animals." By 2001, Aigner-Clark had sold controlling interest in her company to Disney. In 2009, the Baby Einstein brand was estimated to be worth nearly 400 million dollars.

A parent's advocacy group, Campaign for a Commercial Free Childhood, filed a complaint with the Federal Trade Commission (FTC) against Baby Einstein for false advertising. In response, Baby Einstein dropped the word "educational" in their marketing of the DVDs. Although the FTC was satisfied with that response, the advocacy group was not. Lawyers threatened to file a class-action lawsuit against Baby Einstein. The company then announced that it would offer refunds for any of their DVDs purchased between June 2004 and September 2009.

It can be difficult to study the impact of foreground media on children under 2, because of their lack of language skills, but research shows "infants do extract meaningful information from video events and have a range of emotional reactions to them" (Diener et al., 2008, p. 431). However, experiments have demonstrated that infants and toddlers learn *more* from experiencing something in real life than they do from watching a video of the same thing (Diener et al., 2008; Fisch, 2009; Kirkorian, Wartella, & Anderson, 2008; Van Evra, 2004). This *video deficit* is lessened when children watch a video repeatedly (D.R. Anderson et al., 2000; D.R. Anderson & Pempek, 2005). About half of the media exposure for infants is to foreground television; the other half is to background television, which is not designed to attract their attention (D.R. Anderson & Pempek, 2005). Nonetheless, background television does have an impact on this age group. The primary impact seems to be in distracting children from their play, and lessening the quantity and quality of parent–child interactions (D. R. Anderson & Pempek, 2005; Diener et al., 2008).

Age is clearly an important consideration when studying the effects of media on children. Although there are individual differences in the precise timing, researchers have identified several important milestones that children reach with regards to attention to, and comprehension and retention of media content.[5] Researchers have identified age 2½ as a time when language and cognitive development have coalesced to make television content much more comprehensible to children (D. R. Anderson & Pempek, 2005). But young children are still incapable of telling what is real and what is fantasy until they are about 8 years old (Lemish, 2007). They are also unable to understand the intent behind advertising until age 7 or 8 (B. Gunter, Oates, & Blades, 2004; Lemish 2007). The ability to understand certain story-telling devices also develops with age. For example, younger children do not understand the concept of replays; they believe the event is happening over and over again (Van Evra, 2004). Following the events of September 11, 2001, children were particularly upset by repeated replays of the Twin Towers collapsing, because they thought more buildings were continuing to be hit (Kaiser Family Foundation, 2003). Similarly, narrative techniques such as flashbacks are also difficult for children to understand until about age 9 or 10 (Lemish, 2007; Van Evra, 2004).

What Explains Age Differences in Relation to Media Effects?

There are a few explanations for why age differences matter in terms of understanding media effects on children. First, young children have so little experience with the real world that almost everything that they encounter on television may be novel. All this new information may be too difficult for children to assimilate (D. R. Anderson & Collins, 1988). W. A. Collins (1982) also explained that younger children tend to "chunk" television programs into small, discrete units based on scene. Older children, on the other hand, chunk by longer segments, unified by a plot element. The smaller in size, yet large number of chunks may tax the capacity of children's STM, so they remember less. Children can also fail to understand television content if they don't have the required real-world background knowledge. Researchers have shown few effects of indecent media content on children less than 12 years of age because they do not understand basic sexual concepts (Donnerstein, Wilson, & Linz, 1992).

Developmental (age) differences in learning from television are made clearer by Piaget's cognitive development theory (Bryant, Fondren, & Bryant, 2012; Lemish, 2007). Until about age 2, children are seen as in the *sensorimotor stage*. This stage is marked by a lack of reflexive thought – there are no symbolic representations. The child explores objects to learn to distinguish self from the rest of the world. Children may imitate actions that they see, but there is no memory of the action. The next stage (about ages 2 to 7), *preoperational*, involves mental duplication of real-world objects. This stage is marked by "perceptual boundedness," or a rather strict adherence to the physical appearance of a person or object. Most of the limited learning found in prior research occurs in children from this age group. Salience attracts attention and drives learning, because children are not able to think abstractly or think beyond what they see.[6] From ages 7 to 12, children are in the *concrete operations* stage. In this stage, children can separate appearance from reality. They are also able to perform more elaborate cognitive activities, such as relating what is seen to prior knowledge and drawing inferences. It is around this age that researchers begin to identify children's learning from television. After age 12, children enter the adult-like stage of *formal operations*, although their cognitive skills continue to be developed and refined for at least another decade.

Although much research has focused on children's episodic memory, schemas appear to be a necessary prerequisite for memory. Schemas are the organizing framework for long-term memory. W. Schneider and Pressley (1997) summarized some of the research that suggests that even the youngest children have some simple schemas (e.g., they can recognize which household objects belong in the kitchen or the bathroom). But, young children's schemas generally concern events that are common to children's personal experiences, such as eating at a fast food restaurant or going to a birthday party. W. A. Collins (1982) reinforced the importance of schemas in memory for television. Without story schemas, or schemas about television program genres, children answer questions about the order of scenes in programs randomly. Nor can they draw inferences about events that they haven't directly observed.

Meadowcroft and Reeves (1989) supported the importance of story schemas in children's learning from television. Rather than rely solely on age as a surrogate for schema development, the researchers assessed 5- and 8-year-old children's story schema skills. Not surprisingly, children with well-developed story schemas tended to be older. The authors concluded that story schemas do not fully develop until age 7. Consistent with expectations, story schemas aided memory for television programs. Moreover, children with well-developed story schemas were able to pay less attention to television, while still learning more. Story schemas not only reduced the processing demands placed on children while watching television, but also directed attention to central (compared to incidental) story information. Story schemas not only give children a "hook" on which to hang information from television, but also allow them to process the information more efficiently and easily. Collins (1982) concluded that schemas are essential for learning from television. Children need schemas that give them knowledge about the formats of television programs, knowledge about the kinds of stories told, and knowledge about the way that the real world works.

Media and Academic Achievement

The media's impact on academic achievement has been researched consistently since the advent of television (e.g., Ball, Palmer, & Millward, 1986; E. Maccoby, 1954; Schramm, Lyle, & Parker, 1961). Television continues to be the primary medium that is studied in terms of its relationship with academic achievement, because it remains the most prevalent in children's lives. Earlier research showed a small but negative relationship between the amount of television viewed and various measures of academic achievement (e.g., D.R. Anderson & Collins, 1988; Fetler, 1984; S.B. Neuman, 1991). Recent studies have shown, though, that the *content* of television and other electronic media predicts the effects on academic achievement better than simple measures of time spent viewing (Brooks-Gunn & Donahue, 2008; Schmidt & Vandewater, 2008; Kirkorian, Wartella, & Anderson, 2008). Children who watch quality educational programming actually have higher levels of academic achievement than average, while children who watch programs that are violent or that are purely for entertainment perform less well (Schmidt & Vandewater, 2008).

Viewing educational television has been linked to better language skills (Fisch, 2009; Kirkorian, Wartella, & Anderson, 2008), increased literacy and book use (D.R. Anderson et al., 2001; Fisch, 2009), math and science grades (D.R. Anderson et al., 2001; Bickham, Schmidt, & Huston, 2012; Fisch, 2009), and problem solving skills (Fisch, 2009; Lemish, 2007), among other positive academic outcomes. Some research has also shown positive outcomes from educationally oriented video games, including improved spatial skills and eye–hand coordination (Fisch, 2009; Schmidt & Vandewater, 2008).

A lot of emphasis has been placed on preschool educational programming on television. *Sesame Street* was the first such program that was designed to teach a specific curriculum to preschool students (Fisch, Truglio, & Cole, 1999). One of the primary aims of *Sesame Street* from the beginning has been to promote "school readiness" – which encompasses not only academic skills, but also interpersonal skills such as self-confidence and cooperation (Fisch, 2009). *Sesame Street* has served as a model for other preschool television programs such as *Blue's Clues*, in its use of child development experts and educational researchers to help design the programs' content and to conduct ongoing evaluations of its effectiveness (Anderson et al., 2000; Fisch, Truglio, & Cole, 1999). In a review of 30 years of research into the impact of *Sesame Street*, Fisch, Truglio, and Cole (1999) found support for the positive impact of the program on academic achievement and social behavioral goals. Moreover, these positive results were consistent not only over time but also cross-culturally for global adaptations of *Sesame Street* (p. 186).

Researchers have also begun to examine the long-term effects of viewing educational preschool television, particularly *Sesame Street*. Viewing *Sesame Street* at an early age predicts not only school performance in elementary school, but also predicts positive outcomes as far removed as high school grades (D.R. Anderson et al., 2001; Bickham, Schmidt, & Huston, 2012; Fisch, 2009; Fisch, Truglio, & Cole, 1999). This was true "even after the students' early language skills and family background variables were factored out" (Fisch, 2009). Why would watching *Sesame Street* have such a long-lasting impact? Researchers propose it is because good quality educational television, in addition to teaching specific academic skills, also develops children's motivation and interest in learning (Bickham, Schmidt, & Huston, 2012; Fisch, 2009).

But what explains the negative impact on academic achievement for children who primarily watch entertainment television instead? Researchers have proposed a variety of theoretical explanations. The *passivity hypothesis* assumes that, because television viewing (of entertainment programming, at least) is a more mentally passive activity than reading, children become mentally lazy and are less willing to invest mental effort on reading and other academic tasks (Valkenburg & Calvert, 2012; Van Evra, 2004). The *rapid pacing hypothesis* suggests that the fast pacing of most children's programming causes children to have shortened attention spans and weakens their ability to concentrate (Kirkorian, Wartella, & Anderson, 2008; Lemish, 2007; Valkenburg & Calvert, 2012; Van Evra, 2004). Kirkorian, Wartella, and Anderson (2008) point out that educational and entertainment-focused programming differ not only in content but also in terms of the formal features such as pacing (p. 45). Researchers have shown that early viewing of noneducational programming is correlated with later attention problems in children (see, e.g., Zimmerman & Christakis, 2007). A related explanation, the *arousal hypothesis*, also proposes hyperactivity and impulsiveness to be results of watching entertainment television. But rather than the pacing, the effects are posited to result from the level of arousal stimulated by action-oriented programs (Valkenburg & Calvert, 2012). The *visualization hypothesis* suggests that because children do not have to use their mind to imagine what is happening in a story – television provides ready-made images – they do not develop their imagination as much as children using other forms of media (Valkenburg & Calvert, 2012).

The most commonly used explanation for a negative relationship between entertainment television viewing and academic achievement is the *displacement hypothesis*. This hypothesis assumes that television viewing displaces other activities that are more cognitively beneficial to children such as reading or doing homework. The displacement hypothesis is not as simple as it sounds, however. Research has shown that television viewing will not replace any and all activities, only certain types of activities. First, television displaces functionally similar activities (Kirkorian, Wartella, & Anderson, 2008; Lemish, 2007). That is, children will replace television for other activities that fill the same needs, but do not do it as well or as conveniently. So, television viewing has been found to displace radio listening and movie going (Mutz, Roberts, & Van Vuuren, 1993) as well as comic book reading. Similarly, video games and time on the computer have been found to displace television watching and movie going (Valkenburg & Calvert, 2012). Or media use may displace marginal activities that are not very important or salient. It may be that children fill more empty parts of the day, while they are "killing time," with television viewing or video game playing. Neither of these examples should lead directly to reduced academic achievement.

There are several conceptual problems with the displacement hypothesis. First, it assumes that time is spent only on a single activity at a time (Mutz et al., 1993). Most observational studies document that television is often a secondary activity to other tasks (e.g., Bechtel et al., 1972), or that children are using several media simultaneously (Rideout, Foehr, & Roberts, 2010; D. F. Roberts & Foehr, 2008). Television may not displace activities as much as serve as background to them. The displacement hypothesis also typically assumes that television viewing displaces only enriching activities. Television viewing is not necessarily "worse" than the activities it is most likely to displace. And, television viewing may be more mentally enriching than other time fillers, such as solitaire or "hanging out." Researchers posit that the impact of displacement effects depends on what activities television viewing displaced (Fetler, 1984; Schmidt & Vandewater, 2008). For high SES groups, there is a negative relationship between television viewing and academic achievement; for low SES groups, there is a positive relationship (Schmidt & Vandewater, 2008). As Ritchie and his colleagues (Ritchie, Price, & Roberts, 1987) speculated, displacement might be negative when "viewing substitutes for more educationally pertinent conditions or activities (time spent reading, interaction with parents, supportive interpersonal climate, etc.)." Displacement effects might be positive when television "delivers something educationally valuable that would otherwise be missing from the environment (information about the distant world, vocabulary, parasocial interaction)" (p. 312).

G. B. Armstrong and his colleagues (Armstrong, 1993; Armstrong Boiarsky, & Mores, 1991; Armstrong & Greenberg, 1990) propose that television's impact on academic achievement occurs through a distraction process. Based on evidence that television often serves as background to homework and reading (e.g, Lyle & Hoffman, 1972; Patton, Stinard, & Routh, 1983), Armstrong argues that television distracts children from their homework and interferes with their learning. Television can easily distract people from other activities while they are viewing by stimulating an orienting response, by competing for attentional capacity, and by interfering with or taking over the mental activities operations needed to learn new information. These distraction effects should be strongest for the viewers of a lot of television, because it is likely that television viewing should more regularly accompany homework. Research has provided some support for the *distraction hypothesis*. Background television viewing occupies attentional capacity and reduces achievement on more difficult tasks, such as reading comprehension (Armstrong et al., 1991). There is also evidence that background television may interfere with learning by demanding the same types of mental engagement as some mental tasks, such as visual analysis of geometric figures (Armstrong, 1993).

Armstrong and Greenberg (1990) noted that even these findings might underestimate the effects of background television because they used college undergraduates as their research participants. College students, of course, are typically better students and have already reached a higher level of academic achievement. Research has shown that television's distraction effects are stronger with younger children who have not become habituated to watching television and have less prior knowledge and educational experience (Anderson & Pempek, 2005).

All of this research suggests that television can be a potentially potent distraction for children who do their homework while the set is on. Armstrong and his colleagues (1991) found that even when their research participants were instructed to ignore the television in the background, almost 70% reported that they found it difficult to do so.

Headphones at Work?

Are headphones a blessing or a curse when it comes to work productivity? Today's open work environments, designed to facilitate collaboration, can also be loud and distracting. Headphones can help create a sense of your own personal work space, and provide a visual cue to others that you are not to be interrupted. Listening to music you have chosen can improve your mood, and even serve to motivate you to complete a tough task.

However, headphones can also isolate you from your coworkers and the cultural atmosphere of your organization. Other employees can get frustrated if you are not responsive to their attempts to contact you, and being less engaged in the group can hamper career advancement. Another concern about using headphones is that your ability to process necessary work-related information may be compromised by the exposure to task-irrelevant stimuli such as music.

The brain has a limited capacity to process incoming information. When listening to music, in order to focus on a work assignment, part of your brain will have to exert effort to block out the task-irrelevant stimuli to which you are listening. So, the type of task you are trying to complete is an important variable in whether or not using headphones is advisable. If you are filing papers or doing something routine, listening to your favorite music can make that less boring. However, if you are learning new information or need to fully absorb something you are reading, listening to music can inhibit your ability to do so. If you would prefer to listen to music anyway, music with lyrics demand greater cognitive effort than instrumental-only pieces, so classical music may be the best option. Individual characteristics also contribute to one's ability to balance music-listening with work tasks. Introverts, for example, are less able to concurrently process music and learn new information than are extroverts.

A decision whether or not to use headphones at work should hinge on multiple factors: the organizational culture and support for headphone use (or lack thereof), the type of work-related task that needs to be completed, the presence or absence of lyrics in the music, and one's own ability to manage processing multiple stimuli.

Knowledge Gaps

The mass media are a source of information for society as a whole. Public communication campaigns use combinations of different media to spread messages to large groups of people. Information disseminated via the mass media is not learned equally by all societal groups, however. One unintended effect of using the mass media to spread information is the development of knowledge gaps. *Knowledge gaps* are inequities in information, typically based on socioeconomic status (SES).

Tichenor and his colleagues (1970) did not assert that lower SES groups do not learn, only that low SES groups learn at a slower rate than high SES groups, so that gaps between the groups grow larger, as more information is spread via the mass media.

> As the infusion of mass media information into a social system increases, segments of the population with higher socioeconomic status tend to acquire this information at a faster rate than the lower status segments, so that the gap in knowledge between these segments tends to increase rather than decrease. (pp. 159–160)

Knowledge gaps are problems for several reasons. Knowledge is power; so gaps in knowledge translate into gaps in power. Public communication campaigns often use the media to publicize information about health and safety, important to almost everyone in society. Knowledge gaps in these areas mean that health risks will be unequally distributed across SES groups.

The case of the television program, *Sesame Street*, illustrates how the mass media can perpetuate gaps, rather than close them. The program was initiated, in part, because children from lower SES groups were unprepared for school, compared to children from higher SES groups. *Sesame Street*'s first goal was to increase children's intellectual and cultural growth (T. D. Cook et al., 1975). Its important second goal, however, was to stimulate the intellectual growth of disadvantaged preschoolers. Researchers studying the effectiveness of the program were initially pleased with the results: Children learned letters, numbers, and basic concepts that would prepare them for school. Further inquiry, though, found that children of more educated parents tended to watch the program more regularly and tended to learn more from the program (T. D. Cook et al., 1975; Katzman, 1974). So, although there was an overall increase in school preparedness, *Sesame Street* perpetuated the gaps between the advantaged and disadvantaged children.

Tichenor and his colleagues (1970) proposed several explanations for the connection between SES and knowledge gaps. First, SES is associated with education. Higher SES groups tend to be more educated than lower SES groups. With education comes communication skills. The more educated are able to read and comprehend more complex information. Education is associated with background knowledge. When people already have knowledge about a topic, it is easier to understand and assimilate new information. In an experiment using Lang's Limited Capacity Model of Mediated Message Processing (LC3MP, described earlier in the chapter), researchers demonstrated that "the knowledge gap is, at least in part, the product of variance in information processing capacity among education groups" (M. E. Grabe, Kamahawi, & Yegiyan, 2009, p. 106). Higher SES groups also have more relevant social contacts. So, information has more social utility for higher SES individuals; information is the basis for interpersonal discussion and social rewards. Education and SES both lead to more selective seeking of information from the media.

The media system also contributes to knowledge gaps. Because of the reliance on advertising, news media tend to report stories that appeal to higher, rather than lower SES groups. The media system also favors access to those with more economic resources. The best sources of information are not free. Cable television requires monthly payment, newspapers and magazines are paid for by the issue, and online resources require access to an Internet-connected computer or mobile device.

Scholars have identified some conditions that may attenuate knowledge gaps (Viswanath & Finnegan, 1996). *Ceiling effects* diminish knowledge gaps (Ettema & Kline, 1977). Ceiling effects occur when knowledge is less complex and limited. So, because knowing the numbers from 1 to 20 is a fairly defined bit of knowledge, eventually all children will learn, and gaps will disappear. Conflict also reduces knowledge gaps. When there is conflict about an issue, not only is there increased media publicity about that issue – across a full range of media – but the issue becomes more salient to the public. The associated interest and interpersonal discussion can lead to fewer knowledge gaps (Donohue, Tichenor, & Olien, 1975). News diffusion of vitally important events rarely finds awareness gaps (Gaziano, 1985).

Scholars have also found that knowledge gaps can disappear with motivation. That is, individuals from low SES groups can gain knowledge if they see utility in the information and are motivated to acquire it (Ettema & Kline, 1977; Genova & Greenberg, 1979). Individual motivation does appear to close some gaps. In a 2009 meta-analysis of knowledge gap research, there was evidence that knowledge gaps are greater for sociopolitical topics, more so than for health matters; and for international issues more than for local or personal issues (Hwang & Jeong, 2009). The researchers attributed the relatively lower gaps to the increased motivation and interest people have in health topics and issues in close geographic proximity.

The evidence for the influence of motivation is not universal, however. A study of 3,700 people who volunteered to complete a home-based learning project designed to teach diet-related cancer risk reduction strategies (e.g., food shopping and preparation skills) found that this group was a highly motivated group who felt at risk for cancer (Viswanath, Kahn, Finnegan, Hertog, & Potter, 1993). This group did learn more than a control group of unmotivated people in the general population. Knowledge gaps between those with more education and less education, however, persisted. D. M. McLeod and Perse (1994) also noted that SES is still a potent predictor of public affairs knowledge gaps because it is linked to several motivation variables. That is, SES is linked to political interest and a desire to acquire information from news reports.

Concerns about knowledge gaps continue with changes to the media environment. Children, especially, might be the victims of knowledge gaps with the increase of outlets offering children's programming. An initial study found that children with access to only broadcast television had the least diversity and variety of programming available (Wartella, Heintz, Aidman, & Mazzarella, 1990). Cable, digital video players, and Internet access can be expected to increase diversity and variety. Because these media require extra cost, access to children's programming may be limited by SES. Furthermore, children from higher SES homes are more likely to be guided toward watching more educational children's programming (as opposed to purely entertainment programming) and therefore see more learning as a result of their media use.

The growth of the Internet as a source for news and information drives other concerns about knowledge gaps (see, e.g., Jeffres, Neuendorf, & Atkin, 2012; J. A. Yang & Grabe, 2011). Access to information may be limited to those who can afford the hardware and who have knowledge to navigate the Web effectively. But access issues don't tell the whole story. J. A. Yang and Grabe (2011) conducted a study in South Korea, which has a relatively high rate of diffusion in terms of Internet use and access. They recruited participants who had high education levels (a graduate degree), and low education levels (no more than a high school education). But, all of their participants were screened to make sure they had experience accessing news on the Internet. Even with similar news exposure patterns, the participants with more education demonstrated higher levels of knowledge acquisition than participants with less education. Among the general population in the U.S., education and SES do affect access to and ability to use the WWW. More highly educated people also tend to use the Web more for information seeking, rather than for entertainment purposes (Jeffres, Neuendorf, & Atkin, 2012).

Closing knowledge gaps is certainly not an easy task. Research offers some suggestions to developers of public communication campaigns. Perhaps knowledge gaps could be reduced by planning a series of campaigns, each designed to teach fairly discrete and specific bits of knowledge. Ceiling effects could limit knowledge gaps. Campaign designers should also consider ways to increase motivation and interest in the target audience before disseminating information. Increased interest and motivation may also close gaps. Recently, researchers have also provided evidence that routine news coverage – not part of a targeted communication campaign – can also influence the development of knowledge gaps (Jerit, Barabas, & Bolsen, 2006; Slater et al., 2009). Differences in the information environment can exacerbate or alleviate knowledge gaps, with an increase in print coverage heightening knowledge disparities, and increases in television coverage lessening them (Jerit, Barabas, & Bolsen,

2006). Jerit (2009) also demonstrated particular elements of news coverage that influence knowledge gaps. She found that an increase in expert commentary reinforces SES-based knowledge gaps, partly because the language used by experts tends to be confusing to lower SES individuals, but also because norms of objectivity also often mean that news stories include experts with conflicting points of view (p. 443). On the other hand, Jerit (2009) found that the inclusion of contextual information in news stories can lower knowledge gaps. Part of the reason for the existence of knowledge gaps is because higher SES individuals have more background knowledge, so if news stories help provide that background it can even the playing field for lower SES individuals (p. 444). In addition to efforts on the part of news producers and communication campaign developers, problems of access to information and the ability to use it offer special problems that need to be addressed by public policy. The costs and benefits to society in creating equal access to information need to be assessed.

Summary

Learning from the mass media occurs the same way that we learn from other sources. Learning involves both active and passive processes. People learn more completely when they are mentally engaged in learning, by devoting attention to the information, relating it to prior knowledge, and integrating it into mental frameworks. Learning can be stimulated by aspects of the message. Certain message elements can lead to involuntary attention, which might lead to mental engagement if the material is interesting or important.

Active approaches to learning from the media include both conditional and cognitive models. Learning from different media may be conditional on aspects of the audience, such as prior knowledge, age, and cognitive abilities. Learning involves creating new schemas or linking newly encountered information to existing schemas. Passive approaches are more media content centered. The focus is on using media content to attract the involuntary attention of the audience. Weather alerts, for example, use an annoying sound that attracts the inattentive television viewer. Passive approaches also suggest media content that will focus on things that people are interested in – such as sex appeal, celebrities, and so on. This media content centered approach assumes that people need to be pushed to pay attention to media content. Of course, attention is not the only aspect of learning, but it is a prerequisite; once attention is attracted, perhaps more active processes might come into place.

Concerns about the negative impacts of the mass media on learning can be explained by various learning approaches. Children may be hampered in their ability to learn from television, for example, because they have not developed the necessary cognitive skills to learn or the mental organization to store the knowledge. Academic achievement might be limited by television viewing, if heavy viewers try to do homework while watching television. Television can distract children from homework and reduce mental capacity needed to complete certain kinds of mental tasks.

It is clear that prior knowledge and motivation to learn increase learning throughout all groups in society. Knowledge gaps, though, also involve variables that are not under the control of the individual. Societal structure affects the cost of and access to information. For that reason, communication policy needs to address ways to close knowledge gaps.

Notes

1 It is possible to manipulate the length of the bits of information to increase the capacity of STM. Kozma (1991, p. 193) uses this example: The seven words "Lincoln, calculus, criminal, address, differential, lawyer, and Gettysburg" can be rearranged to three chunks: Lincoln Gettysburg address, differential calculus, and criminal lawyer.

2 Interestingly, researchers have also identified formal features which do *not* elicit an orienting response, such as the beginning of slow-motion video and the appearance of text on a computer screen. See Lang, Potter, & Bolls (2009) for a summary.

3 Lang (2000) provides a psychophysiological measurement for assessing what is happening in the brain for the subprocesses of learning: encoding, storage, and retrieval.

4 The AAP "Media and Children" initiative can be accessed at http://www.aap.org/en-us/advocacy-and-policy/aap-health-initiatives/Pages/Media-and-Children.aspx.

5 See Van Evra (2004, chapter 3), for an excellent summary of developmental differences in attention, comprehension, and retention by age.

6 Sparks and Cantor (1986) reported an interesting study of one of the effects of this stage of cognitive development. Children in the concrete operational stage were more likely to be frightened of the television program *The Incredible Hulk* (starring Bill Bixby as David Banner and Lou Ferrigno as the Hulk). Because children at this stage are closely tied to physical appearance, they did not understand that, as Dr. Banner changed to the Hulk, his good character remained. When David Banner got upset about some injustice, he was transformed into the Hulk, a green, muscular, angry character. Young children were frightened by the Hulk, even though he was a "good guy," because of his monster-like appearance.

6   SOCIALIZATION EFFECTS

Through their socialization function, the mass media teach and reinforce societal values. Because socialization involves learning the values and norms of society, for the most part, socialization occurs mainly at certain times of people's lives. Children, because they have had few life experiences, are the main target for socializing messages. But, socialization occurs whenever people enter a new life stage or try a new life style. Adolescence is a period of socialization as children grow to adulthood and experience new freedoms, new relationships, and new responsibilities. Even adults undergo socialization. Newly arrived immigrants, for example, need to be socialized to a new culture and society. When people begin new jobs, they often need to be socialized to the corporate culture of their workplace. And the reinforcement of values is an ongoing process. This chapter builds on Chapter 5, because socialization involves learning the ways, rules, and norms of society.

It is important to remember that the mass media are only one of several sources of socialization. Other societal institutions, such as the family, peer groups, school, and church can offer more immediate and personal socialization. The mass media, though, are easily accessible and attended to by large groups of people. For the youngest children, most concerns about negative effects focus on television because it is the medium that most children use and because it is viewed in the home and requires only limited skills to watch and understand. Children adopt the role models of the media. They imitate the way television characters dress and do their hair; they want lunch boxes and Halloween costumes emblazoned with their favorite characters. Coupled with the realization that some children have limited social contact with other societal institutions, there is a good deal of concern about mass media's potential negative effects on children's knowledge about society.

Acquisition of Stereotypes

Stereotypes are "beliefs about the characteristics and attributes of a group and its members that shape how people think about and respond to the group" (Dovidio, Hewstone, Glick, & Esses, 2010, p. 8). Stereotypes are simplistic representations of social groups that deny any diversity among members of the same group. In most cases, stereotypes are negative and limiting. Children are at risk of being exposed to stereotypes as they watch television because television is replete with stereotyped representations of social groups. Television programs rely on stereotypes because, as a business, they need to attract a large audience, so they must present content that is easily understood by a wide range of people, young and old, educated and uneducated. Much television viewing grows out of a need for relaxation or escape (e.g., Comstock & Scharrer, 1999; A.M. Rubin, 1981a), so content is generally not intellectually challenging. Time limitations of television programs also dictate that character development and identification be rather straightforward. There is no time for subtlety or nuances in characters in programs whose plots must be completed in 30 or 60 minutes (less time with commercials inserted). So, producers rely on stereotypes to present easily understood and identified character types. Even television news relies on stereotypes, because producers need to illustrate news stories with representative examples (Linn, 2003).

Over the years, content analyses have found that television is filled with stereotyped images of many groups – if those groups are depicted at all. Researchers have focused on the concepts of recognition and respect (see, e.g., Lauzen & Dozier, 2005). The question of *recognition* refers to the numerical representation of particular groups in the media, and in particular whether their level of presence in the media conforms to the reality of those groups in society. *Respect* is a more qualitative description of the portrayals, including whether characters are central to story lines, viewed in high or low status occupations, or seen as exhibiting stereotypic behavior for the group to which they belong. Research has emphasized the impact of stereotypes related to age, sex, and ethnicity – in part because these aspects of identity are easily observable and therefore able to be coded reliably (Harwood & Anderson, 2002). Content analyses illustrate that stereotypes on television have been remarkably stable over the past years (e.g., Children Now, 2004; Signorielli, 2012). There are certainly instances of non-stereotypic portrayals on television. But even with any current changes in television content, this does not erase concerns about stereotypes in programs that children watch because television programming has a long life in syndication. Programs created in earlier decades are still aired regularly. Many of these programs are considered "wholesome" because they contain little sex, but they are often filled with outdated stereotypes. And current programming still contains stereotypes, although they may be more subtle in nature than those in older programs.

Stereotypes of Women

It is clear that there are strong, nontraditional female characters on television (e.g., Lauzen, Dozier, & Horan, 2008), but the overwhelming pattern is one of underrepresentation and traditional female images. Females are outnumbered by males by about 2 to 1 on prime-time television programs (Aubrey & Harrison, 2004; Children Now, 2004). This is somewhat dependent on program genre, with women being least represented in action programs and reality television programs, and somewhat more equitably present in situation comedies and dramas (Signorielli, 2012, p. 324). On children's programs, there are even fewer female characters; males outnumber females 4 to 1 (Aubrey & Harrison, 2004; Signorielli, 2012).[1] News programs also underrepresent women. In a report for the Women's Media Center, "The Status of Women in the U.S. Media 2012," Yi and Dearfield (2012) show that only 21.7% of the guests on Sunday morning news programs were women (p. 5). The Global Media Monitoring Project in 2010 reported that about 24% of the sources in the news worldwide are women (Macharia, O'Connor, & Ndganam, 2010).

When fictional women characters appear, they are usually younger than males (Children Now, 2004; Signorielli, 2012; Yi & Dearfield, 2012) and are more often shown in home, family, and romantic contexts (Lauzen et al., 2008) than at work. Family and career do not mix on television; married female characters on television are much less likely to be employed than single or divorced women (Signorielli, 2012). When fictional women characters have careers and family, the programs still usually focus on the interpersonal aspects of their lives (Lauzen et al., 2008). According to Macharia, O'Connor, and Ndganam's "Who Makes the News" report (2010), in news programming, women are identified by their family status at three to four times the rate of male news sources. They argue "identifying women by their family status and at the same time playing down their roles in their communities masks women's other identities as independent, autonomous beings, active participants in the wider society beyond the home" (p. viii).

Commercials also reinforce these patterns of images. Although women are not underrepresented in commercials, they are typically subservient to men. Males are the announcers, spokespersons, and "voices of authority," even in commercials for products that women buy and use. In her book *Housework and Housewives in American Advertising: Married to the Mop*, historian Jessamyn Neuhaus (2011) details the evolution of advertising related to household cleaning products. She describes how women overwhelmingly remain the ones pictured doing housework. Neuhaus argues this reflects that "there remains in our society a widespread assumption about the gendered nature of homemaking" (p. 16). A study of national television commercials shown during prime-time confirms Neuhaus' argument – almost two-thirds of those seen doing chores were women, most of them mothers. And, when men were shown doing housework, it was most often in a humorous light, illustrating their incompetence at such tasks (Scharrer, Kim, Lin, & Liu, 2006). Commercials in children's cartoons also reveal gender stereotyping. Boys in commercials are seen more often, they have more dominant roles in commercials, and are more active. Girls, on the other hand, are shyer, "giggly," and less central to the ads (Browne, 1998).

The stereotype of women presented on television, then, is that women are valued for youth, attractiveness, and filling traditional roles. There is a good deal of research that connects television viewing to children's learning of these gender-role stereotypes. With samples of children as young as 3 years old, several researchers have found that heavier viewers of television are more likely to endorse traditional, stereotypic gender-role statements (e.g., Beuf, 1974; Durkin, 1985; McGhee & Frueh, 1980; Morgan, 1987; Van Evra, 2004). Meta-analysis of this body of literature concludes that television has an overall effect of $r = .101$ on holding gender-role stereotypes across all age groups (Herrett-Skjellum & Allen, 1996). Among children under 3, the average correlation between amount of television and holding gender-role stereotypes is $r = .33$; for children from age 6 to 10, the average correlation is $r = .16$. Young children might be particularly susceptible to the effects of stereotypes given their level of cognitive development (Aubrey & Harrison, 2004).

Stereotypes of the Elderly

Although the cohort of adults over the age of 55 is growing steadily, they continue to be a group consistently underrepresented on television. Analyses of the last two decades of prime-time television programs reveal that there have been few improvements in images of the older adult population (Harwood & Anderson, 2002; Lauzen & Dozier, 2005; J.D. Robinson & Skill, 1995; Signorielli, 2004, 2012). Lauzen and Dozier (2005) found that adults 60 and older were only 4% of the major characters in prime-time television during the 2002–2003 season, despite the fact that they represent 18% of the actual population in the U.S. Also contrary to census figures, older men outnumber older women on television (Harwood & Anderson, 2002; Signorielli, 2004, 2012). When older characters are presented on entertainment television, they tend to be treated disrespectfully or are the subject of humor at their expense (Gerbner, Gross, Signorielli, & Morgan, 1980; J. Walker, 2010).[2] A study of German prime-time television reveals similar patterns of stereotypes (Kessler, Rakoczy, & Staudinger, 2004). Media portrayals outside of prime-time television also underrepresent older adults, including game shows and cartoons (Harwood, 2007). Advertising also tends to underrepresent older adults, although some of the portrayals in advertising are more positive than in other media – perhaps reflecting the increasing market power of this group of consumers (Lee, Carpenter, & Meyers, 2007). News stories about older adults tend to focus on them as victims, as bizarre exceptions to stereotypes (the 80-year-old who is skydiving), or as a group who drain society's resources through government programs like Social Security and Medicare (J. Walker, 2010).

There is very little research on how the media affects children's views of older adults. There is modest evidence that television may imprint stereotypes on heavy viewing children. Gerbner and his colleagues (Gerbner, Gross, Signorielli, & Morgan, 1980) found that viewers who watch a lot of television were more likely to hold negative views of the elderly. The association was even stronger with younger persons who watch a lot of television. They also report that heavy viewers from grade 6 to grade 9 were more likely to estimate that people became "old" when they were age 51; light viewers estimated "old" at age 57. These effects might be limited because so many children do have so many real-life experiences with older family members and neighbors.

Stereotypes of Racial/Ethnic Groups

Content analyses reveal that television's portrayal of racial/ethnic groups is limited. Perhaps the greatest amount of research has focused on the presentation of African Americans on television. It wasn't until the 1980s that African Americans began to be portrayed on television in about the same proportion as they are part of the U.S. population (Gerbner, Gross, Morgan, & Signorielli, 1982). Although African Americans are more consistently represented on television today, there are still concerns about the pattern of portrayals. As early as 1979, Gerbner and Signorielli noted that African Americans were more likely to be characters in situation comedies than in other genres. This trend has not changed, which leads to concern about the limited nature of the types of roles available for African American actors and actresses. Furthermore, prime-time situation comedies are mostly segregated; sitcoms feature casts of a single ethnic group (Children Now, 2004; Mastro, 2009). This means that it would be easy for White viewers not to be exposed to portrayals of African Americans. The other genres of television where African Americans tend to be cast are in mixed-race programs such as reality shows (Children Now, 2004) and crime dramas (Mastro, 2009).

On television news, African Americans are consistently overrepresented as criminals (Dixon, 2007; Mastro, 2009). When compared with actual arrest reports, African Americans are disproportionately depicted as the perpetrators of crime and Whites are underreported as criminals and overrepresented as police officers (Dixon & Linz, 2000; Dixon, 2007). Sports programming also reinforces some stereotypes of African Americans. A content analysis of sports commentary found that announcers were more likely to mention the cognitive abilities of White football players but were more likely to comment on the physical abilities of African American players. And, when announcers made disparaging comments about the cognitive abilities or character of a player, in all cases they were directed toward African American football players (Rada, 1997).

Beyond African Americans, other racial/ethnic groups are conspicuously underrepresented on prime-time television. Outside of Spanish-language media and cable channels, Latino characters have yet to make up more than 6.5% of the characters on television, despite the fact that at 13% of the population they have become the largest racial/ethnic minority group in the United States (Children Now, 2004; Mastro, 2009; Mastro & Behm-Morawitz, 2005). Asian Americans make up 1% to 3% of the characters in prime time, while forming 4% of the U.S. population (Children Now, 2004; Mastro, 2009). Native Americans are portrayed between 0% and 0.4% of the time in prime time, although they are 1% of the population (Children Now,

2004; Mastro, 2009). Arab and Middle Eastern characters are nearly nonexistent, constituting about .3% of the characters featured in shows' opening credits (Children Now, 2004). Minority males uniformly outnumber minority females.

The minority characters that do exist in prime-time programming are often in secondary or nonrecurring roles, and depict stereotypical traits of the groups. Latinos tend to be depicted as criminals, law enforcers, Latin lovers, harlots, or comics/buffoons (Mastro & Behm-Morawitz, 2005; Rivadeneyra, Ward, & Gordon, 2007). They also tend to have lower-level occupations, and are presented as "lazier, less articulate, less intelligent, and more seductively dressed" than other social groups (Mastro, 2009, p. 328; Mastro & Behm-Morawitz, 2005, p. 111). Latinos are also four times more likely to be depicted as domestic workers than other racial/ethnic groups (Children Now, 2004). In a review of racial/ethnic stereotypes, Mastro (2009) finds that Asian Americans are often shown in high status occupations and conservatively attired, while Native American characters are seen as spiritual, as warriors, and as being a social problem. Arab and Middle Eastern characters are overwhelmingly portrayed as criminals when they appear in the media (Children Now, 2004). In a content analysis of over 900 Hollywood movies, communication scholar Jack G. Shaheen finds that viewers are led to equate being Arab with being Muslim, and Arab characters – almost exclusively male – are shown to be "brute murderers, sleazy rapists, religious fanatics, oil-rich dimwits, and abusers of women" (2003, p. 172).

Video games also reinforce stereotypes, particularly of minority males (because there are almost no minority females depicted). In a content analysis of 150 games across nine gaming platforms, Williams, Martins, Consalvo, and Ivory (2009) discovered that video games offer an even more distorted picture than television in terms of the number of female and minority characters portrayed: Women account for about 15% of all characters, and only 10% of all primary characters. Whites are overrepresented, while Blacks, Asians, Native Americans and especially Latinos are underrepresented. In a content analysis of video game magazines and covers of video games, Burgess and her colleagues (2011) found Blacks were portrayed as either professional athletes, or as violent thugs. Latinos were only present in the most violent video games. Asians were depicted as a "model minority" or as martial artists. Arab/Middle Eastern characters were only seen as the enemy in the video games, even in those created prior to September 11, 2001. Not a single minority character in any of the video games was shown being violent in a socially sanctioned setting, as opposed to White characters, who often were portrayed as heroic fighters in the military. Their analysis also showed there were more alien/non-human characters depicted than there were total minority human characters (Burgess et al., 2011).

There are two kinds of potential effects of stereotyped media images of racial/ethnic groups: the creation of stereotypes and prejudice among non-group members and negative effects on the members of racial/ethnic groups themselves, particularly for children who are still in the process of identity formation. Children are aware of stereotyped depictions of racial/ethnic groups in the media. A survey of 1,200 children, age 10 to 17, found that children associate White characters on television with "having lots of money," "being well-educated," "being leaders," "doing well in school," and "being intelligent." Minority characters are described as "breaking the law," "having a hard time financially," "being lazy," and "acting goofy" (Children Now, 1999).

Effects of Media Stereotypes

Stereotypes are sets of "generalized beliefs about a group that are widely held within a particular culture" (Hummert, Shaner, & Garstka, 1995, p. 106). That is, stereotypes are sets of beliefs held and recognized by large groups of people. Researchers once believed that the presence of stereotypes inevitably meant that people would behave in prejudiced ways. But social psychologists have demonstrated that even though knowledge of stereotypes is shared by nearly everyone in a culture, not everyone accepts stereotypes as accurate (see, e.g., Devine, 1989). Even so, stereotypes are cognitive structures that impact the encoding and processing of information (Brown Givens & Monahan, 2005; Dixon, 2007). For example, if a friend said he was going to visit his brother's child, who was attending college on a basketball scholarship, drove a pick-up truck, and liked to go hunting, you would probably conclude that it was his nephew, who came from a rural town. Stereotypes are not idiosyncratic; they are socially shared. In fact, there are only a limited number of stereotypes about any group in a culture. Hummert et al. (1995) summarized the various stereotypes that exist in the United States about the elderly: three positive (golden ager, perfect grandparent, John Wayne conservative) and four negative stereotypes (severely impaired, despondent, recluse, and shrew and/or curmudgeon). Some stereotypes may cut across cultures. Gender-role stereotypes in the United States and Australia, for example, are quite similar (Browne, 1998). Self-presentation behaviors, such as shyness and dominance, are fairly consistently gender stereotyped in most cultures (Browne, 1998).

Stereotypes are not inherently good or bad, even though the term itself carries negative connotations. The stereotype of Asian high school students scoring high on the math section of the Scholastic Aptitude Test (SAT) is certainly not negative. The stereotype of a traditional female is not negative: Being maternal, loving, and good with children are all positive traits. But, even positive stereotypes can have negative consequences, because they are limiting. When people violate stereotypical expectations, they are likely to be evaluated negatively (Rudman & Fairchild, 2004). The Asian high school student who does not excel in math or the woman who decides to give custody of her child to her ex-husband may suffer from violating a stereotype. Stereotypes can present no-win situations in some instances. For example, women who are in high-powered managerial roles can be evaluated negatively if they behave in a traditionally feminine way because they are seen as too nice; but if they act in a more assertive, traditionally masculine way, they are seen as too aggressive (Glick & Rudman, 2010).

Stereotypes are also harmful because they objectify, depersonalize, and deny individuality (Enteman, 1996). The pervasiveness of stereotypes in the mass media drives concerns for effects because these are the dominant, if not only, images in the media of certain groups; there may be few alternative images to counter the stereotypes. These stereotyped images may serve to justify inequitable conditions in society. Negative stereotypes offer potentially adverse effects, because they can be incorporated into our beliefs and attitudes about other groups (Van Evra, 2004). Racial/ethnic stereotypes may lead to fear and limit social interaction among different groups. Stereotypes might also affect how people interact with the elderly. For example, older adults report that physicians sometimes provide them with oversimplified information or talk to their family members instead of talking directly to the elderly patient (J. Walker, 2010).

Cognitive-Transactional Model

Stereotypes can be viewed as person schemas categorized along some dimension, such as gender, age, or ethnicity. As schemas, stereotypes do serve a function: they help people deal with the overwhelming amount of information that they encounter in their daily lives. Stereotypes also help people deal with uncertainty in their environment. For example, if we are stranded late at night in a neighborhood we have never visited and with no cell reception, how do we know if we should go to one of the dwellings to ask for help? Even though we have no direct experience with the neighborhood, we might be more likely to go to the house with the children's bicycle on the porch and the dried flower wreath on the door, instead of the house with a Harley Davidson motorcycle parked in the driveway. Children and flowers seem to offer less threat. And, why do college students want to know the major of people that they meet? Does knowing what someone is studying tell more about the person? Do different majors have different stereotypes?

The cognitive-transactional model offers several explanations for (a) how media content is linked to the acquisition of stereotypes about social groups, (b) how media content affects the development of self-concept, or schemas about ourselves and the groups to which we belong, and (c) how media-primed stereotypes affect responses to members of other groups.

Acquisition of Stereotypes

Media content can lead to the acquisition of new stereotyped schemas, and provide reinforcement of existing schemas. Stereotypes about groups develop from generalizations drawn from actual or mediated experiences with members of that group. People tend to see lots of individuality among others who belong to their "ingroups" but tend to minimize differences among those in "outgroups." Media exposure can be the basis for stereotyped schemas in children. Young children especially have few opportunities to have direct experiences with people outside their own family. And, family members tend to be very much alike. So, young children's sole experience with groups different from their family is most likely vicarious, through television or other media. Because young children are dependent on media for information about other groups, that information is more likely to have an effect (Ball-Rokeach & DeFleur, 1976). Children may develop schemas about groups in society that they have no direct experience with, based on the images they see in the media (Van Evra, 2004).

Are stereotypes developed from television viewing during childhood representative of the schemas that children will carry with them for their entire lives? That is, are these effects from television viewing and other media use long term? Schemas can be modified through experience (Fiske & Taylor, 1991). As children gain experiences, they may attach new knowledge to preexisting schemas, making them more complex. Stereotypes may become more specific, with greater knowledge. In adults, stereotypes tend not to be applied to groups as a whole. Adults recognize the variability among members of a group. Stereotypes, instead, become applied to subgroups that share the characteristics of exemplars of stereotypes (Brown Givens & Monahan, 2005; D. L. Hamilton & Mackie, 1990). For example, Brown Givens and Monahan (2005) found that participants in their study who viewed a video depicting African American women as "jezebels" were quicker to associate an African American job interviewee with sexual terms than were people who viewed videos showing a "mammy" stereotype or a nonstereotyped portrayal of an African American woman. So, as people learn throughout their lives, stereotyped schemas developed in early childhood do develop and become more complex. Real-life interaction with a greater range of diverse groups of people can also lead to changes in stereotypes.[3]

Exposure to counterstereotypes in media can also alter stereotyped schemas (Schiappa, Gregg, & Hewes, 2005). However, because people tend to view counterstereotypes as exceptions, social psychologists have suggested three strategies that can be adopted for presenting effective counterstereotypic information via the mass media to change or reduce stereotypes. First, counterstereotypes should be depicted across a range of characters, so that the counterstereotypes are more generalizable to the group, as a whole (Fiske & Taylor, 1991). Second, the counterstereotyped characters should be otherwise typical of the group, so that they are not seen as exceptions or subcategories (Gaertner, Dovidio, & Houlette, 2010). Third, counterstereotypes should be presented over time; repetition may enhance schema change (S. L. Smith & Granados, 2009). There have been studies demonstrating the ability to alter stereotypes and prejudice following exposure to mass media content (e.g., Ramasubramanian, 2011; Schiappa, Gregg, & Hewes, 2005), but these are primarily studies that were conducted in laboratory settings. The effectiveness of large-scale campaigns to reduce stereotypes and prejudice is much harder to study due to the influences of selective exposure, and the general limitations of correlational research. Also, many people do not want to express prejudiced attitudes because they don't want to appear biased, so researchers must often use indirect measures, such as *reaction times* (Brown Givens & Monohan, 2005). In the case of stereotype research, reaction time measures are gathered by exposing participants to some sort of experimental stimulus and then presenting them with a series of words, one at a time, and asking them to indicate how well each word describes the person shown in the stimulus. If a schema relevant to a particular word has been activated by the stimulus material, participants will answer the question more quickly than for words that are irrelevant to that schema.

Development of Self-Schemas

Just as people hold schemas about others in society, they also hold self-schemas. Self-schemas are mental representations of one's "own personality attributes, social roles, past experience, future goals, and the like" (Fiske & Taylor, 1991, pp. 181–182). Self-schemas are self-concepts. They include attributes that are relevant and important to a person; self-schemas do not include irrelevant material. For example, if weight and physical appearance are important to an adolescent girl, then, they will be part of her self-schema. And, if physical strength is not important to her, the ability to lift weights will not be part of her self-schema. Self-schematic attributes can be positive (e.g., intelligence) or negative (e.g., shyness).

People are attentive to self-schematic information they encounter (Fiske & Taylor, 1991). So, self-relevant constructs are important in selective attention to and perception of media content. There is also mounting evidence that self-schemas may be derived in part from media content. In a longitudinal panel study with preteen Black and White girls and boys, Martins and Harrison (2012) found that "television exposure predicted a decrease in self-esteem for all children except White boys" (p. 351). Rivadeneyra, Ward, and Gordon (2007) found that increased media use is correlated with lower self-esteem in the areas of appearance and social skills, although in their studies it was not related to an overall measure of self-esteem.

If people internalize stereotypes, there can be several consequences. Self-esteem is predictive of other important variables, such as motivation, academic achievement, health of peer relationships, and risk of engaging in unhealthy behaviors (Crocker & Garcia, 2010; Martins & Harrison, 2012). Low self-esteem fostered by acceptance of negative self-stereotypes can thus impact many facets of people's lives. Among older people, a positive self-concept can have physiological effects. B. R. Levy and her colleagues (2002) found that individuals with positive self-perceptions about aging lived 7½ years longer than people with less positive beliefs. Social psychologists have also identified a phenomenon known as *stereotype threat*, where members of a stigmatized group underperform on tasks that are related to stereotypes about groups to which they belong. So, for example, if women are told that past scores on a difficult math test have indicated gender differences, they tend to perform significantly worse on the test than men. However, if the stereotype is removed by telling women that both genders have done equally well on the same test, they perform equally well (Crocker & Garcia, 2010). *Stereotype lift* has also been identified: groups who are supposed to be "better at" something actually perform better when the stereotype is made salient than when it is not (Crocker & Garcia, 2010; Walton & Cohen, 2003). Stereotypes in media are by no means the only source of one's self-concept, but they can contribute to the development and reinforcement of self-schemas.

Responses Based on Media-Activated Stereotypes

Media content can also be an effective prime. That is, media content can activate stereotypes, influencing how subsequent information is processed and thereby affecting how people respond to various groups in society or evaluate themselves against media standards (Dixon, 2007; Mastro, 2009). The priming of stereotypes is a result of automatic mental processing. Stereotypes are based on the most salient characteristics of a person; physical appearance, for example, is a strong cue to a stereotype (D. J. Schneider, Hastorf, & Ellsworth, 1979). So, it is not surprising that television images and other visual media could prime stereotypes. Like other schemas, once a stereotype is activated it guides and filters other incoming information (Oliver & Fonash, 2012). When stereotypes are activated repeatedly, as is often the case with media portrayals of race, gender and age, relevant schemas become more and more easily accessible.

"Hate Speech in Media"

The number of hate groups in the United States has increased 56% since 2000 (Southern Poverty Law Center, n.d.). This rise has been attributed in part to a downturn in the economy and a diminishing White majority – as embodied by the election of Barack Obama to the Presidency. But observers charge that hate speech in media also has helped fuel this rise, and has contributed to an increase in the number of hate crimes. The media forms where hate speech is most prevalent are on the Internet, cable news, and talk radio.

Advocacy groups for the targets of hate speech have launched campaigns to counter hateful content. In 2013 the group "Women, Action, & the Media" (WAM!) began a campaign for Facebook to change its policies regarding gender-based hate speech on its site.

Facebook responded by removing most of the offending content originally identified, but has yet to change its policies. As of 2014, WAM! is posting fresh examples of problematic content on a daily basis. All of the content actively encourages or makes light of violence against women. One example shows a picture of a woman who has been beaten, and the caption reads: "1/3 of women are physically abused. 2/3 of men aren't doing their job." (http://www.womenactionmedia.org/examples-of-gender-based-hate-speech-on-facebook/).

The National Hispanic Media Coalition (NHMC) submitted a request to the Federal Communications Commission (FCC) in 2009 asking for commissioners formally to examine both the prevalence of hate speech in media and the effects of such content. One of the NHMC's primary concerns was anti-immigrant rhetoric by talk radio hosts like Rush Limbaugh. One syndicated talk show host, Michael Savage, for example, wants to place strict rules on any Muslim in the United States: "I have a number of things that I am gonna demand and one of them is that no more Muslim immigrants come into this country. No more mosques be permitted to be built in this country ... and yes we need racial profiling immediately" ("Shock Jock," 2009).

In a 2008 report "Fear and Loathing in Prime Time: Immigration Myths and Cable News," Media Matters reported several of the recurring – and incorrect – myths about immigration being propagated on cable television. Among them: immigrants are more likely to engage in criminal activities, take a disproportionate share of social services without paying their own taxes, and that immigrants have caused a resurgence of diseases like leprosy (p. 2). Further, cable TV hosts regularly claimed that Mexican immigrants are part of a conspiracy to take back the southwestern United States for Mexico (Media Matters, 2008, p. 14).

When stereotypes are activated, research has shown that people's beliefs about and actions toward others are impacted. Dixon (2007) found that people who were exposed to television news stories about a crime where the race of the suspect and the race of the police officer were not specified assumed that the criminal was Black and the police officer White (p. 283). This was especially true of people who are heavy television news viewers. Both pornographic films (Hald, Malamuth, & Yuen, 2010; McKenzie-Mohr & Zanna, 1990) and music videos (Aubrey, Hopper, & Mbure, 2011; C.H. Hansen & R.D. Hansen, 1988) have been found to activate stereotyped gender-role schemas and influence how men respond to women. Two experiments conducted by J.G. Power et al. (1996) support the ability of media content to prime stereotypes. College-student participants read fabricated news articles about a fictitious person, "Chris Miller," who was described in the first study as a Black male in either stereotypic or counterstereotypic terms. After reading the article, participants who had read the stereotypic article were more likely to believe that Rodney King brought on his much-reported beating at the hands of police officers than those who had read the counterstereotypic article. In the second study, "Chris Miller" was described as a female in either stereotypic or counterstereotypic terms. After reading, participants who had read the stereotyped article were less likely to find Anita Hill to be a credible witness against then-nominee for the U.S. Supreme Court Clarence Thomas. The authors concluded that stereotypical or counterstereotypic portrayals subsequently cued specific interpretations of media events (J. G. Power et al., 1996, p. 53).

There is also evidence that some types of media content can activate stereotyped self-schemas. Aubrey, Henson, Hopper, and Smith (2009) found that women who viewed images of female models who were exposing a good deal of skin used more negative descriptors of their own appearance than women who viewed the control images. Geis et al. (1984) noted that college women who saw women in sex-typed commercials were more likely to emphasize homemaking in essays about what their lives would be like in 10 years.

Cumulative Model

Another theory that connects media content and the acquisition of stereotypes is cultivation. Cultivation is a theory of media effects that is explained by the cumulative model. Content analyses consistently reveal that prime-time television content of the major broadcast networks is remarkably similar (Signorielli, 2012). That is, while there certainly are differences between specific television programs, overall, television presents a fairly consistent set of images: Men are overrepresented, women and minorities (except for African Americans) are underrepresented, and violence is pervasive and common. Moreover, groups tend to be presented stereotypically. Because the images are consistent and similar across television channels, greater immersion in the television world leads to believing that the real world resembles the television world. Although cultivation was initially proposed to describe and predict effects of violent media content, it is being used more often to describe how children's socialization is affected by television viewing. So, the cultivation hypothesis predicts that heavier television viewing is linked to holding more stereotyped views of social groups (Morgan et al., 2009). There is support for cultivation. Viewers who watch a lot of television are more likely than other viewers to believe rape myths, and to overestimate the number of false reports of rape (Kahlor & Eastin, 2011). Heavy viewers also are more likely to hold racist beliefs (Mastro, 2009).

Cultivation theory can help to explain the effects of stereotyped television content on children. Certainly repeated exposure to inaccurate images of social groups can contribute to what children learn about society. However, the theory was developed at a time when the broadcast networks provided the majority of content to which people were exposed. Does cultivation theory still have explanatory power in today's media environment? Morgan and colleagues (2009) argue that the proliferation of content options has not led to a major shift in the diversity of portrayals of various social groups (p. 45). Concentration of ownership and the economics of an advertising-supported system have largely meant that patterns of content have remained fairly consistent. There is evidence, too, that other forms of media in addition to broadcast, cable, and satellite television repeat these same stereotypes both in terms of exclusion of particular groups and of stereotyped portrayals of members of minority groups when they do appear. In an analysis of video game magazines and video game covers, Burgess et al. (2011) found that minorities were underrepresented compared to their percentage in the population. In fact, there were more space aliens than there were minority human characters (p. 296). And the minorities that were portrayed were in stereotypic roles – Black men as athletes or thugs; Asians as model minorities or martial artists, and so on. If stereotyped content is repetitious across different media forms, one would expect cultivation effects to be heightened.

Conditional Model

After reviewing the various theories that explain the effects of television content on children, Van Evra (2004) formulated a model that describes the effects as conditional on various aspects of the child (see Figure 6.1).

Van Evra (2004) argued that there are several key individual differences in how social relationship and social category variables are important in understanding if and how television will affect a child:

- Viewing motives, or the reasons that the child watches television (entertainment or information);
- perceived reality, or how real and true-to-life the child believes the television content is;
- the amount of time that the child spends watching television (heavy or light viewing);
- the number of alternative information sources available to the child about the subjects in television programs (e.g., parental discussion, real-life exposure to minority groups, access to other media);
- age, gender, socioeconomic status, program preferences, level of cognitive development.

According to this model, television should have its strongest impact on a child's body of knowledge when the child watches television as a source of information, when the child believes that television content is realistic, when the child watches television a lot, and has few other alternative sources of information. Alternately, television will have its least impact when the child views purely for entertainment and does not believe that television shows are

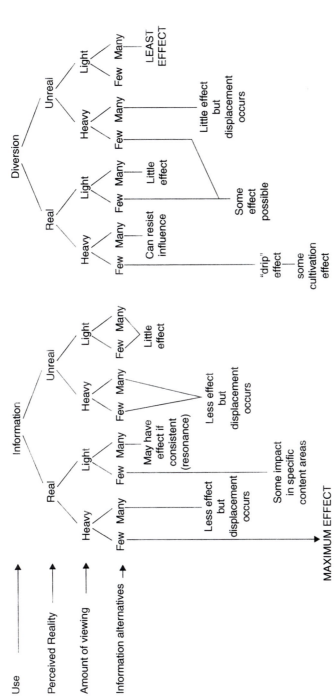

Use ——————→

Perceived Reality ——————→

Amount of viewing ——————→

Information alternatives ——————→

Information

Real

Heavy — Few Many

Less effect but displacement occurs

Some impact in specific content areas

Light — Few Many

May have effect if consistent (resonance)

Unreal

Heavy — Few Many

Less effect but displacement occurs

Light — Few Many

Little effect

MAXIMUM EFFECT

Diversion

Real

Heavy — Few Many

Can resist influence

"drip" effect
some cultivation effect

Light — Few Many

Little effect

Some effect possible

Unreal

Heavy — Few Many

Little effect but displacement occurs

Light — Few Many

LEAST EFFECT

Figure 6.1 Van Evra's conditional model of socialization effects. From: Van Evra, J. (2004). *Television and child development* (3rd edn.). Mahwah, NJ: Lawrence Erlbaum Associates, p. 18. Reprinted with permission.

particularly realistic. Television's effects are particularly minimized when the child does not watch much television and has many other sources of information about the world.

Although all aspects of this model have not been tested, there is theoretical support for several of its linkages. For example, it is clear that children and adolescents watch television for different reasons (e.g., B. S. Greenberg, 1974; Roe & Minnebo, 2007). Lower income children are more likely than higher income children to watch TV for informational purposes, and to have fewer alternative sources for information (Van Evra, 2004). Children also vary in their beliefs about how real television is (e.g., Potter, 1988), and perceived realism does affect acceptance of some media messages (Perse, 1986; Pouliot & Cowen, 2007). Knowledge-gap research (e.g., Tichenor, Donohue, & Olien, 1970, see also Chapter 4, this volume) points out how education and income influence access to different mass media. Children from families with less income, for example, may find their media use limited because of the costs involved with cable, high-speed Internet connections, and smartphones. In all, then, socialization effects can be explained by incorporating the conditional model.

Learning Unhealthy Behaviors

Adolescents are also the subject of concern about socialization effects of the mass media. Adolescence is a period of great change during which there is a tension between childhood and adulthood. During this time, adolescents begin to establish independence from their families, become more oriented toward relationships with friends and integration with peer groups, begin to form their sexual identity, and establish romantic and sexual relationships; also, they begin to move into more adult roles and accept more adult responsibilities (Strasburger, Wilson, & Jordan, 2009). These new roles are accompanied by a great deal of uncertainty. Adolescents spend more time with media than with any other activity, with the exception of sleep (D. F. Roberts & Foehr, 2008). So it should be no surprise that many teens turn to the media for information and advice, particularly about aspects of their developing identity (Strasburger et al., 2009; Van Evra, 2004). Parents and scholars are concerned that the mass media might encourage adolescents to try adult behaviors (like drinking and sex) before they are mature enough to handle the consequences; or, the mass media might provide models for unhealthy behaviors associated with adulthood (e.g., smoking).

Much concern about socialization effects still focuses on television as a source of negative effects, because it remains the most used single medium both for children and adolescents (Rideout, Foehr, & Roberts, 2010; Strasburger, 2004). During the teenage years, the increased use of other media, especially social networking sites, mobile media such as smartphones and tablets, popular music, video games and magazines, means that adolescents are exposed to a greater range of messages about adult behaviors. Between

2005 and 2010, overall media use among 8 to 18 year-olds rose more than an hour per day to over 7½ hours. When factoring in the amount of time this age group is multitasking with multiple forms of media simultaneously, they average nearly 10 hours and 45 minutes per day of media exposure (Rideout et al., 2010).

Nutrition and Eating Disorders

In order to maintain good health, people need to know some of the principles of good nutrition. News stories, public service announcements, web sites, and food packaging rules ensure that more nutritional information is available to the public, yet television programming and commercials, for the most part, negate those positive messages. Food is a common element of programming (Byrd-Bredbenner, Finckenor, & Grasso, 2003) and commercials (Strasbuger et al., 2009). Children's programming especially is surrounded by commercials for sweetened breakfast cereals, processed food product snacks (like pop tarts and fruit roll-ups), and high-fat fast foods. As children grow older, they might watch sports programming, which is flooded with soda, pizza, fast food, and snack food commercials. Ninety-seven % of food advertising viewed by children, and 89% viewed by adolescents are for products high in fat, sugar, and/or salt (Powell, Szczypka, & Chaloupka, 2007). There are few opportunities for children and adolescents to learn healthy eating practices by watching television.

The food industry is increasingly reaching children and adolescents through other forms of media as well: Web sites with activities directed to particular age groups, and URLs to those web sites on packaging, often including codes needed to "unlock" special features (Horgen, Harris, & Brownell, 2012). Social networking sites such as Facebook and Twitter are also used to promote food products targeted at children (Lenhart, Purcell, Smith, & Zickuhr, 2010). Food companies also pay to embed their products in other forms of media. It is no mistake that Coca-Cola cups are placed prominently in front of each judge on *American Idol* (Dawn & Block, 2009). In addition to television programming, product placement of food items appears in movies and video games (FTC, 2008; Horgen et al., 2012). Young people using smartphones or tablets can receive messages directly to their device. Add to that the roughly $186 million food companies devote to in-school advertising, and it is virtually impossible for parents to keep their children from seeing persuasive messages designed to attract them to eat and drink junk food (Horgen et al., 2012).

Media content does seem to have an impact on nutritional knowledge and behavior. A longitudinal study of American elementary school children found that higher levels of television viewing were associated with lower levels of nutritional knowledge and reasoning (Harrison, 2005). In 2006 a thorough review of existing research about the impact of food marketing on children was conducted, and a panel concluded that exposure to television advertisements increases the extent to which children prefer, request their parents to buy, and consume advertised products (IOM, 2006). Researchers are concerned not only about the short-term effects of increased intake of unhealthy food, but also about longer-term effects of misperceptions about nutrition and exercise. In the hopes of avoiding regulation by the Federal Trade Commission, in 2007 the food industry created a self-regulatory body in conjunction with the Better Business Bureau, The Children's Food and Beverage Advertising Initiative (CFBAI). The stated purpose of this group is to "shift the mix of advertising messaging directed to children under 12 to encourage healthier dietary choices and healthy lifestyles" (CFBAI, 2013). However, critics argue that the food industry is simply making positive health claims about unhealthy foods (like "contains vitamins and minerals"), rather than genuinely trying to improve children's food and activity choices (Castonguay, McKinley, & Kunkel, 2013).

Overall, the most common unhealthy effect associated with television viewing is obesity (Castonguay et al., 2013; Strasburger et al., 2009). The more television people watch, the more likely they are to be overweight or obese. There are several possible explanations for this connection (Strasburger et al., 2009). Television viewing is sedentary and burns few calories. Moreover, the more time someone spends watching television, the less time they have for more active pursuits. In addition to displacing activity, snacking often accompanies television viewing (Coon, Goldberg, Rogers, & Tucker, 2001). Zimmerman and Bell (2010), however, found that exposure to television advertising was the best predictor of obesity among children.

As children enter adolescence, new concerns about media effects center on negative body images and eating disorders. Although most of the research in this area focuses on girls, there is an increasing interest in media effects on boys' sense of their bodies, too (Agliata & Tantleff-Dunn, 2004; Field et al., 2005; Ricciardelli et al., 2006). Adolescence marks the onset of puberty, which means that children's bodies are changing and hormones are raging. Adolescence also marks more interest in appearance and a desire to be attractive. Boys want to build muscle and stay lean. Girls want to be thin. Because estrogen helps bind fat, during puberty girls begin to acquire more fat, especially in the breasts and hips. The widespread incidence of anorexia (eating too little food) and bulimia (induced vomiting after overeating) has focused researchers on the media messages about body weight in the mass media.

Researchers examining the development of body image in children argue that media are one element in a group of sociocultural factors shaping perceptions of what bodies *should* look like (Clark & Tiggeman, 2007; M. P. Levine & Harrison, 2009).[4] The media message is clear: thinness is valued in our culture. Magazines, movies, music videos, video games, advertising, and television present images of women with body types that are nearly impossible to achieve (B. S. Greenberg, Eastin, Hofschire, Lachlan, & Brownell, 2003; M. P. Levine & Harrison, 2009; Strasburger et al., 2009). The ideal body type for men is also increasingly unattainable; media images portray men who are tall and lean and extremely muscular (Agliata & Tantleff-Dunn, 2004;

M. P. Levine & Harrison, 2009). People who are overweight or obese are represented far less often than they appear in the real world (M. P. Levine & Harrison, 2009). Furthermore, fatness is portrayed as deviant. Few overweight women are included as main characters in situation comedies, but when they are, male characters frequently criticize their appearance; when overweight men are depicted, they make fun of their own bodies but are not insulted by other characters (Fouts & Burggraf, 2000).

Adolescents may be especially sensitive to media images of thinness because they experience a good deal of anxiety about their physical appearance and attractiveness to potential romantic partners (Clark & Tiggeman, 2006, 2007). Researchers now believe that body dissatisfaction may develop even younger. Clark and Tiggeman (2006) found that 9- to 12-year-old girls are already immersed in "appearance culture," and engaging in discussions about weight and dieting with their peers. Magazines targeting preteen and teenage girls capitalize on these concerns; how to improve physical appearance is the main topic in most of these magazines (Balletine & Ogle, 2005; Strasburger et al., 2009) and on their corresponding web sites (Labre & Walsh-Childers, 2003). The media carry a wealth of messages that reinforce thinness, and also suggest products designed to help shape a "better" body. There has been an increase in women's fitness magazines in recent years that emphasize ways to improve physical appearance. Diet books frequently reach the best-seller lists. Health clubs and diet centers advertise regularly on television. Advertisements of diet products have dramatically increased (Strasburger et al., 2009).

There is some evidence that the mass media contribute to unhealthy negative body image and disordered eating behaviors (M. P. Levine & Harrison, 2009). Studies have found that girls who read fashion magazines are more likely to express body dissatisfaction and lower self-esteem (Clay, Vignoles, & Dittmar, 2005; M. P. Levine & Harrison, 2009). Men and women who internalize the media's appearance standards report higher levels of body dissatisfaction and, for women, higher levels of anorexia nervosa and bulimia (Harrison & Hefner, 2006; Ricciardelli et al., 2006; Strasburger et al., 2009). Among young men, a relationship exists between media use and risky behaviors such as excessive exercise and use of steroids (Smolak, Murnen, & Thompson, 2005). Most of the effects described above are unintentional. However, with the growth of the Internet and then social networking sites, a number of pro-anorexia groups celebrate eating disorders as a lifestyle choice (M. P. Levine & Harrison, 2009; Norris et al., 2006).

Alcohol

Television presents drinking alcoholic beverages as a common, attractive, adult activity. Not only are alcoholic beverages the most common type of drink on television and music videos (Ashby & Rich, 2005; Roberts et al., 2002), they are also the most frequently advertised beverage in televised sports (Center for Alcohol Marketing and Youth, 2003). Drinking is a common element of prime-time television (Gerbner, 2001) and movies (Walsh-Childers & Brown, 2009). Some scholars estimate that children and adolescents see 1,000 to 2,000 ads for beer and wine each year (Jernigan, 2006; American Academy of Pediatrics, 2006). The Center for Alcohol Marketing and Youth (CAMY) found that youth exposure to alcohol advertising increased 71% between 2001 and 2009, in large part because the distilled spirits industry lifted its self-imposed ban against television advertising (CAMY, 2010). Drinkers are typically portrayed as attractive, successful, and adventurous, and alcohol is associated with romance, adventure, camaraderie, and humor (Strasburger et al., 2009). Although drinking is legal only for those age 21 or older, advertising and television programming implies that it is common for young people to drink. Moreover, drinking is most often seen as an activity without any negative consequences (Strasburger et al., 2009). Alcohol companies also attract children through interactive web sites, "give-aways" like clothes and hats with brand logos, and sponsorship of sporting events and concerts (Walsh-Childers & Brown, 2009). Increasingly, teenagers are exposed to pictures on social networking sites of other people drinking or passed out (National Center on Addiction & Substance Abuse, 2012, p. 11).

The pervasiveness and glamor of these images of alcohol lead to concerns about underage drinking and abuse. Research suggests these concerns are legitimate. Several recent studies conclude that exposure to alcohol advertising increases the chances that young people will begin drinking at an earlier age (Ellickson, Collins, Hambarsoomians, & McCaffrey, 2005; Henriksen et al., 2008; Snyder et al., 2006; Stacy et al., 2004). Adolescents who are exposed to a lot of alcohol advertising also believe that drinkers in real life share the characteristics of the people in the ads (attractive, fun loving, sexy), and have more positive "alcohol expectancies" than those youth who are not heavily exposed to such ads (Strasburger et al., 2009; Walsh-Childers & Brown, 2009). Alcohol expectancies are the results that children and adolescents believe will happen if they drink. Positive alcohol expectancies are related to an earlier onset of drinking alcohol, and are also predictive of developing problem drinking behaviors (Jernigan, 2006; Walsh-Childers & Brown, 2009).

Alcohol producers argue that they do not intend to influence the amount of alcohol that young people drink, but rather that the intention of their advertising is simply to influence brand choice (Jernigan, 2006). However, recent longitudinal studies have found connections between exposure to alcohol advertisements and adolescent drinking. Ellickson et al. (2005) found that exposure to alcohol advertising as a 7th grader was predictive of the frequency of alcohol consumption in 9th grade. Another study found that exposure to alcohol ads in 6th grade was related to an intention to drink, or actual drinking, in 7th grade (R. L. Collins, Ellickson, McCaffrey, & Hambarsoomians, et al., 2007). A third piece of research with 7th graders showed that more exposure to alcohol advertising resulted in a 44% increased risk of drinking beer, 34% more risk of drinking wine or hard liquor, and a 26% chance of binge drinking (Stacy et al., 2004).

Tobacco

During 2011, the tobacco industry spent $8.37 billion on advertising and promotions (Federal Trade Commission, 2013). Tobacco companies have to constantly cultivate new smokers to replace those who die or quit smoking (Strasburger, 2012). Given that 90% of smokers begin using cigarettes before the age of 18, these marketing efforts are largely targeted to young people (U.S. Department of Health and Human Services, 2012). And this is despite the passage of the 2009 Family Smoking Prevention and Tobacco Control Act, which gave the Food and Drug Administration (FDA) power to regulate tobacco products including restrictions on marketing to youth. Cigarette advertisements have been banned from broadcast radio and television since the early 1970s, but tobacco companies still had a promotional presence on television in the form of sponsorship of sporting events until the 2009 law went into effect the following year. Companies still continue to advertise in magazines and other traditional media, but there is increasing emphasis on other forms of marketing such as point-of-purchase campaigns in retail stores and gas stations (Henriksen et al., 2010; Walsh-Childers & Brown, 2009). Internet marketing is also prevalent; cigarette and smokeless tobacco companies actively maintain brand-specific web sites with features to attract regular visits such as games, coupons, and information about forthcoming products (Campaign for Tobacco-Free Kids, 2011). Social media such as Facebook and YouTube are also being used to increase the visibility of tobacco products (Campaign for Tobacco-Free Kids, 2011). Increasingly, tobacco products can be purchased from vendors on the Internet, effectively circumventing age restrictions on purchases (Walsh-Childers & Brown, 2009).

Smoking also continues to be prevalent in entertainment media. A content analysis showed that about 20% of television programming features tobacco use, and positive portrayals of smoking outnumber negative ones by a margin of 10 to 1 (Christenson, Henriksen, & Roberts, 2000; Strasburger et al., 2009; Walsh-Childers & Brown, 2009). Furthermore, the characters on TV who are smokers tend to be attractive characters and central to the story line (Strasburger et al., 2009). In music videos tobacco appears only 10% of the time, less often than either alcohol or illicit drugs (Gruber, Thau, Hill, Fisher, & Grube 2005). The presence of smoking in movies, however, has made a resurgence. In a content analysis of a random sample of major films between 1950 and 2002, Glantz, Kacirk, and McCulloch (2004) found that portrayals of smoking were cut almost in half between 1950 and 1982. By 2002, these levels were back up, and even slightly *higher* than they were in the 1950s even though the rate of "real" people smoking in 2002 was nearly half that of the rate in 1950. Smoking is common even in films targeted toward younger children; Ryan and Hoerrner (2004) found that tobacco use was portrayed 106 times in 24 G-rated, animated Disney movies between 1937 and 2000. Although the researchers noted that rates of smoking declined in more recent years, many children still watch older Disney movies repeatedly on video.

Tobacco companies also aggressively use product placement to make sure that their products are used by highly visible and admired film stars (Strasburger et al., 2009). Smoking is presented as the action of glamorous, sexually attractive, independent, healthy, thin, macho, and active people (Strasburger et al., 2009; Walsh-Childers & Brown, 2009). These images may contribute to tobacco use by leading adolescents to form a positive attitude toward smoking.

It is difficult for parents to shield their children from marketing and entertainment featuring smoking. Ads at convenience stores and gas stations are generally placed at eye level for young people, and located in places that might be particularly attractive to them (i.e. near the candy) (Walsh-Childers & Brown, 2009). Researchers have documented that there are more tobacco ads placed in stores where adolescents shop frequently (Henriksen et al., 2004). While magazine advertising now accounts for only 1% of advertising expenditures for the tobacco industry, 1% of $8.37 billion still represents a sizable number of ads (Strasburger, 2012). Movie trailers on TV also contain images of tobacco use; nearly a quarter of R-rated trailers, and 7.5% of trailers for PG-13 and PG movies contain scenes depicting smoking (Healton et al., 2006). Increasingly, young people are seeing tobacco ads online as well. In 2004, 39% of U.S. middle and high school students reported they had seen ads for tobacco online (Centers for Disease Control and Prevention, 2005).

There is substantial evidence to suggest a relationship between exposure to advertising and entertainment featuring tobacco and a variety of risky or incorrect knowledge, attitudes, and behaviors about smoking. Studies show that advertising exposure leads young people to believe that all of their peers are smoking cigarettes, and that they will be more popular if they would smoke, too (Strasburger et al., 2009). Almost 40% of 8th graders believe that smoking a pack of cigarettes daily is unlikely to cause a person serious health problems (L. D. Johnston et al., 2008). Teenagers who are regularly on social networking sites are five times more likely to have used tobacco than young people who aren't on such sites (National Center on Addiction and Substance Abuse, 2012). In both the United States and England, the cigarette brands that are most heavily marketed are the best-sellers for the adolescent market (Strasburger, 2012).

In 2008, the National Cancer Institute released a study which concluded the "total weight of evidence" of many different studies, across multiple disciplines and in different countries, is sufficient to establish a *causal* relationship between exposure to tobacco marketing and portrayal in movies and increased tobacco use among young people (pp. 11–12). In a meta-analysis, Wellman and his colleagues (2006) also concluded the evidence is strong that advertising and other media content contribute to adolescent tobacco use. In fact, they estimate that fully half of young people who begin to smoke are triggered to do so by "exposure to marketing and media" (Wellman et al., 2006, p. 1293).

Sexual Values and Behaviors

Adolescence is a time of growing interest in learning about and experimenting with sex. Unfortunately, most adolescents are under informed about sex. J. D. Brown, Childers, and Waszak (1990) summarized the reasons that media may be a potent source of effects on adolescents' sexual knowledge and behavior: (a) they have little firsthand experience (either in action or observation); (b) their best sources – parents and educators – are reluctant to provide information and adolescents may be embarrassed to approach these sources; and (c) fear of appearing ignorant may lead them to rely on impersonal sources, such as the mass media. Unfortunately, media messages about sex are often inaccurate and incomplete and adolescents' interpretations of media sex may be incorrect and immature. Depictions of and discussions about sex are easily found in almost all media, but are especially prevalent in television, movies, life-style magazines, and on the Internet. The content of the mass media may become a source of effects on sexual knowledge and behavior in adolescents.

P. J. Wright, Malamuth, and Donnerstein (2012) identified two different types of sexual media content: (a) *embedded* sexual content, where the depictions or discussion of sex take place within a context of substantive nonsexual content; and (b) *explicit* sexual content, the primary intent of which is to arouse the audience by showing or describing nudity and/or sexual behaviors (p. 273). This section will primarily address the socialization effects of embedded sexual content, which is commonly found across a variety of media. In their 2005 report for the Kaiser Family Foundation, *Sex on TV 4*, Kunkel and his colleagues found the amount of sexual content on television is increasing, with more than two of three programs containing talk about sex, sexual behavior, or both (Kunkel, Eyal, Finnerty, Biely, & Donnerstein, 2005, p. 20). Because broadcast television is regulated by the Federal Communication Commission, the content on standard prime-time programming contains mostly implied sexual behavior and a lot of sexual talk and innuendo (Harris & Barlett, 2009). Cable television programming has more explicit content, because these channels are not subject to the same level of regulation.

Movies are also featuring a greater quantity and more explicit scenes of sex (Strasburger et al., 2009; Van Evra, 2004; P. J. Wright et al., 2012). In a review of the most popular movies of the last 20 years, almost one-third of these films featured between one and seven scenes of sexual behavior (Gunasekera, Chapman, & Campbell, 2005). Life-style magazines targeted at all ages of adolescents, and at both genders, also contain a good deal of material related to sex (P. J. Wright, 2009; P. J. Wright et al., 2012). Advertising also often uses sexual themes to attract attention and persuade consumers (Strasburger et al., 2009).

Not only is sexual content easily observed in the media, but its lessons are often inaccurate. In the media, sexual activity is more common among unmarried couples (Lemish, 2007; P. J. Wright et al., 2012). The risks and negative consequences of sexual activity are rarely presented or discussed. In examining prime-time television programming, Kunkel and his colleagues found that while about 90% of programs contained sexual talk and/or behavior, only 11% contained any mention or risks or responsibilities (2005). References to contraception are rare throughout the media environment (Strasburger et al., 2009; P. J. Wright et al., 2012). In a review of popular films, Gunasekera and colleagues (2005) found zero mentions of sexually transmitted disease. L. D. Taylor (2005) did not find a single article in his review of male life-style magazines (like *Maxim*) that focused on issues related to consequences of sexual behavior. On the other hand, in magazines aimed at young women, about half of the articles that dealt with sexuality mentioned possible risks such as unplanned pregnancy (Walsh-Childers, Gotthoffer, & Lepre, 2001). Despite recent changes in public opinion, homosexuality is still largely invisible in mainstream media depictions; heterosexuality is still very much the norm (J. L. Kim et al., 2007; Strasburger et al., 2009; Van Evra, 2004). An analysis of characters in prime-time television in the 2011–2012 season showed that only 2.9% of series regulars are lesbian, gay, bisexual, or transgender (GLAAD, 2012).

Concerns about the effects of sexual media content focus on its impact on the development of accurate knowledge, and of healthy sexual attitudes and behaviors. There have been studies reporting positive knowledge gain or instigation of information seeking as a result of exposure to media content (Harris & Barlett, 2009). For example, following an episode of *Friends* where an unplanned pregnancy resulted after a condom failed, 65% of teenagers who watched the show reported learning that condoms could fail (R. L. Collins, Elliott, Berry, Kanouse, & Hunter, 2003). Increased knowledge was particularly strong for teens who talked to an adult about what they saw. More often, however, media use is associated with inaccurate knowledge about sex. Increased media exposure predicts naïve beliefs about risks associated with sexual activity, including the likelihood of teen mothers finishing college and getting good-paying jobs (P. J. Wright et al., 2012). Young people who are heavy media users also overestimate the frequency with which their peers are engaging in sex, and are more likely to believe that having sex would result in positive consequences such as a gain in social status (D. A. Fisher, Hill, Grube, Bersamin, Walker, & Gruber, 2009; Harris & Barlett, 2009; Strasburger et al., 2009; P. J. Wright et al., 2012).

There is modest evidence that exposure to sexual media content is linked to attitudes about sex and sexual behaviors. Researchers have observed that greater exposure to sexual television programs is linked to positive attitudes toward sexual permissiveness and recreational sex (Strasburger et al., 2009; P. J. Wright et al., 2012). Studies of the impact of reality television dating programs such as *The Bachelor(ette)* suggest that viewers who perceive the shows as more "real" are more likely to endorse the attitudes displayed in such shows (Ferris, Smith, Greenberg, & Smith, 2007), including beliefs that dating relationships are inherently adversarial in nature (Zurbriggen & Morgan, 2006). Content analyses suggest that media messages place the responsibility for safe-sex on females rather than males. And an experimental study using television programs with or without depictions of condom use found that safe-sex messages increased female college students' positivity toward condom use, but had no effect on male students' attitudes (Farrar, 2006).

Recent large-scale longitudinal studies support the idea that sexual content in media is a contributing factor to teenagers' sexual behavior. R. L. Collins and colleagues found that young people who have a heavy diet of sexual television were twice as likely as light viewers to have intercourse over the next year – even after controlling for other possible factors (2004). Increased exposure to music, movies and magazines also predicts an earlier initiation of sexual activity (J. D. Brown et al., 2006).

Social Learning Theory

The most commonly invoked theory to explain media effects on learning behaviors is social learning theory (also known as observational learning). Social learning theory is an approach that sees mass communication as a potentially powerful agent in directing human behavior. In the simplest of terms, social learning explains that people can model the actions that they observe in the media. Social learning theory is a cognitive approach that emphasizes the importance of mental activity as a precursor to action. In fact, external factors have an impact on an individual's behavior only through that individual's cognitive activity.

Bandura (2009) pointed out that the range of human knowledge would be severely limited if it were restricted only to what we can learn from our own actions. Human learning is certainly not due solely to operant conditioning, or performing a variety of acts, and learning only those that are reinforced (much as a pigeon learns to peck at a bar in a cage in order to release food pellets). Humans have the ability to conceptualize; so, humans can learn by modeling the behaviors of others that they observe.

Learning is a key element of social learning (see Chapter 5). The theory posits long-term effects as a result of learning observed behaviors. Social learning is not a simple process, based on the simple observation of behavior followed by imitation. Social learning is a complex motivational process marked by four subprocesses: attention, retention, production, and motivation (see Figure 6.2; Bandura, 2009).

The first step in social learning is attention to a behavior presented in the mass media; one cannot learn something that he or she has not paid attention to. Although it is clear that certain media content attributes increase the likelihood of attention (e.g., salience, prevalence), Bandura (2009) pointed out that attention is selective and voluntary, based on one's goals and interests. Media actions that have functional value are more likely to be attended to because they are seen as relevant and useful.

The next subprocess in social learning is retention. This is the mental learning of the observed behavior – integrating it into prior knowledge. Similar to

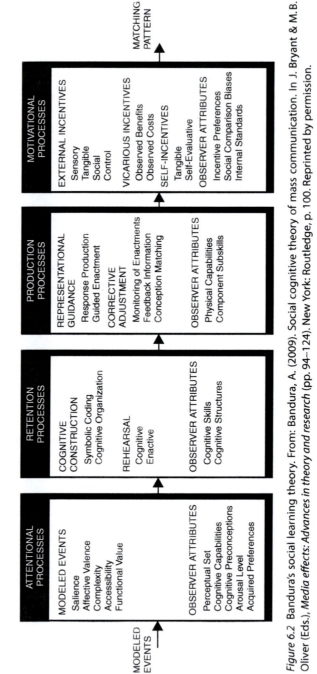

Figure 6.2 Bandura's social learning theory. From: Bandura, A. (2009). Social cognitive theory of mass communication. In J. Bryant & M.B. Oliver (Eds.), *Media effects: Advances in theory and research* (pp. 94–124). New York: Routledge, p. 100. Reprinted by permission.

the active learning models presented in Chapter 5, retention involves cognitive rehearsal, reconstruction, comparing the action to already existing behavioral schemas, and "filing" the behavior into long-term memory.

Learning a behavior does not lead automatically to replicating it. The third subprocess of social learning involves the production of the learned behavior. First, the individual must have the physical abilities and skills to replicate the action. A child might watch a commercial for a particular bouncing toy (such as a pogo stick) over and over, all the while paying a good deal of attention. But, if that child does not have the balance or physical skills to manipulate the toy, he or she will not be able to enact the behavior, even though the behavior may have been socially learned. Moreover, one must have the self-efficacy, or belief that they can enact the behavior, before attempting the action. Bandura (1986, 2009) also pointed out that social learning is more than simply duplicating an action. When the learned behavior is enacted, it often needs to be modified to suit the circumstances, and these modifications typically involve perfecting the learned skills.

Social learning recognizes that even socially learned behaviors that one can replicate may not be enacted unless one is motivated. The fourth subprocess involves various motivational incentives, or rewards (or punishments) associated with the action. If a behavior is rewarded, it is more likely to be produced; if it is punished, it becomes less likely to be produced. The rewards can be direct, self-produced, or vicarious (Bandura, 2009). Direct rewards (or punishments) involve the direct results of the action. Putting one's hand near a flame causes pain, for example; one is less likely to try that a second time. Self-produced rewards are those that emerge from self-satisfaction and a sense of self-worth. After donating blood, for example, most people feel good about themselves. Vicarious rewards (or punishments) are socially observed. A character on a television program may challenge the school bully to a fight and gain the respect of his classmates. After watching that program, that outcome might motivate a school boy to challenge the bully at his own school, even though he knows that there might be some physical pain from the fight. Vicarious reinforcement is heightened by identification with the actor and perceived realism of the media context.

Social learning theory provides a good explanation for the socialization effects of media. Some media images may be especially salient for adolescents. Thin female bodies and sexual actions, especially, can easily attract selective attention. Drinking and smoking, although not necessarily salient, may attract the attention of adolescents who are interested in learning about more adult behaviors (i.e., such actions may have functional value). The repetition of these same sorts of images and behaviors increase the likelihood that they will be learned. But, more important, television provides many more positive than negative reinforcements for harmful behaviors relating to eating, drinking alcohol, smoking, and sex. Although females are often thin, we rarely see the diet and exercise needed to maintain that slim ideal. During the 2012 Olympics, a McDonald's ad campaign featuring Olympic athletes eating fast food was roundly criticized as hypocritical (Associated Press, 2012). Alcohol use is a common occurrence in the media and is associated with celebration and good times. But, television rarely shows any of the harmful effects of drinking; even drunkenness and hangovers are often depicted as comic (Strasburger et al., 2009). Sexual activities are almost always associated with positive reinforcement; young attractive participants who experience pleasure and romance. Negative consequences of sex are essentially invisible (Walsh-Childers & Brown, 2009; P. J. Wright et al., 2012). Media content, then, provides a wealth of opportunities to socially learn inappropriate or unhealthy behaviors. The rewards associated with these behaviors may reduce inhibitions and increase adolescents' motivation to model these behaviors.

Social learning theory is fairly broad in scope. Media content can be the basis for (a) learning novel or new behaviors (change effects), (b) the facilitation or inhibition of already learned behaviors, or (c) the prompting of learned behaviors (both reinforcement effects). But social learning theory is not an omnibus theory to explain all behavioral effects of mass communication. First, social learning theory cannot explain the effects of media content that only infers an action. Direct representation of the behavior is a key component. The behavior must be able to be observed in order to be socially learned: "all modeled information must be symbolically represented if it is to be retained as a guide for future action" (Bandura, 1986, p. 48). Even abstract modeling, or extracting the rules underlying behaviors to apply to innovative situations, involves observation (Bandura, 2009). Abstract modeling involves observing a range of actions, paying attention to rule-relevant aspects of the action, and extracting the underlying rule common to the actions. Bandura (2009) pointed out that abstract modeling is enhanced when "models verbalize their thoughts aloud as they engage in problem-solving activities" (p. 70). So, social learning theory cannot explain the acquisition of behaviors that are not modeled in the mass media, such as bulimia, the use of many birth control devices, or sexual acts (which are not explicitly represented except in pornography).

Second, mere exposure is not sufficient for social learning. Observational learning is an active and motivated learning process that involves far more than simply observing a behavior and imitating it. This is not to say that mere exposure to modeled activities is, in itself, sufficient to produce observational learning. Not all stimulation that impinges on individuals is necessarily observed by them, and even if it is noticed, what is registered may not be retained for any length of time (Bandura, 1986, pp. 76–77). Social learning is a process that involves cognitive action and skills. Because social learning posits long-term effects, the modeled behavior must have some kind of cognitive representation. Some behaviors can be observed many times and not learned. Moreover, even an imitated behavior may not be socially learned. Mimicry is not social learning. Mimicry involves direct imitation of, or matching, a behavior to be imitated. Mimicry is usually a short-term effect, occurring immediately after the behavior. Without cognitive activity and mental representation of the rules underlying the action, the behavior is unlikely to be replicated in the long term. Socialization effects of the mass media are not based on short-term mimicry.

The focus on social learning as the result of cognitive activity also limits social learning to observers who have the necessary cognitive skills to learn. According to Bandura (1986), "observational learning involved acquiring multiple subskills in selective observation, symbolic coding and rehearsal, coordinating sensory-motor and conceptual-motor systems, and judging probable outcomes for adopting another's behavior" (p. 81). Although even infants can mimic adult actions, they do not possess the cognitive abilities to retain, learn, and apply the behaviors in the long term. So, very young children are not likely to socially learn behavior from television. Young children do not have the cognitive abilities to selectively attend to television or remember very much of what they have observed (Van Evra, 2004). Children under age 4 may have difficulty socially learning from television, especially if the behaviors are complex (Fisch, 2009). Bandura et al., (Bandura, Ross, & Ross, 1963) observed evidence of social learning with their sample of nursery school children, but these children averaged over age 4 (53 months). Observed behaviors in children younger than that are probably based on mimicry, not social learning.

Third, media content is only one source of social learning. Children may be exposed to a good deal of media content, but they also typically have a good many opportunities to observe parents, siblings, peers, and teachers. These presumably positive models should exert more influence on children's behavior because of salience, relevance, utility, and motivational factors. When television portrayals contradict what they observe in real life, children tend to reject television models as unrealistic, reducing the likelihood of social learning. Parental coviewing can also have an impact of social learning from television. Parents can make comments that reinforce the salience, relevance, and utility of prosocial behaviors (e.g., "Look what a good girl she is to help her brother") or diminish the reality, relevance, or reward of antisocial behaviors ("Do you think he felt bad when he realized he hurt the puppy?").

Social Learning as a Conditional Model of Effects

Social learning theory has some aspects of the cognitive-transactional model; the nature of the media content is important to understanding media effects. Bandura (2009) pointed out that the action must be observable, salient, and simple enough for the audience to comprehend. It is clear, however, that these media content attributes do not intrude on automatic attention. Social learning is primarily understood as an observer-motivated process. So, it falls clearly in the conditional model of media effects. Audience variables are central to understanding social learning.

Bandura (2009) listed several of these variables; most reflect individual differences: (a) selective exposure based on preferences, arousal level, and perceptual abilities; (b) abilities to learn based on cognitive skills; (c) abilities to replicate the act based on physical capabilities and self-efficacy; and (d) motivation based on perceptions of rewards and preferences for incentives. Social category variables may also have relevance to social learning because social categories affect selective attention to and perception of media content. Age, as a social category, may reflect cognitive abilities and experiences. Social relationships may be important in understanding social learning effects. Social connections with others may serve as alternate, more salient models of behavior. Comments during media exposure may highlight certain behaviors, distract children from other behaviors, or lead children to discount certain behaviors as irrelevant. Social relationships may have their most important impact, however, on motivational processes. The social connections that we have with others can certainly serve as important normative influences that affect our willingness to act and our perceptions about the rewards and punishments associated with our actions (e.g., Fishbein & Ajzen, 1975). Adolescents, for example, may be more likely to drink alcohol or have sex if they expect that their peers will reward them for doing so (Walsh-Childers & Brown, 2009).

What Can be Done?

Every effort to restrict expression – or to encourage more content of a particular sort – reflects a desire to influence the way media affect us. Particularly when children are involved, the government is often asked to develop laws or policies to intervene. There are, for example, rules about the amount and type of advertising that can air during children's programming. Limitations on when, where, and how tobacco and alcohol can be advertised also reflect a desire to minimize children's use of such products.

But the First Amendment guarantee of freedom of speech and of the press strongly limits government regulation of media content. So there are other mechanisms by which we, as a society, try to limit the harm (and encourage positive results) of media messages:

- Government "by raised eyebrow": Members of the government can signal their concern about a particular aspect of media by holding hearings, commissioning a study, or issuing requests for public comments about a topic of concern. The threat that Congress or the Federal Communications Commission (FCC) might take action is often enough to encourage industry members to take their own steps to address the issue. For example, from the early days of television there have been a series of

Congressional hearings about the impact of television violence. In the late 1990s, this ultimately led to television executives agreeing to develop and implement a ratings system which is still in use today.

- Industry self-regulation: Members of media industries, usually under pressure from government or public opinion, can take steps to address concerns about particular aspects of media content. Examples of industry self-regulation include the content ratings systems of movies, television, video games, and music. In 2000, movie industry executives also promised to stop targeting advertising at children who are younger than the ratings of movies deem appropriate as audience members.

- Educational efforts: Undertaken by government bodies, educational institutions, or by public interest groups, many programs exist to help make members of the public more educated about how to protect themselves from the negative consequences of media use. The Media Literacy Project is one of the best-known groups seeking to make children more critical consumers of media, and to encourage them to produce media telling their own stories.

- Advocacy groups: There are many not-for-profit groups that seek to influence government policy about media, or to pressure media industry members to take corrective action. For example, nearly every ethnic group has some sort of organization seeking more or better portrayals of members of their group. The Order Sons of Italy in America, for example, protests the stereotypes of Italian Americans in the media. Other advocacy groups focus on changing media laws and policies; the group Action for Children's Television was instrumental in the passage of the Children's Television Act of 1990.

- Individual strategies: Media scholars also study the effectiveness of individual-level strategies for coping with media effects. One major area of research regards *parental mediation*, or strategies that parents use in interactions with their children about media. There are three commonly recognized forms of parental mediation. The first is often called active mediation, and it refers to parents commenting directly about particular content, sharing their opinions about particular characters or story lines. The second is restrictive guidance, when parents set limits on the amount or type of media exposure. The last form of parental mediation is coviewing, which involves parents and children using media together.

Summary

Scholars of media effects need to be aware of the media content available to children at various ages. We need to be concerned about media content that children have easy access to, including media not specifically designed to attract a child audience. With the ready availability of mobile devices and the Internet, children are increasingly using multiple media simultaneously (Rideout et al., 2010). It is also important to remember that children use and interact with different media at particular times in their lives. Television use, for example, declines as children become older (D. R. Anderson et al., 2001).

It is also important to remember that all socialization effects of the mass media are not negative. Socialization is a positive, functional aspect of the mass media (C. R. Wright, 1986). Television can teach prosocial messages (e.g., Strasburger et al., 2009, pp. 117–144). For example, children's programming can have important, prosocial effects on the development of empathy and tolerance (Lemish, 2007).

Various models of media effects suggest different remedies to negative socialization effects. To reduce the more automatic effects of the cumulative and cognitive-transactional models, there have been suggestions that television programs and other media directed toward children and adolescents be improved. If children have well-produced content made available for them, they may be less likely to watch adult-oriented programs with inappropriate themes. Media producers should also consider the lessons that programs teach; negative as well as positive consequences of behaviors should be depicted.

Models of media effects that focus on active learning as the basis of socialization focus attention on the importance of media literacy. According to the Media Literacy Project, media literacy is a set of skills that provide individuals "the ability to access, analyze, evaluate and create messages of all kinds" (Media Literacy Project, 2014). These skills serve as barriers to negative effects by helping young people (and adults) to (a) understand how media messages create meaning; (b) identify who created a particular media message; (c) recognize what the media maker wants us to believe or do; (d) name the "tools of persuasion" used; (e) recognize bias, spin, misinformation, and lies; (f) discover the part of the story that's not being told; (g) evaluate media messages based on our own experiences, beliefs, and values; (h) create and distribute our own media messages; and (i) become advocates for change in our media system. These skills should lead to a more critical and aware use of the mass media.

Notes

1 Some of the most popular and enduring children's programs over the years have underrepresented women. How many female Muppets have been main characters on *Sesame Street*?

2 Blakeborough (2008), though, describes how *The Simpsons* uses humor and irony to critique and poke fun at the stereotypes about older adults in our culture.

3 This is the central tenet of the "contact hypothesis." For a meta-analysis on the effectiveness of intergroup contact as a method for reducing prejudice and bias, see Pettigrew and Tropp (2006).

4 Other sociocultural factors include parents and peers. Personality and biological factors are also believed to play a role in developing body image in children (Clark & Tiggeman, 2007).

7   EFFECTS OF VIOLENT MEDIA CONTENT

The 2012 Sandy Hook Elementary School shooting in Newtown, Connecticut, capped a year marked by mass violence.[1] Once again, faced with public concerns, politicians moved to identify and eliminate the causes of aggression in the young. Fingers pointed at easy availability of guns and graphic depictions of violence in movies, television, and video games. Congress considered action to increase restrictions on gun sales. Reports that the Sandy Hook shooter practiced his shooting skills with violent video games (e.g., Payne, 2013) focused popular discussion and public policy on the effects of media violence. The National Rifle Association's (NRA) press release following the tragedy blamed "a callous, corrupt and *corrupting* shadow industry that sells, and sows, violence against its own people" (LaPierre, 2012). In the NRA press release, Wayne LaPierre argued that "vicious, violent video games [including "Kindergarten Killers"], "blood-soaked slasher films," and "a thousand music videos that portray life as a joke and murder as a way of life" promote violence in U.S. society.[2]

Widespread concern about media violence is not new. DeFleur and Dennis (1994) reminded us that a "legacy of fear" has surrounded the adoption of almost every new mass medium. In the late 1880s, several states passed laws prohibiting the distribution of books, magazines, and newspapers that described in words or pictures accounts of crime or bloodshed (Saunders, 1996). Even comic books did not escape public scrutiny. In 1954, a Senate judiciary subcommittee led by Estes Kefauver investigated the impact of comic books on juvenile delinquency. And, over the past 50 years, Congress has held over 40 hearings about the impact of media violence (Cooper, 1996; Kenworthy, 2010; Saunders, 1996). Based on the mandate of the 1996 Telecommunications Bill, after January 1, 2000, all television sets with screens 13 inches or larger were equipped with a V-chip, which allowed parents to block programs based on the TV Parental Guidelines ratings system.[3]

Movie Ratings: Is It the Sex or the Violence?

The Motion Picture Association of America has perhaps the most recognized content rating system. This is a purely voluntary system established in 1968 that the MPAA holds serves as a useful tool for parents and as a protection for artistic, creative, and political expression. The system is rather simple; raters (average parents, according to the MPAA) watch films and assign one of these ratings:

- G – General Audiences: All ages admitted
- PG – Parental Guidance Suggested: Some material may not be suitable for children
- PG-13 – Parents Strongly Cautioned: Some material may be inappropriate for children under 13
- R – Restricted. Under 17 requires accompanying parent of adult guardian
- NC-17 – No One 17 and Under Admitted

The ratings system has been criticized. Some argue that there is a "forbidden fruit effect," so that adolescents (especially) find age-restricted movies more appealing. More interesting, however, are assertions that age-restricted ratings are more commonly applied to sexual content than violence content. The findings of two studies support that conclusion. Leone (2002, 2004) conducted a content analysis of 210 scenes and sequences that were part of 13 NC-17 rated versions of films, but not in the R-rated versions. (He assumes that these were removed to gain the more accessible and profitable rating.) Of the deleted sequences, most (61%) were sexual, nonviolent sequences; 25.6% were violent, nonsexual sequences; 13.3% were both sexual and violent. He then found that the MPAA's own descriptions of movies stressed the violent aspects of R-rated films and the sexual aspects of NC-17 rated films: Violence was mentioned in 80.8% of R-rated movie descriptions but in only 30.8% of NC-17-rated ones. Sexuality was mentioned in just over half (57.7%) of R-rated movie descriptions but in 96.2% of NC-17 rated ones. Although most parents find the MPAA ratings useful, there are concerns that the rating system allows easier access to violent content, which can be quite harmful to children.

There are good reasons to be concerned about the effects of media violence. Violence is common in media content. The Cultural Indicators group has analyzed prime-time and weekend daytime television dramatic programming since 1967. Over the years, the findings are remarkably consistent (Signorielli, 2003). Between 1967 and 1985, about three-quarters of all prime-time dramatic programs contained violence; violent acts occurred about 5 times an hour. Between 1993 and 2001, about 60% of all prime-time programs contained violence with about 4.5 acts per hour. Basic cable television programs are even more violent; in 2010 basic cable programs showed 9.1 acts of violence each hour (Signorielli & Shanahan, 2011). Between 1976 and 1985, around 90% of all Saturday morning children's programs included violent acts for an average of about 20 acts per hour. Signorielli (2008) found that 86% of 2007 Saturday morning programs on the broadcast networks, the Cartoon network, Nickelodeon, and Disney showed violent acts. She estimated that a child would see about 23 acts of violence each hour of viewing Saturday morning programs.

The National Television Violence Study (Center for Communication and Social Policy, 1998) found a "strong consistency" in patterns of violence in their three-year study of broadcast and cable television from 1994 to 1997. In all, from 58% to 61% of all television programs contained violence. Programs broadcast on public television were the least violent; only about 1 in 5 showed violent acts. About one-half of the broadcast television programs (51%) included violence. Premium cable, however, was the most violent over the time of the study; just over 4 out of every 5 programs (83%) were violent. In fact, 73% of the programs had so many violent acts (over 9 violent interactions) that they can be consider "saturated" with violence (S.L. Smith, Nathanson, & Wilson, 2002). Clearly, television programming is filled with violence.

More recently, a content analysis of the 50 most popular shows with children during 2006–2007 found that 92% of the shows contained social aggression. Social aggression is not physical violence, but "emotional violence," gossip and critical and disparaging remarks. Social aggression can damage self-esteem and cause psychological or emotional damage. On average, the authors found 14 acts of social aggression per hour, about one every 4 minutes (Martins & Wilson, 2012).

Few analyses have quantified the violence in popular film; however, anyone who has watched action films has noticed how common graphic violence is in this genre. The National Television Violence Study suggests how violent movies are. Of all the program genres, movies (which often are broadcasts of feature films) were the most violent: 89% of movies contained violence. J.T. Hamilton's (1998) summaries of data from the National Coalition on Television Violence illustrated that movies can be quite violent. Although some prime-time television genres, such as action-adventure (27.6 violent acts per hour), western (22.6), science fiction (22.8), and mystery (25.5), as a whole, have more violent acts per hour than movies rated PG (20.1 violent acts per hour) or PG-13 (19.8), R-rated movies are quite a bit more violent than television fare: about 33.1 acts per hour.

Violence appears to be common even in nonviolent film genres. Scholars found that almost 19% of the films in a sample of comic films from 1951 to 2000 contained violence (McIntosh, Murray, Murray, & Manian, 2003). Yokota and Thompson (2000) examined the content of 74 G-rated animated feature films released between 1937 and 1999. They found that every film contained at least one violent act and focused 9.5 minutes on violence. A more recent study analyzed the top three films since 1950 and presence of guns in films with PG-13 ratings since 1985, the first year of that rating (Bushman, Jamieson, Weitz, & Romer, 2013). All these studies discovered that the amount of violence significantly increased over time. Bushman and his colleagues (2013) found that gun violence specifically has more than tripled since 1985 and that "PG-13-rated films have contained as much or more violence as R-rated films" (p. 1014). So, even family-oriented films are becoming more violent.

The mainstreaming of violent video games also raises concerns about the impact of media violence (Power, 2009). The video game industry has responded to concerns about the appropriateness of violence in the games by establishing a voluntary ratings system. But, research shows that even games deemed appropriate for everyone (rated E) include substantial violence: Thompson and Haninger (2001) found that 64% of the E-rated games in their sample contained violent acts. T-rated games (suitable for 13-year-olds) are even more violent: Haninger and Thompson's analysis (2004) observed that 98% of these games include intentional violence, 90% rewarded or required the player to injure characters, 69% rewarded or required the player to kill, and 42% depicted blood.

Public convictions that violent media content contributes to violence in society are supported by anecdotal reports of criminals' media use, naïve beliefs in the connections between crime rates and media violence, media reports of "copycat" crimes, and the publicized reports of some highly visible research. News reports often mention connections between crimes and media content. Television programs, such as *Sopranos*, *Law & Order*, and wrestling, and heavy metal music, such as that by Judas Priest and Ozzy Osbourne, are often blamed for violent imitated acts (Cooper, 2007). Media content is often accused of serving as "training manuals" for violent crime. Video games such as *Grand Theft Auto*, and in the case of the Columbine High School shooters, *Doom*, have been blamed for murder. The Sandy Hook School shooter was reported to play *Call of Duty* and *Starcraft*. Violent scenes in movies such as *Natural Born Killers* and *The Matrix* have been linked to "imitation crimes" (Cooper, 2007; Surette, 1998).

The Matrix Defense

The Matrix was one of the top box office hits of 1999. Its science fiction premise was that humans have been conquered by machines that keep their prisoners docile by having their minds "live" in an artificial reality – the matrix. The plot focuses on the heroes, who use violence to try to escape the matrix. Many thought that the premise of this film was unique. One thing we know: it changed the landscape of legal defenses for violence committed by those who imitate media content.

Defendants over the years have claimed that media content "made" them commit crimes. Ronny Zamora's attorney, for example, argued that his client was "intoxicated" by television and couldn't be held accountable for murdering his 83-year-old neighbor. Lionel Tate, a 12-year-old Florida boy, was convicted for killing a 6-year-old girl. His defense was that he was just wrestling – using the moves he saw on television. Until *The Matrix*, defenses like these failed based on First Amendment grounds or the inability to show that media content "incited" violence. Now, two murder defendants have been acquitted using the "*Matrix* insanity defense" (Cooper, 2007).

Vadim Mieseges, a San Francisco computer science student, killed and dismembered his landlord. He claimed that he had been sucked in the Matrix through his computer. He believed that his landlord was one of the overlord machines. Tonda Ansley, an Ohio woman, shot her land-lord. She claimed that her dreams revealed that her landlord, a vam-pire, was committing arson for profit in the Matrix. Both Mieseges and Ansley were found not guilty by reason of insanity and committed to mental institutions. Although they were not convicted of their crimes, both suffered consequences from their efforts to rid the world of "evil machines."

Perceptions are common that our violent media culture has bred a genera-tion which is desensitized to crime and mayhem. These perceptions, though, are inaccurate. First of all, even though violence in the media has been rather constant over the years, violent crime continues to decline, including in the group most likely to play violent video games, males age 10–24 (see the Bureau of Justice Statistics key facts page, 2011).[4] Overall, violent crime in the U.S. dropped substantially in the 1990s (Levitt, 2004), and continues to be below the high rates of earlier decades. Despite the publicity accompany-ing school shootings, very few young people are in danger at school. Less than 2% of youth homicides occur at school (Dinkes, Cataldi, Lin-Kelly, & Snyder, 2007). The Secret Service analysis of school shooters (Vossekuil, Fein, Reddy, Borum, & Modzeleski, 2002) observed that only 12% of the shooters had an interest in violent video games; 27% had an interest in violent mov-ies. Moreover, there is an inverse relationship between the Nielsen ratings of violent television programs and criminal violence rates across 281 geographic areas (Messner, 1986).

It is clear that the most popular television programs and movies are not the most violent.[5] Most people don't find media violence appealing or entertain-ing (A.J. Weaver, 2011). Advertisers should be concerned about research that suggests that sex and violence in television programs means that viewers are less likely to remember the ads in the programs (Bushman & Bonacci, 2002). But media violence does appeal to certain demographic groups – those most valued by advertisers. The most desirable target audiences are people age 18 to 49, especially women age 18 to 34. Although these age groups spend less

money than older adults, advertisers believe that they are more susceptible
to advertising influence because they have not established product and brand
preferences. Moreover, they watch less television overall, so advertisers are
more interested in funding programs they are likely to watch. Young people are the largest market for media violence. According to Hamilton (1998,
p. 55) "nearly 75% of the heavy viewers of violence programming [e.g., fictional crime, real-life police programs, and action-adventure films] are con-
centrated in three of the demographic groups, males 18–34, females 18–34
(21% of heavy viewers), and males 35–49 (19%)" (p. 55).

Certain scholarly reports capture political and public attention to support the connection between media violence and aggression in society. One
analysis that has received perhaps the most publicity connects television and
homicide rates. Centerwall's (1989a, 1989b) reports compared Western countries' homicide rates between 1945 and 1975 to that of South Africa during
that same time period. Centerwall, a medical doctor, took an epidemiological
approach to the effects of media violence. He explored how the introduction of television into Western societies was associated with an increase in
the homicide rate. He used South Africa as a "control" population; because
of concerns that English-language imported television programming would
undermine the Afrikaans language of the White minority, television broadcasting in South Africa was prohibited until 1975. After controlling for several
alternate explanations, such as economic growth, gun ownership, alcohol-
ism, urbanization, and age distribution of the population, Centerwall found
that the homicide rates among Whites in many Western nations skyrocketed
15 years after television ownership increased, but remained fairly stable in
South Africa. Centerwall concluded that television alone was the cause for
the increase in homicide; he believes that about one-half of the violent crime
in the United States can be attributed to television violence. He explains that
television violence desensitizes child-viewers and makes them more violent.
Centerwall also believes that homicide is committed only by the most violent in society. Television, then, increases the number of children who are
violent enough to kill. As these children become older (accounting for the
15-year lag in homicides), they commit homicides.

Centerwall has been a witness before Congressional hearings at least twice
(Cooper, 1996) and his analyses have been widely cited. Communication
scholars have been relatively uncritical, however, of his findings. Some comments about his work are warranted. Although Centerwall was limited in
locating an industrialized society without television, South Africa might not
have been an accurate comparator to Western nations. Under apartheid, South
Africa was a highly repressive and controlled society. Pally (1994) suggested
that because South African Whites were such an overwhelming minority, a
"siege" mentality might have reduced aggression among that group. Figlio
(n.d.) points out that South Africa's self-isolation and climate of repression
limits the credibility of White crime rates.[6] Centerwall's data ignore some of
the realities of homicide rates. For example, his use of standardized homicide

rates obscures the fact that South Africa had a much higher homicide rate than the United States before television was widely adopted. Moreover, his analyses use data beginning in the mid-1940s, a time of great societal cohesion in Western nations, due to the end of World War II. In fact, homicide rates in the 1940s had dropped dramatically from the 1930s (when homicide rates were among the highest historically).[7] Nor can Centerwall's method explain the current trend of decreasing homicide rates. Because his analytical technique was a relatively simple bivariate graphical analysis, Centerwall's findings could well be the result of a spurious correlation, or a "relationship" between two variables that is really due to the impact of a third variable.[8]

Although politicians and the public rely on anecdotal evidence and widespread beliefs that the preponderance of media violence must be linked to societal aggression, scholars are more convinced by evidence provided by the results of field and laboratory experiments and meta-analyses that consistently demonstrate a connection between exposure to violent media content and aggressive behavior. There is a general and widespread conclusion among most media scholars that there is a connection between media violence and aggressive behavior. Although no reputable media scholar holds that media violence is the largest reason for violence in society, most accept that media violence is a small, but significant contributor to aggressive behavior. This consensus is based on bodies of research and conclusions from large-scale research analyses, including the 1972 Surgeon General's report (Surgeon General's Scientific Advisory Committee, 1972), the 1982 report from the National Institute of Mental Health (NIMH, 1982), Centers for Disease Control (1991), National Academy of Science (1993), the American Psychological Association (1993), the 2001 Surgeon General Report on Youth Violence (Department of Health and Human Services, 2001), and the joint statement of the American Academy of Pediatrics, American Medical Association, the American Academy of Child and Adolescent Psychiatry, and the American Psychological Association (American Academy of Pediatrics, 2000). As summarized in the 1982 NIMH report: "After 10 more years of research, the consensus among most of the research community is that violence on television does lead to aggressive behavior by children and teenagers who watch the programs" (p. 6).

This conclusion is drawn over 35 years of research using a variety of methods and measures. Especially compelling are the results of meta-analyses, a statistical aggregation of research results across a large number of studies that assesses direction and size of effects. Meta-analyses of media violence studies conducted from 1956 through 2007 have consistently found a significant effect of media violence on violent behavior and attitudes (Andison, 1977; Bushman & Anderson, 2001; Christensen & Wood, 2007; Hearold, 1986; Paik & Comstock, 1994; W. Wood et al., 1991). Also notable are the results of longitudinal studies that conclude that television viewing in early years leads to aggressive behavior in later years. The late introduction of television to a Canadian town, for example, gave researchers the chance to observe how children respond to viewing. Among other findings, direct observation of children in playground activities revealed that children became significantly more physically and verbally aggressive 2 years after the introduction of television (Joy et al., 1986). Panel studies, which examined television viewing and aggression in the same children over time, have also concluded that television leads to aggressive behavior (e.g., Huesmann & Eron, 1986; Huesmann, Moise-Titus, Podolski, & Eron, 2003; Lefkowitz, Eron, Walder, & Huesmann, 1977; Robertson, McAnally, & Hancox, 2013).[9]

There are some scholars who deny the causal conclusion between media violence and aggressive behavior (e.g., C. J. Ferguson, Ivory, and Beaver, 2013; Freedman, 1984; Gauntlett, 2005; Olson, 2004; Wurtzel & Lometti, 1987), but most interest in media violence has moved from determining if violent media content has an effect to how its effects occur. The variety of contingent conditions that intervene in the effects of violent media content (e.g., Paik & Comstock, 1994; Van Evra, 2004; T. M. Williams, 1986) pointed out that the dominant model of media effects of media violence is the conditional model. Several theories have evolved to explain the conditions under which viewing violent media content may lead to aggressive behavior.

Theories of Behavioral Effects of Violent Media Content

Cognitive Theories

There is a group of theories that base their explanation for violent media content's effects on a cognitive process. That is, people's aggressive behavior grows out of mental activity generated as a result of, or in response to, violent media content. These theories rely on three types of mental activity as the basis for aggressive behavior: learning, attitude formation, and priming.

Social Learning

The dominant cognitive approach to connecting violent media content and aggressive behavior is based on learning. That is, through exposure to media content, viewers learn how and when to act aggressively. These learning approaches are based on the same learning processes discussed in Chapter 5. Learning is a conditional process that involves mental engagement and effort; it is not the result of passive exposure to media content. Learning also is a relatively long-term effect, so learning approaches assume that effects of learning media violence are fairly enduring.

The most prominent cognitive theory to explain how watching violent media content translates into aggressive behavior is social learning theory (also known as observational learning; see Chapter 6). Bandura (1986, 2009) explained that people learn, not only through direct experience, but also by observing others. Media content provides many opportunities for observational learning; unfortunately, many of these involve antisocial actions. Because violence is so common in the visual media, television, movies, and video provide many models for aggressive actions. There are two keys to social learning: People will be more likely to learn behaviors that are relevant and adaptive.

Relevant behaviors are those that have some connection to one's life. So, social learning is enhanced when viewers perceive the content to be more realistic (e.g., Potter, 1988). In general, violence in film and video is more likely to be learned than animated violence (e.g., Hapkiewicz & Stone, 1974); violence in news has stronger social learning effects than violence in drama (e.g., Atkin, 1983). Social learning is also enhanced when the violent action is depicted as justified. Good reasons for violent actions heighten the perceived utility of violent behavior, making it more likely to be used in the future. In experimental settings, justified violence has been found to have significantly larger effects on aggression than unjustified violence (e.g., Berkowitz & Powers, 1978). Relevance is also increased when the violent actor is similar to the viewer. There is evidence that identification with a violent actor may increase social learning of aggression. Children, for example, are more likely to imitate characters of the same age and gender (e.g., Bandura et al., 1963; Hicks, 1965; Jose & Brewer, 1984).

Another key to social learning is that people learn behaviors that are adaptive, or those that will help them in their own lives. So, people will model violent behavior if it is rewarded; they will not model violent behavior that is punished (Bandura et al., 1963; Lando & Donnerstein, 1978). Social sanctions can be powerful inhibitors of violent behavior. But, there are indications that simple lack of punishment (even in the absence of explicit rewards) is enough to trigger social learning (e.g., Walters & Parke, 1964). Bandura (2009) explained that much media violence makes aggressive behavior appear more adaptive by depicting violence as morally justified, relatively inconsequential, and by depersonalizing the victim and thus reducing the blame on the actor.

Although recent extensions of social learning have suggested that people can learn abstract processes that underlie actions by simply observing the action (Bandura, 2009), social learning theory has its greatest applicability and support in explaining enactments that resemble the media depiction. That is, social learning theory explains why a child might imitate wrestling moves after watching those same moves on televised wrestling. But, it is less successful in explaining why a child punches another after watching a wrestling match in which there is no punching. It is also important to remember that social learning is learning; a process that involves attention, comprehension, and elaboration (Bandura, 2009). Still, visual media offer many images that enhance the likelihood that viewers will socially learn violent acts. Content analyses consistently demonstrate that violence is the behavior of attractive, successful, and rewarded characters (e.g., B.J. Wilson et al., 1997; Potter & Ware, 1987). Moreover, violence is arousing and likely to attract and hold attention, which increases the likelihood that it will be learned (e.g., A. Lang, 1990).

Information-Processing Model

It is clear that not all aggressive behavior associated with media exposure resembles the action in the media. Based on his work on youth violence, Huesmann (1986) articulated another learning model to explain the effects of media violence on aggressive behavior. Huesmann modified social learning theory to move its explanations beyond the impact of media content attributes (e.g., nature of the actor, victim, and reinforcement) and more to the context of the individual learner. The information-processing model is an adaptation of schema theory and network learning models (Chapters 2 and 4) to learning violence. According to this model, learning violent behaviors is the result of learning violent media scripts. These scripts are schemas about courses of action that are stored in memory. When retrieved, they become guides for behavior.

Like the social learning process, this information-processing model requires that media content be salient, and that viewers must pay attention, encode the action, and commit it to long-term memory (LTM). Unlike social learning theory, this approach does not hold that the scripts will be identical to the observed action. Through encoding and elaboration, scripts may become idiosyncratic or combined with other already learned scripts. So, the behaviors may deviate from the models. This approach might provide a better explanation for learning violence in the absence of explicit rewards (Huesmann, 1982). The behavior needs only to be noticeable and useful. Reinforcement also plays a different role in this model. Mental rehearsal reinforces violent scripts, more than actual rewards shown in the media. Evidence for mental rehearsal of violent scripts is found in the connection between violent fantasies and viewing aggressive media content (Huesmann & Eron, 1986).

Huesmann (1986) was clear, however, in pointing out that this information-processing model is a conditional one, based, to a large extent, on children's social development. Huesmann holds that a child's social environment affects violent television viewing as well as the acquisition of violent scripts. For example, children who are violent tend not to be popular. So, they have fewer social activities and might spend more time watching television. Children rejected by their parents might spend less time with them at home, and watch more television. And, these children might act aggressively, out of frustration. So, the acquisition of violent scripts is the interaction of television viewing within the social context.

Priming by Aggressive Media Cues

Another cognitive approach to connecting violent media content with aggressive behavior is one that stresses short-term effects. Based on schema theory and the cognitive-transactional model, violent media content can be a potent prime to activate aggressive mental scripts, which might then lead to aggressive behavior. Scholars who study priming effects of media content (e.g., Jo & Berkowitz, 1994) do not deny the potential long-term effects of social learning or information-processing models. Instead, they recognize that there is another process, a temporary one, by which aggressive cues in media content can stimulate, for a short time, aggressive scripts. Priming is the automatic activation of a preexisting schema by a salient cue in the environment. Once a schema is activated, it is, in a sense, "top of mind," and likely to affect how people think, feel, and act. So, aggressive media cues may stimulate, or prime, aggressive thoughts that can affect how people respond to the social setting.

There is a good deal of research evidence that violent media content can prime, or activate, aggressive scripts. Films with hostile interactions lead to more hostile responses in research participants (e.g., Carver, Ganellen, Froming, & Chambers, 1983). Even violent comic books, comic routines, and video games are associated with temporary aggressive thoughts and feelings (Berkowitz, 1970; Mehrabian & Wixen, 1986). Priming by violent media cues may also be an explanation for some of the short-term violence that accompanies some violent movies and sporting matches.

Further support for the aggressive cue model is provided by research that finds that the use of specific salient objects can cue aggression (Josephson, 1987). In one study, elementary school boys were shown excerpts from either a violent or nonviolent television program. The violent program began with the villains using walkie-talkies. After watching television and being frustrated by not being able to watch promised cartoons, the boys were given a chance to play floor hockey. Before playing, each boy was "interviewed" by a play-by-play commentator using either a tape recorder or a walkie-talkie. Aggression was measured by counting aggressive actions during the game. Consistent with priming, boys who watched the aggressive television program were more aggressive than boys who did not. Interestingly, among those boys who saw the aggressive program, those who were interviewed with the walkie-talkie were the most aggressive. Josephson (1987) explained that the violent television program served to activate aggressive scripts for those boys with higher levels of characteristic aggressiveness. The additional cue of the walkie-talkie, though, was an especially potent prime. Other research suggests that blood can be another aggressive prime. Participants who were high in hostility were significantly more verbally aggressive after playing a violent video game (*Hitman II: Silent Assassin*) with the "blood on" feature than those in a "no gore" condition (Krcmar & Farrar, 2009).[10]

Together with Huesmann's information-processing model, the aggressive cue approach provides a more complete explanation of long-term and short-term effects of media violence based on schematic learning. Exposure to violent media content may be one way that people acquire aggressive scripts. These scripts can become the basis for violent behaviors. People might consciously activate aggressive scripts in controlled mental processing as a way to solve solutions in the real world. Or, salient media cues might prime aggressive scripts that affect how people respond for a short period of time.

Attitude Change

Another cognitive approach to hypothesizing a relationship between violent media content and aggressive behavior focuses on the attitudes that people have toward violence. Exposure to violence in the mass media leads people to be more accepting of violence as a societal norm and as a solution to problems. In a sense, through exposure to media violence, people become disinhibited to violence (as opposed to habituation, which is discussed later in this chapter).

Media content fosters acceptance of violence because much media violence is justified, rewarded, and committed by attractive characters (Potter & Ware, 1987). Moreover, media content rarely shows the consequences of violence, leading some viewers to believe that violence is not so harmful. Research has shown that even short-term exposure to violent media content is associated with greater acceptance of violence (Dominick & Greenberg, 1972; Thomas & Drabman, 1975). Gerbner and his associates (Gerbner, Gross, Jackson-Beeck, Jeffries-Fox, & Signorielli, 1978) found that viewers who watch a lot of television were more likely to agree that it was acceptable to hit someone in anger. Other research has found that heavy television viewing is linked to beliefs that violence is more common (e.g., Morgan, Shanahan, & Signorielli, 2009).

The basis of all research on attitudes is that attitudes are important because they predict behavior (Ajzen & Fishbein, 1980). So, holding positive attitudes about violence should lead to aggressive behavior. It is this connection to aggressive behavior that marks the attitude change approach as a conditional effect of media violence. Research typically finds only a modest connection between attitudes and actions; people don't always act in accordance with their attitudes. One of the earliest studies to demonstrate this lack of correspondence was in the 1930s. In his investigation of racial prejudice, LaPiere (1934) traveled around the United States with a Chinese couple. After visiting 251 hotels and restaurants, they were denied service only once. But, responses to a questionnaire sent to those same establishments about 6 months later recorded that over 90% of respondents would refuse service to Chinese people. Clearly, attitudes and behaviors are not isomorphic. This may illustrate that just because someone holds positive attitudes about violence does not necessarily mean that they will act on those attitudes.

Ajzen and Fishbein's (1980) and Fishbein and Ajzen's (1975) Theory of Reasoned Action (TRA) provides a conditional explanation for how attitudes about violence lead to aggressive behavior. Their formula to describe the connection between attitudes and behavior is:

$$B \sim BI = w_1 A_{act} + w_2 SN_{act}$$

B = a specific behavior
BI = intention to behave
A_{act} = attitude about a specific act
SN_{act} = the attitudes that relevant others hold about the act
w = the situational weights applied in specific contexts

The Theory of Reasoned Action is a cognitive approach that assumes that people have reasons for acting and that attitudes predict behavior, within a social context. Note that Ajzen and Fishbein (1980) held that it is impractical to predict behavior directly. Intentions are not stable; as time passes, intentions can change and situations can intervene that make a specific action less likely. Generally, the shorter the time period between intention formation and opportunity to act, the greater the correspondence between intention and behavior. So, the TRA focuses on predicting intentions to behave (BI).

There are two influences on behavioral intention: attitudes about the specific act and perceptions of subjective norms. The attitude toward the act is a very specific attitude – about a very specific act. In the case of attitudes about violence, an attitude that violence in general is a solution to societal problems is not specific enough to predict specific behavior. If, however, a child holds the attitude that hitting a bully in the playground is a good solution to being bullied, that specific attitude might lead to intentions to punch the bully the next time he or she accosts the child. Subjective norms are perceptions or evaluations of the attitudes held by significant others about the specific act. In other words, subjective norms are beliefs that important others think the behavior is a good or bad idea. So, a child who believes that friends and parents would agree that he or she should punch the bully will probably have greater intention to do so.

In any specific context, however, both attitude and subjective norm are weighted. That is, each is assigned a specific importance, based on the situation. A child might believe that punching bullies in the playground is a good idea but not actually punch the bully because a teacher (who disapproves of punching) is watching. The influence of the subjective norm (the teacher) overrides the positive attitude toward punching. The next recess, however, if that teacher is not in sight, the child might be likely to punch the bully.

Media violence can have an impact on both attitudes toward behaviors and subjective norms. The positive presentation of violence in the mass media as justified, rewarded, and committed by attractive characters might lead to positive attitudes toward specific violent acts. And, media content can also lead to beliefs that society approves of violence in certain settings. But, specific acts based on those attitudes and perceptions are conditional, based on the context in which the act occurs. Even the most violent and provoked person might be hesitant to act aggressively if there are police officers nearby.

Physiological Theories

Another set of theories that hypothesize that aggressive behavior can grow out of exposure to violent media content recognizes that humans react affectively as well as cognitively to their environment. Key to these approaches are physiological responses to violent media content.

Arousal

Arousal is an affective, nonspecific physiological response that is marked by alertness, faster breathing, and increased heart-rate (Lang, 1994). Arousal is a fairly common reaction to media exposure. People become caught up in the action of movies and television programs and become excited (in the case of action films), frightened (horror movies), sad ("tear jerkers"), sexually aroused (pornography), and involved (quiz programs). Certainly one important reason people use the mass media is for excitement and to help relieve boredom (e.g., Perse, 1996; A.M. Rubin, 1983; Zillmann & Bryant, 1985).

Violent media content has the potential to be quite arousing. Based on stimulus generalization, images that depict danger and threat to personal safety can engender arousal. Arousal is an adaptive response because it readies humans to action and increases survival if threats are imminent. Beyond content, the techniques used in violent media content can increase arousal. Fast pacing, numerous cuts and edits, and object movement toward the screen increase arousal (e.g., A. Lang, 1990; A. Lang, Geiger, Strickwerda, & Sumner, 1993). Indeed, researchers have observed evidence of physiological arousal during exposure to violent film clips (e.g., Bushman & Geen, 1990). So, violent media content can increase arousal. Duration of this arousal, though, is fairly short term, lasting anywhere from a few minutes to no more than 1 hour or so (Tannenbaum & Zillmann, 1975). The effects based on arousal, then, are short term.

There are three related mechanisms that explain how the arousal induced by violent media content might be linked to aggressive behavior for a short time. First, arousal simply increases the likelihood of action. Zillmann (1982) conceptualized arousal as "a unitary force that energizes or intensifies behavior that receives direction by independent means" (p. 53). When aroused, "the individual will do as he would ordinarily – but with increased energy and intensity due to the available residual arousal" (Tannenbaum & Zillmann, 1975, p. 161). Arousal, then, leads to more intense behavior. After exposure to arousing violent media content, people may act intensely. People with aggressive tendencies might act even more aggressively. This approach does not argue that aroused action will be aggressive – only that it will be more intense. Actions may be prosocial as well as antisocial. But, if provoked, the antisocial action will be stronger.

The second mechanism that explains the connection between arousal and violent behavior is based on individual differences. Optimal level of arousal is an individual difference variable (Donohew, Finn, & Christ, 1988). That is, people differ on the level of arousal that makes them feel content. When people are below their optimal level of arousal, they feel uncomfortable and bored. When they have exceeded their optimal level of arousal, they also feel uncomfortable; they feel stressed. For some people, with characteristically lower optimal levels of arousal, the arousing aspects of media violence might lead to overstimulation and stress. Overstimulation leads to physical activity to relieve the stress.[11] Once again, this approach does not hold that the physical activity will be necessarily aggressive. Certainly, people pace and fidget when stressed.

The third mechanism is based on the transfer of arousal (Zillmann, 2010). Excitation transfer might increase the likelihood of aggressive action for a short time after exposure to violent media content. Arousal, as a physiological response, is nonspecific. People, however, label their arousal based on their appraisal of the context (Schachter, 1964). For example, an exciting sporting match is associated with a good deal of arousal. A viewer will label that arousal as either positive (happiness or joy) or negative (sadness, disappointment, or anger) based on the outcome of the game. An important implication of excitation transfer is that residual arousal can increase affective reactions to subsequent events. Arousal can be relabeled, based on a changing context. So, arousal produced by an exciting sports contest can first be labeled as disappointment, but then be relabeled as anger, if one is cut off by another car when leaving the stadium parking lot. Excitation transfer provides a theoretical reason to expect aggression to follow arousal as a result of exposure to violent media content. Violent media content produces arousal in a viewer. Three actions might occur as a result of that arousal: (a) the viewer is likely to act more intensely than when unaroused; (b) the viewer may become overstimulated; (c) in the context of media violence, that arousal might be labeled as fear, anger, or hostility. So, for a short time after exposure to violent media content (while the arousal still persists), behavior will be more likely to be intense and grow out of feelings of hostility or anger.

Habituation-Desensitization

Another physiological effect of television violence is habituation. Habituation is an adaptive response to the environment. Stimuli that we regularly encounter lose their ability to arouse us. So, with repeated exposure, stimuli that were initially arousing begin to lose their ability to arouse. With repeated exposure, initially strong arousal reactions to media violence diminish. There is a good deal of evidence that people can become habituated to media violence. Children who are viewers of a lot of television violence show less physiological arousal when watching violence than do viewers of a light amount of television (Cline, Croft, & Courrier, 1973; Thomas, Horton, Lippincott, & Drabman, 1977). College-age males who played violent video games had lower heart rates and physiological arousal when watching films of real violence (Carnagey, Anderson, & Bushman, 2007).

This habituation may have several negative consequences. If people seek out arousing media content to help them achieve optimal levels of arousal, they will need to seek out increasingly more arousing content. Indeed, action film sequels typically become more violent to satisfy repeat viewers (Jhally, 1994). Exposure to increasingly more violent media fare provides fodder for other potential cognitive effects: social learning, aggressive script acquisition, and aggressive cue activation. Moreover, viewing increasingly aggressive media content may lead to callousness, or disregard for the suffering of others as a result of loss of empathy and sympathy. As Zillmann (1991b) hypothesized, viewers might become less disturbed when witnessing violence in real life and, hence, "less inclined to intervene in, and attempt to stop, aggression among others" (p. 120). There is research evidence to support Zillmann's views. After longer-term exposure to violent "slasher" films, research participants began to report fewer emotionally disturbing reactions to later films. When they were asked to review the report of a sexual assault trial, compared to men who had not viewed the films, participants perceived that the victim had suffered less and reported less sympathy for her (Linz, Donnerstein, & Penrod, 1984). Repeated exposure to violence led to calloused perceptions and reactions.

General Aggression Model

The General Aggression Model of violent media effects (C.A. Anderson & Bushman, 2002a) was developed as a theoretical framework integrating earlier theories of media effects into "unified whole" (p. 33). The model falls clearly within the domain of the conditional model. It focuses on aggressive episodes and holds two categories of variables as basic inputs: variables that deal with the person/audience member and those that define the situation. There are three routes to aggressive behavior: cognitive, affective, and arousal-based. According to Anderson and Bushman (2002a), the effects can be mindful and deliberate or impulsive. Effects, then, can be long term or short term. This model is relevant to media effects because it can be applied to aggressive behavior that might result after exposure to violent media content.

Consistent with the conditional model, aspects of the audience member affect whether they will act aggressively within a particular situation. Certain personality traits, such as aggressive personality (e.g., Buss & Perry, 1992) and sex (males are more likely to be aggressive), enhance aggressive behavior. Consistent with attitude-based theories, prior beliefs, attitudes about violence, and beliefs about social norms intervene in aggressive behavior. The scripts that people have developed about aggression and different situations (drawn from information-processing theories) also affect aggressive action.

Characteristics of the situation influence aggressive behavior. The existence of aggressive cues (drawn from priming theories), incentives to act aggressively (drawn from social learning theory), and frustration, pain, and drug/alcohol use (because of disinhibition) stimulate aggressive behavior (e.g., K.D. Williams, 2009).

The routes to aggressive action can be cognitive, through the generation of hostile thoughts or the activation of hostile scripts. The route can be affective, through the creation of bad moods and expressive body movements, such as aggressive gestures and facial expressions. The route can also be through increased arousal, which various arousal theories see as a stimulus to aggression.

Because this is a conditional model, Anderson and Bushman (2002a) point out that aggressive behavior is not inevitable. A mindful view of people suggests that while in the situation, people can appraise the situation and decide to act aggressively or not. But, people are not always mindful; they can act impulsively too.

Summary

Together, these theoretical approaches offer different, but complementary, explanations for aggressive thoughts and behavior as a consequence of exposure to violent media content. Cognitively, people may learn from the violent actions that they watch and model these actions in their daily lives. But, not all aggressive behavior connected to media exposure mimics media action. Viewers may also learn the principles of violence from the mass media and integrate violence into their own behavioral scripts and repertoire. Or, media content may lead to the acquisition of attitudes that might foster violent behavior. Physiologically, violent media content can be arousing. Arousal can stimulate more intense action that might be more likely to grow out of anger or hostility labeled as a result of the context of exposure to violent media content. The General Aggression Model serves a useful integrating function. Research using this model, though, has not been able to test the model as a whole. It is still necessary to assess discrete relationships between variables (e.g., Bartlett, Rodeheffer, Baldassaro, Hinkin, & Harris, 2008; Bushman & Anderson, 2002).

It is important to note that all of these explanations grow out of the conditional model. None holds that exposure to violence leads irrevocably to violent behavior. Whether violent media content becomes the basis for cognitive or physiological processes leading to aggressive behavior depends on many social category, social relationship, and individual difference variables.

Theories of Null Effects

Although most scholars accept that media violence is a small, but significant contributor to aggressive behaviors, thoughts, and feelings, there are some approaches that argue that media content does not cause aggression. Justification holds that there is a connection between exposure to media violence and aggressive behavior, but the causal direction is from aggression to exposure. Catharsis is an approach that holds that not only is there no effect between viewing media violence and aggression, but the relationship is a negative one.

Justification

The justification approach argues that it is aggressive people who watch violent media content to justify their own actions and feelings. In other words, selective exposure accounts for the relationship between aggressive behavior and viewing violent media content. There is some evidence that aggressive tendencies are linked to viewing violence. Huesmann (1982) reported a modest, but significant, connection between aggression and watching violent television a year later. Fenigstein (1979) observed that experimental participants who were given a chance to act aggressively were more likely to select media content that featured violence. Later, Fenigstein and Heyduk (1985) noted that participants who were primed to think violent thoughts by creating imaginary stories including 10 words with aggressive connotations were also more likely to select violent films to watch. McIlwraith and Schallow (1983) found evidence that obsessional emotional daydreaming (i.e., guilt and hostile aggressive daydreams) was linked to reading violent drama and watching television, including violent drama.

There are several theoretical explanations for selective exposure to violent media content as justification. Festinger's (1954) social comparison theory holds that selective exposure is motivated to reduce dissonance, or negative feelings, about one's own actions. Seeing media violence might help aggressive people believe that their own thoughts, feelings, and actions are acceptable. Uses and gratifications might explain that aggressive people might seek out violent media content to get information about how to deal with their own violence or to learn new ways to commit violence. Zuckerman (1996) posited that the arousal potential of violent horror films may appeal to high sensation seekers. Zillmann (1998) offered several other explanations for the appeal of media violence. The appeal of violent content might be found in: (a) notions of protective vigilance, or satisfying curiosity about how to deal with threatening situations (e.g., Boyanowski, 1977); (b) being able to show mastery in social settings by hiding fear (Zillmann et al., 1986); (c) providing a setting for unleashing socially unacceptable emotional responses (e.g., glee at the misfortune of villains); and (d) maximizing entertainment and amusement through excitation transfer, in which the arousal engendered by media violence is transformed into pleasure.

Although justification approaches and research that examines widespread exposure to media violence are relatively unresearched, it is clear that selective exposure offers some valid explanation for the connection between aggressive tendencies and exposure to media violence. Most scholars agree that the connection between aggression and media violence is likely a reciprocal one, in which personal predispositions and media violence are interlinked in patterns of violent life styles.

Catalyst Model

Ferguson and his colleagues (C. J. Ferguson, Rueda, Cruz, Ferguson, Fritz, & Smith, 2008) propose a model of violent media effects that holds that media violence is not the cause of aggression, but instead a "stylistic catalyst." Aggression is the result of nature and nurture. Aggressive people have a predisposition to act violently because of a combination of genetics and environment.

According to the researchers, an aggressive personality is a result of genetics, gender, and temperament. A violent family environment fosters the aggressive personality. Aggression, according to this model, results when there is an environmental catalyst, especially stresses, such as anger, social problems, or reduced inhibitions. Media content provides models for aggression. But, as the authors argue, media content is not the cause for aggression.

> When an individual high in violence proneness decides to act violently, this person may then model violence that he or she has seen in the media. As such, the style or form of violence may be socially modeled but not the desire to act violently itself. Thus, an individual may model violent behaviors he or she has witnessed in a video game, but had that video game been removed from that individual's sphere of modeling opportunities, the violence would still occur in another form. Therefore, video game violence does not cause violent behavior but may have an impact on its form.
>
> (C. J. Ferguson et al., 2008, p. 315)

Using longitudinal data gathered from a large representative sample of adolescent twins, Ferguson and his colleagues (C. J. Ferguson et al., 2013) focused on arrest history as their measure of aggression. The results supported the catalyst model. Genetic factors and gender accounted for a good deal of the variance in arrest history. Media use was not a significant predictor.

The catalyst model does draw attention to important variables in the conditional model and has many similarities to the General Aggression Model (Bushman & Heusmann, 2013). The model, however, has been criticized for its inability to explain the findings of decades of violence research. As Bushman and Heusmann (2013) point out, various studies identify significant effects of media violence even after statistically controlling for aggressive predispositions and family violence, concepts central to the catalyst model. Moreover, the catalyst model cannot explain the scores of studies conducted in laboratories where groups that watch violent media content evidence more aggression than control groups – even without stressors.

Catharsis

Catharsis is an unusual theory connecting media violence and aggressive behavior. Catharsis holds that watching media violence provides a healthy venue for viewers to "purge" their aggressive feelings (Scheele & DuBois, 2006). According to catharsis, the connection between watching media violence and aggressive behavior is a negative one; the more one watches violence, the less aggressive they will be. The notion of catharsis is drawn from dramatic theory as far back as Aristotle. In trying to explain the appeal of tragic drama (e.g., the Greek or Shakespearean tragedies) aestheticians argue that through identification with a great and tragic hero, the audience is able to purge themselves of harmful emotions, and feel relieved and healthier afterward.

The idea that violent media content could be cathartic and healthy was advanced by Feshbach (1955, 1972) who believed that engaging in aggressive fantasies helped reduce aggressive drives. Media content, of course, could help stimulate violent fantasies. There was some limited support for catharsis in a single field study (Feshbach & Singer, 1971). Now, however, catharsis is generally discredited. The overwhelming evidence is that there is a positive, not a negative, relationship between exposure to media violence and aggressive behavior (Paik & Comstock, 1994). Moreover, catharsis is directly counter to priming and arousal theories. Media violence has an arousing not a calming effect on audiences and tends to activate aggressive, not pleasant thoughts.

Some scholars are reluctant to reject catharsis out of hand, however. Comstock et al., (1978) suggested that there are two types of catharsis. Vicarious behavior catharsis, which is based on purging negative emotions simply by participating vicariously in drama, finds few advocates among the scholarly community. It is not considered a valid apology for media violence. Overt behavior catharsis, however, is based on the positive impact of "acting out" emotional responses on purging negative affect. Comstock and his colleagues (1978) summarized the results of several studies that support the effects of overt behavior catharsis. Scheff and Scheele (1980) also presented evidence of overt behavior catharsis. Laughter helps reduce stress and arousal levels. Overt behavior catharsis might explain the appeal of a "good cry" while watching tear jerkers, or how pornography might help reduce sexual tension.

Research on video games, however, has begun to offer some bits of support for the notion of behavioral catharsis. Video games allow gamers to commit aggressive acts. Newer motion-sensing games, such as Nintendo's Wii, allow gamers to physically act out violent behavior, such as punching. After finding a negative meta-analytic relationship between length of game play and aggression, Sherry (2001) wrote: "it is also possible that the players may be using the games to equilibrate their arousal levels. This suggests a drive-reduction or catharsis hypothesis" (p. 425). A recent convention paper (Mahood & Ciccirillo, 2008) offered support for behavioral catharsis: video game play reduced unease, anger, and frustration in male and female college students.

Cultivation

Cultivation is perhaps the body of research with the greatest visibility outside our field. Cultivation is grounded in the evidence of a long-term program of content analysis[12] of dramatic prime-time television content that television presents a pattern of images that deviate from reality: Violence is far more common on television than in reality. Cultivation researchers acknowledge that this television violence may lead to some behavioral effects, but they believe that the most common and subtle effect of television violence is that it shapes viewers' beliefs about the real world. Viewers of a lot of television are more likely to believe that violence is common in the real world, to be fearful of crime and personal injury, to be distrustful of others, and to take precautions to protect themselves against crime (Morgan & Shanahan, 2010; Morgan et al., 2009). According to cultivation, then, the dominant effects of television violence are cognitive (beliefs about social reality) and affective (fear of crime) (Oliver, Bae, Ash, & Chung, 2012).

Cultivation is a media effect that is explained by the cumulative model of media effects. Selective exposure to specific television programs is not relevant for two reasons. First, content analyses demonstrate that the pattern of images pervades all prime-time content, so it is pointless to try to avoid television's dominant message about violence. Second, television is used non-selectively; people watch television by the clock, rather than choosing specific programs (Gerbner & Gross, 1976). Through repeated exposure to similar messages across the range of television channels, viewers of a lot of television begin to adopt television's world as their view of reality.

This perspective was initially grounded in the Marxist view that explained that television's patterns of violence served to reinforce society's existing power structure. Middle-class White males are more likely to be aggressors and women and minorities are more likely to be victims (e.g., Signorielli, 1990). So, television teaches minorities and women their place in society, and threatens them with violence should they try to challenge society's power structure. According to Gerbner and Gross (1976), heavy television viewing should lead to "a heightened sense of risk and insecurity (different for groups of varying power) [that] is more likely to increase acquiescence to and dependence upon established authority, and to legitimize its use of force" (p. 194).

Cultivation research has attracted a good deal of criticism over the years. Scholars and industry representatives questioned the definition of violence that drives the content analyses: "the overt expression of physical force against self or other, compelling action against one's will on pain of being hurt or killed, or actually hurting or killing" (Gerbner & Gross, 1976, p. 184). Because this definition includes unintentional and accidental acts of violence as well as acts of nature, critics argued that the content analyses overestimated the amount of television violence (e.g., Blank, 1977). Cultivation scholars responded that even accidental violence teaches lessons of power (Gerbner et al., 1977).

Still other scholars pointed out that controlling for sociodemographic variables reduces or eliminates cultivation effects (e.g., Hughes, 1980). Cultivation scholars modified their approach to introduce mainstreaming and resonance to account for the impact of sociodemographic characteristics of people (Gerbner, Gross, Morgan, & Signorielli, 1980). With mainstreaming, heavy television viewing overrides views outside the television "mainstream" that are due to sociodemographic characteristics. So, heavy television viewers of all sociodemographic groups tend to be more similar. With resonance, television's messages reinforce real-life experiences of people who watch a lot of television, so that certain sociodemographic groups tend to get a "double dose" from television viewing. These reformulations broaden cultivation's scope, but cultivation research has been criticized for using them only as post-hoc explanations (Hirsch, 1981).

Other critics have questioned whether cultivation effects reflect survey respondents' tendencies to overestimate both their television viewing and their chances of victimization (Wober & Gunter, 1986). In fact, studies note that respondents, as a whole, overestimate (e.g., Perse, 1986; Potter, 1986). There is also evidence that a response bias may account for some cultivation effects; effects are more commonly found with negatively rather than positively phrased questions (A.M. Rubin, Perse, & Taylor, 1988). And, as television viewing becomes more fragmented and selective, cultivation as a cumulative effect might be less common (Perse et al., 1994). Finally, some critics have offered conceptual criticisms (e.g., Zillmann, 1980, 1991b). It seems strange that people would willingly watch media content that leaves them upset and unhappy. Selective exposure research has demonstrated that people watch television to maximize pleasant feelings and minimize negative affect (Zillmann & Bryant, 1985). And, habituation would argue that repeated exposure to violent media content would lead viewers who watch a lot of television to be less affected over time, not more fearful.

These critics have all questioned if the cultivation effect exists. Studies have identified cultivation effects, though, across a wide range of samples and social reality effects (Morgan & Shanahan, 1997). Given the small, but consistent significant effect of television viewing on social reality beliefs, many scholars have assumed that cultivation exists and have attempted to uncover the psychological process that underlies the acquisition of social reality beliefs from television. In general, evidence supports that cultivation may be a result of a psychological process similar to the automatic route of the cognitive-transaction model. That is, cultivated perceptions may be the result of less thoughtful, automatic, heuristic judgments. As Shrum (1997) outlined,

> the cultivation effect can be explained as an instance of the application of the availability heuristic (Tversky & Kahneman, 1973), which posits that people infer the prevalence of a construct (e.g., crime, violence, occupations) from the ease with which relevant examples can be recalled from memory. (p. 350)

For people who watch a lot of television, the easiest examples to recall may be based on television viewing. In a sense, television viewing primes certain notions about the television world. When making judgments about the real world, these viewers have these television notions at top of mind. So, they become the basis of perceptions of social reality.

Support for automatic processing being the basis for cultivation effects is found in experimental studies that show that cultivation effects could be primed by a single exposure, instead of long-term exposure (Tamborini, Zillmann, & Bryant, 1984). Other studies have found that cultivation effects occur when viewers "forget" the source of their information (M. Mares, 1996). Shrum and his colleagues (1998) found that cultivation effects were stronger when participants were not primed to discount television information. Reminding people of television as a source of information significantly reduces cultivation effects (Morgan & Shanahan, 1997). So, a more mindless, ritualistic approach to television viewing is associated with adopting its pattern of images as the source of social reality beliefs.

Effects of Sexually Violent Media Content

Sex is a common theme in most media content.[13] Some type of sexual reference is found in 70% of all television programs (Kunkel, et al., 2005) and in 73% of all music videos (J. S. Turner, 2005).[14] Chapter 6 discussed how this sexual content can play a role in adolescent socialization effects. But, the most commonly available sexual content is often not very explicit. On television, sex is often a topic of conversation or implied in visual euphemisms (e.g., Kunkel et al., 2005). Other media, though, provide more sexually explicit presentations of sexual behavior. R-, X-, NC-17-rated and unrated movies, adult magazines and books, public access cable channels, DVDs, and the Internet all deliver content that depicts graphic sexual acts. It is difficult to get accurate estimates of interest in or exposure to sexually explicit materials, but there are indications that they are widely available and used by a large audience (Bryant & D. Brown, 1989; Peter & Valkenburg, 2009).

Although sexually graphic material can certainly contribute to child and adolescent sexual socialization (see Chapter 6), most graphic material is not as readily available to those audiences as the less explicit content found on television. Parents, educators, and public policy analysts all try to find ways to channel this explicit content, to keep it from being easily accessed by younger children. Because of these restrictions on availability, most of the research on the effects of sexually graphic media content focuses on older adolescents and sexually active adults. Much research on the effects of sexual content focuses on the early initiation of sexual behavior, the development of attitudes about sexual acts, and the impact of sexual content on "family values" and morality (e.g., Kunkel, Farrar, Eyal, Biely, Donnerstein, & Rideout, 2007; Zhang, Miller, & Harrison, 2008), but, there is a body of research that explores the effects of exposure to sexual media content on agression.

Research that focuses on aggression as a result of exposure to sexual media content generally focuses on two types of pornography. As J. B. Weaver (1991d) points out, sexual content with standard nonviolent themes is probably the most common. Even though this category does not contain aggression against women, it is clearly produced with a male audience in mind. As such, it focuses on explicit sexual acts and ignores nonsexual relationships among people. Because the focus is on sexual gratification, foreplay and affection are rarely shown. Women are usually portrayed as sexually available, eager, and promiscuous. In all, this content promotes the view that women's greatest value may be as sexual objects, who satisfy the sexual needs of men, with few needs of their own. Still, common pornography might be considerably more violent than earlier thought. A content analysis of a sample of 50 most rented pornographic videos and DVDs in 2004 and 2005 found that almost 90% of all scenes contained an aggressive act (Bridges, Wosnitzer, Scharrer, Sun, & Liberman, 2010). Aggression included physical aggression, such as choking, biting, spanking, punching/hitting, and bondage, and verbal aggression, such as threats of physical violence and coercive language.

Exposure to this common sort of pornography is linked to aggressive thoughts and actions. Several studies have found that, compared to control groups, experimental groups who have been exposed to sexually explicit material are more likely to accept violence against women (Malamuth & Check, 1981), express less compassion for female rape victims (Zillmann & Bryant, 1982), and recommend lighter prison sentences for convicted rapists (Zillmann & Bryant, 1982). Meta-analyses have found that, in experimental settings, there is an average correlation of $r = .146$ ($N = 2,248$) between exposure to sexual materials and acceptance of rape myths[15] (Allen, Emmers, Gebhardt, & Giery, 1995) and an average correlation of $r = .132$ ($N = 2,040$) between exposure to pornography and behavioral aggression (Allen, D'Alessio, & Brezgel, 1995). Exposure to sexually violent material has also been linked to increased aggression (administering shocks) against women in laboratory settings (Donnerstein & Berkowitz, 1981).

Shope (2004) observed that partners' pornography use increased the likelihood of wife abuse. In fact, 58% of battered women reported that "pornography use affected their abuse" (Shope, 2004, p. 66). Malamuth, Addison, and Koss (2000) concluded that "pornography use is indeed a very good 'marker' of higher sexual aggression levels" (p. 80). They found that men who were "at high risk for sexual aggression (based on the risk factors of HM [hypermasculinity] and SP [sexual promiscuity] . . . were much more likely to have engaged in sexual aggression than their counterparts who consume pornography less frequently" (p. 60). Even exposure to sexual hip-hop music videos can lead to greater acceptance of rape myths (e.g., Kistler & Lee, 2010).

The second type of sexually explicit media content, that with violent or coercive themes, causes considerable concern because of the linkage of sex and violence. Slasher films, or films that depict graphic violence, commonly include violence against women (Molitor & Sapolsky, 1993; J. B. Weaver, 1991a). In fact, in the 1980s, about one-third of all sexual acts in slasher films are accompanied by violence and over 20% of all female victims of violence were killed in sexual circumstances (Molitor & Sapolsky, 1993). An analysis of the most popular slasher films of the 1990s (Sapolsky, Molitor, & Luque, 2003) found that violence against women had increased significantly.[16] This type of media content especially might be linked to cognitive, affective, and behavioral negative effects against women.

Theories That Explain the Effects of Sexually Explicit Media Content

There are few theories proposed to explain specifically the aggressive effects of sexually violent media content. Those theories that explain the effects of media violence can be easily applied to the context of sexually violent media effects.

Social Learning

There is little research that explicitly tests social learning as the theoretical explanation behind the effects of sexually explicit material (Allen, Emmers, et al., 1995). This is understandable, given the focus of social learning on the learning and imitation of specific behaviors depicted in media content (Bandura, 2009). It would be unethical and impractical to assess social learning of private sexual behaviors or sexual violence. But, there are good reasons to suggest that sexually explicit media content might be the basis for social learning (Check & Malamuth, 1981). Sexually explicit behaviors in media content are usually quite salient. That is, they capture the attention of the audience. Much of the audience is quite attentive to sexually explicit action because sexually explicit materials usually present behaviors that are both relevant and adaptive. Sexually explicit media content often has some connection to the audience members' lives. Some individuals expect to be able to learn about sex and get ideas for their own sexual relationship (Duncan, 1990; Perse, 1994). Sexually explicit behavior is usually associated with especially potent rewards: sexual pleasure and satisfaction. Moreover, sexually explicit materials typically present sexual behavior as justified. That is, victims of sexual violence don't appear to suffer; female victims often appear to begin to enjoy the sex and become willing participants (Palys, 1986; Slade, 1984). In all, the salience of the presentation, the utility and rewards of sexual behavior, and the justification of the action suggest that sexually explicit media content may be the basis for social learning of sexual acts as well as sexual violence.

Information Processing

Huesmann's (1986) information-processing model of the effects of violent media content may also provide some explanation for the effects of sexually explicit materials. The information-processing model holds that the connection between media content and subsequent behaviors arises from a learning process. Unlike social learning theory, which explains how specific observed behaviors are learned, this model focuses on the learning of scripts, or patterns of behaviors. According to the information-processing approach, the learned behaviors are not necessarily the same as those observed. Through mental encoding and elaboration, scripts adapted from sexually explicit media content may be combined with preexisting scripts. So, patterns of behavior might resemble the scripts used in sexually explicit materials, and integrate violence against partners, callous disregard for the feelings of others, or actions that objectify and demean women. Although there has been no research to test specifically audiences' learning of scripts based on sexually explicit media content, this process can explain some behavioral effects of exposure.

Priming

A good deal of the research on the effects of sexually explicit violent media content is conducted in laboratory settings, with dependent variables measured shortly after exposure. Much of this evidence of short-term effects of exposure to sexually explicit materials can be explained by priming (Zillmann & Weaver, 1989). Sexually explicit media content is a potent prime. It is salient, and media that features this sort of content uses production techniques, such as close-ups and enhanced sounds to make these images and actions even more prominent. Those who have written about the biological connections between attention to media content and arousal (e.g., Malamuth, 1996) would certainly recognize the biological basis for attention to sexual media. In laboratory settings, especially, where selective exposure is often overridden due to experimental procedures, sexually violent media content may activate schemas in research participants. The sexual violence in pornography might serve as cues to retrieve schemas of sexual violence and coercive sexual behavior (Pollard, 1995), especially among those with higher tendencies toward hypermasculinity (Malamuth, Addison, & Koss, 2000).

Attitude Change

Research supports the conclusion that exposure to sexually explicit media content is linked to calloused attitudes toward women. In both laboratories and natural settings, the more sexually explicit material that men watch, the more likely they are to endorse rape myths and be accepting of sexual violence against women (Allen, D'Alessio, et al., 1995; Allen, Emmers, et al., 1995; Malamuth & Check, 1985; Perse, 1994). Exposure to sexual materials has also been linked to less sympathy toward rape victims (Linz et al., 1984; Zillmann & Bryant, 1982). Sexually explicit media content fosters these attitudes because of the themes and images that cut across pornography. Sexually aggressive behavior is typically enacted by attractive characters and although women initially resist forced sexual advances, they quickly become wanton and willing participants (Palys, 1986; Slade, 1984). With repeated exposure, these themes translate into calloused attitudes toward women and beliefs that rape is not particularly harmful (Zillmann & Bryant, 1982).

Arousal

Physiological and sexual arousal are fairly common reactions to sexually explicit media content (M. Brown, Amoroso, & Ware, 1976; Donnerstein &

Barrett; 1978; Harris, 1994). Arousal might facilitate the effects of sexual materials. As with violent media content, the arousal produced by sexual material might lead to more intense responses (Tannenbaum & Zillmann, 1975). There is evidence that exposure to sexual materials leads to heightened aggression in angered men. Early studies on the impact of violent pornography found that already angered research participants were more likely to administer harmful electric shocks after watching film clips with sexual content (Donnerstein & Berkowitz, 1981; Zillmann, 1971).

Habituation-Desensitization

Just as viewers of violent media content can become less aroused with repeated exposure, so too viewers of sexually explicit media content will find that it loses its potential to arouse. Zillmann and Bryant's research (1984, 1986b) noted that research participants became habituated to more common forms of pornography with repeated exposure. Not only was there evidence of reduced physiological arousal (heart-rate), but research participants seemed to be more likely to seek out more deviant types of pornography than participants who had not been massively exposed to pornography. Beyond evidence to support moralists' desires to suppress pornography, these research findings have some additional implications. The pornography that might be sought out by habituated audiences is likely to depict more arousing types of content, such as less common sexual practices or sexual violence and coercion. This combination of sexual activity and violence might have other, cognitive effects, based on social learning, attitude change, or priming.

Justification

Justification is an approach that holds that the causal direction between negative effects of media content and exposure to that content is based on selective exposure; that is, it is sexually violent or calloused people who prefer sexually explicit media content because it justifies their preexisting beliefs, attitudes, and behavioral tendencies. There may be evidence to support this approach. First, not everyone uses or seeks out sexually explicit media content (Bryant & Brown, 1989). Even accounting for social desirability, different types of media content have different size audiences. Sexually explicit R-rated films are viewed by a large number of people, men's magazines that feature sexually explicit photographs and letters are read by somewhat fewer people, and sexually explicit movies and videos are watched regularly by about a quarter of adults (Bryant & Brown, 1989).

Different types of people have different reactions to sexually explicit media content. Malamuth and Check (1983) observed that men who have a self-admitted high "likelihood of rape" became more sexually aroused when they listened to aggressive, coercive, and nonconsenting sexual acts than when they listened to consenting sex. Check and Guloien (1989) observed differential negative effects of sexually violent and dehumanizing pornography based on psychoticism. Research participants viewed, over a period of 6 days, either three videos containing sexually violent scenes, or three videos with sex in which the woman was objectified and dehumanized, or three videos containing romantic, sexual acts. For those participants low in psychoticism, compared to a no-exposure control group, exposure did not have any effect on their self-admitted likelihood of committing rape or forcing sex acts. But, compared to the control group, those participants high in psychoticism who were exposed to violent and dehumanizing pornography were significantly more likely to say they would rape or force a woman to engage in sex against her will. Based on his research on men who have been convicted of sexually violent crimes, Marshall (1989) believed that sexual criminals have a different use for and reliance on pornography than nonviolent men. There is some evidence that sadistic rapists become more aroused by violent pornography and rapists generate rape fantasies even when they view consenting sexual acts (Marshall, 1989). For certain especially violent men, pornography may serve, in part, as justification for their acts.

Catharsis

It is obvious that vicarious behavior catharsis is not a valid explanation for effects of pornography. All evidence contradicts the proposition that sexual feelings can be purged or satisfied simply by viewing or reading sexually explicit materials. Overt behavior catharsis, however, might be an outcome of use. Overt behavior catharsis is based on the positive impact of "acting out" emotional responses on purging negative affect (Comstock et al., 1978). Sexually explicit media content is used, at times, to generate sexual fantasies, for masturbation, and to reduce sexual tension (Duncan, 1990; Perse, 1994).

Models of Effects

The effects of sexually explicit content draw explanations from all four models of media effects. The almost uniform arousal effects of sexual material point out that sexual content, itself, can evoke automatic, short-term physiological effects. Gender differences might explain how different types of content appeal to males and females, but the predictability of these effects can be explained by innate links between the mind and body (Malamuth, 1996). The cognitive-transactional model is supported by research that demonstrates that salient features of sexually explicit material prime gender-stereotyped schemas that affect, for a short time, real-life appraisals (J. B. Weaver, Masland, & Zillmann, 1984; Jansma, Linz, Mulac, & Imrich, 1997). Content analyses of pornography conclude that there is a good deal of consistency in the kinds of actions that are presented. J. B. Weaver's (1991d) analysis of these studies concludes that 90% of visual pornography involves heterosexual intercourse. The settings and action are stylized and vary little. Moreover, because most of the material is targeted to a male audience, pornography tends to focus on sexual gratification at the expense of expressions of affection and depictions of relationship development. The cumulative model would explain that these consonant and consistent themes and images, over time, might lead to cognitive or attitudinal effects in heavy consumers.

The conditional model explains that effects of sexual materials are indirect, conditional on aspects of the audience. First, although sexually explicit materials are certainly widely available, not everyone chooses to watch or read them (Bryant & Brown, 1989). The social undesirability associated with sexually explicit materials also implies that those who are interested in pornography need to take somewhat active steps to acquire it. So, selective exposure is relevant to effects of use. Some research has suggested that preexisting attitudes about rape (Malamuth & Check, 1983) and personality traits (Check & Guloien, 1989) affected arousal and attitudinal responses to pornography. Perse (1994) found that holding rape myths was, in part, conditional on reasons for using sexual materials. Those respondents who used erotica for sexual release were less likely to hold rape myths; those who used erotica as a substitution for a partner were more likely to hold rape myths. And, using erotica for diversionary, entertainment reasons or for sexual enhancement (information and foreplay) had an indirect impact on rape myths, through respondents' links to greater exposure to sexual materials and through their impact on holding hostile beliefs about women.

Malamuth and Briere (1986) proposed a model of indirect effects of pornography. According to their model, sexually explicit materials can lead indirectly to antisocial effects in the presence of other conditions. They suggest that media content, in connection with individual experiences, such as home environment, social network, and personality characteristics, can be linked to hostility toward women and the acquisition of attitudes that might favor the connections between sexuality and violence. In the presence of opportunity, acute arousal, or forces that lessen inhibition (e.g., alcohol), sexual aggression might result. Marshall's (1989) analysis of research on adult rapists illuminates the indirect influence of pornography on aggression. Research on men who have been convicted of rape and child molestation paints a grim portrait of their early family lives. Rapists are raised typically in violent and abusive homes with alcoholic and neglectful parents. As a result, these boys have low self-esteem and lack the social skills that would allow them to develop normal romantic relationships. Because of their lack of social skills and as a result of the abuse they have suffered, these boys often turn to inappropriate sexual acts. Marshall hypothesizes that pornography has the potential to have a stronger impact on these malsocialized young men. Without adult models of normal male–female relationships, the skewed and inaccurate relationships depicted in pornography might have more potent cognitive and affective effects, leading to beliefs about sexual acts and attitudes about women that mimic those in pornography. Violent pornography, especially, might be more likely to be modeled, because the violence in it mirrors abusive home life. Violent effects of pornography, then, are highly conditional on a host of individual, social, and cultural factors.

Summary

Mass communication scholars overwhelmingly accept that media violence bears some responsibility for violent behavior. Media violence is certainly not the largest contributor to violence in society, but it may be one aspect that is more easily solved. Accumulated research evidence has allowed scholars to identify the aspects of violent media content that are most likely to be associated with aggressive behavior (Donnerstein, Slaby, & Eron, 1994):

when violence is rewarded;
when violence is justified;
when aggressive cues are common in everyday life;
when the aggressor is similar to the audience;
when the audience can identify with the aggressor;
when the violence is motivated by a desire to cause harm;
when the violence has few negative consequences;
when the violence is presented realistically;
when there is little criticism of the violence;
when the violence is physiologically arousing;
when the audience is predisposed to aggression.

Despite this general agreement, the ideas of scholars who are critical of this research are worth noting (e.g., Freedman, 1984; Gauntlett, 2005; Wurtzel & Lometti, 1987). Correlation is not the same as causation. Finding connections between aggressive behavior and exposure to violent media content does not exclude alternate explanations (e.g., selective exposure) or the impact of other influences (e.g., overconsumption of alcohol). Experimental studies can offer evidence of causation, but research ethics do not allow scholars to use measures of realistic aggression. Punching a Bobo doll, administering shocks, or committing fouls in floor hockey are not the kind of violence that our society fears. Research designs may have demonstrated a connection between exposure to violent media content and more socially (or experimenter) acceptable "aggressive" acts, but have been unable to uncover links to real-life violent behavior.[17]

Although most communication scholars are loath to recommend censorship (more communication is generally considered better than less), there have been a number of policy solutions proposed to the problem of media violence. Saunders (1996) suggested limiting the First Amendment protection of media violence by applying the same obscenity exception that is applied to sexual content to violent content. So, "sufficiently explicit and offensive depictions of violence" (p. 4) could be found to be legally obscene. This would allow various levels of government to regulate, or even ban such content. J. T. Hamilton (1998) proposed that media violence be treated as environmental pollution.

Hamilton argues that media violence, like pollution, has negative externalities, or costs, that are borne by society, but not by the producers. This notion suggests solutions, such as programming taxes, to make producers bear some of the costs of their product and to discourage production of harmful content. Another solution might be based on zoning laws that limit the locations and times of operation of certain pollution-producing businesses to reduce their harm. This would involve channeling violent content to hours when children would be less likely to be in the audience. A first attempt to channel violent content was the 1975–1976 Family Viewing Time policy, in which the Federal Communications Commission (FCC) strongly encouraged television broadcasters to limit violence during the first hour of prime time. The policy, though, was overturned in federal court as a result of improper FCC action and seen as a violation of broadcasters' First Amendment rights. Channeling, however, has been more successful with indecent broadcast material.

A solution adopted by government and industry that can limit the impact of media violence is based on the film model. Television programs are now labeled to make parents more aware of age-appropriate programs and to give them information as to what sort of content (i.e., violence, sex, dialogue, or adult situations) makes the program less suitable for children. The 1996 Telecommunications Bill mandates that all television sets with screens 13 inches or larger produced after 2000 include the V-chip, a device that allows parents to block programs with certain ratings.

Another way to limit children's viewing of violent media content is to provide children with other, less violent programming. The popularity of *Sesame Street* and other educational entertainment programs for children shows that violence is not necessary for popularity. Scholars believe that if there were more high quality entertaining and educational children's programs, children would spend their time watching them, instead of less educational, or violent, or adult-oriented programming. One randomized controlled trial found that when parents were encouraged to shift their preschool-age children's television viewing to more age-appropriate and educational programs (e.g., *Sesame Street*, *Dora the Explorer*, *Curious George*, *Super Why*), children seemed to benefit. Compared to a group of children who watched the same amount of television, but whose parents did not modify the programs they watched, children who watched educational programs engaged in fewer emotional and behavioral problems in their children (Christakis et al., 2013).

Research on the effects of violent media content offers guidelines to reduce the negative impact of media violence. Research demonstrates that parental mediation of violent television programming seems to limit aggressive effects (Nathanson, 1999). When parents limit their children's viewing of violent television, there is less exposure to violence. Parents' comments during television viewing also limit aggressive effects. Parents can teach children critical viewing skills, such as reminding them that content is not real, that aggressors are not justified, and that there are real, negative consequences of violent behavior. These can all encourage children to discount television drama as a model. By providing information not included by media producers, parents should be able to minimize the negative impact of media violence. Parents can also provide the normative influence that lets children see that violence is not a socially acceptable solution to problems. As Nathanson (1999) concluded, "parents can socialize children into an orientation toward violent TV that makes them more or less vulnerable to its negative effects" (p. 138). Exposure to violence does not have to lead to negative effects; there are ways to mitigate negative effects and enhance positive effects of media content.

It is clear that it is possible to reduce and even eliminate the negative effects of short-and relatively long-term exposure to sexually violent and demeaning materials (Allen D'Alessio, Emmers, & Gebhardt, 1996; Isaacs & Fisher, 2008). Ethics demand that researchers do not harm their participants. So, studies on the effects of sexually explicit materials always include substantial debriefing: disclosing the purpose of the study, alerting the participants that they might be affected in various ways, and discussing how the messages in the content are inaccurate. Debriefing also involves long-term follow-up to reinforce positive messages (e.g., Linz, Donnerstein, & Penrod, 1984). Debriefing is effective (e.g., Donnerstein & Berkowitz, 1981; Check & Malamuth, 1984; Malamuth & Check, 1984) and its effects appear to be fairly enduring (as long as 7 to 8 months), despite long-term and massive exposure to sexually violent materials. Debriefing appears to cure the effects of exposure to sexually violent materials; prebriefing seems to work as a sort of inoculation protecting people against negative effects.

Outside the laboratory, scholars recommend sex education and media literacy training to reduce the likelihood of negative effects of sexually demeaning and violent media content. Meta-analyses (Allen et al., 1996; Flores & Hartlaub, 1998) found that various educational interventions, such as human sexuality courses, rape education workshops and video interventions, as well as educational briefings and debriefings, reduce acceptance of rape myths. Within our own field, we believe that educated people are more likely to reject effects. Media literacy training will help reduce the negative effects of media content.

The encouraging results of violence interventions and debriefing and prebriefing in pornography recommend that material about pornography and rape myths be part of sex education and media literacy training (Allen et al., 1996). Moreover, these results give scholars, educators, and parents guides to creating educational materials to mitigate the effects of sexually violent or degrading media content:

- Reduce the likelihood that the messages of sexually violent or degrading material will be viewed realistically. Point out the inaccuracies of the material, especially the linkage of sex and violence. Dispel rape myths. Lower perceived realism is associated with fewer effects.
- Reduce the credibility of the material by educating adolescents about the financial aims and intended audiences for sexual materials. Less credible messages have fewer effects.

- Educate about the realities of rape and about the inaccuracies in the depictions of rape in sexually explicit media so that there will be less identification with the aggressors to reduce the likelihood of social learning.
- Create awareness of the typical reactions to the material, so that the audience will know the source of their own reactions. Knowing the source of feelings and thoughts reduces the likelihood that these feelings and thoughts will be generalized beyond the exposure context.

It is important to remember that the prosocial effects of television are stronger and more common than its negative effects (Hearold, 1986; Paik, 1995). As Hearold (1986) concluded,

> Although fewer studies exist on prosocial effects, the effect size is so much larger, holds up better under more stringent conditions, and is consistently higher for boys and girls, that the potential for prosocial effects overrides the smaller but persistent negative effects of antisocial programs.
>
> (p. 116)

Notes

1 In February, 2012, 6 students were shot in a high school in Chardon, Ohio. In April, 7 people were killed in a shooting at Oikos University in Oakland, California. In May, 5 people were killed in a shooting at a Seattle café. In July, 12 people were killed and 58 wounded in a midnight premier of *The Dark Knight Rises* in Aurora, Colorado. In August, 10 were shot at a Sikh temple in Oak Creek, Wisconsin. In September, 6 died in a workplace shooting in Minneapolis. Less than a week before the Sandy Hook School shooting, 3 died in a shooting at a mall in Portland, Oregon.

2 Interestingly, Congress has turned down legislation mandating child-proof locks on guns, but has endorsed the V-chip, which locks children out from objectionable television programming.

3 The TV Parental Guidelines rating system is designed to give information about the program content so that parents can control their children's television viewing. The ratings are: TV-Y (acceptable for all children), TV-Y7 (designed for children age 7 or older), TV-Y7-FV (includes some intense fantasy violence), TV-G (acceptable for general audience, with little violence, strong language, or sexual dialogue or situations), TV-PG (may contain content unsuitable for younger children), TV-14 (contains content not suitable for children under the age of 14), and TV-MA (designed for adults and not suitable for children under the age of 17). TV-PG, TV-14, and TV-MA programs may also carry additional ratings to describe specific content: V (intense violence), S (intense sexual situations), L (strong or coarse language), and D (sexually suggestive dialogue). For more information about and criticisms of the TV Parental Guidelines, see Federman (1998) and Heins (1998).

4 Some reasons for the crime rate drop are: (a) better policing, such as targeting locations that are likely to attract crime with extra police officers; (b) demographics, the aging U.S. population means there are fewer young adults, who commit more crime; and (c) technology, such as security cameras, surveillance cameras, and cell phones, which make it much harder to commit a crime without being observed (Barrett, 2011).

5 The television programs with the highest ratings for the week of July 12, 2010 were the *MLB All-Star Game and Pre-Game, America's Got Talent* (Tuesday and Wednesday editions), *NCIS, The Bachelorette, NCIS-Los Angeles, 60 Minutes, The Big Bang Theory, Two and a Half Men*, and *The Mentalist*. Three of these are crime shows. In 2016, of the 50 most profitable films of all time, none were R-rated (IMDB, 2016).

6 During those years, South Africa was not a member of the World Health Organization, which monitors and records death rates (including homicide) among member nations. There is evidence of deliberate and inadvertent underreporting in some countries (Bialik, 2012).

7 Homicide rates during the Depression were rather high: 8.8 per 100,000 people in 1930, 9.2 (1931), 9.0 (1932), 9.7 (1933), 9.5 (1934). By 1945 (the first year of Centerwall's study), rates were much lower: 5.7 per 100,000 people. After remaining rather low (e.g., 4.7 in 1960), homicide rates climbed dramatically in the 1970s: 10.1 per 100,000 people (1974), 9.9 (1975), 9.0 (1976), 9.1 (1977), 9.2 (1978), 10.0 (1979), and 10.7 (1980; the highest recorded U.S. homicide rate). In 1998, the homicide rate dropped to the lowest rate since 1967: 6 homicides per 100,000 people (U.S. Department of Justice, 1999). Homicide rates have begun to increase a bit since 1999, but they still remain relatively stable and substantially below the rates of the 1960s and 1970s (Bureau of Justice Statistics, 2011).

8 A classic example of a spurious correlation is the strong positive relationship between the number of bars and the number of churches in a town. Although one might be tempted to conclude that drinking leads to repentance and prayer, the relationship is spurious, accounted for in the population of a town. As the number of people in a town increases, so does the number of bars, churches, schools, stores, and so on. Another classic spurious relationship is the one between the size of the big toe and math ability.

9 These panel studies have been widely scrutinized and criticized (e.g., Becker, 1972; Howitt, 1972; Kaplan, 1972; Kay, 1972; Milavsky, Kessler, Stipp, & Rubens, 1982; Sohn, 1982).

10 Because guns are used so often in violent drama and news (S. L. Smith et al., 2004), they might serve as especially potent aggressive cues in the real world.

11 Most of us have observed children who have been watching action-filled cartoons. Often, they cannot sit still.

12 Content analyses of prime-time television have been conducted every year since 1967.

13 Sexually explicit media content is often referred to as pornography, erotica, or obscenity. These terms are often used interchangeably, although they have slightly different meanings and connotations (Hawkins & Zimring, 1988). Erotica, derived from the Greek word *eros* (love), refers to sexually explicit content, without the connotation of degradation. Pornography is derived from the Greek words meaning writings of or about prostitutes. This term tends to define sexual content that includes violence or actions that degrade and demean women (e.g., Longino, 1980). These different terms reflect the different assumptions and views about sexually explicit content that guide research on effects.

Obscenity is a legal term that defines sexual content that is not protected by the First Amendment. The Supreme Court ruled in *Miller v. California* (1973) that obscenity was determined by applying these three rules: (1) the average person, applying contemporary community standards, finds the material, taken as a whole, appeals to prurient interests; (2) the work depicts, in a patently offensive way, sexual conduct defined by the applicable state law; (3) the work lacks any serious literary, artistic, political, or scientific value.

14 This represents a decrease since the first edition of this book (see Baxter, De Riemer, C., Landini, Leslie, & Singletary, 1985; Sherman & Dominick, 1986;

Signorielli, 1987). The Parents Television Council (2007) reported that overall sexual content in all broadcast networks decreased between 1998 and 2002. That study, though, reported that decreases occurred in programming airing between 8:00 p.m. and 10:00 p.m. Hetsroni's (2007) meta-analysis also found that frequency of sexual acts on broadcast television also decreased between 1975 and 2004. These analyses, however, did not examine cable and premium cable networks. Research suggests that these networks carry significantly more sexual content (e.g., D. A. Fisher, Hill, Grube, & Gruber, 2004).

15 Rape myths are stereotyped, inaccurate, outdated, and calloused beliefs about rape and attitudes about women that reflect lack of sympathy for rape victims. Rape myths are usually measured with a scale developed by Burt (1980). Sample items are: "Any healthy woman can successfully resist a rapist if she really wants to," "When women go around braless or wearing short skirts and tight tops, they are just asking for trouble," and "If a girl engages in necking or petting and she lets things get out of hand, it is her own fault if her partner forces sex on her."

16 There are disagreements among scholars about the depiction of violence against women in slasher films. Some argue that women are not singled out as victims in slasher films; they are less likely to be victims than men and are rarely shown as killed after sex (Sapolsky et al., 2003; J. B. Weaver, 1991a). Others argue that women are killed more often in slasher films than in other film genre and in television programs (Linz & Donnerstein, 1994). Moreover, these scholars argue that the significantly longer time that female suffering is on screen (J. B. Weaver, 1991a) emphasizes the focus on female torture (Linz & Donnerstein, 1994).

17 J. B. Weaver (1991c) argues that many of these studies that fail to replicate use flawed methods. Specifically, studies often cue participants by asking them to think about how sexually explicit content demeans and degrades women. Scholars (e.g., M. Mares, 1996; Shrum, 1997) illustrated that when people are aware of the source of information that might be inaccurate (e.g., cultivation effects from inaccurate television content), they are likely to discount it.

8 EFFECTS OF ENTERTAINMENT

Zillmann (2000) calls this the "Entertainment Age." Increases in productivity have created more leisure time. Advances in technology not only deliver a greater variety of different types of entertainment to audiences, but make it easier for them to select and consume the content that appeals to them (e.g., Vorderer, 2000; Zillmann, 2000). Entertainment is the most common use of the mass media. Certainly TV, films, and the Internet are filled with fictional entertainment, but even coverage of real events can be entertaining. Viewers flock to coverage of sporting events; reality programs hold their places as the most watched programs each week. Even news programs can be highly entertaining. For years, *60 Minutes* was one of the highest rated programs; many watched this news program because it was entertaining (e.g., A.M. Rubin, 1981b). Many look forward to Next Media Animation's animated depictions of top news events.[1]

Nielsen reported that people spent 41 hours per week (about 24.4% of the entire week!) watching TV or using the Internet in last quarter of 2009 (Nielsen, 2010). Children spend even more time with the media. The Kaiser Family Foundation (2010) found that:

> 8–18 year-olds devote an average of 7 hours and 38 minutes (7:38) to using entertainment media across a typical day (more than 53 hours a week). And because they spend so much of that time "media multitasking" (using more than one medium at a time), they actually manage to pack a total of 10 hours and 45 minutes (10:45) worth of media content into those 7½ hours. (para. 1)

Theoretical Focus: Uses and Gratifications

Uses and gratifications (E. Katz, Blumler, & Gurevitch, 1974) is a dominant theory that explains the audience's use of entertainment (Bryant & Miron, 2004; Potter & Riddle, 2007). Although uses and gratifications (U&G) was initially developed as a way to explore the appeal of entertainment (e.g., Herzog, 1944), it quickly became clear that U&G was also useful as a theory of media effects, as media content could not have an impact on people who had no use for it (E. Katz, 1959). Uses and gratifications builds on functional approaches to the mass media (e.g., C.R. Wright, 1986) to propose that the reasons that people use media content have an impact on the effects of that content (see A.M. Rubin, 2009). This approach holds that media effects are conditional. That is, effects are based on the reasons that people have for using media content.

U&G research is concerned with:

> the social and psychological origins of needs, which generate expectations of the mass media or other sources, which lead to differential patterns of media exposure (or engagement in other activities), resulting in need gratifications and other consequences, perhaps mostly unintended ones.
>
> (E. Katz et al., 1974, p. 20)

Rosengren's (1974) summary of the U&G model explains how the major concepts are related: People's communication needs, coupled with their personal characteristics and social situations, lead to awareness of various solutions to satisfy those needs. This leads to media use, or other actions, leading to gratification of the needs and/or other consequences.

Several assumptions define U&G (E. Katz et al., 1974; A.M. Rubin, 2009). First, the audience is viewed as actively selecting and using media content. The audience uses mass media to satisfy needs and interests, so media use is goal directed and purposive, motivated by the gratifications that people are seeking. The approach recognizes that people's psychological characteristics and social settings affect media choices and gratifications. Consistent with the conditional model, the audience's media use and gratifications that they receive from that media are seen as more influential in the media effects process than media content. The reasons people use media, their choices, and how they use media content all shape media effects.

U&G research has identified the reasons people have for using the media. People watch television for relaxation, entertainment, to escape daily pressures, to learn, to connect with others, for arousal, for companionship, out of habit, and to pass time (A.M. Rubin, 1981a). People turn to political media for reinforcement, vote guidance, surveillance, and excitement (Blumler & McQuail, 1969). People go on the Internet for interpersonal utility, to pass time, to seek information, for entertainment, and for convenience (Papacharissi & Rubin, 2000). Over the years, scholars have identified the reasons that people listen to talk radio (C.B. Armstrong & Rubin, 1989), surf the Web (D.A. Ferguson & Perse, 2000), use the Web for political information (Kaye & Johnson, 2002), listen to MP3 players (D.A. Ferguson, Greer, & Reardon, 2007; Zeng, 2011), watch YouTube (Bondad-Brown, Rice, & Pearce, 2012; Haridakis & Hanson, 2009), use Facebook (Hunt, Atkin, & Krishnan, 2012; Urista, Dong, & Day, 2009), read blogs (Kaye, 2010), follow Twitter (Greer & Ferguson, 2011), listen to music (Belcher & Haridakis, 2013), and watch reality TV programs (Godlewski & Perse, 2010).

A major modification to U&G grew out of criticisms that audiences weren't always active in selecting and using mass media. Certainly, there is a good deal of evidence that people use television and the Web and its applications to pass time. Now, researchers recognize that audience activity is a variable (A.M. Rubin & Perse, 1987b). That is, audiences can be active – or not – when they select media content and as they consume media content. There are two major types of audience activity (M.R. Levy & Windahl, 1984; Perse, 1990a). Selectivity represents how active and mindful people are when they choose media content. This concept is related to the notion of selective exposure. Involvement represents people's cognitive and affective engagement with the content (M.R. Levy & Windahl, 1984; Perse, 1990a). Involvement is mental or emotional participation with the content or media personalities.

A.M. Rubin (1984) identified two major types of media use: instrumental use, which is an active use of the media, and ritualistic use, which is a more passive use. Instrumental use focuses on using specific media content and is marked by selective exposure to media content and involvement with the content. Ritualistic use, on the other hand, grows out of habit and motives to pass time. It is generally a nonselective use of media, not the content, and little involvement with the content. So, instrumental television users watch more news and information programming (e.g., Rubin, 1984), are more likely to form parasocial relationships with media personalities (Kim & Rubin, 1997; A.M. Rubin, et al., 1985), are more satisfied after watching soap operas (Perse & Rubin, 1988), become more involved with radio talk shows (A.M. Rubin & Step, 2000), and become more involved with the people on reality programs (Godlewski & Perse, 2010). As M.R. Levy and Windahl (1984) explained: "more active individuals not only receive higher amounts of gratification from their media use, but also that they are more affected by such active and gratifying exposure" (pp. 74–75).

Ritualistic use is likely to be linked to some types of Internet addiction (Kim & Haridakis, 2009) and cultivation effects (Bilandzic & Rössler, 2004). Generally, research has found that because instrumental use signals greater involvement with media content, it facilitates effects; ritualistic use is a less engaged and more distracted use of media. Ritualistic use might limit effects because of limited awareness and comprehension of the messages. But, the ritualistic use of television might be compared to the peripheral route to persuasion (Petty & Cacioppo, 1986). Effects might be due to peripheral cues in the content; effects might be unintended (Haridakis, 2002).

There are two major explanations for how U&G accounts for media effects, based on audience motives for using the media and based on audience activity. Motives for media use direct media effects because they guide media selection and use. Information motives, for example, are more likely to lead to selecting news and information-type programming (e.g., D.A. Ferguson & Perse, 2000; A.M. Rubin, 1984; A.M. Rubin et al., 1985). So, audiences are more likely to gain knowledge. Entertainment motives lead people to choose various types of light diversionary programming (A.M. Rubin, 1984). So, these audiences are more likely to be satisfied after media use (e.g., D.A. Ferguson & Perse, 2000; Godlewski & Perse, 2010; Perse & Rubin, 1988).

Motives, though, have their largest impact on the media effects process because they influence audience involvement with the content. Instrumental media use leads to greater cognitive and affective involvement with the content. Cognitive involvement represents mental engagement with media content. People think about the content, elaborate on the implications of what is presented, and think about how the content relates to what they already know (Perse, 1990c, 1998). So, effects derived from media content are more likely. Affective involvement represents the audience's feelings and emotions. People can become caught up in media content. They might become angry while watching a political debate. They might cry while watching a film. They might become nervous while watching the news. They might laugh at a comedy. These emotions can be characterized themselves as media effects. But, research has also shown that emotional responses facilitate identification with media personalities (e.g., Godlewski & Perse, 2010), memory for news (e.g., Newhagen & Reeves, 1992), persuasion (e.g., Nabi, 2007), and aggressive behavior (e.g., C. A. Anderson & Bushman, 2002b).

This chapter focuses on the effects of entertainment, the most widely used type of media content. It focuses on a range of effects that are best explained by applying a uses and gratifications perspective. Because media content cannot affect people who have no use for it (E. Katz, 1959), the chapter applies the conditional model to explain effects from the use of media to produce emotions, for political entertainment, for interpersonal connections, for social comparison, and for dysfunctional and compulsive uses of the media.

Use of the Media to Stimulate Emotions

Mood Regulation

There is a good deal of research evidence that media use results in affective responses. We all know that people laugh at comedies, cry while watching sad films, become frightened by horror movies, and are tense during suspense-filled sporting events. Emotional responses to the media are a functional effect of media use. Mood management research (e.g., Knobloch-Westerwick, 2006; Zillmann, 1988) is a hedonistic approach that holds that people select media content, in part, to maximize pleasurable feelings. Various studies have shown that bored people are more likely to choose exciting television programs and stressed people are more likely to choose arousing programs (e.g., Bryant & Zillmann, 1984). Anxious men and women are more likely to watch comedy programs on television (e.g., D. R. Anderson, Collins, Schmitt, & Jacobvitz, 1996). College students in bad moods are more likely to listen to music that is high-energy and joyful (e.g., Knobloch & Zillmann, 2002). Premenstrual women are more likely to select comedy programs on television (Meadowcroft & Zillmann, 1987).

The most basic assumption underlying mood management theory is that people seek a pleasurable environment. This hedonistic approach holds that people will arrange their environment to minimize discomfort and maximize pleasure. So, we seek out companions that make us feel good; we select food that we like to eat; we take the routes that will take us most easily to our destinations. And, we select media content that will improve our mood.

Mood management effects are based on operant conditioning. Over their lives, people have selected various types of media content and experienced effects on their moods. The content that gives pleasure and helps change negative moods is rewarding and remembered, so that people are likely to select that type of content in the future to change negative moods.

Mood management effects might be explained by the direct effects model. Although people can deliberately select certain types of media content to help change their moods, because of the impact of operant conditioning people do not necessarily need to be aware of the reasons underlying their choices (Knobloch-Westerwick, 2006). It is the attributes of media content that deliver the desired mood-altering effects (Knoblock-Westerwick, 2006; Zillmann, 1988).

The excitatory potential of media content impacts negative moods. That is, arousing content is more likely to energize people when they are feeling bored or need some motivation.[2] Fast music, driving rhythms, television programs with fast pacing, and violent movie special effects all have high excitatory potential, as does media violence and pornography. Calming content, on the other hand, can soothe and relax.

The absorption potential of media content impacts negative moods. Often negative moods are marked by rumination or pondering on the events that created the mood. Media content needs to be absorbing in order to distract attention from the cause of the bad mood, allowing for mood change. Boring content can't be distracting. So, an interesting book or a suspenseful football game is more likely to have mood management effects than a tedious talk show with dull guests. Video games especially can have high absorption potential. Anecdotes in the popular press suggest that gaming can be a break from a reality filled with deadlines, stress, and responsibilities.

Semantic affinity is another media content attribute that affects mood management effects. Media content can remind the viewer about the cause of the bad mood. For example, if someone is stressed about completing a final paper for an international relations class, watching international news will only serve to remind them about the task. Different content, unrelated to the cause of the bad mood, will be distracting. Of course, when one wants to maintain and reinforce positive feelings, one should select content that is semantically similar to the source of the good mood. Watching the highlights of a winning game, for example, can sustain a celebration.

Hedonic value affects mood effects. Happy and cheerful content will boost spirits; sad and unpleasant content will not. So, human interest news stories about successes are more likely to have positive mood effects. News stories about destruction and human tragedy should not. Of course, what is happy for some might not be happy for all. Every sporting event and election has winners and losers. What is good news to someone will be bad news for someone else.

The Paradox of Enjoying Suspense, Horror, and Misery

People use entertainment to improve their moods. Consistent with Stephenson's (1988) play theory that holds that all voluntary media use should be pleasurable, it is easy to see how attributes of media content can help people shift bad moods and improve good ones. Mood management offers an explanation for the appeal for some media content that, on its face, should not be pleasurable. Violence and crime shows often depict gruesome and unpleasant events. But, their absorption potential offers mood shifts. Violent video games not only have high absorption potential, but successful play can bring positive feelings. Selection of other kinds of media content, though, is quite a paradox. Suspense, tear jerkers, and horror are popular entertainment genres. But, they depict situations that, in real life, most all of us avoid. How can these genres be pleasurable?

What's the Appeal of Horror Films?

Horror films are an interesting genre. They are sometimes filled with gruesome and extreme violence (e.g., *Saw*, *Texas Chainsaw Massacre*). Others only hint at violence (e.g., *Psycho*). It is clear that the threat of unknown violence is at the heart of most horror films. Horror films focus on the things that frighten or repulse us. They bring the supernatural, aliens, demons, serial killers, the undead, and rabid animals into our daily lives. Horror films are the stuff that makes nightmares. No horror films (except for the 1975 classic *Jaws*) make the Internet Movie Database Top 100 All-Time U.S. Box Office; however, franchises like the 10 *Halloween* and 9 *Nightmare on Elm Street* movies suggest that they appeal to some large part of the audience. Why do people enjoy seeing gore and disfigurement? Why do they enjoy being frightened?

Steven King (a master of horror himself) gives some good reasons. King (1981) says that horror is one way for society to deal with its fears. So, zombies thrive after a virus decimates society (*28 Days Later*); *Godzilla* is born from a radiation accident. King also believes in a kind of catharsis – that horror films allow us to release our fears so that we can cope with society better.

A media researcher, Dolf Zillmann, offers another theoretical explanation. He points out that horror has been a part of a society's ritualized tales since tribal times (Zillmann & Gibson, 1996). Horror tales were a way to socialize the young men of a tribe so that they could face enemies and hunt and kill ferocious animals. In modern society, horror films are a safe way for adolescents to explore and display gender-role appropriate emotions. So heterosexual men and women enjoy horror films more when they watch with someone of the opposite sex – especially when the "brave" male can comfort the "frightened" woman – a sort of "snuggle" factor (Zillmann & Weaver, 1996).

Suspense

Suspenseful media content is often the most popular and entertaining. One of the most widely watched television programs of all times was the 1980 *Dallas* resolution to the question "Who shot JR?" Movies that keep us on the edge of our seat and football games that are won or lost in the last seconds all rivet audiences to their seats. Suspense is a key element of successful drama. Suspense is generally defined as a state of uncertainty or excitement, as in awaiting a decision or outcome, usually accompanied by a degree of apprehension or anxiety. In real life, suspense and anxiety are not always desirable conditions. It's not pleasant waiting to hear from a college to see if we've been admitted, or from a boyfriend to see if we'll be asked to the prom, or from a doctor to see if our test is positive. It's not pleasant to sit in an airport waiting to see if the weather will break so that our plane can take off. But, in entertainment the suspense and anxiety are pleasant and desirable emotions.

Zillmann (1991a) points out that dramatic suspense is enhanced by a focus on (a) negative outcomes (death, injury, harm, romantic loss, change of economic circumstances), (b) sympathetic characters who are endangered, and (c) a high degree of uncertainty of the negative outcomes. In other words, in order to feel suspense, characters we like must be in positions where it is likely that something terrible will happen to them. Further, suspense is heightened when audiences either identify with or empathize with the protagonist and get "caught up" in the drama (Zillmann, 1991a). Generally, the more suspense, the more audiences feel entertained. But, why is suspense in entertainment so enjoyable when those same feelings in real life cause such distress?

Zillmann (1991a) explains the appeal of suspense by excitation-transfer. Specifically, excitation-transfer holds that emotional reactions to events are influenced by the arousal levels induced by preceding events. This is an arousal-based theory that holds that arousal is key to understanding the appeal of suspense. Arousal is a nonspecific excitement response that is marked by physiological changes such as higher heart rate, faster breathing, and skin conductance (often measured by galvanic skin response or "lie detectors"). Because it is nonspecific, humans label the arousal that they feel according to the context in which they feel it (e.g., Schachter, 1964). For example, if we feel arousal just before giving a speech in class, we are likely to label that arousal as performance fear. If we feel arousal after a romantic embrace, we might label it love. According to excitation-transfer, the elements of suspense all serve to increase arousal in the audience. As suspense increases, arousal increases. In the context of the drama, the arousal is labeled suspense. A second key to excitation-transfer is that arousal does not dissipate quickly. It takes a while for the body to return to an unaroused more normal state. So, arousal induced by prior experiences remains for a while, and can affect perceptions of subsequent events.

Suspense, then, produces arousal. The more successful the dramatic techniques, the greater the arousal; the more that the audience identifies with the protagonist, the greater the arousal. The more that that audience feels distress for the protagonist, the greater the arousal. Because the audience recognizes the dramatic context, the arousal is labeled as "suspense." This arousal itself is distressful, not pleasurable. But, a successful outcome to the drama brings relief and joy. According to excitation-transfer theory, the arousal that still remains is relabeled – as joy and pleasure. So, the greater the arousal, the higher the suspense, and the greater the entertainment after a positive outcome.[3]

There is support for excitation-transfer effects in suspense. Zillmann, Hay, and Bryant (1975) report the results of experimental research that deliberately modified children's television programs to increase the amount of danger threatening the protagonist. The program depicted children on safari with their fathers on the eve of their first lion hunt. The researchers manipulated the amount of danger and suspense with different descriptions of the lion. In the low suspense condition, the lion was described as just a wild lion. In the moderate condition, the lion was described as rather vicious. In the high suspense condition, the lion was described as a ferocious beast that had killed people. The visuals show the lion from far away (low suspense condition) to close-ups of roars and teeth (high suspense). Visuals also showed the boys' reactions, varying amounts of fear. The resolution to the hunt was also manipulated. In the low satisfaction version, the lion escapes and can be heard roaring in the distance. In the high satisfaction version, the boys are able to kill the lion.

A sample of children saw different versions of the program. Trained judges watched the children and marked their facial and verbal expressions of fear and enjoyment. The children were more frightened and excited by the high suspenseful version of the program. After watching, children were asked how much they enjoyed the program. Consistent with excitation-transfer theory, greater suspense led to greater enjoyment – but only in the version with the satisfying ending. So, as threat increases, arousal increases, and the entertainment increases. Excitation-transfer theory, then, supports a hedonistic view of entertainment. People enjoy suspense because it results in pleasure.

Tear Jerkers

Oliver (2008) points out that "tragedies or sad films are perhaps the most obvious paradox, as such films presumably evoke strong negative affective states that mood management characterizes as an outcome typically avoided by viewers" (p. 41). Although some tear jerkers end on optimistic notes, many do not. Jack (along with thousands of others) dies at the end of the *Titanic*, Old Yeller gets rabies and is shot, and Emma dies in *Terms of Endearment*. Moreover, there is evidence some people seek out media content to deliberately maintain sad moods. The broken-hearted often listen to sad songs (see R. Gibson, Aust, & Zillmann, 2000). The lonely sometimes watch television programs about other lonely people (M. Mares & Cantor, 1992).

Oliver has engaged in a line of research that tries to uncover the appeal of sad films. She has found that watching sad films can be consistent with mood management. According to Oliver (1993), there is a distinction between the direct emotional responses to the films and the meta-emotions, or the emotional response to an emotional reaction. In other words, someone might experience positive affect after watching a sad movie, if the emotional reaction is seen as gratifying. (Some people might love a "good cry.") She found that people who enjoy feeling sad while watching sad movies find the movies entertaining and tend to watch more of them, compared to other genres.

It is clear that not all entertainment is happy and jolly. There are several dramatic genres that focus on the ups and downs of human relationships, the connections between people, and the expression of emotion. Sad content often focuses on relationships and the human condition. Oliver (2008) suggests that eudaimonic motivations can direct selection of tear jerkers. That is, people might select sad content in a search for "greater insight, self-reflection, or contemplations of poignancy or meaningfulness" (p. 42). Her research found that tender affective states (e.g., empathy, warmth, kindness, and connections to others) did lead to selection of movies that focus on human drama and poignant and touching films that sometimes included tragic elements.[4] Most recently, her research found that "elevation," a response (e.g., a lump in the throat) to observing moral virtues, "may be experienced in response to sad films that feature characters displaying courage or facing hardship, dramas that grapple with issues of human value, or even more serious romances that depict the power of love in lifting the human spirit" (Oliver, Hartmann, & Woolley, 2012, p. 362).

Horror

The appeal of horror films is difficult to understand. As a genre, they feature depictions of extreme violence and focus on themes of death, destruction, evil, or the supernatural. Unlike typical suspenseful films with satisfying endings, many horror films end with victimization and terror – and indications that the evil antagonist is still alive. The manifest goals of horror are fear and disgust. Although these films are not the most popular of film genres, they have loyal fans, as evidenced by the continued production of sequels such as *Halloween* (9 sequels), *Friday the 13th* (11 sequels), *Nightmare on Elm Street* (7 sequels and a 2010 remake). While some might be motivated by sadistic needs, it is difficult to explain how horror can be entertaining. Scholars, however, have offered three explanations for the appeal of horror (see Tamborini, 2003).

Some writers have suggested excitation-transfer as an explanation for horror's appeal. It is clear that the graphic mayhem, blood, and gore are sources of great arousal. Humans have innate needs to pay attention to and be wary of physical violence (Zillmann, 1998). Excitation-transfer theory suggests that the more arousal (i.e., the more gore and fear), the greater the pleasure after viewing. This hypothesis has been supported – for exposure to horror films with satisfying endings, where the villain is captured or destroyed (C. M. King & Hourani, 2007). But, many horror films don't have happy endings.

There is evidence that excitation-transfer explains positive experiences after viewing horror, for some types of people. Zillmann (1991a) argues that identification with protagonists is key to understanding the appeal of suspense. Research on horror films, however, gives indications that excitation-transfer might be the process of enjoyment only for those viewers low in empathy (C. Hoffner, 2009; C. A. Hoffner & Levine, 2005). Empathy is sympathy or concern for the welfare of others along with feelings of anxiety or discomfort in response to others' suffering (C. Hoffner, 2009). For those low in empathy, the focus on the protagonist might be less relevant to enjoyment. It might not matter who lives or dies. Instead, arousal might be based solely on the physical danger. And, the promise of continuing mayhem and horror might provide the satisfying ending.

A second explanation for the appeal of horror builds on the social gratifications of watching. According to the gender-socialization theory of affect (Zillmann & Weaver, 1996), horror provides an opportunity for adolescents to practice gender-appropriate behaviors that are generally prohibited in other situations. So horror films let adolescent males "prove to their peers, and ultimately to themselves, that they are unperturbed, calm, and collected in the face of terror" (p. 83). Adolescent females can "demonstrate their sensitivity by being appropriately disturbed, dismayed, and disgusted" (p. 83). Consequently, research has found that young men enjoy horror films more when they are with young women (Zillmann, Weaver, Mundorf, & Aust, 1986).

A third explanation for the appeal of horror is based on individual differences in optimal arousal levels, or sensation seeking (e.g., Zuckerman, 1996). Sensation-seeking research is based on the recognition that people have different optimal levels of arousal. Some people prefer calm and placid settings; others prefer commotion and excitement. Sensation seeking is a personality trait that has been defined as "the seeking of varied, novel, complex, and intense sensations and experiences, and the willingness to take physical, social, legal, and financial risks for the sake of such experience" (Zuckerman, 1996, p. 148). High sensation seekers seek arousal in all circumstances, even in media use. The characteristics of horror films especially can help high sensation seekers reach their optimal level of arousal (Zuckerman, 1996). For those high in sensation seeking, the high arousal itself is rewarding and entertaining.

Scholars have found strong support for the relationship between high sensation seeking and preference for horror films (P. A. Lawrence & Palmgreen, 1996; Zuckerman & Litle, 1986) as well as between sensation seeking and enjoyment of horror films (C. A. Hoffner & Levine, 2005). For high sensation seekers, the high arousal gained from horror can be quite entertaining.

Summary

Mood management might not be the sole reason for media use. As uses and gratifications holds, there are other gratifications that people seek from the media. Watching bad news might make viewers feel tense and upset, but serve their need for information (e.g., watching TV coverage during tragedies and disasters). Predictions of extreme weather draw attention, even though they instill fright, because people need to be prepared. Watching others experience tragedies might facilitate downward social comparison (Festinger, 1954). Mood enhancement can result from comparisons to those who are worse off. So, we might get some relief from watching tragedy or listening to songs about loneliness and heartbreak.

Fear in Children

Fear is "an immediate emotional response that is typically of relatively short duration, but that may endure, on occasion, for several hours or days, or even longer" (Cantor, 2009, p. 287). Fear is not necessarily a negative effect of media violence. Studies using nonchild samples show that fear is one of the appeals of certain media genres. Suspense, for example, is a highly sought-after aspect of television programs and movies. Generally, more suspenseful movies are more successful movies because suspense produces enjoyment (Zillmann, 1980). Even horror movies have their fans – those who like being scared (e.g., P. A. Lawrence & Palmgreen, 1996). For children, however, fear is not necessarily pleasurable. There is much concern that some children become quite frightened by some media content, and that fear will have some enduring, negative effects.

Over the years, there has been a good deal of research and anecdotal evidence that children do become frightened by some media content. In one of the Payne Fund studies, Blumer (1933) concluded that some children were so affected emotionally by the movies that they were "emotionally possessed." Fear was one of the common emotional reactions to the movies. Over the years, certain movies and television programs have been anecdotally linked to childhood fear. Some movies (e.g., *Indiana Jones and the Temple of Doom* and *Gremlins*), rated PG, were so frightening that another category to the MPAA movie code was created in 1984: PG-13. Parents were cautioned to keep children from watching *Jurassic Park*, a popular 1993 film about a rampage of cloned dinosaurs in a modern-day theme park, because of the fearful situations they depicted. The *Harry Potter* movies have scenes, situations, and characters that can certainly frighten the younger readers of the series. Even animated programs designed for the youngest children can evoke fear. *Bambi* and *Lion King* depict the death of beloved parents. The *Wizard of Oz* is filled with wicked witches and flying monkeys. Cantor and her colleagues (Cantor, Bryne, Moyer-Gusé, & Riddle, 2010) found that these and many other family movies and television programs frightened children.[5]

Children become frightened by dangers and injuries (a large part of television drama, reality programs, and news), monsters and "unnatural" creatures, distortions of natural forms (e.g., deformed people and extra-large creatures), and by witnessing fear and danger to others (Cantor, 2009). Concerns about childhood fears have increased as technical expertise and computer effects have increased distortions and the graphic portrayal of violence.

It is not always possible to predict when children will be frightened. Movies such as *Poltergeist* and the Stephen King miniseries *It* have left some children afraid of clowns, for example. Research has shown that children's cognitive immaturity can lead to fear reactions. Sparks and Cantor (1986), for example, noted that young children were quite frightened by the television program *The Incredible Hulk*, in which a scientist transforms into a super-strong green monster to correct injustices. The Hulk was a good character, but he frightened children because he looked scary. At young ages, appearances lead to fear, regardless of the motives or underlying character. As children grow older, they are more likely to be frightened by real, rather than fantasy media content (Cantor, 2009). With cognitive maturity, children realize that fiction is not real. But, frightening real-world characters and events can be great sources of fear. For older children, the realistic violence of reality programs and news may be more frightening than drama (e.g., J. Cantor, Mares, & Oliver, 1993).

Political Entertainment

Traditional mass communication research focuses on the effects of news, public affairs programming, and political campaigns (see Chapter 4). A growing body of research, however, is beginning to focus specifically on the impact that entertainment has on people's political thoughts, agendas, and actions. Humorists have always created satire to critique political parties and politics. Benjamin Franklin, Mark Twain, and Will Rogers are some early examples of political satirists; *The Onion*, *The Daily Show*, and *The Colbert Report* are some current examples. Comedians have been inspired by politics: The Smothers Brothers, Lenny Bruce, Lewis Black, Johnny Carson, Jay Leno, Bill Maher, Dennis Miller, and David Letterman all led their audiences to laugh at politicians' "logic" and actions. Over the years, "fake" news programs, such as *That was the Week that Was, Saturday Night Live*'s *Weekend Update*, and *The Daily Show* have made fun of people in the media spotlight, as well as the journalists who report the news. Real-life political and news events inspire the plots of movies and television shows, such as *All the President's Men, Erin*

Brokovich, Black Hawk Down, The China Syndrome, Blood Diamond, and the *Law & Order* franchise ("ripped from the headlines").

Research on the political effects of entertainment programming is increasing. Scholars have found that exposure to movies (Holbert & Hansen, 2006), to crime dramas (Holbrook & Hill, 2005), and late-night television (Moy, Xenos, & Hass, 2006) can prime political thoughts. Research also shows that exposure to nonnews entertainment programming has significant effects on attitudes that are likely to affect political decisions and on evaluations of political candidates.

Effects on Political Attitudes

Cultivation is a theoretical perspective that holds that exposure to the consistent violent content of television drama leads heavy viewers to feel more afraid, distrust others, and to endorse the political mainstream (e.g., Morgan, Shanahan, & Signorielli, 2009). Recent research has expanded cultivation to the study of media's impact on environmental values and actions (e.g., Hart, Nisbett, & Shanahan, 2011; Shanahan Morgan, & Stenbjerre, 1997).

Agenda setting is another theoretical explanation for political effects of entertainment programs. Holbrook and Hill's (2005) experiment assessed the impact of exposure to crime drama programs (e.g., *Third Watch, Without a Trace, Robbery Homicide Division*) on beliefs that crime was one of the most serious problems facing America. These results were reinforced with a follow-up survey that also linked *NYPD Blue* viewing to greater concern that crime was a serious problem facing America. Holbrook and Hill (2005) argue that the frequency and consistency of crime drama programs prime concerns about crime and make those concerns chronically accessible.

Other research has found similar sorts of effects. Holbert, Shah, and Kwak (2003) found that exposure to progressive dramas (e.g., *Law & Order, ER*), sitcoms (e.g., *Friends, Seinfeld*), and traditional dramas (*Touched by an Angel, Dr. Quinn, Medicine Woman*) all lead to support for women's rights. Holbert et al. (2004) found that viewing police reality shows (e.g., *Cops, America's Most Wanted*) was related to support for the death penalty and handgun ownership. Crime drama viewing (e.g., *NYPD Blue, Law & Order*) was related to support for capital punishment. Eyal and her colleagues (Eyal, Metzger, Lingsweiler, Mahood, & Yao, 2006) found that watching violent television programs (e.g., *Cops, The Shield, Sopranos*) predicted holding aggressive political opinions, or those that support "positions that involve forceful resolution to social or political issues" (p. 399), such as support for capital punishment, endorsing gun rights, the use of military force, and vigilantism. Holbert and his colleagues (Holbert et al., 2003) found that the television program *The West Wing* primes positive views of the Presidency as an institution, resulting in increased approval for both Presidents Bill Clinton and George W. Bush. It might be interesting to see if the positive images of U.S. health care presented in entertainment television (e.g., Kaiser Family Foundation, 2008) affect people's attitudes about health care policy.

Effects on Evaluations of Candidates

Presidential candidate Richard Nixon's 1968 appearance on *Laugh In* ("Sock it to *me*?") might be one of the first examples of a politician using a television entertainment program to advance his campaign. Now, entertainment media are important to politicians. Bill Clinton played the saxophone on *The Arsenio Hall Show* in 1992. In the 2000 Presidential campaign, both Al Gore and George W. Bush visited talk shows such as *The Late Show with David Letterman* and *The Tonight Show with Jay Leno*. In the 2004 Presidential campaign, candidates made 25 appearances on television talk shows, including *Real Time with Bill Maher*, *The Late Show with David Letterman*, *The Tonight Show with Jay Leno*, and *The Daily Show with Jon Stewart* (Center for Media and Public Affairs, 2008). By the 2008 campaign, candidates made 110 appearances (Center for Media and Public Affairs, 2008). Two even declared their candidacy on late-night talk shows: John McCain declared on the *Letterman* show; Fred Thompson declared on *The Tonight Show*. On election eve, John McCain and Sarah Palin both appeared on a special election edition of *Saturday Night Live*.

These candidate appearances are strategic. These programs typically get high ratings, ensuring that the candidates are seen by many, even those who would not normally watch public affairs and campaign programming – less involved voters who make decisions based on the peripheral route, candidate image, and emotional responses (see Chapter 4). Moreover, these appearances are hosted by congenial entertainment personalities who focus on personal questions and humor to entertain. Appearances on friendly talk shows allow candidates to avoid the questions, probes, and criticisms of press conferences and debates.

Research on candidate appearances on late-night talk programs shows that these appearances with affable hosts do have positive effects on voters. George W. Bush's favorability ratings increased among viewers after his appearance on the *Letterman* show. Moy and her colleagues (Moy et al., 2006) found that viewers were more likely to base their evaluations of George W. Bush on character traits after he appeared on the *Letterman* show where the interview focused on Bush's ownership of the Texas Rangers and his assertions that he was a "people person."

The 2008 campaign reinforces the impact of entertainment programs on voters' candidate impressions. Sarah Palin, a relative unknown, became the Republican nominee for Vice President. One part of the rush to "define" her included several Tina Fey impressions on *Saturday Night Live*. Writers were concerned that the "one-dimensional" impressions would have a negative effect on Palin (a "Fey effect," e.g., Sands, 2008). There is evidence that the *SNL* skits affected mainstream media coverage of Palin. After the skit spoofing Palin's interview with Katie Couric, there was an increase in the number of news stories questioning Palin's qualifications to be Vice President (Abel & Barthel, 2013). Research by Esralew and Young (2012) explored how those parodies influenced voters' impressions of Palin. Consistent with their hypotheses, they found that the group who watched one of the parodies were more likely to see Palin's "rural" qualities, such as small-town, hick, back-country, and folksy. The authors explained that this effect was pronounced because she was unknown; the parodies were likely to become part of voters' schematic impressions of Palin.

Beyond cultivation and agenda setting, there are some other theoretical explanations for the political effects of entertainment programming. D. G. Young (2008) found that political humor reduces scrutiny of arguments in messages. It is likely that entertainment motives for watching political entertainment would also lead audiences to expend less cognitive effort while watching the programs (e.g., Eveland, 2001) and so follow peripheral routes (see Chapter 4). This less critical approach to political messages in entertainment programming might lead to attitudinal and political effects (e.g., Nabi, Moyer-Guse, & Bryne, 2007).

Political entertainment might also have a "sleeper effect." This is a phenomenon identified in persuasion research. Highly credible sources typically are more persuasive than less credible sources. But, audiences can forget the sources of messages even though they remember the content (Allen & Stiff, 1989). If the discounting effect of the less credible source (entertainment content) is forgotten, then audiences might be affected by the information in the programs.

Effects of "Fake News"

There is growing evidence that a particular kind of political entertainment might have unique effects on the audience. Satirical political entertainment that takes the form of fake news pokes fun at politicians and journalists. *The Daily Show* had adapted the form of a cable news program; *The Colbert Report* has adapted the form of the cable news personality commentary program. These programs use satire to encourage their audiences "to examine, evaluate, and re-situate the genre and its practices" (Baym, 2005, p. 269).

When Fake News has Real Political Effects

Stephen Colbert is a satirist who hosted a daily late-night fake news program, *The Colbert Report*, on Comedy Central network. *The Colbert Report* is a parody of cable news "personality programs." Colbert hosts the program in the character of a right-wing host, said to be modeled on Fox News' Bill O'Reilly ("Papa Bear"). He's adopted that persona and used it many times with some political effect. He received, for example, a chilly reception at the 2006 White House Correspondents' Association dinner; many saw it as a criticism of President Bush and his administration – and the press. Colbert "tested the waters" for a Presidential bid in the 2008 election. He testified before the House Judiciary Subcommittee on Immigration, Citizenship, and Border Security about working with migrant workers. He sponsored his own rally "To Restore Fear" alongside Jon Stewart's October 2010 "Rally to Restore Sanity." And, in 2012, he established his own political action committee, Citizens for a Better Tomorrow, Tomorrow.

Political Action Committees (PAC) are organizations that campaign for (or against) candidates or issues. After the 2010 *Citizens United* decision, corporations and unions were allowed to make contributions to PACs, but not directly to candidates. Other rulings paved the way for "super PACs," which can raise unlimited funds from unions, corporations, and individuals and spend these unlimited funds to support (or fight) candidates and issues – as long as they are not directly associated with the campaign. In June 2012, Restore Our Future, a super PAC that supported Mitt Romney's candidacy for President, was the largest super PAC (with about $46 million). American Crossroads, backed by Karl Rove, is another well-known super PAC.

Stephen Colbert's Citizens for a Better Tomorrow, Tomorrow hasn't raised as much as the big super PACs, but it has had an effect. He's raised awareness of super PACs among his viewers as he's discussed his political work on his program. Citizens for a Better Tomorrow, Tomorrow has stimulated others to set up super PACs. In response to a college student's query about how to set up a super PAC, Colbert offered a $99 "Super PAC Super Fun Kit" for sale on his website. Several college students started their own super PACs. Although these super PACs aren't on a par with American Crossroads, Politico reports that in May 2012, 2.5% of all super PACs are "spawn" of Citizens for a Better Tomorrow, Tomorrow (Levinthal, 2012). Stephen Colbert's lampoon of campaign finance might be leading young people toward political action.

Research on these programs has expanded in the past few years. Many believe that these programs are a prime source of political information for younger viewers, who are turned off by mainstream news (Baym, 2010), just at the time when they are politically socialized and involved (e.g., D.G. Young & Tisinger, 2006). Moreover, high-profile political and celebrity guests draw the attention of the mainstream news media. Jon Stewart himself was a guest on CNN's *Crossfire* in 2004. *The Daily Show* attracts a relatively large regular audience, considering that it is on a basic cable channel. The Pew Research Center's Project for Excellence in Journalism (Pew Research Center for the People & the Press, 2008) reported that in 2007 Jon Stewart ranked as the fourth most admired news journalist, tied with Brian Williams (then *NBC Nightly News* anchor), Tom Brokaw (former anchor of *NBC Nightly News*), Dan Rather (former anchor of *CBS Evening News*), and cable host Anderson Cooper (CNN news personality). In 2008, *The Daily Show* had an average audience of about 1.8 million.[6]

Scholars argue that these two programs differ from other types of political entertainment (e.g., Hoffman & Young, 2011). First, audiences of the programs know that they are humor and the messages are designed to be satirical.[7] The audiences tend to be younger than those of other late-night programs (Pew Research Center for the People & the Press, 2008). The audiences also tend to have higher levels of political knowledge (e.g., D. Young & Tisinger, 2006) and political efficacy (Hoffman & Young, 2011).[8]

The programs present a good deal of political and public affairs information. Cao (2010) reported that over a third of the jokes in *The Daily Show*'s headline dealt with political issues in the 2004 campaign. A content analysis of *The Daily Show* in 2005 found that more than half of the news stories covered political topics; almost half covered world affairs (Brewer & Marquardt, 2007). The authors conclude that these programs' political effects are an important area to study. The programs have become a regular stop for high-profile politicians and news makers. Recent guests include President Barack Obama, Vice President Joe Biden, former Presidents Jimmy Carter and Bill Clinton. Foreign heads of state visit: Tony Blair and Gordon Brown, both former Prime Ministers of the United Kingdom, Pervez Musharraf, former President of Pakistan, and Abdullah II, the King of Jordan. Other guests include political candidates, senators, representatives, governors, cabinet members, and journalists.

Although most of *The Daily Show*'s "on-location" live reports occur in the studio in front of a blue screen, correspondents travel to the places where news is made and cover real news stories. Ed Helms reported from "the free speech zone" at the 2004 Democratic convention in Boston. Jason Jones visited Wasilla, Alaska, to report on the duties of the mayor. Rob Riggle, a former Marine who served in Liberia, Kosovo, and Afghanistan, visited with the U.S. troops in Iraq and covered the 2008 Beijing Olympics.

Young people approach the programs as both entertainment and news. D. G. Young (2012) found that 81% of her college-student sample watched the programs because they were entertaining. But, 42% watched to learn about news and politics. Another 39% watched because it made learning about news and politics fun. A smaller group watch because they find the programs unbiased and a truthful source for news (10%); another 9% watch to get context for the news they already know. These results signal that a good portion of the young audience is watching for instrumental reasons (e.g., A.M. Rubin, 1984). The informational orientation is likely to lead to political effects (e.g., Eveland, 2001).

Research has shown that watching *The Daily Show* is associated with increased attention to politics. Feldman and Young (2008) noted that exposure to *The Daily Show* was linked to attention to the 2004 campaign – even after controlling for exposure to newspapers and network, cable, and local news. Cao (2010) found that, among the most apolitical viewers of *The Daily Show*, exposure was related to increased attention to politics and the war in Afghanistan. Similarly, among younger people, watching *The Daily Show* was linked to higher political knowledge (Cao, 2008; Hollander, 2005). Other research found that watching *The Daily Show* was associated with young people reporting more confidence in their ability to understand politics (Baumgartner & Morris, 2006). And, among the less politically involved, experimental exposure to clips from *The Daily Show* led to more interest in the news and higher knowledge (Xenos & Becker, 2009).

These indications that *The Daily Show*'s most noticeable effects appear to occur among the young, especially those less knowledgeable and politically involved support Baum's "gateway hypothesis" (2003). According to Baum, exposure to soft news and comedy, like *The Daily Show*, makes it easier for people to gain information. Especially among those people who are less motivated to seek information, entertainment and humor reduce the opportunity costs associated with information seeking. So, watching *The Daily Show* can lead to increased knowledge for the less motivated, greater knowledge for those who don't watch other kinds of news, and perhaps even serve to motivate people to seek out additional news. There is indirect support for the gateway hypothesis; D. G. Young and Tisinger (2006) found that for many viewers of *The Daily Show*, the program is a supplement to other news sources. Although there has not been consistent support for the gateway hypothesis (e.g., Feldman & Young, 2008), others find strongest effects for the programs among the least politically engaged (e.g., Cao, 2010, Hollander, 2005; Xenos & Becker, 2009). Research on the gateway hypothesis supports research efforts that focus on the impact of entertainment programming. Perhaps humor and entertainment "wrapping" of more serious content is a way to overcome some of the barriers identified in knowledge-gap research (e.g., Tichenor, Donohue, & Olien, 1970). Humor may overcome the impact of education and motivation to lead to increased prosocial media effects.

Use of Entertainment to Form Interpersonal Connections

Disposition theory (Raney, 2006) explains that entertainment depends on our emotional connections to the characters in drama. Enjoyment increases when good things happen to characters we like; it decreases when characters we like suffer (Raney, 2006). The importance of the audience's involvement with characters has been supported in studies of humor (e.g., Zillmann & Cantor, 1972), drama (e.g., Zillmann & Cantor, 1977), crime stories (e.g., Raney, 2005), and sports (e.g., Zillmann, Bryant, & Sapolsky, 1989). According to disposition theory, then, the characters in the media are central to entertainment. As Raney (2006) points out, "disposition-based theories contend that media enjoyment starts with and is driven by the viewer's feelings about characters" (p. 145).

It is clear that our feelings for media characters do not end when the program or movie ends. There is a good deal of evidence that people form attachments to media personalities. Fans of the *Twilight* series are drawn to Bella, Edward, and Jacob. News viewers feel comfortable getting the news from their familiar local anchors. Eyal and Cohen (2006) observed that fans of *Friends* felt "distress" after viewing the last episode. The authors suggest that fans felt sadness at the "parasocial breakup." Children also identify with media personalities and imitate their actions and fashions (J. Cohen, 2001; C. Hoffner, 1996).[9]

The widespread adoption of television in the 1950s led Horton and Wohl (1956) to notice the interpersonal connections that the audience members formed with the media personalities. Most media consumption is personalized by the audience, as it takes place in familiar settings and focuses on attractive people. Producers take steps to encourage interpersonal connections between personalities and the audience. They use camera angles that give the illusion of interpersonal distance. Talk show hosts and news anchors talk directly to the audience, simulating conversation. Several television programs "break the fourth wall" (e.g., Auter & Davis, 1991) and feature characters who talk directly to the audience, seemingly erasing the artificiality of the medium.[10] Most recently, there is evidence that celebrities' and politicians' use of Twitter and social networking sites enhances parasocial feelings because they give the feeling of actual conversations (E. Lee & Jang, 2012).

Horton and Wohl (1956) proposed that people engage in "parasocial interaction" and form "parasocial relationships" with media personalities. Parasocial interaction is a one-sided relationship between audience members and media personalities that is characterized as a pseudofriendship. As a result of regular exposure to the program and consistent presentations by the personalities, audience members come to feel that they "know" the media personality just like they know their real-life friends. Repeated exposure also allows viewers to develop a "sense of history" with the performer. There is evidence that people form parasocial relationships with news anchors (e.g., A.M. Rubin et al., 1985), with radio talk show hosts (e.g., A.M. Rubin & Step, 2000), television characters (e.g., J. Cohen, 2002), characters in telenovelas (Shefner-Rogers, Rogers, & Singhal, 1998) and soap operas (e.g., A.M. Rubin & Perse, 1987b), athletes (e.g., Earnheardt & Haridakis, 2009; Kassing & Sanderson, 2009), and music video performers (e.g., Auter, Ashton, & Soliman, 2008).

Initially, writers believed that parasocial interaction was an abnormal and extreme response to television. Parasocial interaction was viewed as a way for lonely and socially isolated audiences to find social connections to others (e.g., Rosengren & Windahl, 1972; A.M. Rubin et al., 1985). It became clear, however, that parasocial responses to media characters were common. Now, parasocial interaction is conceptualized as evidence of an active audience that is involved with the characters on the programs (e.g., J. Kim & Rubin, 1997; A.M. Rubin & Perse, 1987a). Parasocial relationships are similar to social relationships. Audiences are attracted to appealing characters (R. B.

Rubin & McHugh, 1987) who share their attitudes and backgrounds (J.R. Turner, 1993). The parasocial relationship develops over time. Because regular viewing allows audience members to self-disclose as well as react to various settings and other characters, regular viewing leads audiences to feel that they "know" the character the way that they know their social friends (Perse & Rubin, 1989). Keys to the development of parasocial relationships, then, are (a) active and involved audience members, (b) appealing and attractive media personalities, (c) regular and consistent exposure to the personalities, and (d) media production techniques that encourage interpersonal connections.

Identification refers to an emotional and cognitive process whereby a viewer imagines himself or herself as a particular character (Moyer-Gusé & Nabi, 2010, p. 29). It includes a good deal of involvement and absorption with a character (J. Cohen, 2001). It is conceptualized as a typical response to entertainment and has a long history in the study of the mass media. As Cohen (2001) notes, viewers often speak of the strong identification with characters (Liebes & Katz, 1990), children remember more about characters with whom they identify (E.E. Maccoby & Wilson, 1957), college students who identify with celebrities are more affected by their health messages (Basil, 1996), children are more likely to model aggressive behavior of those characters with which they identify (Huesmann, Lagerspetz, & Eron, 1984).

Identification is encouraged by some media production techniques. Unlike parasocial interaction, identification is likely to be encouraged by dramatic and narrative media content that lets audiences forget that they are in an audience. So, techniques like "breaking the fourth wall" should limit identification. Like parasocial interaction, though, likeable and attractive characters encourage identification (C. Hoffner, 1996). Cohen suggests that emotional characters will also increase identification as well as "realistic" characters (J. Cohen, 2001).

Like parasocial interaction, identification develops over time. As Cohen (2001) remarked "the longer an audience member is exposed to a character, the more likely he or she is to be able to imagine being that character" (p. 259). Demographic and attitudinal similarity increased identification; it is easier for audience members to imagine being someone like themselves.

Parasocial interaction and identification are outcomes of media exposure that are interesting in themselves. Parasocial interaction and identification are functional. They increase enjoyment and entertainment. There are also commercial effects. When audiences have relationships with characters, they might be more likely to watch them on other programs and in other settings (A.M. Rubin et al., 1985). Advertisers also believe that popular personalities can be successful product endorsers.

Along with the encouragement of media content, the effects are best characterized as growing from the conditional model. Audience activity becomes an important variable, as do social category and individual difference variables. There is evidence that males and females find different types of characters appealing (C. Hoffner, 1996). Age also affects the kinds of characters that children chose to identify with (e.g., C. Hoffner, 1996). Most importantly, though, just as each of us chooses different types of people as friends, there are individual differences in the characters that we find attractive, similar, and appealing.

There is growing evidence that both parasocial interaction and identification can be significant facilitators of other media effects. Social learning theory (Bandura, 2009) holds that vicarious reinforcement encourages people to adopt the behaviors that they observe in the media. Similarity and identification enhance social learning (Bandura, 2009). Cohen (2006) summarized several other effects that should be facilitated by identification. First, because identification increases exposure to the programs of the favored character, people might be more likely to be affected by repeated exposure to the content. Identification has been linked to stronger memories about the character, so the effects might be longer-term. Persuasive effects might also be more enduring because identification leads to internalization of attitudes (Kelman, 1961). Identifying with celebrities has already been shown to be linked to adopting their attitudes toward health practices and causes (Basil, 1996; W. J. Brown, Basil, & Bocarnea, 2003). Moyer-Gusé and Nabi (2010) found that identification increases the effects of education-entertainment programs because it reduces counterarguing with persuasive messages.

There are also indications that parasocial interaction facilitates some media effects. Moyer-Gusé and Nabi (2010) found that parasocial interaction with television characters in a drama about teenage pregnancy led to fewer reactive strategies to the persuasive message. Parasocial interaction led to less resistance to messages about safe sex. Another study found that identification with television characters in *Sex in the City* facilitated discussion about sexually transmitted diseases (Moyer-Gusé, Chung, & Jain, 2011).

The parasocial contact hypothesis (Schiappa, Gregg, & Hewes, 2005) argues that parasocial interaction can function similarly to real social contact to reduce intergroup stereotypes and conflict. Allport's (1954) interpersonal contact theory is founded on the belief that stereotypes and negative attitudes about groups are based on incomplete or inaccurate information. Prejudice, he believes, can be reduced by learning more about people. The theory states that "under appropriate conditions interpersonal contact is one of the most effective ways to reduce prejudice between majority and minority group members" (Schiappa et al., 2005, p. 92).

Schiappa and his colleagues (2005) point out that prejudice tends to lead people to avoid contact with groups that are viewed unfavorably. Media depictions, however, can be a nonthreatening way for people to experience groups about which they hold prejudices. The parasocial contact hypothesis, then, argues that exposure to pleasing characters should reduce prejudice. There is some support for the parasocial contact hypothesis. A reduced prejudice about gay men was linked to exposure to popular programs that featured gay men (e.g., *Six Feet Under* and *Queer Eye for the Straight Guy*, Schiappa et al., 2005; Schiappa, Gregg, & Hewes, 2006).

A recent study found that parasocial interaction has an impact on the effects of depictions of thin models in the media on body dissatisfaction (Oxley, 2010). Based on social comparison theory (Festinger, 1954) Oxley hypothesized that college-aged women would be more likely to socially compare themselves with thin personalities with whom they had a parasocial relationship. Her hypothesis was supported; parasocial interaction increased social comparison. Moreover, parasocial interaction was directly linked to body dissatisfaction after seeing photos of thin celebrities; there was a positive connection between parasocial interaction with a celebrity and feeling fat after viewing her photo.

For Social Comparison: Effects on Body Satisfaction

According to Festinger (1954), humans have a desire to evaluate themselves. People can use objective means for evaluation, but if these are not available, they will compare themselves to others – social comparison. Festinger (1954) first focused on the social comparison of opinions, attitudes, and performances, but the theory has been expanded to include social comparison of abilities, traits, values, and physical appearance (e.g., J. V. Wood, 1989). Social comparison is a common feature of daily life that probably has roots in evolutionary biology. Social comparison is central to social adaptation. We assess the abilities of our competitors to make decisions about strategies to succeed (e.g., Gilbert, Price, & Allan, 1995).

There are two general types of social comparison depending on the motives that drive the comparison. Upward social comparison is driven by desires for self-improvement or self-enhancement. In this case, people compare themselves to ideals or models for inspiration and motivation (Blanton, Buunk, Gibbons, and Kuyper, 1999). Downward social comparison, on the other hand, is motivated by desires for reassurance and comfort. In that case, people will compare themselves to others who are less successful or appealing (e.g., Buunk & Gibbons, 2007).

Media content provides many models for both upward and downward social comparison. News reports stories about successes for those seeking upward comparison as well as stories of failures for those seeking downward comparison. Sports coverage allows comparison of physical strength and abilities. Medical programs can comfort the infirm through comparison with stories about illness. Romantic comedies invite comparison of relationship strategies and success. And, the images in advertising can serve as anchors to judge one's appearance (e.g., Jonason, Krcmar, & Sohn, 2009; López-Guimerà, Levine, Sánchez-Carracedo, & Fauquet, 2010).

Images in the media invite social comparison. First, there is a wide range of content to appeal to people seeking different gratifications from the media (e.g., A.M. Rubin, 1981a). Characters are central to most media content. News, for example, focuses on the personalities in the news; sports coverage highlights the success and failures of the athletes; drama is typically person centered. Disposition theory (Raney, 2006) reinforces the importance of social action to entertainment. Second, because of the profit nature of the media, media producers place a good deal of emphasis on "ideal" characters. Production techniques and make-up ensure that media models look almost flawless and present an ideal that is just about impossible to achieve (Levine & Harrison, 2009). Third, the emphasis on thin and beautiful models can serve to make those attributes more salient and desirable, activating schemata (Dittmar, Halliwell, & Stirling, 2009) and motivating social comparison (e.g., Harrison, 2003). Last, upward social comparison especially is more likely when the comparison can be made in private, with the target being unaware of the comparison (e.g., Ybema & Buunk, 1993). Media exposure allows private comparison.

One of the fastest-growing areas of media effects research is based on the use of the mass media for social comparison of body image. This research is driven not only by theoretical interest in understanding media effects, but by public health concerns. Researchers hypothesize that exposure to thin, flawless, and unrealistic models in the mass media leads to body dissatisfaction, which then leads to disordered eating. Researchers and public health officials are concerned that the consistent presentation of thin and flawless models in the media leads to perceptions that these are social norms (e.g., Levine & Harrison, 2004; Wasylkiw, Emms, Meuse, & Poirier, 2009) and internalization of the "thin beauty ideal" (Stice, 1998). Studies show that body dissatisfaction is widespread even among adolescent females who are not overweight (e.g., Pritchard, King, & Czajika-Narins, 1997). (See Chapter 6 for discussions of body image effects for children and adolescents.)

Eating disorders are a serious health problem. A National Institute for Mental Health funded study (Hudson, Hiripi, Pope, & Kessler, 2007) found that 0.9% of women and 0.3% of men reported having anorexia at some time in their lives; 1.5% of women and 0.5% of men reported having bulimia; 3.5% of women and 2% of men reported having a binge-eating disorder at some point in their lives. Levine and Harrison (2009) report that "a reasonable, conservative estimate of the prevalence of [disordered eating behavior] that produces *significant* physical, psychological, and social problems, but does not meet the full criteria of [anorexia nervosa] or [bulimia nervosa], is 6% to 8%" (p. 491). Eating disorders are more common in younger women, but have been increasing among adolescent males (Smolak, Murnen, & Thompson, 2005). Eating disorders are associated with severe psychological and social costs. Medical consequences of eating disorders can be life-threatening.

There is growing evidence that media exposure is a significant factor in body dissatisfaction. Meta-analyses point out modest but consistent effects of exposure to media showing thin models and body dissatisfaction. Groesz, Levine, and Murnen's (2002) meta-analysis of 25 experimental studies found an overall effect size of $d = -.31$,[11] a drop in body satisfaction after exposure to thin-ideal media content. An update of that study found an overall effect of $d = -.28$ (S. Grabe, Ward, & Hyde, 2008). The effect was stronger in correlational studies ($d = -.42$) than experiments ($d = -.21$). The authors also found stronger effects for studies published after 2000. They speculate that either media effects have gotten stronger over time, or methods and designs have become more sensitive.

Despite the consistent evidence of the impact of media content, social comparison effects are best explained by the conditional model of media effects. Media content is widely viewed, but affects only a small part of the audience. Clearly, there are variables that make the effects conditional on certain aspects of the audience. Levine and Harrison (2009) summarize the different variables that can increase or decrease the effects of media content on disordered eating. Meta-analyses have found that social categories play a strong role in the process. Effects are stronger for females than males, for White, European-Americans than those of other racial-ethnic backgrounds; younger adolescents are more susceptible than young adults. There is some evidence that some individual difference variables are important to understanding these effects. High self-esteem, for example, has been found to be a barrier to effects (López-Guimerà et al., 2010; Oxley, 2010). Social relationship variables, though, seem to be especially important to understanding the effects. It is important to recognize that media impact on parents and peers can also have indirect effects on adolescents through the influence of social relationships (e.g., López-Guimerà et al., 2010). Levine and Harrison (2009) propose that family environment, especially family norms and communication between parents and children, enhance or mitigate the effects. As López-Guimerà and her colleagues (2010) note:

> parents and peers play an important role in the transmission, reinforcement, and modeling of the thin beauty ideals and disordered eating behaviors and beliefs or – in an opposite sense, their social support could be a protective factor from the adverse effects of the media. (p. 408)

Compulsive Media Use: Media Addiction

There is no single, agreed-upon definition of addiction, but the concept includes notions of compulsion and lack of control. McIlwraith (1998), for example, defines television addiction as "heavy television watching that is subjectively experienced as being to some extent involuntary, displacing more productive activities, and difficult to stop or curtail" (p. 372). Although study of addiction began with ingestion of drugs (e.g., nicotine, alcohol, heroin), there is now evidence of behavioral addictions, such as gambling, sex, and exercise (M. D. Griffiths, 2005). There is a good deal of concern about addiction to different types of media, television addiction (e.g., Horvath, 2004; Smith, 1986), Internet addiction (e.g., Caplan, 2002; Kim & Haridakis, 2009), and video game addiction (e.g., Brunborg et al., 2013; M. D. Griffiths, 2008; K. M. Lee, Peng, & Park, 2009). Media use can be addictive because it offers "partial reinforcement," a critical psychological aspect of addiction. Partial reinforcement is receiving rewards (or reinforcement) intermittently. Partial reinforcement means that addictions are harder to overcome, because the next action might provide reward, even if the last one did not (Harrington, 1999).

Media addiction is a dysfunctional use of the media. Television addiction is marked by heavy viewing that causes relationship problems, craving television, and withdrawal symptoms when not watching television (Horvath, 2004). Video game addiction (or problematic use) is characterized by compulsion to play, conflict between play and other activities, positive emotions ("buzz") while playing, finding that the game dominates thoughts, and believing that playing games is the most important daily activity (Oggins & Sammis, 2012). Problematic Internet use is marked by compulsive use and having negative life outcomes because of use (e.g., missing school or social engagements, feeling guilty, Caplan, 2002).

Research has identified many negative outcomes of various media addic-tions: spending less time with friends and family, spending less time participat-ing in productive and healthier activities, less engagement in critical thought, sleep disturbances, withdrawal symptoms, conflicts with family, friends, and relationship partners, lower levels of academic achievement, and guilt (Caplan, 2002; Foss & Alexander, 1996; Kubey, Lavin, & Barrows, 2001).

McIlwraith, Jacobvitz, Kubey, and Alexander (1991) point out that addic-tion is a content-irrelevant effect of media use: "Television addiction does not mean being 'hooked' on particular TV content. TV addiction means depend-ence on the television medium itself, regardless of whatever content happens to be on" (p. 104). But, it is likely that addictions can be associated with content-dependent effects. As McIlwraith (1998) points out, addiction "might be the first in a chain of other effects" (p. 372). Addiction "opens the gates" to the effects of heavy media use, such as displacement of other activities, desensitization, and reduction of imaginative play (McIlwraith, 1998). Tel-evision addicted viewers might be more likely to be cultivated to television's dominant messages (e.g., Morgan et al., 2009). Video game addicts might have more aggressive thoughts and tendencies because they are immersed in violent scenarios (e.g., C. A. Anderson & Bushman, 2002a).

Key to the study of media addiction is identifying what leads people to become addicted to different types of media. There is some evidence that social categories can explain some television addiction (Horvath, 2004). Males report more addiction to television (Horvath, 2004), to video games (M. D. Griffiths & Hunt, 1998) and to the Internet (Kubey et al., 2001). Older people report more addiction to television; education is negatively related to television addiction (Horvath, 2004). Some individual difference variables have been connected to media addictions: depression (R. A. Davis, 2001), neuroticism, psychoticism, and inability to pay attention (McIlwraith, 1998).

Social relationship variables appear to have a stronger connection to media addictive thoughts and behaviors. People who report having fewer social con-nections with others are more likely to report media addictions. Loneliness, for example, has been linked to Internet addiction (R. A. Davis, 2001; Kubey et al., 2001). Caplan (2005) also found that less comfort and fewer skills in interpersonal settings are linked to compulsive Internet use and negative outcomes of using the Internet.

Uses and gratifications is a fruitful avenue to understanding media addictions. Many scholars have pointed out that heavy use is not the same as addiction. Addiction to media use is influenced to a large extent by the reasons that people use the media. Various studies have found connections between media use motives and media addictions. McIlwraith (1998), for example, found that compared to nonaddicts, TV addicts used television more to alleviate anxious moods and to fill empty time. Kubey and his colleagues (2001) noted that Internet addicts sought significantly more Internet entertainment than nonaddicts. Morahan-Martin and Schumacher (2000) found that problematic Internet use was motivated by desires to meet new people and to seek emotional support.

LaRose, Lin, and Eastin (2003) provide a sound theoretical explanation for a uses and gratifications account for media addiction. They propose a model in which an active audience uses the media for self-reactive reasons, or to overcome loneliness, pass time, and escape problems. Media use provides gratifications that reinforce media use. These gratifications then motivate similar behavior to overcome stressful and anxious mood states. For those audience members who have stressful lives and fewer satisfying social connections with others, the dysphoric mood states might be fairly common. Media use, then, as a response to those states then becomes habitual and compulsive – and less active (less likely to be under conscious control).

There is support for this model of media addiction. First, prior research supports the connection between unhappy mood states, poor social skills, depression, loneliness, and media addiction (e.g., Caplan, 2005; R. A. Davis, 2001; McIlwraith, 1998). Second, partial gratifications are a key to understanding the development and endurance of addictive behaviors (Harrington, 1999). LaRose and his colleagues (2003) confirmed several of their theoretical hypotheses. Depression was linked to self-reactive motives for using the Internet. Self-reactive motives were then related to deficient self-regulation of Internet use (their measure of Internet addiction). Later research found that companionship and diversionary motives predicted tendencies toward Internet addiction (Indeok Song, LaRose, Eastin, & Lin, 2004).

Summary

Entertainment is the most common use of the mass media. It is associated with a variety of media effects – even beyond the socialization effects explained in Chapter 6 and the effects of media violence summarized in Chapter 7. People seek out entertainment and are affected by the themes, the plots, the images, and the ideas that are the basis for the comedy and drama that we all enjoy.

The uses and gratifications perspective provides an explanation for the effects of entertainment. According to this theoretical perspective, media can only affect people who have use for the content. So, uses and gratifications suggests that most effects of entertainment content are explained by the conditional model: The types of effects are dependent on the reasons people have for using the media.

Entertainment can help people regulate their moods. Pleasant, cheerful content reinforces happy feelings and good moods. But, people can seek out exciting and absorbing content to distract them from gloomy feelings and bad moods. Political drama and comedy not only serve to amuse the audience. There is a good deal of evidence that plots that deal with issues such as crime, health, capital punishment, and political intrigue can affect political attitudes and even have some agenda-setting effects. The increase in political figures' appearances on talk shows affects viewers' attitudes and impressions of these figures.

Audiences find a good deal of appeal in personalities that populate entertainment. People commonly become involved with the characters, form parasocial relationships with them, and identify with the people in their favorite programs. These pseudo-personal relationships not only enhance audience enjoyment, but can facilitate other effects, such as acceptance of persuasive messages and reduction of prejudice.

Finally, the appeal of entertainment can have a dark side. Research has shown that using characters with idealized physical attributes as the basis for social comparison can lead to negative effects on body image. And, writers hold that excessive media use can result in addictive behaviors and their associated negative life outcomes. All these effects of entertainment are explained by the conditional model. The reasons that people have for turning to the media and their content influence the effects of that content.

Notes

1 Next Media Animation (NMA) of Taiwan's depiction of Tiger Wood's car accident was a hit on YouTube and shown on several news stations.
2 Consider the excitatory potential of music that is played in gyms during workouts or the music performed by marching bands during football games.
3 Note that a negative outcome after suspense should also lead to great sadness and despair, but that is not often the case in dramatic entertainment.
4 Two of these films were *The Prince of Tides* and *Winter People*.
5 Some of these movies and TV programs were *The Wizard of Oz, Harry Potter I & III, Finding Nemo, 101 Dalmatians, Rudolf the Red-Nosed Reindeer, Peter Pan, Star Wars*, and *Scooby Doo*.
6 In comparison, Fox News' *Hannity & Colmes* had an average audience of 1.9 million and CNN's Election Center (its highest rated news program of 2008) reported 1.2 million viewers (Pew Research Center's Project for Excellence in Journalism, 2008).
7 *The Colbert Report* might be an exception to this statement. LaMarre, Landreville, and Beam (2009) found that some conservative audience members interpreted the program's content literally, as a criticism of liberal political views.
8 Jon Stewart's "Rally to Restore Sanity," a response to Glenn Beck's "Rally to Restore Honor," showed how politically active the program's viewers could be. The October 2010 rally drew an estimated 200,000 participants.

9 This imitation is a concern, because children and adolescents can imitate harmful, as well as positive actions. Much of the concern about smoking and drinking in PG and PG-13 films, for example, is based on concerns for underage adoption of those habits (e.g., Sargent et al., 2002).

10 The characters in *The Office* and *Modern Family* regularly talk directly to the audience. Perhaps the earliest example was the 1950s program *The Burns and Allen Show*, starring George Burns and his wife Gracie Allen. George was the straight man who often turned to the audience to comment on his wife's nonsensical actions and interpretations of the world. Many Mel Brooks movies (e.g., *Blazing Saddles*, *Spaceballs*) also include characters breaking the fourth wall. In *Ferris Beuller's Day Off* the lead character, played by Matthew Broderick, even scolds the audience for staying until the end of the credits when the movie was clearly over.

11 *d* is a standardized measure of effect size. *d* represents the difference between the experimental and control groups. It indicates the size of the difference in terms of standard deviations. So, in this case, body satisfaction of groups that saw thin-promoting media content was .31 of standard deviation lower than groups that did not.

REFERENCES

Abel, A.D., & Barthel, M. (2013). Appropriation of mainstream news: How *Saturday Night Live* changed the political discussion. *Critical Studies in Mass Communication, 30,* 1–6.

Abrams, J.R., & Giles, H. (2007). Viewing and avoiding television among African Americans: A group vitality and social identity gratifications perspective. *Media Psychology, 9,* 115–134.

Abrams, J.R., & Giles, H. (2009). Hispanic television activity: Is it related to vitality perceptions? *Communication Research Reports, 26,* 247–252.

Agliata, D., & Tantleff-Dunn, S. (2004). The impact of media exposure on males' body image. *Journal of Clinical and Social Psychology, 23*(1), 7–22.

Aikat, D., & Yu, J. (2005). News on the Web: Agenda setting of online news in web sites of major newspaper, television and online news services, paper presented to the International Communication Association Annual Meeting, New York.

Ajzen, I., & Fishbein, M. (1980). *Understanding attitudes and predicting social behavior.* Englewood Cliffs, NJ: Prentice-Hall.

Alexander, A., Ryan, M.S., & Munoz, P. (1984). Creating a learning context: Investigations on the interaction of siblings during television viewing. *Critical Studies in Mass Communication, 1,* 345–364.

Allen, M., D'Alessio, D., & Brezgel, K. (1995). A meta-analysis summarizing the effects of pornography II: Aggression after exposure. *Human Communication Research, 22,* 258–283.

Allen, M., D'Alessio, D., Emmers, T.M., & Gebhardt, L. (1996). The role of educational briefings in mitigating effects of experimental exposure to violent sexually explicit material: A meta-analysis. *Journal of Sex Research, 33,* 135–141.

Allen, M., Emmers, T.M., Gebhardt, L., & Giery, M.A. (1995). Exposure to pornography and acceptance of rape myths. *Journal of Communication, 45*(1), 5–26.

Allen, M., & Stiff, J. (1989). Testing three models for the sleeper effect. *Western Journal of Speech Communication, 53,* 411–426.

Allport, G.W. (1954). *The nature of prejudice.* Cambridge, MA: Perseus Books.

Althaus, S.L. (2002). American news consumption during times of national crisis. *PS: Political Science and Politics, 35,* 517–521.

Althaus, S.L., & Largio, D.M. (2004). When Osama became Saddam: Origins and consequences of the change in America's public enemy #1. *PS: Political Science and Politics, 37,* 795–799.

American Academy of Pediatrics, Committee on Communications. (2006). Policy statement: Children, adolescents and advertising. *Pediatrics, 118*(6), 2563–2569.

American Academy of Pediatrics. (2000, July 26). *Joint Statement on the Impact of Entertainment Violence on Children.* Retrieved from: http://www2.aap.org/advocacy/releases/jstmtevc.htm.

American Psychological Association. (1993). *Violence and youth: Psychology's response*. Washington, DC: Author.

American Red Cross. (2011, Summer). *Social media in disasters and emergencies*. Retrieved from: http://www.redcross.org/www-files/Documents/pdf/SocialMediain Disasters.pdf.

Anderson, C.A., & Bushman, B.J. (2002a). Human aggression. *Annual Review of Psychology, 53*, 27–51.

Anderson, C.A., & Bushman, B.J. (2002b). The effects of media violence on society. *Science, 295*, 2377–2379.

Anderson, D.R., Alwitt, L.F., Lorch, E.P., & Levin, S.R. (1979). Watching children watch television. In G. Hale & M. Lewis (Eds.), *Attention and cognitive development* (pp. 331–361). New York: Plenum Press.

Anderson, D.R., Bryant, J., Wilder, A., Santomero, A., Williams, M., & Crawley, A.M. (2000). Researching *Blue's Clues*: Viewing behavior and impact. *Media Psychology, 2*(2), 179–194.

Anderson, D.R., & Burns, J. (1991). Paying attention to television. In J. Bryant & D. Zillmann (Eds.), *Responding to the screen: Reception and reaction processes* (pp. 3–25). Hillsdale, NJ: Lawrence Erlbaum Associates.

Anderson, D.R., & Collins, P.A. (1988). The impact on children's education: Television's influence on cognitive development (Working paper No. 2). Washington, DC: U.S. Department of Educational Research and Improvement, U.S. Department of Education.

Anderson, D.R., Collins, P.A., Schmitt, K.L., & Jacobvitz, R.S. (1996). Stressful life events and television viewing. *Communication Research, 23*, 243–260.

Anderson, D.R., Huston, A.C., Schmitt, K.L., Linebarger, D.L., Wright, J.C., & Larson, R. (2001). Early childhood television viewing and adolescent behavior: The recontact study. *Monographs of the Society for Research in Child Development, 66*(1), 1–154.

Anderson, D.R., & Levin, S.R. (1976). Young children's attention to *Sesame Street*. *Child Development, 47*, 806–811.

Anderson, D.R., Lorch, E.P., Collins, P.A., Field, D.E., & Nathan, J.G. (1986). Television viewing at home: Age trends in visual attention and time with TV. *Child Development, 57*, 1024–1033.

Anderson, J.A., & Meyer, T.P. (1988). *Mediated communication: A social action perspective*. Newbury Park, CA: SAGE.

Anderson, D.R., & Pempek, T.A. (2005). Television and very young children. *American Behavioral Scientist, 48*(5), 505–522.

Anderson, J.R. (1995). *Cognitive psychology and its implications* (4th edn.). New York: W.H. Freeman.

Andison, F.S. (1977). TV violence and viewer aggression: A cumulation of study results 1956–1976. *Public Opinion Quarterly, 41*, 314–331.

Andreasen, M. (1985). Listener recall for call-in versus structured interview radio formats. *Journal of Broadcasting & Electronic Media, 29*, 421–430.

Andsager, J.L., & White, H.L. (2007). *Self versus others: Media, messages, and the third-person effect*. New York: Routledge.

Arbitron. (2009). *Radio today: How America listens to the radio*. Columbia, MD: Author.

Armstrong, C.B., & Rubin, A.M. (1989). Talk radio as interpersonal communication. *Journal of Communication, 39*, 84–94.

Armstrong, G.B. (1993). Cognitive interference from background television: Structure effects on verbal and spatial processing. *Communication Studies, 44*, 56–70.

Armstrong, G.B., Boiarsky, G.A., & Mores, M. (1991). Background television and reading performance. *Communication Monographs*, 58, 235–253.

Armstrong, G.B., & Greenberg, B.S. (1990). Background television as an inhibitor of cognitive processing. *Human Communication Research*, 16, 355–386.

Asch, S.E. (1956). Studies of independence and conformity: I. A minority of one against a unanimous majority. *Psychological Monographs*, 70(9), 1–70.

Ashby, S.L. & Rich, M. (2005). Video killed the radio star: The effects of music videos on adolescent health. *Adolescent Medicine Clinics*, 16(2), 371–393.

Associated Press. (May 3, 2012). McDonald's criticized as Olympic sponsor; Docs said ads may worsen obesity epidemic. Retrieved from: http://www.nydailynews.com/life-style/health/uk-doctors-criticize-mcdonal-olympic-sponsorship-ads-worsen-obesity-epidemic-article-1.1071819.

Atkin, C.K. (1983). Effects of realistic TV violence vs. fictional violence on aggression. *Journalism Quarterly*, 60, 615–621.

Atkin, C.K., Hocking, J., & Block, M. (1984). Teenage drinking: Does advertising make a difference? *Journal of Communication*, 34(20), 157–167.

Attorney General's Commission on Pornography. (1986). *Final report*. Washington, DC: U.S. Department of Justice.

Aubrey, J.S., & Harrison, K. (2004). The gender-role content of children's favorite television programs and its link to their gender-related perceptions. *Media Psychology*, 6(2), 111–146.

Aubrey, J.S., Henson, J.R., Hopper, K.M., & Smith, S.E. (2009). A picture is worth twenty words (about the self): Testing the priming influence of visual sexual objectification on women's self-objectification. *Communication Research Reports*, 26(4), 271–284.

Aubrey J.S, Hopper, K.M. & Mbure, W.G. (2011). Check that body! The effects of sexually objectifying music videos on college men's sexual beliefs. *Journal of Broadcasting & Electronic Media*, 55(3), 360–379.

Austin, E.W., Bolls, P., Fujioka, Y., & Engelbertson, J. (1999). How and why parents take on the tube. *Journal of Broadcasting & Electronic Media*, 43, 175–192.

Auter, P.J, Ashton, E., & Soliman, M.R. (2008). A study of Egyptian and American young adult parasocial "relationships" with music video personae. *Journal of Arab & Muslim Media Research*, 1, 131–144.

Auter, P.J., & Davis, D.M. (1991). When characters speak directly to viewers: Breaking the fourth wall in television. *Journalism Quarterly*, 68, 165–171.

Axsom, D., Yates, S., & Chaiken, S. (1987). Audience response as a heuristic cue in persuasion. *Journal of Personality and Social Psychology*, 53, 30–40.

Baker, S.M., & Petty, R.E. (1994). Majority and minority influences: Source-position imbalance as a determinant of message scrutiny. *Journal of Personality and Social Psychology*, 67, 5–19.

Ball, S., & Bogatz, G.A. (1970). *The first year of Sesame Street: An evaluation*. Princeton, NJ: Educational Testing Services.

Ball, S., Palmer, P., & Millward, E. (1986). Television and its educational impact: A reconsideration. In J. Bryant & D. Zillmann (Eds.), *Perspectives on media effects* (pp. 129–142). Hillsdale, NJ: Lawrence Erlbaum Associates.

Ball-Rokeach, S. (2001). The politics of studying media violence: Reflections 30 years after the Violence Commission. *Mass Communication & Society*, 4, 3–18.

Ball-Rokeach, S.J., & DeFleur, M.L. (1976). A dependency model of mass-media effects. *Communication Research*, 3, 3–21.

Ballentine, L.W., & Ogle, J.P. (2005). The making and unmaking of body problems in *Seventeen* magazine, 1992–2003. *Family and Consumer Sciences Research Journal*, 33(4), 281–307.

Bandura, A. (1986). *Social foundations of thought and actions: A social cognitive theory*. Englewood Cliffs, NJ: Prentice-Hall.

Bandura, A. (2009). Social cognitive theory of mass communication. In J. Bryant & M.B. Oliver (Eds.), *Media effects: Advances in theory and research* (3rd edn., pp. 94–124). New York: Routledge.

Bandura, A., Ross, D., & Ross, S.A. (1963). Imitation of film-mediated aggressive models. *Journal of Abnormal and Social Psychology, 66*, 3–11.

Baran, S.J., & Davis, D.K. (2009). *Mass communication theory: Foundations, ferment, and future* (5th edn.). Boston, MA: Wadsworth Cengage.

Baran, S.J., & Blasko, V.J. (1984). Social perceptions and the by-products of advertising. *Journal of Communication, 34*(3), 12–20.

Bargh, J.A. (1988). Automatic information processing: Implications for communication and affect. In L. Donohew, H.E. Sypher, & E.T. Higgins (Eds.), *Communication, social cognition, and affect* (pp. 9–32). Hillsdale, NJ: Lawrence Erlbaum Associates.

Baron, L., & Straus, M.A. (1984). Sexual stratification, pornography, and rape in the United States. In N.M. Malamuth & E. Donnerstein (Eds.), *Pornography and sexual aggression* (pp. 186–209). Orlando, FL: Academic Press.

Barrett, D. (2011, December 20). Crime down across nation. *Wall Street Journal*, A8.

Bartlett, C., Rodeheffer, C.D., Baldassaro, R., Hinkin, M.P., & Harris, R.J. (2008). The effect of advances in video game technology and content on aggressive cognitions, hostility, and heart rate. *Media Psychology, 11*, 540–565.

Bartlett, F.A. (1932). *A study in experimental and social psychology*. New York: Cambridge University Press.

Basil, M.D. (1996). Identification as a mediator of celebrity effects. *Journal of Broadcasting & Electronic Media, 40*, 478–495.

Bassiouni, M.C. (1982). Media coverage of terrorism: The law and the public. *Journal of Communication, 32*(2), 128–143.

Bauder, D. (2011, August 30). All Irene all weekend: Storm of TV criticism. *Philadelphia Inquirer*, D3.

Baum, M.A. (2003). *Soft news goes to war: Public opinion & American foreign policy*. Princeton, NJ: Princeton University Press.

Baumgartner, J., & Morris, J.S. (2006). *The Daily Show* effect: Candidate evaluations, efficacy, and American youth. *American Politics Research, 34*, 341–367.

Baumgartner, J.C., & Morris, J.S. (2008). One "nation" under Stephen? The effects of *The Colbert Report* on American youth. *Journal of Broadcasting & Electronic Media, 52*, 622–643.

Baxter, R.L., De Riemer, C., Landini, A., Leslie, L., & Singletary, M.W. (1985). A content analysis of music videos. *Journal of Broadcasting & Electronic Media, 29*, 245–257.

Baym, G. (2005). *The Daily Show*: Discursive integration and the reinvention of political journalism. *Political Communication, 22*, 259–276.

Baym, G. (2010). *From Cronkite to Colbert: The evolution of broadcast news*. Boulder, CO: Paradigm Publishers.

Bechtel, R.B., Achelpohl, C., & Akers, R. (1972). Correlates between observed behavior and questionnaire response on television viewing. In E.A. Rubenstein, G.A. Comstock, & J.P. Murray (Eds.), *Television and social behavior: Vol. 4. Television in day-to-day life, patterns of use* (DHEW publication HSM 72–9059, pp. 274–344). Washington, DC: Government Printing Office.

Becker, G. (1972). Causal analysis in R-R studies: Television violence and aggression. *American Psychologist, 27*, 967–968.

Belcher, J.D., & Haridakis, P. (2013). The role of background characteristics, music-listening motives, and music selection on music discussion. *Communication Quarterly, 61*, 375–396.

Bem, D.J. (1965). An experimental analysis of self-persuasion. *Journal of Experimental Social Psychology, 1*, 199–218.

Bem, S.L. (1981). Gender schema theory: A cognitive account of sex typing. *Psychological Review, 88*, 354–364.

Bemmaor, A.C. (1984). Testing alternative econometric models on the existence of advertising threshold effect. *Journal of Marketing Research, 21*, 298–308.

Bennett, W.L. (2011). News polls: Constructing an engaged public. In R.Y. Shapiro & L.R. Jacobs (Eds.), *The Oxford Handbook of American Public Opinion and the Media.* New York: Oxford University Press.

Bennett, W.L., & Iyengar, S. (2008). A new era of minimal effects? The changing foundations of political communication. *Journal of Communication, 58*, 707–731.

Benoit, W.L., Hansen., G.J., & Verser, R.M. (2003). A meta-analysis of the effects of viewing U.S. presidential debates. *Communication Monographs, 70*, 335–350.

Benoit, W.L., Leshner, G.M., & Chattopadhyay, S. (2007). A meta-analysis of political advertising. *Human Communication, 10*, 507–522.

Berelson, B. (1959). The state of communication research. *Public Opinion Quarterly, 23*, 1–17.

Berkowitz, L. (1970). Aggressive humor as a stimulus to aggressive responses. *Journal of Personality and Social Psychology, 16*, 710–717.

Berkowitz, L., & Alioto, J.T. (1973). The meaning of an observed event as a determinant of its aggressive consequences. *Journal of Personality and Social Psychology, 28*, 206–217.

Berkowitz, L., & Powers, P.C. (1978). Effects of timing and justification of witnessed aggression on the observers' punitiveness. *Journal of Research in Personality, 13*, 71–80.

Berkowitz, L., & Rogers, K.H. (1986). A priming effect analysis of media influences. In J. Bryant & D. Zillmann (Eds.), *Perspectives on media effects* (pp. 57–81). Hillsdale, NJ: Lawrence Erlbaum Associates.

Berlyne, D.E. (1960). *Conflict, arousal, and curiosity.* New York: McGraw-Hill.

Berlyne, D.E. (1970). Attention as a problem in behavior theory. In D.I. Mostofsky (Ed.), *Attention: Contemporary theory and analysis* (pp. 25–49). New York: Appleton Century Crofts.

Bernard, R.M., & Coldevin, G.O. (1985). Effects of recap strategies on television news recall and retention. *Journal of Broadcasting & Electronic Media, 29*, 407–419.

Berry, C. (1983). Learning from television news: A critique of the research. *Journal of Broadcasting, 27*, 359–370.

Beuf, A. (1974). Doctor, lawyer, household drudge. *Journal of Communication, 24*(2), 142–154.

Beullens, K., Roe, K., & Van den Bulck, J. (2011). The impact of adolescents' news and action movie viewing on risky driving behavior: A longitudinal study. *Human Communication Research, 37*, 488–508.

Beullens, K., & Van den Bulck, J. (2013). Predicting young driver's car crashes: The role of music video viewing and the playing of driving games. Results from a prospective cohort study. *Media Psychology, 16*, 88–114.

Bialik, C. (2012, January 28–29). Fuzzy facts can make crime rankings suspect. *Wall Street Journal*, A2.

Bickham, D.S., Schmidt, M.E., & Huston, A.C. (2012). Attention, comprehension, and the educational influences of television and other electronic media. Chapter 6 in D.G. Singer & J.L Singer (Eds.), *Handbook of children and the media* (2nd edn.). Los Angeles: SAGE.

Bilandzic, H., & Rössler, P. (2004). Life according to television: Implications of genre-specific cultivation effects. The gratification/cultivation model. *Communications: The European Journal of Communication Research, 29*, 295–326.

Bishop, G. F., Oldendick, R. W., Tuchfaber, A. J., & Bennett, S. E. (1980). Pseudo-opinions on public affairs. *Public Opinion Quarterly, 44,* 198–209.

Blakeborough, D. (2008). "Old people are useless": Representations of aging on *The Simpsons. Canadian Journal on Aging, 27*(1), 57–67.

Blank, D. M. (1977). The Gerbner violence profile. *Journal of Broadcasting, 21,* 273–279.

Blanton, H., Buunk, B. P., Gibbons, F. X., & Kuyper, H. (1999). When better-than-others compare upward: Choice of comparison and comparative evaluation as independent predictors of academic performance. *Journal of Personality and Social Psychology, 76,* 420–430.

Blumer, H. (1933). *Movies and conduct.* New York: Macmillan.

Blumer, H. (1946). Collective behavior. In A.M. Lee (Ed.), *New outlines of the principles of sociology* (pp. 167–222). New York: Barnes and Noble.

Blumler, J. G., & McQuail, D. (1969). *Television in politics: Its uses and influence.* Chicago, IL: University of Chicago Press.

Bogart, L. (1989). *Press and public: Who reads what, when, where, and why in American newspapers* (2nd edn.). Hillsdale, NJ: Lawrence Erlbaum Associates.

Bondad-Brown, B. A., Rice, R. E., & Pearce, K. E. (2012). Influences on TV viewing and online user-shared video: Demographics, generations, contextual age, media use, motivations, and audience activity. *Journal of Broadcasting & Electronic Media, 56,* 471–493.

Booth-Butterfield, S., & Welbourne, J. (2002). The elaboration likelihood model: Its impact on persuasion theory and research. In J. P. Dillard & M. Pfau (Eds.), *The persuasion handbook: Developments in theory and practice.* Thousand Oaks, CA: SAGE.

Borzekowski, D. L. G., & Robinson, T. N. (2005). The remote, the mouse, and the no. 2 pencil: The household media environment and academic achievement among third grade students. *Archives of Pediatrics & Adolescent Medicine, 150,* 607–613.

Boston Women's Health Book Collective. (1973). *Our bodies ourselves.* New York: Simon & Schuster.

Bowen, G. L. (1989). Presidential action in public opinion about U.S. Nicaraguan policy: Limits to the rally round the flag syndrome. *PS: Political Science and Politics, 22,* 793–800.

Box Office Mojo. (2010). *Yearly box office.* Retrieved from: http://boxofficemojo.com/yearly/

Boyanowski, E. O. (1977). Film preference under conditions of threat: Whetting the appetite for violence, information, or excitement? *Communication Research, 4,* 133–145.

Boyle, M. P., McLeod, D. M., & Rojas, H. (2008). The role of ego enhancement and perceived message exposure in third-person judgments concerning violent video games. *American Behavioral Scientist, 52*(2), 165–185.

Bracken, C. C. (2005). Presence and image quality: The case of high-definition television. *Media Psychology, 7,* 191–205.

Bracken, C. C. (2006). Perceived source credibility of local television news: The impact of television form and presence. *Journal of Broadcasting & Electronic Media, 50,* 723–741.

Bradley, S. D. (2007). Dynamic, embodied, limited-capacity attention and memory: Modeling cognitive processing of mediated stimuli. *Media Psychology, 9*(1), 211–239.

Brannigan, A. (1987). Pornography and behavior: Alternate explanations. *Journal of Communication, 37*(3), 185–189.

Brannigan, A., & Goldenberg, S. (1987). The study of aggressive pornography: The vicissitudes of relevance. *Critical Studies in Mass Communication, 4,* 262–283.

Brannigan, A., & Kapardis, A. (1986). The controversy over pornography and sex crimes: The criminological evidence and beyond. *Australian & New Zealand Journal of Criminology, 19,* 259–284.

Braverman, J. (2008). Testimonials versus informational persuasive messages: The moderating effect of delivery mode and personal involvement. *Communication Research, 35*(5), 666–694.

Brewer, P.R., & Marquardt, E. (2007). Mock news and democracy: Analyzing *The Daily Show. Atlantic Journal of Communication, 15,* 249–267.

Bridges, A., Wosnitzer, R., Scharrer, E., Sun, C., & Liberman, R. (2010). Aggression and sexual behavior in best-selling pornography videos: A content analysis update. *Violence Against Women, 16,* 1065–1085.

Brigham, J.C., & Giesbrecht, L.W. (1976). All in the family: Racial attitudes. *Journal of Communication, 26*(4), 69–74.

Brinson, M.E., & Stohl, M. (2012). Media framing of terrorism: Implications for public opinion, civil liberties, and counterterrorism policies. *Journal of International and Intercultural Communication, 5,* 270–290.

Brock, R.C., & Balloun, J.L. (1967). Behavioral receptivity to dissonant information. *Journal of Personality and Social Psychology, 6,* 413–428.

Brooks-Gunn, J., & Donahue, E.H. (2008). Introducing the issue. *Future of Children, 18*(1), 3–10.

Brosius, H., Donsbach, W., & Birk, M. (1996). How do text–picture relations affect the informational effectiveness of television newscasts? *Journal of Broadcasting & Electronic Media, 40,* 180–195.

Brosius, H., & Kepplinger, H.M. (1990). The agenda-setting function of television news. *Communication Research, 17,* 183–211.

Bross, M. (1985). Mitigating the effects of mass media sexual violence. Unpublished Master's thesis, University of Wisconsin-Madison.

Brown, D., & Bryant, J. (1989). The manifest content of pornography. In D. Zillmann & J. Bryant (Eds.), *Pornography: Research advances & policy considerations* (pp. 3–24). Hillsdale, NJ: Lawrence Erlbaum Associates.

Brown, J. (1958). Some tests of the decay theory of immediate memory. *Quarterly Journal of Experimental Psychology, 10,* 12–21.

Brown, J.D., Childres, K.W., & Waszak, C.S. (1990). Television and adolescent sexuality. *Journal of Adolescent Health Care, 11,* 62–70.

Brown, J.D., L'Engle, K.L., Pardun, C.J., Guo, G., Kenneavy, K., & Jackson, C. (2006). Sexy media matter: Exposure to sexual content in music, movies, television, and magazines predicts black and white adolescents' sexual behavior. *Pediatrics, 117*(4), 1018–1027.

Brown, M., Amoroso, D.M., & Ware, E.E. (1976). Behavioral effects of viewing pornography. *Journal of Social Psychology, 98,* 235–245.

Brown, W.J., Basil, J.D., & Bocarnea, M.C. (2003). The influence of famous athletes on health beliefs and practices: Mark McGwire, child abuse prevention, and Androstenedione. *Journal of Health Communication, 8,* 41–57.

Brown, W.J., Bocarnea, M., & Basil, M. (2002). Fear, grief, and sympathy response to the attacks. In B.S. Greenberg (Ed.), *Communication and terrorism: Public and media responses to 9/11* (pp. 245–259). Cresskill, NJ: Hampton Press.

Brown Givens, S.M., & Monahan, J.L. (2005). Priming mammies, jezebels, and other controlling images: An examination of the influence of mediated stereotypes on perceptions of an African American woman. *Media Psychology, 7*(1), 87–106.

Browne, B.A. (1998). Gender stereotypes in advertising on children's television in the 1900s: A cross-national analysis. *Journal of Advertising, 27,* 83–96.

Bryant, J., & Brown, D. (1989). Uses of pornography. In D. Zillmann & J. Bryant (Eds.), *Pornography: Research advances & policy considerations* (pp. 25–55). Hillsdale, NJ: Lawrence Erlbaum Associates.

Bryant, J., Fondren, W., & Bryant, J.A. (2012).Creating vigilance for better learning from television. Chapter 9 in D.G. Singer & J.L. Singer (Eds.), *Handbook of children and the media* (2nd edn.). Los Angeles: SAGE.

Bryant, J., & Miron, D. (2004). Theory and research in mass communication. *Journal of Communication, 54*(4), 662–704.

Bryant, J., & Oliver, M.B. (Eds.). (2009). *Media effects: Advances in theory and research* (3rd edn.). New York: Routledge.

Bryant, J., & Rockwell, S.C. (1994). Effects of massive exposure to sexually oriented prime-time television programming on adolescents' moral judgment. In D. Zillmann, J. Bryant, & A.C. Huston (Eds.), *Media, children, and the family* (pp. 183–195). Hillsdale, NJ: Lawrence Erlbaum Associates.

Bryant, J., & Zillmann, D. (1984). Using television to alleviate boredom and stress: Selective exposure as a function of induced excitational states. *Journal of Broadcasting, 28,* 1–20.

Bryant, J., & Zillmann, D. (Eds.). (1994). *Media effects: Advances in theory and research*. Hillsdale, NJ: Lawrence Erlbaum Associates.

Bryant, J., & Zillmann, D. (2009). A retrospective and prospective look at media effects. In R.L. Nabi & M.B. Oliver (Eds.), *The SAGE handbook of media processes and effects* (pp. 9–17). Los Angeles: SAGE Publications.

Bryant, J., Zillmann, D., & Brown, D.F. (1983). Entertainment features in children's educational television: Effects on attention and information acquisition. In J. Bryant & D.R. Anderson (Eds.), *Children's understanding of television: Research on attention and comprehension* (pp. 221–240). New York: Academic Press.

Bucy, E.P., & Newhagen, J.E., eds. (2004). *Media access: Social and psychological dimensions of new technology use*. Mahwah: Lawrence Erlbaum Associates.

Budd, R.W., MacLean, M.S., Jr., Barnes, A.M. (1966). Regularities in the diffusion of two major news events. *Journalism Quarterly, 43,* 221–230.

Bureau of Justice Statistics. (1998a). Criminal victimization 1998: Changes 19997098 with trends 1993–98. Retrieved: http://www.bjs.gov/content/pub/pdf/cv98.pdf.

Bureau of Justice Statistics. (1998b). Serious violent crime levels continued to decline in 1997. Retrieved from: http://www.ojp.usdoj.gov/bjs/glace/cv2.htm.

Bureau of Justice Statistics. (1999). Firearm death by intent, 1991–96. Retrieved from: http://www.ojp.usdoj.gov/bjs/glace/frmdth.txt.

Bureau of Justice Statistics. (2011). Rate of violent victimization declined 13 percent in 2010. Washington, DC: Author. Retrieved: http://www.bjs.gov/content/pub/press/cv10pr.cfm.

Bureau of Labor Statistics. (2009). Leisure time on an average day. *American time use study*. Retrieved from: http://www.bls.gov/tus/charts/chart9.pdf.

Burgess, M.C.R., Dill, K.E., Stermer, S.P., Burgess, S.R., & Brown, B.P. (2011). Playing with prejudice: The prevalence and consequences of racial stereotypes in video games. *Media Psychology, 14*(3), 289–311.

Burt, M.R. (1980). Cultural myths and supports for rape. *Journal of Personality and Social Psychology, 38,* 217–230.

Bushman, B.J. (1995). Moderating role of trait aggressiveness in the effects of violent media on aggression. *Journal of Personality and Social Psychology, 69,* 950–960.

Bushman, B.J., & Anderson, C.A. (2001). Media violence and the American public. *American Psychologist, 56,* 477–489.

Bushman, B.J., & Anderson, C.A. (2002). Violent video games and hostile expectations: A test of the General Aggression Model. *Personality and Social Psychology Bulletin, 28,* 1679–1686.

Bushman, B. J., & Bonacci, A. M. (2002). Violence and sex impair memory for television ads. *Journal of Applied Psychology, 87,* 557–564.

Bushman, B. J., & Geen, R. G. (1990). Role of cognitive-emotional mediators and individual difference in the effects of media violence on aggression. *Journal of Personality and Social Psychology, 58,* 156–163.

Bushman, B. J., & Huesmann, L. R. (2013). Twenty-five years of research on violence in digital games and aggression revisited: A reply to Elson & Ferguson (2013). *European Psychologist.* Advance online publication.

Bushman, B. J., Jamieson, P. E., Weitz, I., & Romer, D. (2013). Gun violence trends in movies. *Pediatrics, 132,* 1014–1018.

Buss, A. H., & Perry, M. (1992). The Aggression Questionnaire. *Journal of Personality and Social Psychology, 63,* 452–459.

Busselle, R. W. (2001). Television exposure, perceived realism, and exemplar accessibility in the social judgment process. *Media Psychology, 3,* 43–67.

Buunk, A. P., & Gibbons, F. X. (2007). Social comparison: The end of a theory and the emergence of a field. *Organizational Behavior and Human Decision Processes, 102,* 3–21.

Byrd-Bredbenner, C., Finckenor, M., & Grasso, D. (2003). Health related content in prime-time Television programming. *Journal of Health Communication: International Perspectives, 8*(4), 329–341.

Cacioppo, J. T., & Petty, R. E. (1979). Effects of message repetition and position on cognitive response, recall, and persuasion. *Journal of Personal and Social Psychology, 37,* 97–109.

Cacioppo, J. T., & Petty, R. E. (1982). The need for cognition. *Journal of Personality and Social Psychology, 42,* 116–131.

Cacioppo, J. T., Petty, R. E., Kao, C., & Rodriguez, R. (1986). Central and peripheral routes to persuasion: An individual difference perspective. *Journal of Personality and Social Psychology, 51,* 1032–1043.

Campaign for Tobacco Free Kids. (2011). *Tobacco product marketing on the Internet.* Retrieved from: http://www.tobaccofreekids.org/research/factsheets/pdf/0081.pdf.

Campbell, W. J. (2010). *Ten of the greatest misreported stories in American journalism.* Berkeley, CA: University of California Press.

Cantor, J. (2009). Fright reactions to mass media. In J. Bryant & M. B. Oliver (Eds.), *Media effects: Advances in theory and research* (3rd ed., pp. 287–303). New York: Routledge.

Cantor, J., Byrne, S., Moyer-Gusé, E., & Riddle, K. (2010). Descriptions of media-induced fright reactions in a sample of US elementary school children. *Journal of Children and Media, 4,* 1–17.

Cantor, J., Mares, M. L., & Oliver, M. B. (1993). Parents' and children's emotional reactions to televised coverage of the Gulf War. In B. Greenberg & W. Gantz (Eds.), *Desert storm and the mass media* (pp. 325–340). Cresskill, NJ: Hampton Press.

Cantril, H., Gaudet, H., & Herzog, H. (1940). *The invasion from Mars: A study in the psychology of panic.* Princeton, NJ: Princeton University Press.

Cao, X. (2008). Political comedy shows and knowledge about primary campaigns: The moderating effects of age and education. *Mass Communication & Society, 11,* 43–61.

Cao, X. (2010). Hearing it from Jon Stewart: The impact of *The Daily Show* on public attentiveness to politics. *International Journal of Public Opinion Research, 22,* 26–46.

Caplan, S. E. (2002). Problematic Internet use and psychosocial well-being: Development of a theory-based cognitive-behavioral measurement instrument. *Computers in Human Behavior, 18,* 553–575.

Caplan, S. E. (2005). A social skill account of problematic Internet use. *Journal of Communication, 55,* 721–736.

Carey, J. (2003). The functions and uses of media during September 11 crisis and its aftermath. In A.M. Noll (Ed.), *Crisis communications: Lessons from September 11* (pp. 1–16). Lanham, MD: Rowman & Littlefield.

Carnagey, N.L., Anderson, C.A., & Bushman, B.J. (2007). The effect of video game violence on physiological desensitization to real-life violence. *Journal of Experimental Social Psychology, 43*, 489–496.

Carrocci, N.M. (1985). Diffusion of information about cyanide-laced Tylenol. *Journalism Quarterly, 62*, 630–633.

Carver, C.S., Ganellen, R.J., Froming, W.J., & Chambers, W. (1983). Modeling: An analysis in terms of category accessibility. *Journal of Experimental Social Psychology, 19*, 402–421.

Carveth, R., & Alexander, A. (1985). Soap opera viewing motivations and the cultivation process. *Journal of Broadcasting & Electronic Media, 29*, 259–273.

Castonguay, J., McKinley, C., & Kunkel, D. (2013). Health-related messages in food advertisements targeting children. *Health Education, 113*(5), 420–432.

Ceci, S.J., & Kain, E.L. (1982). Jumping on the bandwagon with the underdog: The impact of attitude polls on polling behavior. *Public Opinion Quarterly, 46*, 228–242.

Center for Alcohol Marketing and Youth (CAMY). (2003). *Alcohol advertising on sports television, 2001–2003*. Baltimore, MD: John Hopkins Bloomberg School of Public Health.

Center for Alcohol Marketing and Youth (CAMY). (2010). *Youth exposure to alcohol advertising on television, 2001–2009*. Baltimore, MD: John Hopkins Bloomberg School of Public Health.

Center for Communication and Social Policy, ed. (1998). *National television violence study 3*. Thousand Oaks, CA: SAGE.

Center for Media and Public Affairs. (2008). The comedy campaign: The role of late-night tv shows in Campaign '08. *Media Monitor, 22*(3), 1–7.

Center for Responsive Politics. (2014). OpenSecrets.org *Election overview: Stats at a glance*. Retrieved from: OpenSecrets.org web site: https://www.opensecrets.org/overview/.

Centers for Disease Control. (1991). *Position papers from the Third National Injury Conference: Setting the national agenda for injury control in the 1990s*. Washington, DC: Department of Health and Human Services.

Centers for Disease Control and Prevention. (2005, April 1). Tobacco use, access, and exposure to tobacco in media among middle and high school students – United States, 2004. *Morbidity and Mortality Weekly Report, 54*(12), 297–301.

Centerwall, B.S. (1989a). Exposure to television as a cause of violence. In G. Comstock (Ed.), *Public communication and behavior* (Vol. 2, pp. 1–58). Orlando, FL: Academic Press.

Centerwall, B.S. (1989b). Exposure to television as a risk factor for violence. *American Journal of Epidemiology, 129*, 643–652.

Chaffee, S.H. (1977). Mass media effects: New research perspectives. In D. Lerner & L.M. Nelson (Eds.), *Communication research. A half-century appraisal* (pp. 210–241). Honolulu: University of Hawaii Press.

Chaffee, S.H. (1992). Review of *Is anyone responsible? How television frames political issues. Journal of Broadcasting & Electronic Media, 36*, 239–241.

Chaffee, S.H., & Hochheimer, J.L. (1982). The beginnings of political communication research in the United States: Origins of the "limited effects" model. In E.M. Rogers & F. Balle (Eds.), *The media revolution in America and western Europe* (pp. 267–296). Norwood, NJ: Ablex.

Chaffee, S.H., McLeod, J.M., & Atkin, C.K. (1971). Parental influences on adolescent media use. *American Behavioral Scientist, 14*, 323–340.

Chaffee, S. H., McLeod, J. M., & Wackman, D. B. (1973). Family communication patterns and adolescent political participation. In J. Dennis (Ed.), *Socialization to politics: A reader* (pp. 349–364). New York: Wiley.

Chaffee, S. H., & Metzger, M. J. (2001). The end of mass communication? *Mass Communication & Society, 4*(4), 365–379.

Chaffee, S. H., & Schleuder, J. (1986). Measurement and effects of attention to media news. *Human Communication Research, 13,* 76–107.

Chaiken, S. (1979). Communicator physical attractiveness and persuasion. *Journal of Personality and Social Psychology, 37,* 1387–1397.

Chang, H. (1998). The effect of news teasers in processing TV news. *Journal of Broadcasting & Electronic Media, 42,* 327–339.

Check, J. V. P., & Guloien, T. H. (1989). Reported proclivity for coercive sex following repeated exposure to sexually violent pornography, nonviolent pornography, and erotica. In D. Zillmann & J. Bryant (Eds.), *Pornography: Research advances & policy considerations* (pp. 159–184). Hillsdale, NJ: Lawrence Erlbaum Associates.

Check, J. V. P., & Malamuth, N. M. (1981). Pornography and social aggression: A social learning theory analysis. In M. L. McLaughlin (Ed.), *Communication Yearbook 9* (pp. 181–213). Beverly Hills, CA: SAGE.

Check, J. V. P., & Malamuth, N. (1984). Can there be positive effects of participation in pornography experiments? *Journal of Sex Research, 20,* 14–31.

Chertoff, M., & Lawrence, D. (2013, April 23). Investigation terror in the age of twitter. *Wall Street Journal,* A23.

Chew, F., & Palmer, S. (1994). Interest, the knowledge gap, and television programming. *Journal of Broadcasting & Electronic Media, 38,* 271–287.

Children Now. (1999). *A different world: Children's perceptions of race and class in media.* Oakland, CA: Children Now. Retrieved from: http://www.readwritethink.org/files/resources/lesson_images/lesson96/different_world.pdf.

Children Now. (2004). *Fall colors: 2003–2004 prime time diversity report.* Oakland, CA: Children Now. Retrieved from: http://www.bus.iastate.edu/emullen/mgmt472/Prime%20time%20diversity%20report.pdf.

The Children's Food and Beverage Advertising Initiative (CFBAI). (2013). Retrieved from: https://www.bbb.org/council/the-national-partner-program/national-advertising-review-services/childrens-food-and-beverage-advertising-initiative/.

Chong, D., & Druckman, J. N. (2007). A theory of framing and opinion formation in competitive elite environments. *Journal of Communication, 57*(1), 99–118.

Chou, S.-Y., Rashad, I., & Grossman, M. (2008). Fast-food restaurant advertising on television and its influence on childhood obesity. *Journal of Law and Economics, 51,* 599–618.

Chozick, A. (2010, April 7). What your TV is telling you to do, *Wall Street Journal,* D1, D3.

Christakis, D. A., Garrison, M. M., Herrenkohl, T., Haggerty, K., Rivara, F. P., Zhou, C., & Liekweg, K. (2013). Modifying media content for preschool children: A randomized controlled trial. *Pediatrics,* 431–438.

Christensen, F. (1986). Sexual callousness: Re-examined. *Journal of Communication, 36*(1), 174–184.

Christensen, P. N., & Wood, W. (2007). Effects of media violence on viewers' aggression in unconstrained social interaction. In R. W. Preiss, B. M. Gayle, N. Burrell, M. Allen, & J. Bryant (Eds.), *Mass media effects research: Advances through meta-analysis* (pp. 145–168). Mahwah, NJ: Erlbaum.

Christenson, P. G., Henriksen, L., & Roberts, D. F. (2000). *Substance use in popular prime time television.* Washington, D.C.: Office of National Drug Control Policy & Mediascope Macro International, Inc.

Clark, L., & Tiggemann, M. (2006). Appearance culture in 9- to 12-year-old girls: Media and peer influences on body dissatisfaction. *Social Development, 15*(4), 628–643.

Clark, L., & Tiggemann, M. (2007). Sociocultural influences and body image in 9- to 12-year-old girls: The role of appearance schemas. *Journal of Clinical Child & Adolescent Psychology, 36*(1), 76–86.

Clay, D., Vignoles, V.L., & Dittmar, H. (2005). Body image and self-esteem among adolescent girls: Testing the influence of sociocultural factors. *Journal of Research on Adolescence, 15*(4), 451–477.

Cline, V.B., Croft, R.G., & Courrier, S. (1973). Desensitization of children to television violence. *Journal of Personality and Social Psychology, 27,* 360–365.

Cohen, B. (1963). *The press and foreign policy.* Princeton, NJ: Princeton University Press.

Cohen, F., Ogilvie, D.M., Solomon, S., Greenberg, J., & Pyszczynski, T. (2005). *Analyses of Social Issues and Public Policy, 5,* 177–187.

Cohen, J. (1988). *Statistical power analysis for the behavioral sciences* (2nd edn.). Hillsdale, NJ: Lawrence Erlbaum Associates.

Cohen, J. (2001). Defining identification: A theoretical look at identification of audiences with media characters. *Mass Communication & Society, 4,* 245–264.

Cohen, J. (2002). Deconstructing Ally: Explaining viewers' interpretations of popular television. *Media Psychology, 4,* 253–277.

Cohen, J. (2006). Audience identification with media characters. In J. Bryant & P. Vorderer (Eds.), *Psychology of entertainment* (pp. 183–197). New York: Routledge.

Cohen, J. (2009). Mediated relationships and media effects: Parasocial interaction and identification. In R.L. Nabi & M.B. Oliver (Eds.), *The SAGE handbook of media processes and effects* (pp. 223–236). Los Angeles: SAGE.

Cohen, J., & Davis, R.G. (1991). Third-person effects and the differential impact in negative political advertising. *Journalism Quarterly, 68,* 680–688.

Cohen, J., & Weimann, G. (2000). Cultivation revisited: Some genres have some effects on some viewers. *Communication Reports, 13,* 99–114.

Coleman, R., & McCombs, M. (2007). The young and agenda-less? Exploring age-related difference in agenda setting on the youngest generation, baby boomers, and the civic generation. *Journalism & Mass Communication Quarterly, 84,* 495–508.

Coleman, S., & Blumler, J.G. (2009).*The Internet and democratic citizenship: Theory, practice, and policy.* New York: Cambridge University Press.

Coles, C.D., & Shamp, M.J. (1984). Some sexual, personality, and demographic characteristics of women readers of erotic romances. *Archives of Sexual Behavior, 13*(3), 187–209.

Collins, R.L., Ellickson, P.L., McCaffrey, D., & Hambarsoomians, K. (2007). Early adolescent exposure to alcohol advertising and its relationship to underage drinking. *Journal of Adolescent Health, 40,* 527–534.

Collins, R.L., Elliott, M.N., Berry, S.H., Kanouse, D.E., & Hunter, S.B. (2003). Entertainment television as a health sex educator: The impact of condom-efficacy information in an episode of *Friends. Pediatrics, 112*(5), 1115–1121.

Collins, R.L., Elliott, M.N., Berry, S.H., Kanouse, D.E., Kunkel, D., Hunter, S.B., & Miu, A. (2004). Watching sex on television predicts adolescent initiation of sexual behavior. *Pediatrics, 114*(3), e280–e289.

Collins, W.A. (1982). Cognitive processing in television viewing. In D. Pearl, L. Bouthilet, & J. Lazar (Eds.), *Television and behavior: Ten years of scientific progress and implications for the eighties* (DHHS Publication No. ADM 82–1196, Vol. 2, pp. 9–23). Washington, DC: U.S. Government Printing Office.

Commission on Obscenity and Pornography. (1970). *The report of the Commission on Obscenity and Pornography.* Washington, DC: U.S. Government Printing Office.

Comstock, G., Chaffee, S., Katzman, N., McCombs, M., & Roberts, D. (1978). *Television and human behavior*. New York: Columbia University Press.

Comstock, G., & Scharrer, E. (1999). *Television: What's on, who's watching, and what it means*. San Diego, CA: Academic Press.

Condry, J. (1989). *The psychology of television*. Hillsdale, NJ: Lawrence Erlbaum Associates.

Converse, P.E. (1975). Public opinion and voting behavior. In F. Greenstein & N. Polsby (Eds.), *Handbook of political science* (Vol. 4, pp. 75–169). Reading, MA: Addison-Wesley.

Cook, R.F., & Fosen, R.H. (1971). *Pornography and the sex offender: Patterns of exposure and immediate arousal effects of pornographic stimuli. Technical report of the Commission on Obscenity and Pornography* (Vol. 7, pp. 149–162). Washington, DC: U.S. Government Printing Office.

Cook, T.D., Appleton, H., Conner, R.F., Shaffer, A., Tamkin, G., & Weber, S.J. (1975). *Sesame Street revisited: A case study in evaluation research*. New York: Russell Sage.

Coon, K.A., Goldberg, J., Rogers, B.L., & Tucker, K.L. (2001). Relationships between use of television during meals and children's food consumption patterns. *Pediatrics*, *107*(1), E7.

Cooper, C.A. (1996). *Violence on television: Congressional inquiry, public criticism and industry response. A policy analysis*. Lanham, MD: University Press of America.

Cooper, C.A. (2007). *Violence in the media and its influence on criminal defense*. Jefferson, NC: McFarland & Company.

Coser, L.A. (1956). *The functions of social conflict*. New York: Free Press.

Cotton, J.L. (1985). Cognitive dissonance in selective exposure. In D. Zillmann & J. Bryant (Eds.), *Selective exposure to communication* (pp. 11–33). Hillsdale, NJ: Lawrence Erlbaum Associates.

Craft, S., & Wanta, W. (2004). U.S. public concerns in the aftermath of 9/11: A test of second level agenda setting. *International Journal of Public Opinion Research*, *16*, 456–463.

Craik, F.I.M., & Lockhart, R.S. (1972). Levels of processing: A framework for memory research. *Journal of Verbal Learning and Verbal Behavior*, *11*, 671–684.

Crenshaw, D. (2008). *The myth of multitasking: How "doing it all" gets nothing done*. Sana Francisco, CA: Jossey-Bass.

Crocker, J., & Garcia, J.A. (2010). Internalized devaluation and situational threat. In J.F. Dovidio, M. Hewstone, P. Glick, & V.M. Esses (Eds.), *The Sage handbook of prejudice, stereotyping and discrimination*. Thousand Oaks, CA: SAGE.

Cummins, R.G. (2009). The effects of subjective camera and fanship on viewers' experience of presence and perception of play in sports telecasts. *Journal of Applied Communication Research*, *37*, 374–396.

Cummins, R.G., Keene, J.R., & Nutting, B.H. (2012). The impact of subjective camera in sports on arousal and enjoyment. *Mass Communication and Society*, *15*, 74–97.

Curran, J., Gurevitch, M., & Woollacott, J. (1982). The study of the media: Theoretical approaches. In M. Gurevitch, T. Bennett, J. Curran, & J. Woollacott (Eds.), *Culture, society and the media* (pp. 11–29). New York: Methuen.

Czarny, M., Faden, R.R., & Sugarman, J. (2010). Bioethics and professionalism in popular television medical dramas. *Journal of Medical Ethics*, *36*, 203–206.

Daniels, G.L., & Loggins, G.M. (2007). Conceptualizing continuous coverage: A strategic model for wall-to-wall local television weather broadcasts. *Journal of Applied Communication Research*, *35*, 48–66.

Das, E., Bushman, B.J., Bezemer, M.D., Kerkhof, P., & Vermeulen, I.E. (2009). How terrorism news reports increase prejudice against outgroups: A terror management account. *Journal of Experimental Social Psychology*, *45*, 452–459.

David, P., & Johnson, M.A. (1998). The role of self in third-person effects about body image. *Journal of Communication, 48*(4), 37–58.

Davis, D.K., & Robinson, J.P. (1986). News story attributes and comprehension. In J.P. Robinson & M.R. Levy (Eds.), *The main source: Learning from television news* (pp. 179–210). Beverly Hills: SAGE.

Davis, R.A. (2001). A cognitive-behavioral model of pathological Internet use. *Computers in Human Behavior, 17*, 187–195.

Davison, W.P. (1983). The third-person effect in communication. *Public Opinion Quarterly, 47*, 1–15.

Dawn, R., & Block, A.B. (2009, May 12). Brands Take the "American Idol" Stage. *Adweek.*

Dayan, D., & Katz, E. (1992). *Media events: Live broadcasting of history.* Cambridge, MA: Harvard University Press.

Dearing, J.W., & Rogers, E.M. (1996). *Communication concepts 6: Agenda-setting.* Thousand Oaks, CA: SAGE.

Deemers, D.P., Craff, D., Choi, Y., & Pessin, B.M. (1989). Issue obtrusiveness and the agenda-setting effects of national network news. *Communication Research, 16*, 793–812.

DeFleur, M.L. (1987). The growth and decline of research on the diffusion of the news, 1945–1985. *Communication Research, 14*, 109–130.

DeFleur, M.L., & Ball-Rokeach, S. (1989). *Theories of mass communication* (5th edn.). New York: Longman.

DeFleur, M.L., & Dennis, E.E. (1994). *Understanding mass communication: A liberal arts perspective* (5th edn.). Dallas: Houghton Mifflin.

Dennis, E.E., Stebenne, D., Pavlik, J., Thalhimer, M., LaMay, C., Smillie, D., FitzSimon, M., Gazsi, S., & Rachlin, S. (1991). *The media at war: The press and the Persian Gulf conflict.* New York: Gannett Foundation.

Department of Health and Human Services. (2001). *Youth violence: A report of the Surgeon General.* Rockville, MD: Office of the Surgeon General.

Detenber, B.H., & Reeves, B. (1996). A bio-informational theory of emotion: Motion and image size effects on viewers. *Journal of Communication, 46*(3), 66–84.

Devine, P.G. (1989). Stereotypes and prejudice: Their automatic and controlled components. *Journal of Personality and Social Psychology, 56*(1), 5–18.

De Vreese, C.H. (2004). The effects of frames in political television news on issue interpretation and frame salience. *Journalism & Mass Communication Quarterly, 81*(1), 36–52.

Diamond, E., & Bates, S. (1992). *The spot: The rise of political advertising on television* (3rd edn.). Cambridge, MA: MIT Press.

Diamond, M., & Uchiyama, A. (1999). Pornography, rape, and sex crimes in Japan. *International Journal of Law and Psychiatry, 22*, 1–11.

Diaz-Castillo, L. (2005). Bandwagon and underdog effects on a low-information, low-involvement election. Unpublished dissertation, The Ohio State University, Columbus, OH.

Diener, M.L., Pierroutsakos, S.L., Troseth, G.L., & Roberts, A. (2008). Video versus reality: Infants' attention and affective responses to video and live presentations. *Media Psychology, 11*(3), 418–441.

DiFranza, J.R., Richards, J.W., Paulman, P.M., Wolf-Gillespie, N., Fletcher, C., Jaffe, R.D., & Murray, D. (1991). RJR Nabisco's cartoon camel promotes Camel cigarettes to children. *JAMA, 266*, 3149–3153.

Dimmick, J., Chen, Y., & Li, Z. (2004).Competition between the Internet and traditional news media: The gratification-opportunities niche dimension. *The Journal of Media Economics, 17*(1), 19–33.

Dimock, M., Doherty, C., & Tyson, Al. (2013). *Most expect "occasion acts of terrorism" in the future*. Washington, DC: The Pew Research Center for the People & The Press.

Dinkes, R., Cataldi, E. F., Lin-Kelly, W., & Snyder, T. D. (2007). *Indicators of school crime and safety: 2007* (NCES 2008–021/NCJ 219553). Washington, DC: National Center for Education statistics, Institute of Education Sciences, U.S. Department of Education, and Bureau of Justice Statistics, Office of Justice Programs, U.S. Department of Justice.

Dittmar, H., Halliwell, E., & Stirling, E. (2009). Understanding the impact of thin media models on women's body-focused affect: The role of thin-ideal internalization and weight-related self-discrepancy activation in experimental exposure effects. *Journal of Social and Clinical Psychology, 28*, 43–72.

Dixon, T. L. (2007). Black criminals and white officers: The effects of racially misrepresenting law breakers and law defenders on television news. *Media Psychology, 10*(2), 270–291.

Dixon, T. L., & Linz, D. (2000). Overrepresentation and underrepresentation of African Americans and Latinos as lawbreakers on television news. *Journal of Communication, 50*(2), 131–154.

Dobkin, B. A. (1992). *Tales of terror: Television news and the construction of the terrorist threat*. New York: Praeger.

Dominick, J. R. (1984). Videogames, television violence, and aggression in teenagers. *Journal of Communication, 34*(2), 136–147.

Dominick, J. R., & Greenberg, B. S. (1972). Attitudes towards violence: The interaction of television, exposure, family attitudes, and social class. In G. A. Comstock & E. A. Rubinstein (Eds.), *Television and social behavior: Vol. 3. Television and adolescent aggressiveness* (pp. 314–335). Washington, DC: U.S. Government Printing Office.

Donnerstein, E. (1984). Pornography: Its effects on violence again women. In N. Malamuth & E. Donnerstein (Eds.), *Pornography and sexual aggression* (pp. 53–81). New York: Academic Press.

Donnerstein, E., & Barrett, G. (1978). The effects of erotic stimuli on male aggression towards females. *Journal of Personality and Social Psychology, 36*, 180–188.

Donnerstein, E., & Berkowitz, L. (1981). Victim reactions in aggressive-erotic films as a factor in violence against women. *Journal of Personality and Social Psychology, 41*, 710–724.

Donnerstein, E., Linz, D., & Penrod, S. (1987). *The question of pornography: Research findings and policy implications*. New York: Free Press.

Donnerstein, E., Slaby, R. G., & Eron, L. D. (1994). The mass media and youth aggression. In L. D. Eron, J. H. Gentry, & P. Schlegel (Eds.), *Reason to hope: A psychosocial perspective on violence & youth* (pp. 219–250). Washington, DC: American Psychological Association.

Donnerstein, E., Wilson, B., & Linz, D. (1992). On the regulation of broadcast indecency to protect children. *Journal of Broadcasting & Electronic Media, 36*, 111–117.

Donohew, L., Finn, S., & Christ, W. G. (1988). "The nature of news." revisited: The roles of affect, schemas, and cognition. In L. Donohew, H. E. Sypher, & E. T. Higgins (Eds.), *Communication, social cognition, and affect* (pp. 195–218). Hillsdale, NJ: Lawrence Erlbaum Associates.

Donohue, G. A., Tichenor, P. J., & Olien, C. N. (1975). Mass media and the knowledge gap: A hypothesis reconsidered. *Communication Research, 2*, 3–23.

Donsbach, W. (2001). *Who's afraid of election polls? Normative and empirical arguments for the freedom of pre-election surveys*. Amsterdam: European Society for Opinion and Marketing Research.

Doob, A. N., & Macdonald, G. E. (1979). Television viewing and fear of victimization: Is the relationship causal? *Journal of Personality and Social Psychology*, 37, 170–179.

Dorr, A. (1986). *Television and children: A special medium for a special audience.* Beverly Hills, CA: SAGE.

Dovidio, J. F., Hewstone, M., Glick, P., & Esses, V. M. (2010). Prejudice, stereotyping and discrimination: Theoretical and empirical overview. In J. F. Dovidio, M. Hewstone, P. Glick, & V. M. Esses (Eds.), *The SAGE handbook of prejudice, stereotyping and discrimination.* Thousand Oaks, CA: SAGE.

Driscoll, P. D. & Salwen, M. B. (1997). Self-perceived knowledge of the O. J. Simpson trial: Third-person perception and perceptions of guilt. *Journalism & Mass Communication Quarterly*, 74, 541–556.

Duncan, D. (1990). Pornography as a source of sex information for university students. *Psychological Reports*, 66, 442.

Dunkel, C. S. (2002). Terror management theory and identity: The effect of the 9/11 terrorist attacks on anxiety and identity change. *Identity: An International Journal of Theory and Research*, 2, 287–301.

Dunstan, D. W. et al. (2010). Television viewing time and mortality. *Circulation*, 121, 384–391.

Durkheim. E. (1964). *The division of labor in society* (G. Simpson, Trans.). New York: Free Press. (Original work published 1893.)

Durkin, K. (1985). Television and sex-role acquisition. 2: Effects. *British Journal of Social Psychology*, 24, 191–210.

Dutta-Bergman, M. (2005). Depression and news gathering after September 11: The interplay of affect and cognition. *Communication Research Reports*, 22, 7–14.

Dynes, R. (1970). *Organized behavior in disaster.* Lexington, MA: Heath Lexington.

Eagly, A. H., & Chaiken, S. (1993). *The Psychology of Attitudes.* Fort Worth, TX: Harcourt Brace.

Earnheardt, A. C., & Haridakis, P. M. (2009). An examination of fan–athlete interaction: Fandom, parasocial interaction, and identification. *Ohio Communication Journal*, 47, 27–53.

Edwards, E. D. (1991). The ecstasy of horrible expectations: Morbid curiosity, sensation seeking, and interest in horror movies. In B. A. Austin (Ed.), *Current research in film: Audiences, economics, and law* (Vol. 5, pp. 19–38). Norwood, NJ: Ablex.

Edwards-Levy, A. (2012, December 4). Chris Christie's approval rating, reelection prospects high: Poll. *The Huffington Post*. Retrieved from: http://www.huffington post.com/2012/12/04/christie-approval-rating-poll_n_2237190.html.

Edwardson, M., Grooms, D., & Proudlove, S. (1981). Television news information gain from interesting video vs. talking heads. *Journal of Broadcasting*, 25, 15–24.

Edwardson, M., Kent, K., & McConnell, M. (1985). Television news information gain: Videotex versus a talking head. *Journal of Broadcasting & Electronic Media*, 29, 367–378.

Edy, J. A., & Meirick, P. C. (2007). Wanted, dead or alive: Media frames, frame adoption, and support for the war in Afghanistan. *Journal of Communication*, 57(1), 119–141.

Eggerton, J. (2007, September 26). NBC, Telemundo to cut snack ads from educational kids' shows. *Broadcasting & Cable*. Retrieved from: http://www.broadcastingcable.com/article/110489-NBC_Telemundo_to_Cut_Snack_Ads_from_Educational_Kids_Shows.php.

Ellickson, P. L., Collins, R. L., Hambarsoomians, K., & McCaffrey, D. F. (2005). Does alcohol advertising promote adolescent drinking? Results from a longitudinal assessment. *Addiction*, 100, 235–246.

Elliott, P. (1974). Uses and gratifications research: A critique and sociological alternative. In J.G. Blumler & E. Katz (Eds.), *The uses of mass communication: Current perspectives on gratifications research* (pp. 249–268). Beverly Hills, CA: SAGE.

Endestad, T., Heim, J., Kaare, B., Torgersen, L., & Brandtzaeg, P.B. (2011). Media user types among young children and social displacement. *Nordicom Review, 32,* 17–30.

Ennemoser, M., & Schneider, W. (2007). Relations of television viewing and reading development: Findings from a 4-year longitudinal study. *Journal of Educational Psychology, 99,* 349–368.

Enteman, W.F. (1996). Stereotyping, prejudice, and discrimination. In P.W. Lester (Ed.), *Images that injure: Pictorial stereotypes in the media* (pp. 10–14). Westport, CN: Praeger.

Entman, R.M. (1993). Framing: Toward clarification of a fractured paradigm. *Journal of Communication, 43*(4), 51–58.

Esralew, S., & Young, D.G. (2012). The influence of parodies on mental models: Exploring the Tina Fey-Sarah Palin phenomenon. *Communication Quarterly, 60,* 338–352.

Ettema, J.S., & Kline, F.G. (1977). Deficits, difference, and ceilings: Contingent conditions for understanding knowledge gap. *Communication Research, 4,* 179–202.

Eveland, W.P., Jr. (1997). Interactions and nonlinearity in mass communication: Connecting theory and methodology. *Journalism and Mass Communication Quarterly, 74,* 400–416.

Eveland, W.P., Jr. (2001). The cognitive mediation model of learning from the news: Evidence from nonelection, off-year election, and presidential election contexts. *Communication Research, 28,* 571–601.

Eveland, W.P., & Dunwoody, S. (2000). Examining information processing on the World Wide Web using think aloud protocols. *Media Psychology, 2*(3), 219–244.

Eveland, W.P., & Dunwoody, S. (2001). User control and structural isomorphism or disorientation and cognitive load? Learning from the Web versus print. *Communication Research, 28*(1), 48–78.

Eveland, W.P., McLeod, D.M., & Signorielli, N. (1995). Actual and perceived U.S. public opinion: The spiral of silence during the Persian Gulf War. *International Journal of Public Opinion Research, 7,* 91–109.

Eveland, W.P., Seo, M., & Martin, K. (2002). Learning from the news in campaign 2000: An experimental comparison of TV news, newspapers, and online news. *Media Psychology, 4,* 355–380.

Eyal, K., & Cohen, J. (2006). When good friends say goodbye: A parasocial breakup study. *Journal of Broadcasting & Electronic Media, 50,* 502–523.

Eyal, K., Metzger, J.J., Lingsweiler, R.W., Mahood, C., & Yao, M.Z. (2006). Aggressive political opinions and exposure to violent media. *Mass Communication & Society, 9,* 399–428.

Eysenck, M.W. (1993). *Principles of cognitive psychology.* Hillsdale, NJ: Lawrence Erlbaum Associates.

Eysenck, M.W., & Keane, M.T. (1992). *Cognitive psychology: A student's handbook.* Hillsdale, NJ: Lawrence Erlbaum Associates.

Fahri, P. (2013, September 17). News outlets stumble during early coverage. *Wilmington News Journal,* A8.

Faiola, A. (2004, August 9). Youth violence has Japan struggling for answers. *Washington Post,* A01.

Farrar, K.M. (2006). Sexual intercourse on television: Do safe sex messages matter? *Journal of Broadcasting & Electronic Media, 50*(4), 635–650.

Federal Election Commission. (1998). About elections and voting. Retrieved from: http://www.fec.gov/pages/electpg.htm.

Federal Trade Commission (FTC). (2008). *Marketing food to children and adolescents: A review of industry expenditures, activities, and self-regulation.* Retrieved from: http://www.ftc.gov/reports/marketing-food-children-adolescents-review-industry-expenditures-activities-self-regulation.

Federal Trade Commission (FTC). (2013). *Cigarette report for 2011.* Retrieved from: http://www.ftc.gov/reports/federal-trade-commission-cigarette-report-2011.

Federman, J. (1998). Media ratings systems: A comparative review. In M. E. Price (Ed.), *The V-chip debate: Content filtering from television to the Internet* (pp. 99–132). Mahwah, NJ: Lawrence Erlbaum Associates.

Feldman, L., & Young, D. G. (2008). Late-night comedy as a gateway to traditional news: An analysis of time trends in news attention among late-night comedy viewers during the 2004 presidential primaries. *Political Communication, 25,* 401–422.

Feng, G. C., & Guo, S. Z. (2012). Support for censorship: A multilevel meta-analysis of the third-person effect. *Communication Reports, 25*(1), 40–50.

Fenigstein, A. (1979). Does aggression cause a preference for viewing media violence? *Journal of Personality and Social Psychology, 37,* 2307–2317.

Fenigstein, A., & Heyduk, R. G. (1985). Thought and action as determinants of media exposure. In D. Zillmann & J. Bryant (Eds.), *Selective exposure to communication* (pp. 113–139). Hillsdale, NJ: Lawrence Erlbaum Associates.

Ferguson, C. J., Ivory, J. D., & Beaver, K. M. (2013). Genetic, maternal, school, intelligence, and media use predictors of adult criminality: A longitudinal test of the Catalyst Model in adolescence through early adulthood. *Journal of Aggression, Maltreatment & Trauma, 22,* 447–460.

Ferguson, C. J., Rueda, S. M., Cruz, A. M., Ferguson, D. E., Fritz, S., & Smith, S. M. (2008). Violent video games and aggression: Causal relationship or byproduct of family violence and intrinsic violence motivation? *Criminal Justice and Behavior, 35,* 311–332.

Ferguson, D. A., Greer, C. F., & Reardon, M. E. (2007). Uses and gratifications of mp3 players by college students: Are iPods more popular than radio? *Journal of Radio Studies, 14,* 102–121.

Ferguson, D. A., & Perse, E. M. (1993). Media and audience influences on channel repertoire. *Journal of Broadcasting & Electronic Media, 37,* 31–47.

Ferguson, D. A., & Perse, E. M. (2000). The World Wide Web as a functional alternative to television. *Journal of Broadcasting & Electronic Media,* 155–174.

Ferris, A. L., Smith, S. W., Greenberg, B. S., & Smith, S. L. (2007). The content of reality dating shows and viewer perceptions of dating. *Journal of Communication, 57,* 490–510.

Feshbach, S. (1955). The drive-reducing function of fantasy behavior. *Journal of Abnormal and Social Psychology, 50,* 3–11.

Feshbach, S. (1972). Reality and fantasy in filmed violence. In J. P. Murray, E. A. Rubinstein, & G. A. Comstock (Eds.), *Television and social behavior. Vol. 2: Television and social learning* (pp. 318–345). Rockville, MD: National Institute of Mental Health.

Feshbach, S., & Singer, R. D. (1971). *Television and aggression: An experimental field study.* San Francisco: Jossey-Bass.

Festinger, L. (1954). A theory of social comparison. *Human Relations, 7,* 117–140.

Festinger, L. (1957). A *theory of cognitive dissonance.* Stanford, CA: Stanford University.

Fetler, M. (1984). Television viewing and school achievement. *Journal of Communication, 34*(2), 104–118.

Field, A. E., Austin, S. B., Camargo, C. A., Jr., Taylor, C. B., Striegel-Moore, R. H., Loud, K. J., & Colditz, G. C. (2005). Exposure to the mass media, body shape concerns, and use of supplements to improve weight and shape among male and female adolescents. *Pediatrics, 116*(2), e214–e220.

Figlio, R. M. (n.d.). Review and critique: Report to the American Broadcasting Company regarding: Centerwall, Brandon S., Exposure to television as risk factor for violence. Unpublished report, University of California-Riverside, Department of Sociology.

Findahl, O., & Höijer, G. (1985). Some characteristics of news memory and comprehension. *Journal of Broadcasting & Electronic Media, 29,* 379–396.

Fisch, S. M. (2000). A capacity model of children's comprehension of educational content on television. *Media Psychology, 2*(1), 63–91.

Fisch, S. M. (2009). Educational television and interactive media for children: Effects on academic knowledge, skills, and attitudes. In J. Bryant & M. B. Oliver (Eds.), *Media effects: Advances in theory and research.* New York: Routledge.

Fisch, S. M., Truglio, R. T., & Cole, C. F. (1999). The impact of *Sesame Street* on preschool children: A review and synthesis of 30 years' research. *Media Psychology, 1*(2), 165–190.

Fishbein, M., & Ajzen, I. (1975). *Belief, attitude, intention and behavior: An introduction to theory and research.* Reading, MA: Addison-Wesley.

Fishbein, M., & Hornik, R., eds. (2008). Measuring exposure: Papers from the Annenberg media exposure workshop [Special Issue]. *Communication Methods and Measures, 2*(1–2).

Fisher, D. A., Hill, D. L., Grube, J. W., Bersamin, M. M., Walker, S., & Gruber, E. L. (2009). Televised sexual content and parental mediation: Influences on adolescent sexuality, *Media Psychology, 12*(2), 121–147.

Fisher, D. A., Hill, D. L., Grube, J. W., & Gruber, E. L. (2004). Sex on American television: An analysis across program genres and network types. *Journal of Broadcasting & Electronic Media, 48,* 529–553.

Fisher, W. A., & Barak, A. (1989). Sex education as a corrective: Immunizing against possible effects of pornography. In D. Zillmann (Ed.), *Pornography: Research advances & policy considerations* (pp. 289–320). Hillsdale, NJ: Lawrence Erlbaum Associates.

Fiske, S. T., & Kinder, D. R. (1991). Involvement, expertise, and schema sue: Evidence from political cognition. In N. Cantor & J. F. Kihlstrom (Eds.), *Personality, cognition, and social interaction* (pp. 171–190). Hillsdale, NJ: Lawrence Erlbaum Associates.

Fiske, S. T., & Taylor, S. E. (1991). *Social cognition* (2nd edn.). New York: McGraw-Hill.

Flavell, J. H. (1963). *The developmental psychology of Jean Piaget.* New York: Van Nostrand.

Flores, S. A., & Hartlaub, M. G. (1998). Reducing rape-myth acceptance in male college students: A meta-analysis of intervention studies. *Journal of College Student Development, 39,* 438–448.

Fogel, J., & Kovalenko, L. (2013). Reality television shows focusing on sexual relationships are associated with college students engaging in one-night stands. *Journal of Cognitive and Behavioral Psychotherapies, 13,* 321–331.

Fogel, J., & Krausz, F. (2013). Watching reality television beauty shows is associated with tanning lamp use and outdoor tanning among college students. *Journal of the American Academy of Dermatology, 68,* 784–789.

Foss, K. A., & Alexander, A. F. (1996). Exploring the margins of television viewing. *Communication Reports, 9,* 61–68.

Fouts, G., & Burggraf, K. (2000). Television situation comedies: Female weight male negative comments, and audience reactions. *Sex Roles, 42*(9/10), 925–932.

Fowles, J. (1992). *The case for television violence.* Los Angeles: SAGE.

Fox, J., Chung, Y., Lee, S., Schwartz, N., Haverhals, L., Wang, Z., Lang, A., & Potter, D. (2003). *Picture this: Effects of graphics on the processing of television news.* International Communication Association; 2003 Annual Meeting, San Diego, CA.

Frankovic, K.A. (1998). Public opinion and polling. In D. Graber, D. McQuail, & P. Norris (Eds.), *The politics of news: The news of politics* (pp. 150–170). Washington, DC: Congressional Quarterly Press.

Frankovic, K.A. (2005). Reporting "the polls" in 2004. *The Public Opinion Quarterly, 69(5),* 682–697.

Freedman, J.L. (1984). Effect of television violence on aggressiveness. *Psychological Bulletin, 96,* 227–246.

Fuchs, D.A. (1966). Election-day radio-television and western voting. *Public Opinion Quarterly, 30,* 226–236.

Funkhouser, G.R. (1973a). The issues of the sixties: An exploratory study in the dynamics of public opinion. *Public Opinion Quarterly, 37,* 62–75.

Funkhouser, G.R. (1973b). Trends in media coverage of the issues of the sixties. *Journalism Quarterly, 50,* 533–538.

Gaertner, S.L., Dovidio, J.F., & Houlette, M.A. (2010). Social categorization. In J.F. Dovidio, M. Hewstone, P. Glick, & V.M. Esses (Eds.), *The SAGE handbook of prejudice, stereotyping and discrimination.* Thousand Oaks, CA: SAGE.

Gallup Organization. (1991, January). *Buildup to war.* Monthly Report, pp. 2–13.

Gantz, W. (1978). How uses and gratifications affect recall of television news. *Journalism Quarterly, 55,* 664–672, 681.

Gantz, W. (1983). The diffusion of news about the attempted Reagan assassination. *Journal of Communication, 33(1),* 56–66.

Gantz, W., Krendl, K.A., & Robertson, S.R. (1986). Diffusion of a proximate news event. *Journalism Quarterly, 63,* 282–287.

Gantz, W., & Tokinoya, H. (1987). Diffusion of news about the assassination of Olof Palme: A trans-continental, two-city comparison of the process. *European Journal of Communication, 2,* 197–210.

Garner, P.E., & Garfinkel, P.E. (1979). The Eating Attitudes Test: An index of symptoms of anorexia nervosa. *Psychological Medicine, 9,* 273–279.

Garramone, G.M. (1983). Issue versus image orientation and effects of political advertising. *Communication Research, 18,* 59–76.

Gartner, M. (1976). Endogenous bandwagon and underdog effects. *Public Choice, 25,* 83–89.

Gauntlett, D. (1998). *Ten things wrong with the "effects model."* Retrieved from: http://theory.org.uk/effects.htm.

Gauntlett, D. (2005). *Moving experiences: Media effects and beyond* (2nd edn.). Eastleigh, UK: John Libbey Publishing.

Gaziano, C. (1985). The knowledge gap: An analytical review of media effects. In M. Gurevitch & M. Levy (Eds.), *Mass communication review yearbook* (Vol. 5, pp. 462–501). Beverly Hills: SAGE.

Gaziano, C. (1988). How credible is the credibility crisis? *Journalism Quarterly, 65,* 267–278, 375.

Gaziano, C., & McGrath, K. (1986). Measuring the concept of credibility. *Journalism Quarterly, 63,* 451–462.

Geis, F.L., Brown, V., Walstedt, J., & Porter, N. (1984). TV commercials as achievement scripts for women. *Sex Roles, 10,* 513–525.

Genova, B.K.L., & Greenberg, B.S. (1979). Interests in news and the knowledge gap. *Public Opinion Quarterly, 43,* 79–91.

Gerbner, G. (2001). Drugs in television, movies, and music videos. In Y.R. Kamalipour & K.R. Rampal (Eds.), *Media, sex, violence and drugs in the global village.* Lanham, MD: Rowman & Littlefield.

Gerbner, G., & Gross, L. (1976). Living with television: The violence profile. *Journal of Communication, 26(2),* 173–199.

Gerbner, G., Gross, L., Eleey, M., Jackson-Beeck, M., Jeffries-Fox, S., & Signorielli, N. (1977). The Gerbner violence profile. An analysis of the CBS report. *Journal of Broadcasting, 21,* 280–286.

Gerbner, G., Gross, L., Jackson-Beeck, M., Jeffries-Fox, S., & Signorielli, N. (1978). Cultural indicators: Violence profile no. 9. *Journal of Communication, 28*(3), 176–207.

Gerbner, G., Gross, L., Morgan, M., & Signorielli, N. (1980). The "mainstreaming" of America: Violence profile no. 11. *Journal of Communication, 30*(3), 10–29.

Gerbner, G., Gross, L., Morgan, M., & Signorielli, N. (1982). Charting the mainstream: Television's contributions to political orientations. *Journal of Communication, 32*(2), 100–127.

Gerbner, G., Gross, L., Morgan, M., & Signorielli, N. (1986). Living with television: The dynamics of the cultivation process. In J. Bryant & D. Zillmann (Eds.), *Perspectives on media effects* (pp. 17–40). Hillsdale, NJ: Lawrence Erlbaum Associates.

Gerbner, G., Gross, L., Signorielli, N., & Morgan, M. (1980). Aging with television: Images on television drama and conceptions of social reality. *Journal of Communication, 30*(1), 37–47.

Gerbner, G., & Signorielli, N. (1979). *Women and minorities in television drama 1969–1978.* Philadelphia: Annenberg School for Communication, University of Pennsylvania.

Ghanem, S. (1997). Filling in the tapestry: The second level of agenda setting. In M. McCombs, D. L. Shaw, & D. Weaver (Eds.), *Communication and democracy: Exploring the intellectual frontiers in agenda-setting theory* (pp. 3–14). Mahwah, NJ: Lawrence Erlbaum Associates.

Gibson, J. L., & Caldeira, G. A. (2009). *Citizens, courts, and confirmations: Positivity theory and the judgments of the American people.* Princeton, NJ: Princeton University Press.

Gibson, R., Aust, C. F., & Zillmann, D. (2000). Loneliness of adolescents and their choice and enjoyment of love-celebrating versus love-lamenting popular music. *Empirical Studies of the Arts, 18,* 421–433.

Giessner, S. R., Ryan, M. K., Schubert, T. W., & Van Quaquebeke, N. (2011). The power of pictures: Vertical picture angles in power pictures. *Media Psychology, 14,* 442–464.

Gilbert, P., Price, J. S., & Allan, S. (1995). Social comparison, social attractiveness and evolution: How might they be related. *New Ideas in Psychology, 13,* 149–165.

Gitlin, T. (1978). Media sociology: The dominant paradigm. *Theory and Society, 6,* 205–253.

Gitlin, T. (1980). *The whole world is watching: Mass media and the making and unmaking of the new left.* Berkeley: University of California Press.

GLAAD (Gay & Lesbian Alliance Against Defamation). (2012). *Where we are on TV.* Retrieved from: http://www.glaad.org/publications/whereweareontv11.

Glantz, S. A., Kacirk, K. W., & McCulloch, C. (2004). Back to the future: Smoking in movies in 2002 compared with 1950 levels. *American Journal of Public Health, 94*(2), 261–263.

Glick, P., & Rudman, L. A. (2010). *Sexism.* Chapter 20 in J. F. Dovidio, M. Hewstone, P. Glick, & V. M. Esses (Eds.), *The SAGE handbook of prejudice, stereotyping and discrimination.* Los Angeles: SAGE.

Glynn, C. J., Hayes, A. F., & Shanahan, J. (1997). Perceived support for one's opinions and willingness to speak out: A meta-analysis of survey studies on the "spiral of silence." *Public Opinion Quarterly, 61,* 452–463.

Glynn, C. J., & McLeod, J. M. (1985). Implications of the spiral of silence theory of communication and public opinion research. In K. R. Sanders, L. L. Kaid, & D. Nimmo (Eds.), *Political communication yearbook 1984* (pp. 43–65). Carbondale, IL: Southern Illinois University Press.

Godlewski, L. R., & Perse, E. M. (2010). Audience activity and reality television: Identification, online activity, and satisfaction. *Communication Quarterly, 58*, 148–169.

Goffman, E. (1974). *Frame analysis: An essay on the organization of experience.* New York: Harper & Row.

Golan, G. J., & Day, A. J. (2008). The first-person effect and its behavioral consequences: A new trend in the 25-year history of third-person effect research. *Mass Communication & Society, 11*(4), 539–556.

Goldberg, M. E., Gorn, G. J., & Gibson, W. (1978). TV messages for snack and breakfast foods: Do they influence children's preferences? *Journal of Consumer Research, 5*, 73–81.

Goldman, K., & Reilly, P.M. (1992, September 10). Untold story: Media's slow grasp of hurricane's impact helped delay response. *Wall Street Journal*, A1, A9.

Goltz, J. D. (1984). Are the news media responsible for the disaster myth? A content analysis of emergency response imagery. *International Journal of Mass Emergencies and Disasters, 2*, 345–368.

González, H. (1988). Mass media and the spiral of silence: The Philippines from Marcos to Aquino. *Journal of Communication, 38*(4), 33–48.

Gortmaker, S. L., Must, A., Sobol, A.M., Peterson, K., Colditz, G.A., & Dietz, W. H. (1996). Television viewing as a cause of increasing obesity among children in the United States, 1986–1990. *Archive of Pediatrics & Adolescent Medicine, 150*(4), 356–362.

Grabe, M. E., Kamhawi, R., & Yegiyan, N. (2009). Informing citizens: How people with different levels of education process television, newspaper, and web news. *Journal of Broadcasting & Electronic Media, 53*(1), 90–111.

Grabe, M. E., Lang, A., Zhou, S., & Bolls, P. (2000). Cognitive access to negatively arousing news: An experimental investigation of the knowledge gap. *Communication Research, 27*(1), 3–26.

Grabe, S., Ward, L. M., & Hyde, J. S. (2008). The role of the media in body image concerns among women: A meta-analysis of experimental and correlational studies. *Psychological Bulletin, 134*, 460–476.

Graber, D. A. (1982). The impact of media research on public opinion studies. In D.C. Whitney, E. Wartella, & S. Windahl (Eds.), *Mass communication review yearbook* (Vol. 3, pp. 555–563). Beverly Hills: SAGE.

Graber, D. A. (1988). *Processing the news: How people tame the information tide* (2nd edn.). New York: Longman.

Graber, D. A. (1989). *Mass media and American politics* (3rd edn.). Washington, DC: Congressional Quarterly Press.

Graber, D. A. (1990). Seeing is remembering: How visuals contribute to learning from television news. *Journal of Communication, 40*(3), 134–155.

Graber, D. A. (2001). *Processing politics: Learning from television in the Internet age.* Chicago: University of Chicago Press.

Graber, D. A. (2007). The road to public surveillance: Breeching attention thresholds. In W. R. Neuman, G. E. Marcus, M. Mackuen, & A.N. Crigler (Eds.), *The affect effect: dynamics of emotion in political thinking and behavior.* Chicago: University of Chicago Press.

Graber, D. A. (2009). *Mass Media and American Politics* (8th edn.). Washington, DC: CQ Press.

Graber, D. A. (2010). *American politics and the mass media* (8th edn.). Washington, DC: CQ Press.

Graves, S. B. (1993). Television, the portrayal of African Americans, and the development of children's attitudes. In G. L. Berry & J. K. Asamen (Eds.), *Children & television: Images in a changing sociocultural world* (pp. 179–190). Newbury Park, CA: SAGE.

Greenberg, B.S. (1965). Diffusion of news about the Kennedy assassination. In B.S. Greenberg & E.B. Parker (Eds.), *The Kennedy assassination and the American public: Social communication in crisis* (pp. 89–98). Stanford, CA: Stanford University Press.

Greenberg, B.S. (1974). Gratifications of television viewing and their correlates for British children. In J.G. Blumler & E. Katz (Eds.), *The uses of mass communications: Current perspectives on gratifications research* (pp. 71–92). Beverly Hills: SAGE.

Greenberg, B.S. (1988). Some uncommon television images and the drench hypothesis. In S. Oskamp (Ed.), *Applied social psychology annual. Vol. 8: Television as a social issue* (pp. 88–102). Newbury Park, CA: SAGE.

Greenberg, B.S. (1994). Content trends in media sex. In D. Zillmann, J. Bryant, & A.C. Huston (Eds.), *Media, children, and the family: Social scientific, psychodynamic, and clinical perspectives* (pp. 165–182). Hillsdale, NJ: Lawrence Erlbaum Associates.

Greenberg, B.S., Cohen, E., & Li, H. (1993). How the U.S. found out about the war. In B.S. Greenberg & W. Gantz (Eds.), *Desert Storm and the mass media* (pp. 145–152). Cresskill, NJ: Hampton.

Greenberg, B.S., Eastin, M., Hofschire, L., Lachlan, K., & Brownell, K.D. (2003). Portrayals of overweight and obese individuals on commercial television. *American Journal of Public Health, 93*(8), 1342–1348.

Greenberg, B.S., Hofschire, L., & Lachlan, K. (2002). Public perceptions of media functions at the beginning of the war on terrorism. In B.S. Greenberg (Ed.), *Communication and terrorism: Public and media responses to 9/11* (pp. 3–16). Cresskill, NJ: Hampton Press.

Greenberg, J., Pyszczynski, T., & Solomon, S. (1986). The causes and consequences of a need for self-esteem: A terror management theory. In R.F. Baumeister (Ed.), *Public and private self* (pp. 189–212). New York: Springer-Verlag.

Greenwald, A.G., & Leavitt, C. (1984). Audience involvement in advertising: Four levels. *Journal of Consumer Research, 11*, 581–592.

Greer, C.F., & Ferguson, D.A. (2011). Following local television news personalities on Twitter: A uses and gratifications approach to social marketing. *Electronic News, 5*(3), 145–157.

Griffith, R. (1986). *Battle in the Civil War: Generalship and tactics in America 1861–65.* Camberley, England: Fieldbooks.

Griffiths, M. (1997). Video games and aggression. *The Psychologist, 9*, 397–401.

Griffiths, M.D. (2005). A "components" model of addiction within a biopsychosocial framework. *Journal of Substance Abuse, 10*, 191–197.

Griffiths, M.D. (2008). Videogame addiction: Further thoughts and observations. *International Journal of Mental Health and Addiction, 6*, 182–185.

Griffiths, M.D., & Hunt, N. (1998). Dependence on computer games by adolescents. *Psychological Reports, 82*, 475–480.

Groesz, L.M., Levine, M.P., & Murnen, S.K. (2002). The effect of experimental presentation of thin media images on body satisfaction: A meta-analytic review. *International Journal of Eating Disorders, 31*, 1–16.

Großer, J., & Schram, A. (2010). Public opinion polls, voter turnout, and welfare: An experimental study. *American Journal of Political Science, 54*(3), 700–717.

Grube, J.W., & Wallack, L. (1994). Television beer advertising and drinking knowledge, beliefs, and intentions among school children. *American Journal of Public Health, 84*, 254–259.

Gruber, E.L., Thau, H.M., Hill, D.L., Fisher, D.A., & Grube, J.W. (2005). Alcohol, tobacco and illicit substances in music videos: A content analysis of prevalence and genre. *Journal of Adolescent Health, 37*, 81–83.

Guarino, M. (2011, December 8). Virginia Tech tests emergency plans developed after 2007 rampage. *Christian Science Monitor*. Retrieved from: http://www.csmonitor.com/USA/2011/1208/Virginia-Tech-shooting-tests-emergency-plans-developed-after-2007-rampage.

Guhn, M., Hamm, A., & Zenter, M. (2007). Physiological and musico-acoustic correlates of the chill response. *Music Perception, 24*, 473–483.

Gunasekera, H., Chapman, S., & Campbell, S. (2005). Sex and drugs in popular movies: An analysis of the top 200 films. *Journal of the Royal Society of Medicine, 98*, 464–470.

Gunter, B. (1987). *Poor reception: Misunderstanding and forgetting broadcast news*. Hillsdale, NJ: Lawrence Erlbaum Associates.

Gunter, B., Oates, C., & Blades, M. (2004). *Advertising to children on TV: Content, impact and regulation*. Mahwah, NJ: Erlbaum.

Gunter, G. (1985). New sources and news awareness: A British survey. *Journal of Broadcasting & Electronic Media, 29*, 397–406.

Gunther, A.C. (1995). Overrating the X-rating: The third-person perception and support censorship of pornography. *Journal of Communication, 45*(1), 27–38.

Gunther, A.C., & Chia, S.C. (2001). Predicting pluralistic ignorance: The hostile media perception and its consequences. *Journalism & Mass Communication Quarterly, 78*(4), 688–701.

Gunther, A.C., & Mundy, P. (1993). Biased optimism and the third-person effect. *Journalism Quarterly, 70*, 58–67.

Gunther, A.G., & Thorson, E. (1992). Perceived persuasive effects of product commercials and public service announcements: Third-person effects in new domains. *Communication Research, 19*, 574–596.

Gurevitch, M., & Blumler, J.G. (1990). Political communication systems and democratic values. In J. Lichtenberg (Ed.), *Democracy and the mass media: A collection of essays* (pp. 269–289). Cambridge: Cambridge University Press.

Gurevitch, M., Coleman, S., & Blumler, J.G. (2009). Political communication: Old and new media relationships. *The Annals of the American Academy of Political and Social Science, 625*(1), 164–181.

Ha, S. (2011). Attribute priming effects and presidential candidate evaluation: The conditionality of political sophistication. *Mass Communication & Society, 14*, 315–342.

Hamilton, D.L., & Mackie, D.M. (1990). Specificity and generality in the nature and use of stereotypes. In T.K. Srull & R.S. Wyer, Jr. (Eds.), *Advances in social cognition: Vol. III. Content and process specificity in the effects of prior experiences* (pp. 99–110). Hillsdale, NJ: Lawrence Erlbaum Associates.

Hamilton, J. (2004). *All the news that's fit to sell: How the market transforms information into news*. Princeton, NJ: Princeton University Press.

Hamilton, J.T. (1998). *Channeling violence: The economic market for violent television programming*. Princeton, NJ: Princeton University Press.

Haninger, K., & Thompson, K.M. (2004). Content and ratings of teen-rated video games. *Journal of the American Medical Association, 291*(7), 856–865.

Hansen, C.H. (1989). Priming sex-role stereotypic event schemas with rock music videos: Effects on impression favorability, trait inferences, and recall of a subsequent male–female interaction. *Basic and Applied Social Psychology, 10*, 371–391.

Hansen, C.H., & Hansen, R.D. (1988). How rock music videos can change what is seen when boy meets girl: Priming stereotypic appraisal of social interaction. *Sex Roles, 19*, 287–316.

Hapkiewicz, W.G., & Stone, R.D. (1974). The effect of realistic versus imaginary aggressive models on children's interpersonal play. *Child Study Journal, 4*(2), 47–58.

Hardmeier, S. (2008). The effects of published polls on citizens. In W. Donsbach & M. W. Traugott (Eds.), *The SAGE Handbook of Public Opinion Research*. Los Angeles: SAGE Publications.

Haridakis, P. M. (2002). Viewer characteristics, exposure to television violence, and aggression. *Media Psychology, 4*, 323–352.

Haridakis, P. M., & Hanson, G. (2009). Social interaction and coviewing with YouTube: Blending mass communication reception and social connection. *Journal of Broadcasting & Electronic Media, 53*, 317–335.

Harrington, A. (1999). *The placebo effect: An interdisciplinary exploration*. Cambridge, MA: Harvard University Press.

Harris, R. J. (1994). The impact of sexually explicit media. In J. Bryant & D. Zillmann (Eds.), *Media effects: Advances in theory and research* (pp. 247–272). Hillsdale, NJ: Lawrence Erlbaum Associates.

Harris, R. J., & Barlett, C. P. (2009). Effects of sex in the media. In J. Bryant & M. B. Oliver (Eds.), *Media effects: Advances in theory and research*. New York: Routledge.

Harrison, K., (2003). Television viewers' ideal body proportions: The case of the curvaceously thin woman. *Sex Roles, 48*, 255–264.

Harrison, K. (2005). Is "fat free" good for me? A panel study of television viewing and children's nutritional knowledge and reasoning. *Health Communication, 17*(2), 117–132.

Harrison, K., & Cantor, J. (1997). The relationship between media consumption and eating disorders. *Journal of Communication, 47*(1), 40–67.

Harrison, K., & Hefner, V. (2006). Media exposure, current and future body ideals, and disordered eating among preadolescent girls: A longitudinal panel study. *Journal of Youth and Adolescence, 35*(2), 153–163.

Hart, P. S., Nisbet, E. C., & Shanahan, J. E. (2011). Use influence predispositions for public engagement in wildlife management decision making. *Society & Natural Resources: An International Journal, 24*, 276–291.

Harwood, J. (1999). Age identification, social identity gratifications, and television viewing. *Journal of Broadcasting & Electronic Media, 43*, 123–136.

Harwood, J. (2007). *Understanding communication & aging: Developing knowledge and awareness*. Thousand Oaks, CA: SAGE.

Harwood, J., & Anderson, K. (2002). The presence and portrayal of social groups on prime-time television. *Communication Reports, 15*(2), 81–97.

Hastie, R. (1981). Schematic principles in human memory. In E. T. Higgins, C. P. Herman, & M. P. Zanna (Eds.), *Social cognition: The Ontario Symposium* (Vol. 1, pp. 39–88). Hillsdale, NJ: Lawrence Erlbaum Associates.

Hastorf, A. H., & Cantril, H. (1954). They saw a game: A case study. *Journal of Abnormal and Social Psychology, 49*, 129–134.

Haugtvedt, C. P., Petty, R. E., & Cacioppo, J. T. (1992). Need for cognition and advertising: Understanding the role of personality variables in consumer behavior. *Journal of Consumer Psychology, 1*(3), 239–260.

Hawkins, G., & Zimring, F. E. (1988). *Pornography in a free society*. Cambridge: Cambridge University Press.

Hawkins, R. P., & Pingree, S. (1982). Television's influence on social reality. In D. Pearl, L. Bouthilet, & J. Lazar (Eds.), *Television and behavior: Ten years of scientific progress and implications for the eighties* (DHHS Publication No. ADM 82-1196, Vol. 2, pp. 224–247). Washington, DC: U.S. Government Printing Office.

Healton, C., Farrelly, M. C., Weitzenkamp, D., Lindsey, D., & Haviland, M. L. (2006). Youth smoking prevention and tobacco industry revenue. *Tobacco Control, 15*(2), 103–106.

Hearold, S. (1986). A synthesis of 1043 effects of television on social behavior. In G. Comstock (Ed.), *Public communication and behavior* (Vol. 1, pp. 65–133). Orlando, FL: Academic Press.

Hebditch, D., & Anning, N. (1988). *Porn gold: Inside the pornography business*. London: Faber & Faber.

Heeter, C., Brown, N., Soffin, S., Stanley, C., & Salwen, M. (1989). Agenda-setting by electronic text news. *Journalism Quarterly, 66*, 101–106.

Heins, M. (1998). Three questions about television ratings. In M. E. Price (Ed.), *The V-chip debate: Content filtering from television to the Internet* (pp. 47–58). Mahwah, NJ: Lawrence Erlbaum Associates.

Helregel, B. K., & Weaver, J. B. (1989). Mood-management during pregnancy through selective exposure to television. *Journal of Broadcasting & Electronic Media, 33*, 15–33.

Henriksen, L., Feighery, E. C., Schleicher, N. C., & Fortmann, S. P. (2008). Receptivity to alcohol marketing predicts initiation of alcohol use. *Journal of Adolescent Health, 42*, 28–35.

Henriksen, L., Feighery, E. C., Schleicher, N. C., Haladjian, H. H., & Fortmann, S. P. (2004). Reaching youth at the point of sale: Cigarette marketing is more prevalent in stores where adolescents shop frequently. *Tobacco Control, 13*(3), 315–318.

Henriksen, L., & Flora, J. A. (1999). Third-person perception and children: Perceived impact of pro and anti-smoking ads. *Communication Research, 26*, 643–665.

Henriksen, L., Schleicher, N. C., Feighery, E. C., & Fortmann, S. P. (2010). A longitudinal study of exposure to retail cigarette advertising and smoking initiation. *Pediatrics, 126*(2), 232–238.

Henshel, R. L., & Johnston, W. (1987). The emergence of bandwagon effects: A theory. *Sociological Quarterly, 28*, 493–511.

Herman, E. S., & Chomsky, N. (1988). *Manufacturing consent: The political economy of the mass media*. New York: Pantheon Books.

Herman, E. S., & Chomsky, N. (2002). *Manufacturing consent: The political economy of the mass media*. New York: Pantheon Books.

Herrmann, J. W., Rand, W., Schein, B., & Vodopivec, N. (2013, August). An agent-based model of urgent diffusion in social media. Paper presented at the Computational Social Science Society of the Americas (CSSSA) Conference, Santa Fe, New Mexico. Retrieved from: http://www.isr.umd.edu/~jwh2/papers/csssa2013.pdf.

Herrett-Skjellum, J., & Allen, M. (1996). Television programming and sex stereotyping: A meta-analysis. In B. R. Burleson (Ed.), *Communication yearbook* (Vol. 19, pp. 157–185). Thousand Oaks, CA: SAGE.

Herzog, H. (1944). What do we really know about daytime serial listeners? In P. F. Lazarsfeld & F. N. Stanton (Eds.), *Radio research 1942–1943* (pp. 3–33). New York: Duell, Sloan & Pearce.

Hether, H. J., Huang, G. C., Beck, V., Murphy, S. T., & Valente, T. W. (2008). Entertainment-education in a media saturated environment: Examining the impact of single and multiple exposures to breast cancer stories on two popular medical dramas. *Journal of Health Communication, 13*, 808–823.

Hetsroni, A. (2007). Three decades of sexual content on prime-time network programming: A longitudinal meta-analytic review. *Journal of Communication, 57*, 318–348.

Hickman, H. (1991). Public polls and election participants. In P. J. Lavrakas & J. K. Holley (Eds.), *Polling and presidential election coverage* (pp. 100–133). Newbury Park, CA: SAGE.

Hicks, D. J. (1965). Imitation and retention of film-mediated aggressive peer and adult models. *Journal of Personality and Social Psychology, 2*, 97–100.

Hill, D. B. (1985). Viewer characteristics and agenda setting by television news. *Public Opinion Quarterly, 49,* 340–350.

Hill, D. B., & Dyer, J. A. (1981). Extent of diversion of newscasts from distant stations by cable viewers. *Journalism Quarterly, 58,* 552–555.

Hill, R. J., & Bonjean, C. M. (1964). News diffusion: A test of the regularity hypothesis. *Journalism Quarterly, 41,* 336–342.

Hirsch, P. (1981). On not learning from one's own mistakes: A reanalysis of Gerbner et al.'s findings on cultivation analysis: Part II. *Communication Research, 8,* 3.17.

Hirschburg, P. L., Dillman, D. A., & Ball-Rokeach, S. J. (1986). Media system dependency theory: Responses to the eruption of Mount St. Helens. In S. J. Ball-Rokeach & M. G. Cantor (Eds.), *Media, audience, and social structure* (pp. 117–126). Newbury Park, CA: SAGE.

Hirschman, E. C. (1987). Consumer preferences in literature, motion pictures, and television programs. *Empirical Studies of the Arts, 5,* 31–46.

Ho, S. S., Detenber, B. H., Malik, S., & Neo, R. L. (2012). The roles of value predispositions, communication, and third person perception on public support for censorship of films with homosexual content. *Asian Journal of Communication, 22*(1), 78–97.

Hoffman, L. H., & Young, D. G. (2011). Satire, punch lines, and the nightly news: Untangling media effects on political participation. *Communication Research Reports, 28,* 159–168.

Hoffner, C. (1996). Children's wishful identification and parasocial interaction with favorite television characters. *Journal of Broadcasting & Electronic Media, 40,* 389–402.

Hoffner, C. (2009). Affective responses and exposure to frightening films: The role of empathy and different types of content. *Communication Research Reports, 26,* 285–296.

Hoffner, C., Fujioka, Y., Ibrahim, A., & Ye, J. (2002). Emotion and coping with terror. In B. S. Greenberg (Ed.), *Communication and terrorism: Public and media responses to 9/11* (pp. 229–244). Cresskill, NJ: Hampton Press.

Hoffner, C., Fujioka, Y., Ye, J., & Ibrahim, A. (2009). Why we watch: Factors affecting exposure to tragic television news. *Mass Communication & Society, 12,* 193–216.

Hoffner, C. A., & Levine, K. J. (2005). Enjoyment of mediated fright and violence: A meta-analysis. *Media Psychology, 7,* 207–237.

Hogben, M. (1998). Factors moderating the effect of televised violence on viewer behavior. *Communication Research, 25,* 220–247.

Holbert, R. L., Garrett, R. K., & Gleason, L. S. (2010). A new era of minimal effects? A response to Bennett and Iyengar. *Journal of Communication, 60,* 15–34.

Holbert, R. L., & Hansen, G. J. (2006). Fahrenheit 9–11, need for closure and the priming of affective ambivalence: An assessment of intra-affective structures by party identification. *Human Communication Research, 32,* 109–129.

Holbert, R. L., Shah, D. V., & Kwak, N. (2003). Political implications of prime-time drama and sitcom use: Genres of representation and opinions concerning women's rights. *Journal of Communication, 53,* 45–60.

Holbert, R. L., Shah, D. V., & Kwak, N. (2004). Fear, authority, and justice: The influence of TV news, police reality, and crime drama viewing on endorsements of capital punishment and gun ownership. *Journalism & Mass Communication Quarterly, 81,* 343–363.

Holbrook, R. A., & Hill, T. (2005). Agenda-setting and priming in prime time television: Crime dramas as political cues. *Political Communication, 22,* 277–295.

Hollander, B. A. (2005). Late-night learning: Do entertainment programs increase political campaign knowledge for young viewers? *Journal of Broadcasting & Electronic Media, 49,* 402–415.

Holloway, S., Tucker, L., & Hornstein, H.A. (1977). The effects of social and nonsocial information on interpersonal behavior of males: The news makes news. *Journal of Personality and Social Psychology, 35*, 514–522.

Horgen, K., Harris, J., & Brownell, K. (2012). Food advertising: Targeting children in a toxic environment. Chapter 22 in D.G. Singer & J.L. Singer (Eds.), *Handbook of children and the media* (2nd edn.). Los Angeles: SAGE.

Hornstein, H.A., LaKind, E., Frankel, G., & Manne, S. (1975). Effects of knowledge about remote social events on prosocial behavior, social conceptual, and mood. *Journal of Personality and Social Psychology, 32*, 1038–1046.

Horton, D., & Wohl, R.R. (1956). Mass communication and para-social interaction: Observations on intimacy at a distance. *Psychiatry, 19*, 215–229.

Horvath, C.A. (2004). Measuring television addiction. *Journal of Broadcasting & Electronic Media, 48*, 378–398.

Hotz, R.L. (2011, October 1–2). Decoding our Twitter. *Wall Street Journal*, C1–C2.

Houston, J.B. (2009). Media coverage of terrorism: A meta-analytic assessment of media use and posttraumatic stress. *Journalism & Mass Communication Quarterly, 86*, 844–861.

Houston, J.B., Pfefferbaum, B., & Reyes, G. (2008). Experiencing disasters indirectly: How traditional and new media disaster coverage impacts youth. *The Prevention Researcher, 15*, 14–17.

Hovland, C.I., Janis, I.L., & Kelley, J.J. (1953). *Communication and persuasion*. New Haven, CT: Yale University.

Hovland, C.I., Luchins, A.S., Mandell, W., Campbell, E.H., Brock, T.C., McGuire, W.J., Feierabend, R.L., & Anderson, N.H. (1957). *The order of presentation in persuasion*. New Haven, CT: Yale University Press.

Hovland, C.I., Lumsdaine, A.A., & Sheffield, F.D. (1949). *Experiments on mass communication*. Princeton, NJ: Princeton University Press.

Hovland, C.I., & Mandell, W. (1952). An experimental comparison of conclusion-drawing by the communicator and by the audience. *Journal of Abnormal and Social Psychology, 47*, 581–588.

Howard, D.J. (1990). Rhetorical question effects on message processing and persuasion: The role of information availability and the elicitation of judgment. *Journal of Experimental Social Psychology, 26*, 217–239.

Howard, P.N., & Hussain, M.M. (2011). The Upheavals in Egypt and Tunisia: The role of digital media. *Journal of Democracy, 22*(3), 35–48.

Howitt, D. (1972). Television and aggression: A counterargument. *American Psychologist, 27*, 969–970.

Hsu, M.L., & Price, V. (1993). Political expertise and affect. *Communication Research, 20*, 671–695.

Huberman, B.A., Pirolli, P.L.T., Pitkow, J.E., & Lukose, R.M. (1998, April 3). Strong regularities in World Wide Web surfing. *Science, 280*, 95–97.

Hudson, J.I., Hiripi, E., Pope, H.G., & Kessler, R.C. (2007). The prevalence and correlates of eating disorders in the national comorbidity survey replication. *Biological Psychiatry, 61*, 348–358.

Huesmann, L.R. (1982). Television and violence and aggressive behavior. In D. Pearl, L. Bouthilet, & J. Lazar (Eds.), *Television and behavior: Ten years of scientific progress and implications for the eighties* (DHHS Publication No. ADM 82–1196, Vol. 2, pp. 126–137). Washington, DC: Government Printing Office.

Huesmann, L.R. (1986). Psychological processes promoting the relation between exposure to media violence and aggressive behavior by the viewer. *Journal of Social Issues, 42*(3), 125–140.

Huesmann, L.R., & Eron, L.D. (1986). The development of aggression in American children as a consequence of television violence viewing. In L.R. Huesmann &

L.D. Eron (Eds.), *Television and the aggressive child: A cross-national comparison* (pp. 45–80). Hillsdale, NJ: Lawrence Erlbaum Associates.

Huesmann, L.R., Eron, L.D., Klein, R., Brice, P., & Fischer, P. (1983). Mitigating the imitation of aggressive behavior by changing children's attitudes about media violence. *Journal of Personality and Social Psychology, 44*, 899–910.

Huesmann, L.R., Lagerspetz, K., & Eron, L.D. (1984). Intervening variables in the TV violence–aggression relation: Evidence from two countries. *Developmental Psychology, 20*, 746–775.

Huesmann, L.R., Moise-Titus, J., Podolski, C., & Eron, L.D. (2003). Longitudinal relations between children's exposure to TV violence and their aggressive and violent behavior in young adulthood: 1977–1992. *Developmental Psychology, 39*, 201–221.

Hughes, M. (1980). The fruits of cultivation analysis: A reexamination of some effects of television watching. *Public Opinion Quarterly, 44*, 287–302.

Hummert, M.L., Shaner, J.L., & Garstka, T.A. (1995). Cognitive processes affecting communication with older adults: The case for stereotypes, attitudes, and beliefs about communication. In J.F. Nussbaum & J. Coupland (Eds.), *Handbook of communication and aging research* (pp. 105–131). Mahwah, NJ: Lawrence Erlbaum Associates.

Hunt, D., Atkin, D., & Krishnan, A. (2012). The influence of computer–media communication apprehension on motives for Facebook use. *Journal of Broadcasting & Electronic Media, 56*, 187–202.

Huston, A.C., Wright, J.C., Wartella, E., Rice, M.L., Watkins, B.A., Campbell, T., & Potts, R. (1981). Communicating more than content: Formal features of children's television programs. *Journal of Communication, 31*(3), 32–48.

Huston, A.C., & Wright, J.C. (1983). Children's processing of television: The informative functions of formal features. In J. Bryant and D.R. Anderson (Eds.), *Children's understanding of television: Research on attention and comprehension* (pp. 35–68). New York: Academic Press.

Hutcheson, J., Domke, D., Billeaudeaux, A., & Garland, P. (2004). U.S. national identity, political elites, and a patriotic press following September 11. *Political Communication, 21*, 27–50.

Hwang, Y., & Jeong, S.H. (2009). Revisiting the knowledge gap hypothesis: A meta-analysis of thirty-five years of research. *Journalism & Mass Communication Quarterly, 86*(3), 513–532.

Hyde, T.S., & Jenkins, J.J. (1973). Recall for words as a function of semantic, graphic, and syntactic orienting tasks. *Journal of Verbal Learning and Verbal Behavior, 12*, 471–480.

Ibrahim, Ye, & Hoffner, C. (2008). Diffusion of news of the shuttle Columbia disaster: The role of emotional responses and motives for interpersonal communication. *Communication Research Reports, 25*, 91–101.

Immerwahr, J., & Doble, J. (1982). Public attitudes toward freedom of the press. *Public Opinion Quarterly, 46*, 177–194.

Indeok Song, B.A., LaRose, R., Eastin, M.S., & Lin, C.A. (2004). Internet gratifications and Internet addiction: On the uses and abuses of new media. *CyberPsychology & Behavior, 7*, 384–394.

Institute of Medicine (IOM). (2006). *Food marketing to children and youth: Threat or opportunity?* Washington, DC: The National Academies Press.

Internet Movie Data Base. (2016). *The 50 highest grossing movies of all time.* Retrieved from: http://www.imdb.com/list/ls000021718/.

Isaacs, C.R., & Fisher, W.A. (2008). A computer-based education intervention to address potential negative effects of Internet pornography. *Communication Studies, 59*, 1–18.

Itons-Peterson, M.J., & Roskos-Ewoldsen, B., Thomas, L., Shirley, M., & Blut, D. (1989). Will educational materials reduce negative effects of exposure to sexual violence? *Journal of Social and Clinical Psychology, 50,* 455–457.

Iyengar, S. (1991). *Is anyone responsible: How television frames political issues.* Chicago: University of Chicago Press.

Iyengar, S. (2009). Framing research: The next steps. In B.F. Schaffner & P.J. Sellers (Eds.), *Winning with words: The origins & impact of political framing.* New York: Routledge.

Iyengar, S., & Kinder, D.R. (1987). *News that matters: Television and American public opinion.* Chicago: University of Chicago Press.

Iyengar, S., Peters, M.D., & Kinder, D.R. (1982). Experimental demonstrations of the "not-so-minimal" consequences of television news programs. *American Political Science Review, 76,* 848–858.

Iyengar, S., & Simon, A. (1993). News coverage of the gulf crisis and public opinion. *Communication Research, 20,* 365–383.

Izard, R. (2010). NBC News: Covering a tale of human suffering. In R. Izard & J. Perkins (Eds.), *Covering disaster: Lessons from media coverage of Katrina and Rita* (pp. 31–38). New Brunswick, NJ: Transaction.

Jackson, J.E. (1983). Election night reporting and voter turnout. *American Journal of Political Science, 27,* 615–635.

Jaglom, L.M., & Gardner, H. (1981). The preschool television viewer as anthropologist. In H. Kelly & H. Gardner (Eds.), *Viewing children through television* (pp. 9–30). San Francisco: Jossey-Bass.

Jamieson, K.H., & Birdsell, D.W. (1988). *Presidential debates: The challenge of creating an informed electorate.* New York: Oxford.

Jansma, L.L., Linz, D.G., Mulac, A., & Imrich, D.J. (1997). Men's interactions with women after viewing sexually explicit films: Does degradation make a difference? *Communication Monographs, 64,* 1–24.

Jeffres, L.W., Neuendorf, K., & Atkin, D.J. (2012). Acquiring knowledge from the media in the Internet age. *Communication Quarterly, 60*(1), 59–79.

Jensen, J.D., Bernat, J.K., Wilson, K.M., & Goonewardene, J. (2011). The delay hypothesis: The manifestation of media effects over time. *Human Communication Research, 37,* 509–528.

Jensen, J.D., & Hurley, R.J. (2005). Third-person effects and the environment: Social distance, social desirability, and presumed behavior. *Journal of Communication, 55*(2), 242–256.

Jerit, J. (2009). Understanding the knowledge gap: The role of experts and journalists. *The Journal of Politics, 71*(2), 442–456.

Jerit, J., Barabas, J., & Bolsen, T. (2006). Citizens, knowledge, and the information environment. *American Journal of Political Science, 50*(2), 266–282.

Jernigan, D.H. (2006). Importance of reducing youth exposure to alcohol advertising. *Archives of Pediatrics & Adolescent Medicine, 160*(1), 100–102.

Jha, S. (2007). Exploring internet influence on the coverage of social protest: Content analysis comparing protest coverage in 1967 and 1999. *Journalism & Mass Communication Quarterly, 84,* 40–57.

Jhally, S. (Producer and Director). (1994). *The killing screens* [Film]. Northampton, MA: Media Education Foundation.

Jo, E., & Berkowitz, L. (1994). A priming effect analysis of media influences: An update. In J. Bryant & D. Zillmann (Eds.), *Media effects: Advances in theory and research* (pp. 43–60). Hillsdale, NJ: Lawrence Erlbaum Associates.

Johansen, M.S., & Joslyn, M.R. (2008). Political persuasion during times of crisis: The effects of education and news media on citizens' factual information about Iraq. *Journalism & Mass Communication Quarterly, 85,* 591–608.

Johnson, B. T., & Eagly, A. H. (1990). Involvement and persuasion: Types, traditions, and the evidence. *Psychological Bulletin*, 107, 375–384.

Johnson, E. (2011, March 11). Foreign media take flak for fanning fears: Sensationalist reports spark debate on timid domestic press. *The Japan Times Online*. Retrieved from: http://www.japantimes.co.jp/text/nn20110321f1.html.

Johnson, W. T., Kupperstein, L. R., & Peters, J. J. (1971). *Sex offenders. experience with erotica. Technical report of the Commission on Obscenity and Pornography* (Vol. 7, pp. 163–171). Washington, DC: U.S. Government Printing Office.

Johnston, A., & Kaid, L. L. (2002). Image ads and issue ads in presidential advertising: Using videostyle to explore stylistic differences in televised political ads from 1952 to 2000. *Journal of Communication*, 52, 281–300.

Johnston, E. (2011). *The Tohoku Earthquake and Tsunami, the Fukushima Nuclear Reactor, and How the World's Media Reported Them*. Tokyo, Japan: Japan Times.

Johnston, L. D., O'Malley, P. M., Bachman, J. G., & Schulenberg, J. E. (2008). *Monitoring the future national survey results on drug use, 1975–2012: Volume 1, secondary school students*. Ann Arbor: Institute for Social Research, The University of Michigan.

Jonason, P. K., Krcmar, M., & Sohn, S. (2009). Male body image: The role of muscle magazine exposure, body mass index, and social comparison in men's body satisfaction. *Social Behavior & Personality: An International Journal*, 37, 627–629.

Jones, J. M. (2009, January 26). Obama's Initial Approval Ratings in Historical Context. *The Gallup Poll*. Retrieved from: http://www.gallup.com/poll/113968/obama-initial-approval-ratings-historical-context.aspx.

Jones, S., & Rainie, L. (2002). Internet use and the terror attacks. In B. S. Greenberg (Ed.), *Communication and terrorism: Public and media responses to 9/11* (pp. 27–37). Cresskill, NJ: Hampton Press.

Jordan, A., Trentacoste, N., Henderson, V., Manganello, J., & Fishbein, M. (2007). Measuring the time teens spend with media: Challenges and opportunities. *Media Psychology*, 9, 19–41.

Jose, P. E., & Brewer, W. G. (1984). Development of story liking: Character identification, suspense, and outcome resolution. *Developmental Psychology*, 20, 911–924.

Josephson, W. L. (1987). Television violence and children's aggression: Testing the priming, social script, and disinhibition predictions. *Journal of Personality and Social Psychology*, 53, 882–890.

Jowett, G. S., Jarvie, I. C., & Fuller, K. H. (1996). *Children and the movies: Media influence and the Payne Fund controversy*. New York: Cambridge University Press.

Joy, L. A., & Kimball, M. M., & Zabrack, M. L. (1986). Television and children's aggressive behavior. In T. M. Williams (Ed.), *The impact of television: A natural experiment in three communities* (pp. 303–360). Orlando, FL: Academic Press.

Kahlor, L., & Eastin, M. S. (2011). Television's role in the culture of violence toward women: A study of television viewing and the cultivation of rape myth acceptance in the United States. *Journal of Broadcasting & Electronic Media*, 55(2), 215–231.

Kahneman, D. (1973). *Attention and effort*. Englewood Cliffs, NJ: Prentice-Hall.

Kahneman, D., & Tversky, A. (1984). Choices, values, and frames. *American Psychologist*, 39, 341–350.

Kaid, L., & Bystrom, D. G., eds. (1999). *The electronic election: Perspectives on the 1996 campaign communication*. Mahwah, NJ: Lawrence Erlbaum Associates.

Kaid, L. L., Harville, B., Ballotti, J., & Wawrzyniak, M. (1993). Telling the Gulf War story: Coverage in five papers. In B. S. Greenberg & W. Gantz (Eds.), *Desert Storm and the mass media* (pp. 61.–73). Cresskill, NJ: Hampton Press.

Kaiser Family Foundation. (Spring 2003). *Children and the news: Coping with terrorism, war and everyday violence*. Menlo Park, CA: The Henry J. Kaiser Family Foundation.

Kaiser Family Foundation. (2010, January 20). Daily media use among children and teens up dramatically from 5 years ago. Retrieved from: http://kff.org/disparities-policy/press-release/daily-media-use-among-children-and-teens-up-dramatically-from-five-years-ago/.

Kaiser Family Foundation (KFF), & The USC Annenberg Norman Lear Center's Hollywood, Health, & Society. (2008). How healthy is prime time? An analysis of health content in popular prime time television programs. Retrieved from: ttp://www.kff.org/entmedia/upload/7764.pdf.

Kanihan, S. F., & Gale, K. L. (2005). Within 3 hours, 97 percent learn about 9/11 attacks. In E. K. Grusin & S. H, Utt (Eds.), *Media in American crisis: Studies of September 11, 2001* (pp. 207–218). Lanham, MD: University Press of America.

Kantar Media/CMAG with analysis by the Wesleyan Media Project. (2014). Ad spending in 2014 elections poised to break $1 billion. Retrieved from: http://mediaproject.wesleyan.edu/category/releases/2014-elections/.

Kaplan, R. M. (1972). On television as a cause of aggression. *American Psychologist*, 27, 968–969.

Kassing, J. W., & Sanderson, J. (2009). "You're the kind of guy that we all want for a drinking buddy": Expressions of parasocial interaction on Floydlandis.com. *Western Journal of Communication*, 73, 182–203.

Katz, D. (1960). The functional approach to the study of attitudes. *Public Opinion Quarterly*, 24, 163–204.

Katz, E. (1959). Mass communication research and the study of popular culture. *Studies in Public Communication*, 2, 1–6.

Katz, E. (1968). On reopening the question of selectivity in exposure to mass communications. In R. P. Abelson, E. Aronson, W. J. McGuire, T. M. Newcomb, M. J. Rosenberg, & P. H. Tannenbaum (Eds.), *Theories of cognitive consistency: A sourcebook* (pp. 788–796). Chicago: Rand McNally.

Katz, E. (1980). Media events: The sense of occasion. *Studies in Visual Anthropology*, 6, 84–89.

Katz, E. (1987). Communication research since Lazarsfeld. *Public Opinion Quarterly*, 51, S25–S45.

Katz, E., Adoni, H., & Parness, P. (1977). Remembering the news: What the picture adds to recall. *Journalism Quarterly*, 54, 231–239.

Katz, E., Blumler, J. G., & Gurevitch, M. (1974). Utilization of mass communication by the individual. In J. G. Blumler & E. Katz (Eds.), *The uses of mass communications* (pp. 19–32). Beverly Hills, CA: SAGE.

Katz, E., & Lazarsfeld, P. F. (1955). *Personal influence: The part played by people in the flow of mass communications*. New York: Free Press.

Katz, E., & Liebes, T. (2007). "No more peace!": How disaster, terror and war have upstaged media events. *International Journal of Communication*, 1, 157–166.

Katzman, N. (1974). The impact of communication technology: Promises and prospects. *Journal of Communication*, 24(4), 47–58.

Kay, H. (1972). Weaknesses in the television-causes-aggression analysis by Eron et al. (1972). *American Psychologist*, 27, 970–973.

Kaye, B. K., (2010). Going to the blogs: Toward a development of a uses and gratifications measurement scale for blogs. *Atlantic Journal of Communication*, 18, 194–210.

Kaye, B. K., & Johnson, T. J. (2002). Online and in the know: Uses and gratifications of the web for political information. *Journal of Broadcasting & Electronic Media*, 46, 54–71.

Kellerman, K. (1985). Memory processes in media effects. *Human Communication Research*, 12, 83–131.

Kellner, D. (1993). The crisis in the Gulf and the lack of critical media discourse. In B.S. Greenberg & W. Gantz (Eds.), *Desert Storm and the mass media* (pp. 37–47). Cresskill, NJ: Hampton Press.

Kellner, D. (2003). *From 9/11 to terror war: The dangers of the Bush legacy.* Lanham, MD: Rowman & Littlefield.

Kelman, H.C. (1961). Process of opinion change. *Public Opinion Quarterly, 25,* 57–78.

Kennamer, J.D. (1990). Self-serving biases in perceiving the opinions of others: Implications for the spiral of silence. *Communication Research, 17,* 393–404.

Kenski, K., & Stroud, N.J. (2006).Connections between Internet use and political efficacy, knowledge, and participation. *Journal of Broadcasting & Electronic Media, 50*(2), 173–192.

Kenworthy, B. (2010). *Timeline: TV, regulation and broadcast violence.* First Amendment Center. Retrieved from: http://www.firstamendmentcenter.org/about.aspx?id=19525.

Kepplinger, H.M. (1997). Political correctness and academic principles: A reply to Simpson. *Journal of Communication, 47*(4), 102–117.

Kerlinger, F.N., & Lee, H.B. (2000). *Foundations of behavioral research* (4th edn.). Fort Worth, TX: Harcourt College Publishers.

Kessler, E.M., Rakoczy, K., & Staudinger, U.M. (2004). The portrayal of older people in prime time television series: The match with gerontological evidence. *Aging & Society, 24,* 531–552.

Kim, J., & Haridakis, P.M. (2009). The role of Internet user characteristics and motives in explaining three dimensions of Internet addiction. *Journal of Computer-Mediated Communication, 14,* 988–1015.

Kim, J., & Rubin, A.M. (1997). The variable influence of audience activity on media effects. *Communication Research, 24,* 107–135.

Kim, J.L., Sorsoli, C.L., Collins, K., Zylbergold, B.A., Schooler, D., & Tolman, D.L. (2007). From sex to sexuality: Exposing the heterosexual script on primetime network television. *Journal of Sex Research, 44*(2), 145–157.

Kim T., & Biocca, F. (1997). Telepresence via television: Two dimensions of telepresence may have different connections to memory and persuasion. *Journal of Computer-Mediated Communication, 3.* Retrieved from: http://jcmc.indiana.edu/vol3/issue2/kim.html.

Kinder, D.R., & Sanders, L.M. (1990). Mimicking political debate with survey questions: The case of white opinion on affirmative action for blacks. *Social Cognition, 8,* 73–103.

Kinder, D.R., & Sears, D.O. (1985). Public opinion and political action. In G. Lindzey & E. Aronson (Eds.), *Handbook of social psychology: Vol. 2. Special fields and applications* (pp. 659–741). New York: Random House.

King, C.M., & Hourani, N. (2007). Don't tease me: Effects of ending type on horror film entertainment. *Media Psychology, 9,* 473–492.

King, S. (1981). *Danse macabre.* New York: Berkley.

Kiousis, S. (2004). Explicating media salience: A factor analysis of *New York Times* issue coverage during the 2000 U.S. presidential election. *Journal of Communication, 54*(1), 71–87.

Kipper, P. (1986). Television camera movement as a source of perceptual information. *Journal of Broadcasting & Electronic Media, 30,* 295–307.

Kirkorian, H.L., Wartella, E.A., & Anderson, D.R. (2008). Media and young children's learning. *Future of Children, 18*(1), 39–61.

Kister, M.E., & Lee, M.J. (2010). Does exposure to sexual hip-hop music videos influence the sexual attitudes of college students? *Mass Communication and Society, 13,* 67–86.

Klapper, J. T. (1960). *The effects of mass communication*. New York: Free Press.

Klatzky, R. L. (1980). *Human memory: Structures and processes* (2nd edn.). New York: W. H. Freeman.

Kohut, A., Doherty, C., Dimock, M., & Keeter, S. (2010). *Ideological news sources: Who watches and why? Americans spending more time following the news*. Washington, DC: Pew Research Center.

Kohut, A., Morin, R., & Keeter, S. (2007). *What Americans know: 1989–2007. Public knowledge of current affairs little changes by news and information revolutions*. Washington, DC: Pew Research Center.

Kozma, R. B. (1991). Learning with media. *Review of Educational Research*, 61, 179–211.

Knobloch, S., & Zillmann, D. (2002). Mood management via the digital jukebox. *Journal of Communication*, 52(3), 351–366.

Knobloch-Westerwick, S. (2006). Mood management theory, evidence, and advancements. In J. Bryant & P. Vorderer (Eds.), *Psychology of entertainment* (pp. 239–254). New York: Routledge.

Kraft, R. N. (1987). The influence of camera angle on comprehension and retention of pictorial events. *Memory & Cognition*, 15, 291–307.

Kraus, S. (1996). Winners of the first 1960 televised presidential debate between Kennedy and Nixon. *Journal of Communication*, 46(4), 78–96.

Kraut, R., Patterson, M., Lundmark, V., Kiesler, S., & Mukopadhyay, R., & Scherlis, W. (1998). Internet paradox: A social technology that reduces social involvement and psychological well-being? *American Psychologist*, 53, 1017–1031.

Krcmar, M., & Farrar, K. (2009). Retaliatory aggression and the effects of point of view and blood in violent video games. *Mass Communication and Society*, 12, 115–138.

Krugman, H. E. (1965). The impact of television advertising: Learning without involvement. *Public Opinion Quarterly*, 29, 349–356.

Krugman, H. E. (2000). Memory without recall, exposure without perception. *Journal of Advertising Research*, 40(6), 49–54.

Kubey, R., & Csikszentmihalyi, M. (1990). *Television and the quality of life: How viewing shapes everyday experience*. Hillsdale, NJ: Lawrence Erlbaum Associates.

Kubey, R. W., Lavin, M. J., & Barrows, J. R. (2001). Internet use and collegiate academic performance decrements: Early findings. *Journal of Communication*, 51, 366–382.

Kubey, R. W., & Peluso, T. (1990). Emotional response as a cause of interpersonal news diffusion: The case of the space shuttle tragedy. *Journal of Broadcasting & Electronic Media*, 34, 69–76.

Kueneman, R. M., & Wright, J. E. (1975). New policies of broadcast stations for civil disturbances and disasters. *Journalism Quarterly*, 52, 670–677.

Kull, S., Ramsey, C., & Lewis, E. (2002). Misperceptions, the media and the Iraq war. *Political Science Quarterly*, 118, 569–598.

Kunkel, D., Eyal, K., Finnerty, K., Biely, E., & Donnerstein, E. (2005). *Sex on TV 4*. Menlo Park, CA: Kaiser Family Foundation.

Kunkel, D., Farrar, K. M., Eyal, K., Biely, E., Donnerstein, E., & Rideout, V. (2007). Sexual socialization messages on entertainment television: Comparing content trends 1997–2002. *Media Psychology*, 9, 595–622.

Kunzmann, U., & Gruhn, D. (2005). Age differences in emotional reactivity: The sample case of sadness. *Psychology and Aging*, 20, 47–59.

Kutchinsky, B. (1991). Pornography and rape: Theory and practice? Evidence from crime data in four countries where pornography is easily available. *International Journal of Law and Psychiatry*, 14, 147–164.

Labre, M. P., & Walsh-Childers, K. (2003). Friendly advice? Beauty messages in web sites of teen magazines. *Mass Communication & Society*, 6(4), 379–396.

Lachlan, K. A., Spence, P. R., Lin, X., & Del Greco, M. (2014). Screaming into the wind: Twitter use during Hurricane Sandy. Communication Studies, 65, 500–518.

LaMarre, H. L., Landreville, K. D., & Beam, M. A. (2009). The irony of satire: Political ideology and the motivation to see what you want to see in *The Colbert Report*. *International Journal of Press/Politics*, 14, 212–231.

Lamb, B., & Associates. (1988). *C-SPAN: American's town hall*. Washington, DC: Acropolis Books.

Landau, M. J., Solomon, S., Greenberg, J., Cohen, F., Pyszczynski, T., Arndt, J., et al. (2004). Deliver us from evil: The effects of mortality salience and reminders of 9/11 on support for President George W. Bush. *Personality and Social Psychology Bulletin*, 30, 1136–1150.

Lando, H. A., & Donnerstein, E. I. (1978). The effects of a model's success or failure on subsequent aggressive behavior. *Journal of Research in Personality*, 12, 225–234.

Lang, A. (1990). Involuntary attention and physiological arousal evoked by structural features and emotional content in TV commercials. *Communication Research*, 17, 275–299.

Lang, A. (1994). What can the heart tell us about thinking? In A. Lang (Ed.), *Measuring psychological responses to media* (pp. 99–111). Hillsdale, NJ: Lawrence Erlbaum Associates.

Lang, A. (1995). Defining audio/video redundancy from a limited capacity information processing perspective. *Communication Research*, 22, 86–115.

Lang, A. (2000). The limited capacity model of mediated message processing. *Journal of Communication*, 50, 46–70.

Lang, A., Geiger, S., Strickwerda, M., & Sumner, J. (1993). The effects of related and unrelated cuts on television viewers' attention, processing capacity, and memory. *Communication Research*, 20, 4–29.

Lang, A., Newhagen, J., & Reeves, B. (1996). Negative video as structure: Emotion, attention, capacity, and memory. *Journal of Broadcasting & Electronic Media*, 40, 460–477.

Lang, A., Potter, R. F., & Bolls, P. (2009). Where psychophysiology meets the media: Taking the effects out of mass media research. In J. Bryant & M. B. Oliver (Eds.), *Media effects: Advances in theory and research*. New York: Routledge.

Lang, K., & Lang, G. E. (1968). *Voting and nonvoting: Implications of broadcasting returns before polls are closed*. Waltham, MA: Blaisdell.

Lang, K., & Lang, G. E. (1984). The impact of polls on public opinion. *Annals of the American Academy of Political and Social Science*, 472, 129–142.

LaPiere, R. T. (1934). Attitudes vs. actions. *Social Forces*, 13, 230–237.

LaPierre, W. (2012, December 21). NRA Press Conference. Retrieved from: http://www.nytimes.com/interactive/2012/12/21/us/nra-news-conference-transcript.html.

Lapinski, M. K., & Nwulu, P. (2008). Can a short film impact HIV-related risk and stigma perceptions? Results from an experiment in Abuja, Nigeria. *Health Communication*, 23, 403–412.

LaRose, R., Lin, C. A., & Eastin, M. S. (2003). Unregulated Internet usage: Addiction, habit, or deficient self-regulation? *Media Psychology*, 5, 225–253.

Larson, J. F. (1980). A review of the state of the art in mass media disaster reporting. In *Disasters and the mass media: Proceedings of the Committee on Disasters and the Mass Media Workshop* (pp. 75–136). Washington, DC: National Academy of Sciences.

Lasorsa, D. (2003). News media perpetuate few rumors about 9/11 crisis. *Newspaper Research Journal*, 24, 10–21.

Lasorsa, D. L. (1989). Real and perceived effects of "Amerika." *Journalism Quarterly*, 66, 373–378, 529.

Lasswell, H. (1927). *Propaganda technique in the world war*. New York: Knopf.

Lasswell, H. D. (1948). The structure and function of communication in society. In L. Bryson (Ed.), *The communication of ideas* (pp. 37–51). New York: Harper.

Lau, R. R. (1986). Political schemata, candidate evaluations, and voting behavior. In R. R. Lau & D. O. Sears (Eds.), *Political cognition: The 19th Annual Carnegie Symposium on Cognition* (pp. 95–126). Hillsdale, NJ: Lawrence Erlbaum Associates.

Lau, R. R., & Sears, D. O. (1986). Social cognition and political cognition: The past, the present, and the future. In R. R. Lau & D. O. Sears (Eds.), *Political cognition: The 19th Annual Carnegie Symposium on Cognition* (pp. 347–366). Hillsdale, NJ: Lawrence Erlbaum Associates.

Lauzen, M. M., Dozier, D. M., & Horan, N. (2008). Constructing gender stereotypes through social roles in prime-time television. *Journal of Broadcasting & Electronic Media*, 52(2), 200–214.

Lavrakas, P. J., Holley, J. K., & Miller, P. V. (1991). Public reactions to polling news during the 1988 presidential election campaign. In P. J. Lavrakas & J. K. Holley (Eds.), *Polling and presidential election coverage* (pp. 151–183). Newbury Park, CA: SAGE.

Lawrence, K., & Herold, E. S. (1988). Women's attitudes toward and experience with sexually explicit materials. *Journal of Sex Research*, 24, 161–169.

Lawrence, P. A., & Palmgreen, P. C. (1996). A uses and gratifications analysis of horror film preference. In J. B. Weaver, III, & R. Tamborini (Eds.), *Horror films: Current research on audience preferences and reactions* (pp. 161–178). Mahwah, NJ: Lawrence Erlbaum Associates.

Lawrence, V. W. (1991). Effect of socially ambiguous information on white and black children's behavioral and trait perceptions. *Merrill-Palmer Quarterly*, 37, 619–630.

Lazarsfeld, P. F., Berelson, B., & Gaudet, H. (1968). The people's choice: How the voter makes up his mind in a presidential election (3rd edn.). New York: Columbia University Press.

Lazarsfeld, P. F., & Merton, R. K. (1948). Mass communication, popular taste and organized social action. In L. Bryson (Ed.), *The communication of ideas* (pp. 95–118). New York: Harper.

Ledingham, J. A., & Walters, L. M. (1989). The sound and the fury: Mass media and hurricanes. In L. M. Walters, L. Wilkins, & T. Walters (Eds.), *Bad tidings: Communication and catastrophe* (pp. 35–45). Hillsdale, NJ: Lawrence Erlbaum Associates.

Lee, A., & Lee, E. B. (1939). *The fine art of persuasion: A study of Father Coughlin's speeches*. New York: Harcourt, Brace.

Lee, E., & Jang, J. (2012). Not so imaginary interpersonal contact with public figures on social network sites: How affiliative tendency moderates its effects. *Communication Research*, 40, 27–51.

Lee, K. M. (2004). Presence, explicated. *Communication Theory*, 14, 27–50.

Lee, K. M., Peng, W., & Park, N. (2009). Effects of computer/video games and beyond. In J. Bryant & M. B. Oliver (Eds.), *Media effects: Advances in theory and research* (3rd edn., pp. 551–566). New York: Routledge.

Lee, M. M., Carpenter, B., & Meyers, L. S. (2007). Representations of older adults in television advertisements. *Journal of Aging Studies*, 21, 23–30.

Lee, T. K., & Taylor, L. D. (2014). The motives for and consequences of viewing television medical dramas. *Health Communication*, 29, 13–22.

Lee, Y.-K. & Chang, C.-T. (2010). Framing public policy: The impacts of political sophistication and nature of public policy. *The Social Science Journal*, 47, 69–89.

Lefkowitz, M. L., Eron, L., Walder, L., & Huesmann, L. R. (1977). *Growing up to be violent: A longitudinal study of the development of aggression*. New York: Pergamon Press.

Lemish, D. (2007). *Children and television: A global perspective*. Malden, MA: Blackwell Publishing.

Lenhart, A., Purcell, K., Smith, A., & Zickuhr, K. (2010). Social media & mobile internet use among teens and young adults. A project of the Pew Internet & American Life Project. Retrieved from: http://pewinternet.org/~/media//Files/Reports/2010/PIP-Teens-and-Mobile-2010-with-topline.pdf.

Len-Rios, M. E., & Qiu, Q. (2007). Negative articles predict clinical trial reluctance, *Newspaper Research Journal, 28*, 24–39.

Leone, R. (2002). Contemplating ratings: An examination of what the MPAA considers "too far for R" and why. *Journal of Communication, 52*, 938–954.

Leone, R. (2004). Rated sex: The MPAA's use of R and NC-17 ratings. *Communication Research Reports, 21*, 68–74.

Levin, S. R., & Anderson, D. R. (1976). The development of attention. *Journal of Communication, 26*(2), 126–135.

Levine, M. P., & Harrison, K. (2009). Effects of media on eating disorders and body image. In J. Bryant & M. B. Oliver (Eds.), *Media effects: Advances in theory and research* (3rd edn., pp. 490–516). New York: Routledge.

Levine, R. R., Asada, K. J., & Carpenter, C. (2009). Sample sizes and effects sizes are negatively correlated in meta-analyses: Evidence and implications of a publication bias against nonsignificant findings. *Communication Monographs, 76*, 286–302.

Levinthal, D. (2012, May 4). Stephen Colbert's super PAC spawns mini PACs. Poltiico. Retrieved from: http://www.politico.com/news/stories/0512/75942.html.

Levitt, S. D. (2004). Understanding why crime fell in the 1990s: Four factors that explain the decline and six that do not. *Journal of Economic Perspectives, 18*, 163–190.

Levy, B. R., Slade, M. D., Kunkel, S. R., & Kasl, S. V. (2002). Longevity increased by positive self-perceptions of aging. *Journal of Personality and Social Psychology, 83*(2), 261–270.

Levy, M. R. & Windahl, S. (1984). Audience activity and gratifications: A conceptual clarification and exploration. *Communication Research, 11*, 51–78.

Liebes, T., & Katz, E. (1990). *The export of meaning: Cross-cultural readings of Dallas*. New York: Oxford University Press.

Linn, T. (2003). Media methods that lead to stereotypes. In P.M. Lester & S. D. Ross (Eds.), *Images that injure: Pictorial stereotypes in the media* (2nd edn.). Westport, CT: Praeger Publishers.

Linz, D. (1985). Sexual violence in the media: Effects on male viewers and implications for society. Doctoral dissertation, University of Wisconsin-Madison. Dissertation Abstracts International, 46, 4604B.

Linz, D., & Donnerstein, E. (1988). The methods and merits of pornography research. *Journal of Communication, 38*(2), 180–184.

Linz, D., & Donnerstein, E. (1994). Sex and violence in slasher films: A reinterpretation. *Journal of Broadcasting & Electronic Media, 38*, 243–246.

Linz, D., Donnerstein, E., & Penrod, S. (1984). The effects of multiple exposures to filmed violence against women. *Journal of Communication, 34*(3), 130–147.

Linz, D., Fuson, I. A., & Donnerstein, E. (1990). Mitigating the negative effects of sexually violent mass communications through preexposure briefings. *Communication Research, 17*, 641–674.

Linz, D., & Malamuth, N. (1993). *Pornography*. Newbury Park: CA: SAGE.

Lippmann, W. (1922). *Public opinion*. New York: Macmillan.

Litle, P., & Zuckerman, M. (1986). Sensation seeking and music preference. *Personality and Individual Differences, 4*, 575–577.

Livingston, S. (2007). The Nokia effect: The re-emergence of amateur journalism and what it means for international affairs. In D. D. Perlmutter & J. M. Hamilton (Eds.), *From pigeons to news portals: Foreign reporting and the challenge of new technology*. Baton Rouge: Louisiana State University Press.

Lombard, M., Reich, R. D., Grabe, M. E., Bracken, C. C., & Ditton, T. B. (2000). Presence and television: The role of screen size. *Human Communication Research, 26*(1), 75–98.

Longino, H. E. (1980). Pornography, oppression, and freedom: A closer look. In L. Lederer (Ed.), *Take back the night: Women on pornography* (pp. 40–54). New York: William Morrow.

López-Guimerà, G., Levine, M. P., Sánchez-Carracedo, D., & Fauquet, J. (2010). Influence of mass media on body image and eating disordered attitudes and behaviors in females: A review of effects and processes. *Media Psychology, 13*, 387–416.

Lorch, E. P., Anderson, D. R., & Levin, S. R. (1979). The relationship of visual attention to children's comprehension of television. *Child Development, 50*, 722–727.

Low, R., & Sweller, J. (2005). The modality principle in multimedia learning. In R. E. Mayer (Ed.), *The Cambridge handbook on multimedia learning*. New York: Cambridge University Press.

Lowrey, W. (2004). Media dependency during a large-scale social disruption: The case of September 11. *Mass Communication & Society, 7*, 339–357.

Lowry, D., Nio, T. C. J., & Leitner, D. (2003). Setting the public fear agenda: A longitudinal analysis of network TV crime reporting, public perceptions of crime, and FBI crime statistics. *Journal of Communication, 53*(1), 61–73.

Lyle, J., & Hoffman, H. R. (1972). Children's use of television and other media. In E. A. Rubinstein, G. A. Comstock, & J. P. Murray (Eds.), *Television and social behavior: Vol. 4. Television in day-to-day life: Patterns of use* (DHEW publication HSM 72–9059, pp. 129–256). Washington, DC: U.S. Government Printing Office.

Maccoby, E. (1954). Why do children watch television? *Public Opinion Quarterly, 18*, 239–244.

Maccoby, E. E., & Wilson, W. C. (1957). Identification and observational learning from films. *Journal of Abnormal and Social Psychology, 55*, 76–87.

Machariah, S., O'Connor, D., & Ndangam, L. (2010). *Who Makes the News?* London: Global Media Monitoring Project of the World Association for Christian Communication.

MacKuen, M. B., & Coombs, S. L. (1981). *More than news: Media power in public affairs*. Beverly Hills: SAGE.

Maher, T. M. (2001). An emerging paradigm, or a phase of agenda setting? In S. D. Reese, O. H. Gandy, Jr., & A. E. Grant (Eds.), *Framing public life: Perspectives on media and our understanding of the social world*. Mahwah, NJ: Erlbaum.

Mahood, C., & Cicchirillo, V. (2008. November). The combined effect of physical activity and violent content in motion-sensing video games on affective aggression: A reexamination of the catharsis hypothesis. Paper presented at the National Communication Association annual conference, San Diego, CA.

Malamuth, N. M. (1996). Sexually explicit media, gender differences, and evolutionary theory. *Journal of Communication, 46*(3), 8–31.

Malamuth, N. M., Addison, T., & Koss, M. (2000). Pornography and sexual aggression: Are there reliable effects and can we understand them? *Annual Review of Sex Research, 11*, 26–91.

Malamuth, N. M., & Briere, J. (1986). Sexual violence in the media: Indirect effects on aggression against women. *Journal of Social Forces, 42*, 75–92.

Malamuth, N. M., & Check, J. V. P. (1980). Penile tumescence and perceptual responses to rape as a function of the victim's perceived reactions. *Journal of Applied Social Psychology*, 10, 528–547.

Malamuth, N. M., & Check, J. V. P. (1981). The effects of mass media exposure on acceptance of violence against women: A field experiment. *Journal of Research in Personality*, 15, 436–446.

Malamuth, N. M., & Check, J. V. P. (1983). Sexual arousal to rape depictions: Individual differences. *Journal of Abnormal Psychology*, 92, 55–67.

Malamuth, N. M., & Check, J. V. P. (1984). Debriefing effectiveness following exposure to pornographic rape depictions. *Journal of Sex Research*, 20, 14–31.

Malamuth, N. M., & Check, J. V. P. (1985). The effects of aggressive pornography on beliefs in rape myths: Individual differences. *Journal of Research in Personality*, 19, 299–320.

Malamuth, N. M., Haber, S., & Feshbach, S. (1980). Testing hypotheses regarding rape: Exposure to sexual violence, sex differences, and the "normality" of rapists. *Journal of Research in Personality*, 14, 121–137.

Malamuth, N., & Huppin, M. (2005). Pornography and teenagers: The importance of individual differences. *Adolescent Medicine Clinics*, 16, 315–326.

Mares, M. (1996). The role of source confusions in television's cultivation of social reality judgments. *Human Communication Research*, 23, 278–297.

Mares, M., & Cantor, J. (1992). Elderly viewers' responses to televised portrayals of old age: Empathy and mood management versus social comparison. *Communication Research*, 19, 459–478.

Mares, M. L., & Sun, Y. (2010). The multiple meanings of age for television content preferences. *Human Communication Research*, 36, 372–396.

Marsh, C. (1984). Do polls affect what people think? In C. F. Turner & E. Martin (Eds.), *Surveying subjective phenomena* (Vol. 2, pp. 565–591). New York: Russell Sage Foundation.

Marshall, W. L. (1989). Pornography and sex offenders. In D. Zillmann & J. Bryant (Eds.), *Pornography: Research advances & policy considerations* (pp. 185–214). Hillsdale, NJ: Lawrence Erlbaum Associates.

Martin, H. H. (1984). President Reagan's return to radio. *Journalism Quarterly*, 61, 817–821.

Martins, N., & Harrison, K. (2012). Racial and gender differences in the relationship between children's television use and self-esteem: A longitudinal panel study. *Communication Research*, 39(3), 338–357.

Martins, N., & Wilson, B. J. (2012). Mean on the screen: Social aggression in programs popular with children. *Journal of Communication*, 62, 991–1009.

Mastro, D. E. (2009). Effects of racial and ethnic stereotyping. In J. Bryant, & M. B. Oliver (Eds.), *Media effects: Advances in theory and research*. New York: Routledge.

Mastro, D. E., & Behm-Morawitz, E. (2005). Latino representation on primetime television. *Journalism & Mass Communication Quarterly*, 82(1), 110–130.

Matthes, J., Morrison, K. R., & Schemer, C. (2010). A spiral of silence for some: Attitude certainty and the expression of political minority opinions. *Communication Research*, 37(6), 774–800.

Mayer, M. E., Gudykunst, W. B., Perrill, N. K., & Merrill, B. D. (1990). A comparison of competing models of the news diffusion process. *Western Journal of Speech Communication*, 54, 113–123.

McArthur, L. Z., & Post, D. L. (1977). Figural emphasis and person perception. *Journal of Experimental Social Psychology*, 13, 520–535.

McArthur, L. Z., & Solomon, L. K. (1978). Perceptions of an aggressive encounter as a function of the victim's salience and perceiver's arousal. *Journal of Personality and Social Psychology*, 36, 1278–1290.

McCain, T.A., Chilberg, J., & Wakshlag, J. (1977). The effect of camera angle on source credibility and attraction. *Journal of Broadcasting, 21*, 35–46.

McClure, R.D., & Patterson, T.E. (1974). Television news and political advertising: The impact of exposure on voter beliefs. *Communication Research, 1*, 3–31.

McCombs, M. (2004). *Setting the agenda: The mass media and public opinion.* Malden, MA: Blackwell Press.

McCombs, M. (2005). A look at agenda-setting: Past, present and future. *Journalism Studies, 6*(4), 543–557.

McCombs, M., & Ghanem, S.I. (2001). The convergence of agenda-setting and framing. In S.D. Reese, O.H. Gandy, Jr., & A.E. Grant (Eds.), *Framing public life: Perspectives on media and our understanding of the social world.* Mahwah, NJ: Erlbaum.

McCombs, M., & Reynolds, A. (2009). How the news shapes our civic agenda. In J. Bryant & M.B. Oliver (Eds.), *Media effects: Advances in theory and research* (3rd edn., pp. 1–16). New York: Routledge.

McCombs, M.E., & Shaw, D.L. (1972). The agenda-setting function of mass media. *Public Opinion Quarterly, 36*, 176–187.

McCombs, M.E., & Weaver, D.H. (1985). Toward a merger of gratifications and agenda-setting research. In K.E. Rosengren, L.A. Wenner, & P. Palmgreen (Eds.), *Media gratifications research: Current perspectives* (pp. 95–108). Beverly Hills, CA: SAGE.

McDevitt, M., Kiousis, S., & Wahl-Jorgensen, K. (2003). Spiral of moderation: Opinion expression in computer-mediated communication. *International Journal of Public Opinion Research, 15*, 454–470.

McDonald, I.R., & Lawrence, R.G. (2004). Filling the 24 x 7 news hole: Television news coverage following September 11. *American Behavioral Scientist, 48*, 327–340.

McGhee, P.E., & Frueh, T. (1980). Television viewing and the learning of sex-role stereotypes. *Sex Roles, 6*, 179–188.

McGloin, R., Farrar, K., & Krcmar, M. (2013). Video games, immersion, and cognitive aggression: Does the controller matter? *Media Psychology, 16*, 65–87.

McGuire, A.J. (1985). Attitudes and attitude change. In G. Lindzey & E. Aronson (Eds.), *The handbook of social psychology: Vol 2. Special fields and applications* (3rd edn., pp. 233–346). New York: Random House.

McGuire, W.J. (1986). The myth of massive media impact: Savagings and salvagings. In G. Comstock (Ed.), *Public communication and behavior* (Vol. 1, pp. 173–257). Orlando, FL: Academic Press.

McIntosh, W.D., Murray, J.D., Murray, R.M., & Manian, S. (2003). What's so funny about a poke in the eye? The prevalence of violence in comedy films and its relationship to social and economic threat in the United States, 1951–2000. *Mass Communication and Society, 6*, 345–360.

McIlwraith, R.D. (1998). "I'm addicted to television": The personality, imagination, and TV watching patterns of self-identified TV addicts. *Journal of Broadcasting & Electronic Media, 42*, 371–386.

McIlwraith, R.D., Jacobvitz, R.S., Kubey, R., & Alexander, A. (1991). Television addiction: Theories and data behind the ubiquitous metaphor. *American Behavioral Scientist, 35*, 104–121.

McIlwraith, R.D., & Schallow, J.R. (1983). Adult fantasy life and patterns of media use. *Journal of Communication, 33*(1), 78–91.

McKenzie, R. (1993). Comparing breaking TV newscasts of the 1989 San Francisco earthquake: How socially responsible was the coverage? *World Communication, 22*, 13–20.

McKenzie-Mohr, D., & Zanna, M.P. (1990). Treating women as sexual objects: Look to the (gender schematic) male who has viewed pornography. *Personal and Social Psychology Bulletin, 16*, 296–308.

McLaughlin, B. (1965). "Intention" and "incidental" learning in human subjects: The role of instructions to learn and motivation. *Psychological Bulletin, 63,* 359–376.

McLeod, D.M. (1995). Communicating deviance: The effects of television news coverage of social protest. *Journal of Broadcasting & Electronic Media, 39,* 4–19.

McLeod, D.M., & Detenber, B.H. (1999). Framing effects of television news coverage of social protest. *Journal of Communication, 49*(3), 3–23.

McLeod, D.M., Eveland, W.P., Jr., & Nathanson, A.I. (1997). Support for censorship of violent and misogynic rap lyrics: An analysis of the third-person effect. *Communication Research, 24,* 153–174.

McLeod, D.M., Eveland, W.P., Jr., & Signorielli, N. (1994). Conflict and public opinion: Rallying effects of the Persian Gulf War. *Journalism Quarterly, 72,* 20–31.

McLeod, D.M., & Hertog, J.K. (1992). The manufacture of public opinion by reporters: Informal cues for public perceptions of protest groups. *Discourse and Society, 3,* 259–275.

McLeod, D.M., & Perse, E.M. (1994). Direct and indirect effects of socioeconomic status on public affairs knowledge. *Journalism Quarterly, 71,* 433–442.

McLeod, D.M., Perse, E., Signorielli, N., & Courtright, J.A. (1993). Public perceptions and evaluations of the functions of the media in the Persian Gulf War. In B.S. Greenberg & W. Gantz (Eds.), *Desert Storm and the mass media* (pp. 197–212). Cresskill, NJ: Hampton Press.

McLeod, D.M., Perse, E.M., Signorielli, N., & Courtright, J.A. (1999). Public hostility toward freedom of expression during international conflicts: A case study of public opinion during the Persian Gulf War. *Free Speech Yearbook, 36,* 104–117.

McLeod, J.M., Becker, L.B., & Byrnes, J.E. (1974). Another look at the agenda-setting function of the press. *Communication Research, 1,* 131–166.

McLeod, J.M., Kosicki, G.M., & Pan, A. (1991). On understanding and misunderstanding media effects. In J. Curran & M. Gurevitch (Eds.), *Mass media and society* (pp. 235–266). London: Edward Arnold.

McLeod, J.M., & McDonald, D.G. (1985). Beyond simple exposure: Media orientation and their impact on political processes. *Communication Research, 12,* 3–33.

McLeod, J.M., & Reeves, B. (1980). On the nature of mass media effects. In S. Withey & R. Abels (Eds.), *Television and social behavior: Beyond violence and children* (pp. 17–54). Hillsdale, NJ: Lawrence Erlbaum Associates.

McQuail, D. (2010). *McQuail's mass communication theory* (6th edn.). Los Angeles: SAGE Publications.

McQuail, D., & Windahl, S. (1993). *Communication models: For the study of mass communication* (2nd edn.). New York: Longman.

Meadowcroft, J.M., & Reeves, B. (1989). Influence of story schema development on children's attention to television. *Communication Research, 16,* 352–374.

Meadowcroft, J.M., & Zillmann, D. (1987). Women's comedy preferences during the menstrual cycle. *Communication Research, 14,* 204–218.

Media Literacy Project. (2014). *What is media literacy?* Retrieved from: http://medialiteracyproject.org/learn/media-literacy.

Media Matters. (2008). *Fear and loathing in prime time: Immigration myths and cable news.* Washington, DC: Media Matters Action Network.

Mehrabian, A., & Wixen, W.J. (1986). Preference for individual video games as a function of their emotional effects on players. *Journal of Applied Social Psychology, 16,* 3–15.

Mendelsohn, H. (1964). Broadcast and personal sources of information in emergent public crises: The presidential assassination. *Broadcasting, 8,* 147–156.

Mendelsohn, H. (1966). Western voting and broadcasts of results on presidential election day. *Public Opinion Quarterly, 30,* 212–225.

Merton, R.K. (1946). *Mass persuasion: The social psychology of a war bond drive.* New York: Harper.

Merton, R.K. (1949). Patterns of influence: A study of interpersonal influence and communication behavior in a local community. In P.F. Lazarsfeld & F.N. Stanton (Eds.), *Communications research 1948–49* (pp. 180–219). New York: Harper.

Merton, R.K. (1968). *Social theory and social structure.* New York: Free Press.

Messaris, P. (1986). Parents, children, and television. In G. Gumpert & R. Cathcart (Eds.), *Inter/media: Interpersonal communication in a media world* (3rd edn., pp. 519–536). New York: Oxford.

Messaris, P., & Kerr, D. (1983). Mothers' comments about TV: Relation to family communication patterns. *Communication Research, 10,* 175–194.

Messner, S.E. (1986). Television violence and violent crime: An aggregate analysis. *Social Problems, 33,* 218–235.

Metz, E., & Youniss, J. (2003). September 11 and service: A longitudinal study of high school students' views and responses. *Applied Developmental Science, 7,* 148–155.

Meyers-Levy, J., & Peracchio, L.A. (1992). Getting an angle in advertising: The effect of camera angle on product evaluations. *Journal of Marketing Research, 29,* 454–461.

Meyrowitz, J. (1982). Television and interpersonal behavior: Codes of reception and response. In G. Gumpert & R. Cathcart (Eds.), *Inter/media: Interpersonal communication in a media world* (2nd edn., pp. 221–241). New York: Oxford.

Meyerowitz, J. (1985). *No sense of place: The impact of electronic media on social behavior.* New York: Oxford.

Milavsky, J.R., Kessler, R., Stipp, H., & Rubens, W.S. (1982). Television and aggression: Results of a panel study. In D. Pearl, L. Bouthilet, & J. Lazar (Eds.), *Television and behavior: Ten years of scientific progress and implications for the eighties* (DHHS Publication No. ADM 82–1196, Vol. 2, pp. 138–157). Washington, DC: U.S. Government Printing Office.

Milgram, S. (1974). *Obedience to authority: An experimental view.* New York: Harper & Row.

Mill, J.S. (1978). On Liberty. In E. Rapaport (Ed.), *On Liberty.* Indianapolis, IN: Hackett Publishing Co. (Original work published 1859.)

Miller v. California, 413 U.S. 15 (1973).

Miller, J.M. & Krosnick, J.A. (2000). News media impact on the ingredients of presidential evaluations: Politically knowledgeable citizens are guided by a trusted source. *American Journal of Political Science, 44*(2), 301–315.

Milton, J. (1890). Aeropagitica: A Defence of the Liberty of Unlicensed Printing. In H. Morley (Ed.), *Famous Pamphlets.* London: George Routledge and Sons. (Original work published 1644.)

Mitchell, J.T., Thomas, D.S.K., Hill, A.A., & Cutter, S.L. (2000). Catastrophe in reel life versus real life: Perpetuating disaster myth through Hollywood films. *International Journal of Mass Emergencies and Disasters, 18,* 383–402.

Mindak, W.H., & Hursh, D. (1965). Television functions on the assassination weekend. In B.S. Greenberg & E.B. Parker (Eds.), *The Kennedy assassination and the American public: Social communication in crisis* (pp. 130–141). Stanford, CA: Stanford University Press.

Molitor, F., & Sapolsky, B.S. (1993). Sex, violence, and victimization in slasher films. *Journal of Broadcasting & Electronic Media, 37,* 233–242.

Montani, M.C. (2006). The germs of terror – Bioterrorism and science communication after September 11. *Journal of Science Communication, 5,* 1–8.

Moore, D. (2001). Bush job approval highest in Gallup history. Gallup News Service. Retrieved from: http://www.gallup.com/poll/4924/bush-job-approval-highest-gallup-history.aspx.

Moore, J. (2011, June 30). Social media day: Did Twitter and Facebook really build a global revolution? *The Christian Science Monitor*.

Morahan-Martin, J., & Schumacher, P. (2000). Incidence and correlates of pathological Internet use among college students. *Computers in Human Behavior, 16,* 13–29.

Morgan, M. (1986). Television and the erosion of regional diversity. *Journal of Broadcasting & Electronic Media, 30,* 123–139.

Morgan, M. (1987). Television, sex-role attitudes, and sex-role behavior. *Journal of Early Adolescence, 7,* 269–282.

Morgan, M., & Shanahan, J. (1991). Do VCRs change the TV picture? VCRs and the cultivation process. *American Behavioral Scientist, 35,* 122–135.

Morgan, M., & Shanahan, J. (1997). Two decades of cultivation research: An appraisal and meta-analysis. In B. R. Burleson (Ed.), *Communication yearbook 20* (pp. 1–45). Thousand Oaks, CA: SAGE.

Morgan, M., & Shanahan, J. (2010). The state of cultivation. *Journal of Broadcasting & Electronic Media, 54,* 337–355.

Morgan, M., Shanahan, J., & Signorielli, N. (2009). Growing up with television: Cultivation processes. In J. Bryant & M. B. Oliver (Eds.), *Media effects: Advances in theory and research* (3rd ed., pp. 34–49). New York: Routledge.

Morwitz, V. G., & Pluzinski, C. (1996). Do polls reflect opinions or do opinions reflect polls? The impact of political polling on voters' expectations, preferences, and behavior. *Journal of Consumer Research, 23,* 53–67.

Mosher, D. L. (1971). Sex callousness toward women. In *Technical report of the Commission on Obscenity and Pornography* (Vol. 7, pp. 313–325). Washington, DC: U.S. Government Printing Office.

Mosher, D. L., & Tompkins, S. S. (1988). Scripting the macho man: Hypermasculine socialization and enculturation. *Journal of Sex Research, 25,* 60–84.

Movieweb. (1999). Top 50 all-time highest grossing movies. Retrieved from: http://www.movieweb.com/movie/alltime.html.

Moy, P., Xenos, M. A., & Hess, V. K. (2006). Priming effects of late-night comedy. *International Journal of Public Opinion Research, 18,* 198–210.

Moyer-Gusé, E., Chung, A. H., & Jain, P. (2011). Identification with characters and discussion of taboo topics after exposure to an entertainment narrative about sexual health. *Journal of Communication, 61,* 387–406.

Moyer-Gusé, E., & Nabi, R. L. (2010). Explaining the effects of narrative in an entertainment television program: Overcoming resistance to persuasion. *Human Communication Research, 36,* 26–52.

Mueller, J. E. (1970). Presidential popularity from Truman to Johnson. *American Political Science Review, 64,* 18–34.

Mukherji, J. (2005). Maternal communication patterns, advertising attitudes and mediation behaviours in urban India. *Journal of Marketing Communications, 11,* 247–262.

Mullainathan, S., & Shleifer, A. (2005). The market for news. *The American Economic Review, 95*(4), 1031–1053.

Mullin, C., Imrich, D. J., & Linz, D. (1996). The impact of acquaintance rape stories and cast-specific pre-trial publicity on juror decision making. *Communication Research, 23,* 100–135.

Mutz, D. C., Roberts, D. F., & Van Vuuren, D. P. (1993). Reconsidering the displacement hypothesis: Television influence on children's time use. *Communication Research, 20,* 51–75.

Myers, P. N., Jr., & Biocca, F. A. (1992). The elastic body image: The effect of television advertising and programming on body image distortions in young women. *Journal of Communication, 42*(3), 108–133.

Myers-Levy, J., & Peracchio, L. A. (1992). Getting an angle in advertising: The effect of camera angle on product evaluations. *Journal of Marketing Research*, 29, 454–461.

Naaman, M., Zhang, A. X., Brody, S., & Lotan, G. (2012, May 20). On the study of diurnal urban routines on Twitter. Paper presented at the International AAAI Conference on Weblogs and Social Media, Dublin, Ireland. Retrieved from: http://sm.rutgers.edu/pubs/naaman-twitterpatterns-icwsm2012.pdf.

Nabi, R. L. (2007). Emotion and persuasion: A social cognitive perspective. In S. R. Roskos-Ewoldson & J. Monahan (Eds.), *Social cognition and communication: Theories and methods* (pp. 377–398). Mahwah, NJ: Lawrence Erlbaum Associates.

Nabi, R. L. (2009). Cosmetic surgery makeover programs and intentions to undergo cosmetic enhancements: A consideration of three models of media effects. *Human Communication Research*, 35, 1–27.

Nabi, R. L., Moyer-Gusé, E., & Byrne, S. (2007). All joking aside: A serious investigation into the persuasive effect of funny social issue messages. *Communication Monographs*, 74, 29–54.

Nabi, R. L., & Oliver, M. B. (2009). *The SAGE handbook of media processes and effects*. Los Angeles: SAGE Publications.

Nacos, B. L. (1990). *The press, presidents, and crises*. New York: Columbia University Press.

Nakonezny, P. A., Reddick, R., & Rodgers, J. L. (2004). Did divorces decline after the Oklahoma City bombing? *Journal of Marriage and the Family*, 66, 90–100.

Nathanson, A. I. (1999). Identifying and explaining the relationship between parental mediation and children's aggression. *Communication Research*, 26, 124–143.

Nathanson, A. I. (2001). Parents versus peers: Exploring the significance of peer mediation of antisocial television. *Communication Research*, 28, 251–274.

National Academy of Science. (1993). *Understanding and preventing violence*. Washington, DC: National Academy Press.

National Cancer Institute. (2008). *The role of the media in promoting and reducing tobacco use*. Tobacco Control Monograph No. 19. Bethesda, MD: U.S. Department of Health and Human Services, National Institutes of Health, National Cancer Institute. NIH Pub. No. 07–6242.

National Center on Addiction and Substance Abuse. (2012). *National survey of American attitudes on substance abuse XVII: Teens*. New York: Columbia University.

National Institute for Mental Health (NIMH). (1982). *Television and behavior: Ten years of scientific progress and implications for the eighties. Vol. 1: Summary report* (DHHS Pub. No. ADM 82–1195). Washington, DC: U.S. Government Printing Office.

Nawy, H. (1973). In the pursuit of happiness? Consumers of erotica in San Francisco. *Journal of Social Issues*, 29(3), 147.161.

Nelson, T. E. (2011). Issue Framing. In R. Y. Shapiro & L. R. Jacobs (Eds.), *The Oxford handbook of American public opinion and the media*. New York: Oxford University Press.

Nelson, T. E., Oxley, Z. M., & Clawson, R. A. (1997). Toward a psychology of framing effects. *Political Behavior*, 19(3), 221–246.

Nestvold, K. J. (1964). Oregon radio.TV response to the Kennedy assassination. *Journal of Broadcasting*, 8, 141–146.

Neuendorf, K. A., & Fennell, R. (1988). A social facilitation view of the generation of humor and mirth reactions: Effects of a laugh track. *Communication Studies*, 39, 37–48.

Neuhaus, J. (2011). *Housework and housewives in American advertising: Married to the mop*. New York: Palgrave MacMillan.

Neuman, R. (1976). Patterns of recall among television news viewers. *Public Opinion Quarterly*, 40, 115–123.

Neuman, S.B. (1991). *Literacy in the television age: The myth of the TV effect* (2nd edn.). Norwood, NJ: Ablex.

Neuman, W.R., Just, M.R., & Crigler, A.N. (1992). *Common knowledge: News and the construction of political meaning*. Chicago: University of Chicago Press.

Newhagen, J.E. (1994). The relationship between censorship and the emotional and critical tone of television news coverage of the Persian Gulf War. *Journalism Quarterly, 71*, 32–42.

Newhagen, J.E., & Reeves, B. (1992). The evening's bad news: Effects of compelling negative television news images on memory. *Journal of Communication, 42*(2), 25–41.

Nielsen. (2009). Americans watching more TV than ever; web and mobile video up too. Nielsenwire. Retrieved from: http://blog.nielsen.com/nielsenwire/online_mobile/americans-watching-more-tv-than-ever/.

Nielsen. (2010). *Television audience report*. Retrieved from: http://blog.nielsen.com/nielsenwire/wp-content/uploads/2010/04/TVA_2009-for-Wire.pdf.

Nisbet, M.C. (2010). Knowledge into action: Framing the debates over climate change and poverty. In P. D'Angelo, & J.A. Kuypers (Eds.), *Doing news framing analysis: Empirical and theoretical perspectives*. New York: Routledge.

Noelle-Neumann, E. (1973). Return to the concept of powerful mass media. *Studies in Broadcasting, 9*, 68–105.

Noelle-Neumann, E. (1984). *The spiral of silence: Public opinion. Our social skin*. Chicago: University of Chicago Press.

Noelle-Neumann, E. (1991). The theory of public opinion: The concept of the spiral of silence. In J.A. Anderson (Ed.), *Communication yearbook* (Vol. 14, pp. 256–287). Newbury Park, CA: SAGE.

Noelle-Neumann, E. (1993). *The spiral of silence: Public opinion. Our social skin* (2nd edn.). Chicago: University of Chicago Press.

Norris, M.L., Boydell, K.M., Pinhas, L., & Katzman, D.K. (2006). Ana and the Internet: A review of pro-anorexia web sites. *International Journal of Eating Disorders, 39*(6), 443–447.

Oggins, J., & Sammis, J. (2012). Notions of video game addiction and their relation to self-reported addiction among players of World of Warcraft. *International Journal of Mental Health and Addiction, 10*, 210–230.

O'Keefe, D.J. (2009). Theories of persuasion. In R.L. Nabi & M.B. Oliver (Eds.), *The SAGE handbook of media processes and effects* (pp. 269–282). Los Angeles: SAGE Publications.

O'Keefe, M.T., & Kissel, B.C. (1971). Visual impact: An added dimension in the study of news diffusion. *Journalism Quarterly, 48*, 298–303.

Oliver, M.B. (1993). Exploring the paradox of the enjoyment of sad films. *Human Communication Research, 19*, 315–342.

Oliver, M.B. (2008). Tender affective states as predictors of entertainment preference. *Journal of Communication, 58*, 40–61.

Oliver, M.B., Bae, K., Ash, E., & Chung, M. (2012). New developments in analyses of fear and crime. In M. Morgan, J. Shanahan, & N. Signorielli (Eds.), *Living with television now: Advances in cultivation theory and research* (pp. 17–37). New York: Peter Lang.

Oliver, M.B., & Fonash, D. (2002). Race and crime in the news: Whites' identification and misidentification of violent and nonviolent criminal suspects. *Media Psychology, 4*(2), 137–156.

Oliver, M.B., Hartmann, T., & Woolley, J.K. (2012). Elevation in response to entertainment portrayals of moral virtue. *Human Communication Research, 38*, 360–378.

Olson, C.K. (2004). Media violence research and youth violence data: Why do they conflict? *Academic Psychiatry, 28*, 144–150.

Olsson, W. (2010). Defining crisis news events. *Nordicom Review, 31*, 87–101.

Oppliger, P. (2007). Effects of gender stereotyping on socialization. In R. W. Preiss, B. M. Gayle, N. Burrell, M. Allen, & J. Bryant (Eds.), *Mass media effects research: Advances through meta-analysis* (pp. 199–214). Mahwah, NJ: Erlbaum.

Oxley, L. M. (2010). Parasocial comparison: The analysis of a new social comparison target when looking at body satisfaction. Unpublished Master's thesis. Department of Communication, University of Delaware, Newark, DE.

Paik, H. (1995). Prosocial television programs and altruistic behavior: A meta-analysis. *Mass Communication Review, 22*, 147–165.

Paik, H., & Comstock, G. (1994). The effects of television violence in antisocial behavior. *Communication Research, 21*, 516–546.

Palazzolo, J. (2012, November 5). @The Slammer: The perils of sending false tweets. *Wall Street Journal*, B1.

Pally, M. (1994). *Sex & sensibility: Reflections on forbidden mirrors and the will to censor*. Hopewell, NJ: Ecco Press.

Palmgreen, P., Wenner, L. A., & Rayburn, J. D., III. (1980). Relations between gratifications sought and obtained: A study of television news. *Communication Research, 7*, 161–192.

Palmgreen, P., Wenner, L. A., & Rayburn, J. D., III. (1981). Gratifications discrepancies and news program choice. *Communication Research, 8*, 451–478.

Palys, T. S. (1986). Testing the common wisdom: The social content of video pornography. *Canadian Psychology, 27*, 22–35.

Pan, Z., Abisaid, J. L., Paek, H.-J., Sun, Y., & Houden, D. (2006). Exploring the perceptual gap in perceived effects of media reports of opinion polls. *International Journal of Public Opinion Research, 18*(3), 340–350.

Papacharissi, A., & Rubin, A. M. (2000). Predictors of Internet use. *Journal of Broadcasting & Electronic Media, 44*, 175–196.

Parents Television Council. (2007). *Sex loses its appeal: A state of the industry report on sex on TV*. Los Angeles: Author.

Pariser, E. (2011). *The filter bubble: What the Internet is hiding from you*. New York: Penguin Press.

Patton, J., Stinard, T., & Routh, D. (1983). Where do children study? *Journal of Educational Research, 76*, 280–286.

Paul, B., Salwen, M. B., & Dupagne, M. (2000). The third-person effect: A meta-analysis of the perceptual hypothesis. *Mass Communication & Society, 3*, 57–85.

Payne, E. (2013, February 13). Report: Sandy Hook shooter tried to emulate Norway massacre. Retrieved from: http://www.cnn.com/2013/02/19/justice/connecticut-newtown-shooting/index.html.

Peffley, M., Shields, T., & Williams, B. (1996). The intersection of race and crime in television news stories: An experimental study. *Political Communication, 13*, 309–327.

Peled, T., & Katz, E. (1974). Media functions in wartime: The Israel home front in October 1973. In J. G. Blumler & E. Katz (Eds.), *The uses of mass communication: Current perspectives on gratifications research* (pp. 49–69). Beverly Hills, CA: SAGE.

Peña, J., Hancock, J. T., & Merola, N. A. (2009). The priming effects of avatars in virtual settings. *Communication Research, 36*, 838–856.

Peralta, E. (2013, July 15). Asiana will sue TV station over bogus flight crew names. *NPR.org*. Retrieved from: http://www.npr.org/blogs/thetwo-way/2013/07/15/202314953/asiana-will-sue-tv-station-over-bogus-flight-crew-names.

Perloff, R., Wartella, E., & Becker, L. (1982). Increasing learning from TV news. *Journalism Quarterly, 59*, 83–86.

Perloff, R. M. (2009). Mass media, social perception, and the third-person effect. In J. Bryant & M. B. Oliver (Eds.), *Media effects: Advances in theory and research* (3rd edn., pp. 252–268). New York: Routledge.

Persch, J. A. (2009, September 9). "House" effect: TV doc has real impact on care. Retrieved from: http://www.msnbc.msn.com/id/32745079/ns/health.

Perse, E. M. (1986). Soap opera viewing patterns of college students and cultivation. *Journal of Broadcasting & Electronic Media, 30,* 175–193.

Perse, E. M. (1990a). Audience selectivity and involvement in the newer media environment. *Communication Research, 17,* 675–697.

Perse, E. M. (1990b). Cultivation and involvement with local television news. In N. Signorielli & M. Morgan (Eds.), *Cultivation analysis: New directions in media effects research* (pp. 51–69). Newbury Park, CA: SAGE.

Perse, E. M. (1990c). Involvement with local television news: Cognitive and emotional dimensions. *Human Communication Research, 16,* 556–581.

Perse, E. M. (1990d). Media involvement and local news effects. *Journal of Broadcasting & Electronic Media, 34,* 17–36.

Perse, E. M. (1990e). Predicting attention to local television news: Need for cognition and motives for viewing. *Communication Reports, 5,* 40–49.

Perse, E. M. (1994). Uses of erotica and acceptance of rape myths. *Communication Research, 21,* 488–515.

Perse, E. M. (1996). Sensation seeking and the use of television for arousal. *Communication Reports, 9,* 37–48.

Perse, E. M. (1998). Implications of cognitive and affective involvement for channel changing. *Journal of Communication, 48*(3), 49–68.

Perse, E. M., & Courtright, J. A. (1993). Normative images of communication media: Mass and interpersonal channels in the new media environment. *Human Communication Research, 19,* 485–503.

Perse, E. M., Ferguson, D. A., & McLeod, D. M. (1994). Cultivation in the newer media environment. *Communication Research, 21,* 79–104.

Perse, E. M., & Rubin, A. M. (1988). Audience activity and satisfaction with favorite television soap opera. *Journalism Quarterly, 65,* 368–375.

Perse, E. M., & Rubin, R. B. (1989). Attribution in social and parasocial relationships. *Communication Research, 16,* 59–77.

Perse, E., Signorielli, N., Courtright, J., Samter, W., Caplan, S., Lambe, J., & Cai, X. (2002). Public perceptions of media functions at the beginning of the war on terrorism. In B. S. Greenberg (Ed.), *Communication and terrorism: Public and media responses to 9/11* (pp. 39–52). Cresskill, NJ: Hampton Press.

Peter, J., & Valkenburg, P.M. (2009). Adolescents' exposure to sexually explicit Internet material and sexual satisfaction: A longitudinal study. *Human Communication Research, 35,* 171–194.

Pettigrew, T. F., & Tropp, L. (2006). A meta-analytic test of intergroup contact theory. *Journal of Personality and Social Psychology, 90*(5), 751–783.

Petty, R. E., Briñol, P., & Priester, J. R. (2009). Mass media attitude change: Implications of the elaboration likelihood model of persuasion. In J. Bryant & M. B. Oliver (Eds.), *Media effects: Advances in theory and research.* New York: Routledge.

Petty, R. E., & Cacioppo, J. T. (1980). Effects of issue involvement on attitudes in an advertising context. In G. Gorn & M. Goldberg (Eds.), *Proceedings of the Division 23 program* (pp. 75–79). Montreal: American Psychological Association.

Petty, R. E., & Cacioppo, J. T. (1984). The effects of involvement on responses to argument quantity and quality: Central and peripheral routes to persuasion. *Journal of Personality and Social Psychology, 46,* 69–81.

Petty, R. E., & Cacioppo, J. T. (1986). *Communication and persuasion: Central and peripheral routes to attitude change*. New York: Springer-Verlag.

Petty, R. E., Cacioppo, J. T., & Goldman, R. (1981). Personal involvement as a determinant of argument-based persuasion. *Journal of Personality and Social Psychology, 41*, 847–855.

Petty, R. E., Cacioppo, J. T., & Heesacker, M. (1981). The use of rhetorical questions in persuasion: A cognitive response analysis. *Journal of Personality and Social Psychology, 40*, 432–440.

Petty, R. E., Cacioppo, J. T., Strathman, A. J., & Priester, J. R. (2005). To think or not to think: Exploring two routes to persuasion. In T. C. Brock & M. C. Green (Eds.), *Persuasion: Psychological insights and perspectives*. Thousand Oaks, CA: SAGE.

Petty, R. E., Kasmer, J. A., Haugtvedt, C. P., & Cacioppo, J. T. (1987). Source and message factors in persuasion: A reply to Stiff's critique of the elaboration likelihood model. *Communication Monographs, 54*(3), 233–249.

Petty, R. E., Ostrom, T. M., & Brock, T. C. (1981). *Cognitive responses in persuasion*. Hillsdale, NJ: Lawrence Erlbaum Associates.

Petty, R. E., & Priester, J. R. (1994). Mass media attitudes change: Implications of the Elaboration Likelihood Model of Persuasion. In J. Bryant & D. Zillmann (Eds.), *Media effects: Advances in theory and research* (pp. 91–122). Hillsdale, NJ: Lawrence Erlbaum Associates.

Petty, R. E., Wegener, D. T., Fabrigar, L. R., Priester, J. R., & Cacioppo, J. T. (1993). Conceptual and methodological issues in the Elaboration Likelihood Model of persuasion: A reply to the Michigan State critics. *Communication Theory, 3*, 336–362.

Pew Research Center for the People & the Press. (2005, September 8). Two-in-three critical of Bush's relief efforts: Huge racial divide over Katrina and its consequences. Retrieved from: http://www.people-press.org/2005/09/08/two-in-three-critical-of-bushs-relief-efforts/.

Pew Research Center for the People & the Press. (2008). *News consumption and believability study*. Washington, DC: Author.

Pew Research Center for the People & the Press. (2010). *Public's Top Stories of the Decade – 9/11 and Katrina*. Washington, DC: Author.

Pew Research Center for the People & the Press. (2011, January 4). Internet gains on television as public's main news source. Retrieved from: http://pewresearch.org/pubs/1844/poll-main-source-national-international-news-internet-television-newspapers.

Pew Research Center's Project for Excellence in Journalism. (2008, May). Journalism, Satire or Just Laughs? "*The Daily Show* with Jon Stewart," Examined. Retrieved from: http://www.journalism.org/node/10953#fn5.

Pfau, M., Haigh, M., Gettle, M., Donnelly, M., Scott, G., Warr, D., & Wittenburg, E. (2004). Embedding journalists in military combat units: Impact on newspaper story frame and tones. *Journalism & Mass Communication Quarterly, 81*, 74–88.

Picard, R. G. (1993). *Media portrayals of terrorism: Functions and meaning of news coverage*. Ames: Iowa State University Press.

Pierce, J. P., Gilpin, E., Burns, D. M., Whalen, E., Rosbrook, B., Shopland, D., & Johnson, M. (1991). Does tobacco advertising target young people to start smoking? *JAMA, 266*, 3154–3158.

Pierce, J. P., Lee, L., & Gilpin, E. A. (1994). Smoking initiation by adolescent girls, 1944 through 1988. *JAMA, 217*, 608–611.

Platow, M. J., Haslam, S. A., Both, A., Chew, I., Cuddon, M., Goharpey, N., Maurer, J., Rosini, S. Tsekouras, A., & Grace, D. M. (2005). "It's not funny if *they're* laughing": Self-categorization, social influence, and responses to canned laughter. *Journal of Experimental Social Psychology, 41*, 542–550.

Plouffe, D. (2009). *The audacity to win: The inside story and lessons of Barack Obama's historic victory*. New York: Viking/Penguin.

Plunkett, J. W. (2009). *Plunkett's entertainment and media industry almanac 2009: Entertainment and media industry market research, statistics, trends and leading companies*. Houston, TX: Plunkett Research.

Politicalmaps.org. (2008, October 16). Spending on television by 2008 presidential campaigns. Retrieved from: http://politicalmaps.org/spending-on-television-advertising-by-the-2008-presidential-campaigns/.

Pollard, P. (1995). Pornography and sexual aggression. *Current Psychology*, *14*, 200–221.

Pooley, J. (2008). The new history of mass communication research. In D. W. Park & J. Pooley (Eds.), *The history of media and communication research* (pp. 43–69). New York: Peter Lang.

Postman, N. (1985). *Amusing ourselves to death: Public discourse in the age of show business*. New York: Penguin.

Potter, W. J. (1986). Perceived reality and the cultivation hypothesis. *Journal of Broadcasting & Electronic Media*, *30*, 159–174.

Potter, W. J. (1988). Perceived reality in television effects research. *Journal of Broadcasting & Electronic Media*, *32*, 23–41.

Potter, W. J. (1998). *Media literacy*. Thousand Oaks, CA: SAGE.

Potter, W. J., & Riddle, K. (2007). A content analysis of the media effects literature. *Journalism & Mass Communication Quarterly*, *84*, 90–104.

Potter, W. J., & Ware, W. (1987). An analysis of the contexts of antisocial acts on prime-time television. *Communication Research*, *14*, 664–686.

Pouliot, L., & Cowen, P. S. (2007). Does perceived realism really matter in media effects? *Media Psychology*, *9*, 241–259.

Powell, L. M., Szczypka, G., Chaloupka, F. J., & Braunshweig, C. L. (2007). Nutritional content of television food advertisements seen by children and adolescents in the United States. *Pediatrics*, *120*(3), 576–583.

Power, J. G., Murphy, S. T., & Coover, G. (1996). Priming prejudice: How stereotypes and counter-stereotypes influence attribution of responsibility and credibility among ingroups and outgroups. *Human Communication Research*, *23*, 36–58.

Power, M. R. (2009). Video games and a culture of conflict. *Journal of Children and Media*, *3*, 90–94.

Preiss, R. W., Gayle, B. M., Burrell, N., Allen, M., & Bryant, J. (2007). *Mass media effects research: Advances through meta-analysis*. Mahwah, NJ: Erlbaum.

Price, V. (1992). *Communication concepts 4: Public opinion*. Newbury Park, CA: SAGE.

Price, V., & Allen, S. (1990). Opinion spirals, silent and otherwise: Applying small group research to public opinion phenomena. *Communication Research*, *17*, 369–392.

Price, V., & Czilli, E. J. (1996). Modeling patterns of news recognition and recall. *Journal of Communication*, *46*(2), 55–78.

Price, V., & Tewksbury, D. (1997). News values and public opinion: A theoretical account of media priming and framing. In G. Barnett & F. J. Boster (Eds.), *Progress in communication sciences* (Vol. 13, pp. 173–212). Greenwich, CT: Ablex.

Price, V., Tewksbury, D., & Huang, L. (1998). Third-person effects on publication of a holocaust-denial advertisement. *Journal of Communication*, *48*(2), 3–26.

Price, V., Tewksbury, D., & Powers, E. (1997). Switching trains of thought: The impact of news frames on readers' cognitive responses. *Communication Research*, *24*, 481–506.

Price, V., & Zaller, J. (1993). Who gets the news? Alternative measures of news reception and its implications for research. *Public Opinion Quarterly*, *57*, 133–164.

Prior, Markus (2007). *Post-Broadcast Democracy*. New York: Cambridge University Press.

Pritchard, M.E., King, S.L., & Czajika-Narins, D.M. (1997). Adolescent body mass indices and self-perception. *Adolescence*, *32*, 863–880.

Purcell, K., Raine, L., Mitchell, A., Rosenstiel, T., & Olmstead, K. (2010). Understanding the participatory news consumer: How Internet and cell phone users have turned news into a social experience. Pew Internet & American Life Project. Retrieved from: http://www.pewinternet.org/Reports/2010/Online-News.aspx.

Quarantelli, E.L. (1981). The command post view in local mass communication systems. *International Journal of Communication Research*, *7*, 57–73.

Rada, J.A. (1997). Color blind-sided: Racial bias in network television's coverage of professional football games. In S. Biagi & M. Kern-Foxworth (Eds.), *Facing difference: Race, gender, and mass media* (pp. 23–29). Thousand Oaks, CA: Pine Forge Press.

Ramasubramanian, S. (2011). The impact of stereotypical versus counterstereotypical media exemplars on racial attitudes, causal attributions, and support for affirmative action. *Communication Research*, *38*(4), 497–516.

Raney, A.A. (2005). Punishing media criminals and moral judgment: The impact of enjoyment. *Media Psychology*, *7*, 145–163.

Raney, A.A. (2006). The psychology of disposition-based theories of media enjoyment. In J. Bryant & P. Vorderer (Eds.), *Psychology of entertainment* (pp. 137–150). New York: Routledge.

Rappoport, P.N., & Alleman, J. (2003). The Internet as a news medium for the crisis news of terrorist attacks in the United States. In A.M. Noll (Ed.), *Crisis communications: Lessons from September 11* (pp. 149–166). Lanham, MD: Rowman & Littlefield.

Ravaja, N. (2004). Effects of Image Motion on a Small Screen on Emotion, Attention, and Memory: Moving-Face Versus Static-Face Newscaster. *Journal of Broadcasting & Electronic Media*, *48*(1), 108–133.

Rayburn, J.D., II, Palmgreen, P., & Acker, T. (1984). Media gratifications and choosing a morning news program. *Journalism Quarterly*, *61*, 149–156.

Record-Breaking TV audience. (1991, January 28). *Newsweek*, 6.

Reed, C. (2004, Nov. 6). "Moral values" doomed the democrats; electoral tactician Karl Rove's brilliant strategy worked wonders for Bush. *The Business Times Singapore*.

Reese, S. (1984). Visual verbal redundancy effects on television news learning. *Journal of Broadcasting*, *28*, 79–87.

Reese, S.D. (2010). Finding frames in a web of culture: The case of the war on terror. In P. D'Angelo, & J.A. Kuypers (Eds.), *Doing news framing analysis: Empirical and theoretical perspectives*. New York: Routledge.

Reeves, B., Lang, A., Kim, E.Y., & Tatar, D. (1999). The effects of screen size and message content on attention and arousal. *Media Psychology*, *1*, 49–67.

Reeves, B., Newhagen, E., Mailbach, E., Basil, M., & Kurz, K. (1991). Negative and positive television messages: Effects of message type and message context on attention and memory. *American Behavioral Scientist*, *34*, 679–694.

Reeves, B., Thorson, E., & Schleuder, J. (1986). Attention to television: Psychological theories and chronometric measures. In J. Bryant & D. Zillmann (Eds.), *Perspectives on media effects* (pp. 251–279). Hillsdale, NJ: Lawrence Erlbaum Associates.

Rhee, J.W., & Cappella, J.N. (1997). The role of political sophistication in learning from news: Measuring schema development. *Communication Research*, *24*, 197–233.

Ricciardelli, L.A., McCabe, M.P., Lillis, J., & Thomas, K. (2006). A longitudinal investigation of the development of weight and muscle concerns among preadolescent boys. *Journal of Youth and Adolescence*, *2*, 177–187.

Rich, M. (2007, July 11). Potter has limited effect on reading habits. *New York Times*. Retrieved from: http://www.nytimes.com/2007/07/11/books/11potter.html.

Riddle, K. (2013). Transportation into vivid media violence: A focus on attention, emotions, and mental rumination. *Communication Quarterly*, 61, 446–462.

Rideout, V. J., Foehr, U. G., & Roberts, D. F. (2010). *Generation M2: Media in the lives of 8- to 18-year-olds*. Menlo Park, CA: Kaiser Family Foundation.

Riffe, D., & Stovall, J. G. (1989). Diffusion of news of shuttle disaster: What role for emotional response? *Journalism Quarterly*, 66, 551–556.

Ritchie, D., Price, V., & Roberts, D. F. (1987). Television, reading, and reading achievement: A reappraisal. *Communication Research*, 14, 292–315.

Rivadeneyra, R., Ward, L. M., & Gordon, M. (2007). Distorted reflections: Media exposure and Latino adolescents' conceptions of self. *Media Psychology*, 9(2), 261–290.

Roberts, C. (2012, November 18). Chris Christie hits Saturday Night Live in his infamous blue fleece. *Daily News*. Retrieved from: http://www.nydailynews.com/news/national/chris-christie-hits-saturday-night-live-infamous-blue-fleece-article-1.1204037.

Roberts, D. F., Christenson, P. G., Henriksen, L., & Bandy, E. (2002). *Substance use in popular music videos*. Washington, DC: Office of National Drug Control Policy.

Roberts, D. F., & Foehr, U. G. (2008). Trends in media use. *Future of Children*, 18(1), 11–37.

Robertson, L. A., McAnally, H. M., & Hancox, R. J. (2013). Childhood and adolescent television viewing and antisocial behavior in early adulthood. *Pediatrics*, 131, 439–446.

Robinson, J. D., & Skill, T. (1995). The invisible generation: Portrayals of the elderly on prime-time television. *Communication Reports*, 8, 111–119.

Robinson, J. P., & Levy M. R., eds. (1986). *The main source: Learning from television news*. Beverly Hills, CA: SAGE.

Robinson, J. P., & Levy, M. R. (1996). New media use and the informed public: A 1990s update. *Journal of Communication*, 46(2), 129–135.

Roe, K., & Minnebo, J. (2007). Antecedents of adolescents' motives for television use. *Journal of Broadcasting & Electronic Media*, 51(2), 305–315.

Rogers, E. M. (1994). *A history of communication study: A biographical approach*. New York: Free Press.

Rogers, E. M. (2003a). *Diffusion of innovations* (5th edn.). New York: Free Press.

Rogers, E. M. (2003b). Diffusion of news of the September 11 terrorist attacks. In A.M. Noll (Ed.), *Crisis communications: Lessons from September 11* (pp. 17–30). Lanham, MD: Rowman & Littlefield.

Rojas, H., Shah, D. V., & Faber, R. J. (1996). For the good of others: Censorship and the third-person effect. *International Journal of Public Opinion Research*, 8, 163–186.

Roper Starch Worldwide. (1995). *America's watching: Public attitudes toward television*. New York: Author.

Rosengren, K. E. (1974). Uses and gratifications: A paradigm outlined. In J. G. Blumler & E. Katz (Eds.), *The uses of mass communications* (pp. 269–286). Beverly Hills, CA: SAGE.

Rosengren, K. E. (1987). Conclusion: The comparative study of news diffusion. *European Journal of Communication*, 2, 227–255.

Rosengren, K. E., McQuail, D., & Blumler, J. G. (1987). News diffusion [Special issue]. *European Journal of Communication*, 2(2).

Rosengren, K. E., & Windahl, S. (1972). Mass media consumption as a functional alternative. In D. McQuail (Ed.), *Sociology of mass communications* (pp. 166–194). New York: Penguin.

Rosenstiel, T. (2005). Political polling and the new media culture: A case of more being less. *The Public Opinion Quarterly*, 69(5), 698–715.

Rosenthal, R. (1979). The "file drawer problem" and tolerance for null results. *Psychological Bulletin, 86,* 638–641.

Rosenthal, R. (1984). *Meta-analytic procedures for social research.* Newbury Park, CA: SAGE.

Rosenthal, R., & Rubin, D. B. (1982). A simple, general purpose display of magnitude of experimental effect. *Journal of Educational Psychology, 74,* 708–712.

Roskos-Ewoldsen, D. R., Roskos-Ewoldsen, B., & Carpentier, F. D. (2009). Media priming: An updated synthesis. In J. Bryant & M. B. Oliver (Eds.), *Media effects: Advances in theory and research* (3rd edn., pp. 74–93). New York: Routledge.

Ross, S. D., & Bantimaroudis, P. (2006). Frame shifts and catastrophic events: The attacks of September 11, 2001, and *New York Times*'s portrayals of Arafat and Sharon. *Mass Communication & Society, 9,* 85–101.

Rothenbuhler, E. W. (1988). The living room celebration of the Olympic games. *Journal of Communication, 38*(4), 61–81.

Rothschild, M. L., & Ray, M. L. (1974). Involvement and political advertising effects: An exploratory experiment. *Communication Research, 1,* 264–283.

Rowland, W. D., Jr. (1983). *The politics of TV violence: Policy uses of communication research.* Beverly Hills, CA: SAGE.

Rubin, A. M. (1981a). An examination of television viewing motivations. *Communication Research, 8,* 141–165.

Rubin, A. M. (1981b). A multivariate analysis of "60 Minutes" viewing motivations. *Journalism Quarterly, 58,* 529–534.

Rubin, A. M. (1983). Television uses and gratifications: The interactions of viewing patterns and motivations. *Journal of Broadcasting, 27,* 37–51.

Rubin, A. M. (1984). Ritualized and instrumental television viewing. *Journal of Communication, 34*(3), 66–77.

Rubin, A. M. (1986). Age and family control influences on children's television viewing. *The Southern Speech Communication Journal, 52,* 35–51.

Rubin, A. M. (2009). Uses-and-gratifications perspective on media effects. In J. Bryant & M. B. Oliver (Eds.), *Media effects: Advances in theory and research* (3rd edn., pp. 165–184). New York: Routledge.

Rubin, A. M., & Bantz, C. R. (1987). Utility of videocassette recorders. *American Behavioral Scientist, 30,* 471–485.

Rubin, A. M., & Perse, E. M. (1987a). Audience activity and television news gratifications. *Communication Research, 14,* 58–84.

Rubin, A. M., & Perse, E. M. (1987b). Audience activity and television news gratifications. *Communication Research, 14,* 58–84.

Rubin, A. M., Perse, E. M., & Powell, R. A. (1985). Loneliness, parasocial interaction, and local television news viewing. *Human Communication Research, 12,* 155–180.

Rubin, A. M., Perse, E. M., & Taylor, D. S. (1988). A methodological examination of cultivation. *Communication Research, 15,* 107–134.

Rubin, A. M., & Step, M. M. (2000). Impact of motivation, attraction and parasocial interaction on talk radio listening. *Journal of Broadcasting & Electronic Media, 44,* 635–654.

Rubin, R. B., & McHugh, M. P. (1987). Development of parasocial interaction relationships. *Journal of Broadcasting & Electronic Media, 31,* 279–292.

Rucinski, D., & Salmon, C. T. (1990). The "other" as the vulnerable voter: A study of the third person effect in the 1988 U.S. presidential campaign. *International Journal of Public Opinion Research, 2,* 345–368.

Rudman, L. A. & Fairchild, K. (2004). Reactions to counterstereotypic behavior: The role of backlash in cultural stereotype maintenance. *Journal of Personality and Social Psychology, 87*(2), 157–176.

Ruggiero, T., & Glascock, J. (2002). Tracking media use and gratifications. In B.S. Greenberg (Ed.), *Communication and terrorism: Public and media responses to 9/11* (pp. 65–74). Cresskill, NJ: Hampton Press.

Rutenberg, J., & Calmes, J. (2009, Aug. 14). False "death panel" rumor has some familiar roots. *New York Times*, A1.

Ryan, E.L., & Hoerrner, K.L. (2004). Let your conscience be your guide: Smoking and drinking in Disney's animated classics. *Mass Communication & Society*, 7(3), 261–278.

Salmon, C.T., & Kline, F.G. (1985). The spiral of silence ten years later. In K.R. Sanders, L.L. Kaid, & D. Nimmo (Eds.), *Political communication yearbook 1984* (pp. 3–30). Carbondale, IL: Southern Illinois University Press.

Salmon, C.T., & Neuwirth, K. (1990). Perceptions of opinion "climates" and willingness to discuss the issue of abortion. *Journalism Quarterly*, 67, 567–577.

Salomon, G. (1983). The differential investment of mental effort in learning from different sources. *Educational Psychologist*, 18, 42–50.

Salomon, G., & Leigh, T. (1984). Predispositions about learning from print and television. *Journal of Communication*, 34(2), 119–135.

Salwen, M.B., & Driscoll, P.D. (1997). Consequences of third-person perception in support of press restrictions in the O.J. Simpson trial. *Journal of Communication*, 47(2), 60–78.

Sands, D.R. (2008, October 9). As Palin's star dims, Fey turns superstar. *The Washington Times*. Retrieved from: http://www.washingtontimes.com/news/2008/oct/09/as-palins-star-dims-fey-turns-superstar/.

Sapolsky, B.S., Molitor, F., & Luque, S. (2003). Sex and violence in slasher films: Re-examining the assumptions. *Journalism & Mass Communication Quarterly*, 80, 28–38.

Sargent, J.D., Dalton, M.A., Beach, M.L., Mott, L.A., Tickle, J.J., Ahrens, M.B., & Heatherton, T.F. (2002). Viewing tobacco use in movies: Does it shape attitudes that mediate adolescent smoking? *American Journal of Preventive Medicine*, 22, 137–145.

Saunders, K.W. (1996). *Violence as obscenity: Limiting the media's First Amendment protection.* Durham, NC: University of North Carolina Press.

Scanlon, J. 2009. Research about the mass media and disaster: Never (well hardly ever) the twain shall meet. In D.A. McEntire (Ed.), *Disciplines, disasters and emergency management textbook*. Retrieved from: http://www.training.fema.gov/emiweb/downloads/scanlonjournalism.pdf.

Schachter, S. (1964). The interaction of cognitive and physiological determinants of emotional state. In L. Berkowitz (Ed.), *Advances in experimental social psychology* (Vol. 1, pp. 49–80). New York: Academic Press.

Schaffner, B.F., & Sellers, P.J. (2009). *Winning with words: The origins & impact of political framing.* New York: Routledge.

Scharrer, E., Kim, D.D., Lin, K., & Liu, Z. (2006). Working hard or hardly working? Gender, humor, and the performance of domestic chores in television commercials. *Mass Media & Society*, 9(2), 215–238.

Scheele, B., & DuBois, F. (2006). Catharsis as a moral form of entertainment. In J. Bryant & P. Vorderer (Eds.), *Psychology of entertainment* (pp. 405–422). New York: Routledge.

Scheff, T.J., & Scheele, S.C. (1980). Humor and catharsis: The effect of comedy on audiences. In P.H. Tannenbaum (Ed.), *The entertainment functions of television* (pp. 165–182). Hillsdale, NJ: Lawrence Erlbaum Associates.

Schenck v. United States, 249 U.S. 47 (1919).

Scheufele, D.A. (1999). Framing as a theory of media effects. *Journal of Communication*, 49(1), 103–122.

Scheufele, D. A., & Moy, P. (2000). Twenty-five years of the spiral of silence: A conceptual review and empirical outlook. *International Journal of Public Opinion Research*, 12(1), 3–28.

Scheufele, D. A., Nisbet, M. C., & Ostman, R. E. (2005). September 11 news coverage, public opinion, and support for civil liberties. *Mass Communication & Society*, 8, 197–218.

Scheufle, D. A., & Tewksbury, D. (2007). Framing, agenda setting, and priming: The evolution of three media effects models. *Journal of Communication*, 57(1), 9–20.

Schiappa, E., Gregg, P. B., & Hewes, D. E. (2005). The parasocial contact hypothesis. *Communication Monographs*, 72, 92–115.

Schiappa, E., Gregg, P. B., & Hewes, D. B. (2006). Can one TV show make a difference? *Will & Grace* and the parasocial contact hypothesis. *Journal of Homosexuality*, 5(4), 15–37.

Schleuder, J. D., White, A. V., & Cameron, G. T. (1993). Priming effects of television news bumpers and teasers on attention and memory. *Journal of Broadcasting & Electronic Media*, 37, 437–452.

Schmidt, M. E., & Vandewater, E. A. (2008). Media and attention, cognition, and school achievement. *Future of Children*, 18(1), 63–85.

Schneider, D. J., Hastorf, A. H., & Ellsworth, P. C. (1979). *Person perception* (2nd edn.). Reading, MA: Addison-Wesley.

Schneider, W., & Pressley, M. (1997). *Memory development between two and twenty* (2nd edn.). Mahwah, NJ: Lawrence Erlbaum Associates.

Schramm, W. (1965). Communication in crisis. In B. S. Greenberg & E. B. Parker (Eds.), *The Kennedy assassination and the American public: Social communication in crisis* (pp. 1–25). Stanford, CA: Stanford University Press.

Schramm, W., Lyle, J., & Parker, E. (1961). *Television in the lives of our children*. Stanford, CA: Stanford University Press.

Schuman, H., & Presser S. (1996). *Questions and answers in attitude surveys: Experiments on question form, wording, and context*. Thousand Oaks, CA: SAGE Publications.

Schwartz, D. A. (1973–1974). How fast does news travel? *Public Opinion Quarterly*, 37, 625–627.

Schwarz, N. (1990). Feelings as information: Informational and motivational functions of affective states. In E. T. Higgins & R. M. Sorrentino (Eds.), *Handbook of motivation and cognition: Foundations of social behavior* (Vol. 2, pp. 527–561). New York: Guilford Press.

Shafer, J. (2012, October 30). The strange allure of disaster porn. *Reuters*. Retrieved from: http://blogs.reuters.com/jackshafer/2012/10/30/the-strange-allure-of-disaster-porn/.

Shaheen, J. G. (2003). Reel bad Arabs: How Hollywood vilifies a people. *The ANNALS of the American Academy of Political and Social Science*, 588, 171–193.

Shanahan, J., Morgan, M., & Stenbjerre, M. (1997). Green or brown? Television and the cultivation of environmental concern. *Journal of Broadcasting & Electronic Media*, 41, 305–323.

Shannon, C. E., & Weaver, W. (1949). *The mathematical theory of communication*. Urbana: University of Illinois Press.

Shapiro, A. M. (2005). The site map principle in multimedia learning. In R. E. Mayer (Ed.), *The Cambridge handbook on multimedia learning*. New York: Cambridge University Press.

Shapiro, R. Y., & Jacobs, L. R. (2011). The democratic paradox: The waning of popular sovereignty and the pathologies of American politics. In R. Y. Shapiro & L. R. Jacobs (Eds.), *The Oxford handbook of American public opinion and the media*. New York: Oxford University Press.

Sharkey, J. (1991). *Under fire: U.S. military restrictions on the media from Grenada to the Persian Gulf*. Washington, DC: Center for Public Integrity.

Sheatsley, P.B., & Feldman, J.J. (1965). A national survey on public reactions and behavior. In B.S. Greenberg & E.B. Parker (Eds.), *The Kennedy assassination and the American public: Social communication in crisis* (pp. 149–177). Stanford, CA: Stanford University Press.

Shefner-Rogers, C.L., Rogers, E.M., & Singhal, A. (1998). Parasocial interaction with the television soap operas *"Simplemente María"* and *"Oshin." Keio Communication Review, 20*, 3–18.

Sherif, C.W., Sherif, M., & Nebergall, R.E. (1965). *Attitude and attitude change: The social judgment-involvement approach.* Philadelphia: Saunders.

Sherman, B.L., & Dominick, J.R. (1986). Violence and sex in music videos: TV and rock 'n' roll. *Journal of Communication, 36*(1), 79–93.

Sherry, J.L. (2001). The effects of violent video games on aggression: A meta-analysis. *Human Communication Research, 27*, 409–431.

Sherry, J.L. (2007). Violent video games and aggression: Why can't we find effects? In R.W. Preiss, B.M. Gayle, N. Burrell, M. Allen, & J. Bryant (Eds.), *Mass media effects research: Advances through meta-analysis* (pp. 245–262). Mahwah, NJ: Erlbaum.

Shin, D.H. & Kim, J.K. (2011). Alcohol product placements and the third-person effect. *Television & New Media, 12*(5), 412–440.

Shin, N. (2004). Exploring pathways from television viewing to academic achievement in school age children. *The Journal of Genetic Psychology: Research and Theory on Human Development, 165*(4), 367–382.

Shock jock Michael Savage: Panel of quotes. (2009, May 7). *The Telegraph.* Retrieved from: http://www.telegraph.co.uk/news/politics/5287820/Shock-jock-Michael-Savage-panel-of-quotes.html.

Shoemaker, P.J. (1989). Predicting media uses. In F. Williams (Ed.), *Measuring the information society* (pp. 229–242). Newbury Park, CA: SAGE.

Shoemaker, P.J. (1996). Hardwired for news: Using biological and cultural evolution to explain the surveillance function. *Journal of Communication, 46*(3), 32–47.

Shope, J.H. (2004). When words are not enough: The search for the effect of pornography on abused women. *Violence Against Women, 10*, 56–72.

Shrum, L.J. (1997). The role of source confusion in cultivation effects may depend on processing strategy: A comment on Mares (1996). *Human Communication Research, 24*, 349–358.

Shrum, L.J., Wyer, R.S., Jr., & O.Guinn, T.C. (1998). The effects of television consumption on social perceptions: The use of priming procedure to investigate psychological processes. *Journal of Consumer Research, 24*, 447–458.

Signorielli, N. (1987). Drinking, sex, and violence on television: The cultural indicators perspective. *Journal of Drug Education, 17*, 245–260.

Signorielli, N. (1990). Television's mean and dangerous world: A continuation of the Cultural Indicators Perspective. In N. Signorielli & M. Morgan (Eds.), *Cultivation analysis: New directions in media effects research* (pp. 85–106). Newbury Park, CA: SAGE.

Signorielli, N. (2003). Violence on television 1993–2001: Has the picture changed? *Journal of Broadcasting & Electronic Media, 47*(1), 36–57.

Signorielli, N. (2004). Aging on television: Messages relating to gender, race, and occupation in prime-time. *Journal of Broadcasting & Electronic Media, 48*(2), 279–301.

Signorielli, N. (2008, November). Children's programs in 2007: Basic demography and violence. Paper presented at the National Communication Association annual convention, San Diego, CA.

Signorielli, N. (2012). Television's gender-role images and contribution to stereotyping: Past, present, future. Chapter 16 in D.G. Singer & J.L. Singer (Eds.), *Handbook of children and the media* (2nd edn.) Los Angeles: SAGE.

Signorielli, N., & Shanahan, J. (2011, November). The voice of television violence: The violence profile in the 21st century. Paper presented at the National Communication Association annual convention, New Orleans.

Simon, A. F. (1997). Television news and international earthquake relief. *Journal of Communication, 47*(3), 82–93.

Simon, H. A. (1974). How big is a chunk? *Science, 183*, 482–488.

Simpson, C. (1994). *Science of coercion: Communication research & psychological warfare 1945–1960*. New York: Oxford University Press.

Simpson, C. (1996). Elisabeth Noelle-Neumann's "spiral of silence" and historical context of communication theory. *Journal of Communication, 46*(3), 149–173.

Simpson, C. (1997). Response to Kepplinger. *Journal of Communication, 47*(4), 139–141.

Singer, J. (1980). The power and limitations of television: A cognitive-affective analysis. In P. H. Tannenbaum (Ed.), *The entertainment functions of television* (pp. 31–65). Hillsdale, NJ: Lawrence Erlbaum Associates.

Singhal, A., Cody, M. J., Rogers, E. M., & Sabido, M. (2004). *Entertainment-education and social change: History, research, and practice*. Mahwah, NJ: Lawrence Erlbaum.

Singhal, A., & Rogers, E. M. (1989). Prosocial television for development in India. In R. E. Rice & C. K. Atkin (Eds.), *Public communication campaigns* (2nd edn., pp. 331–350). Newbury Park, CA: SAGE.

Slade, J. W. (1984). Violence in the hard-core pornographic film: A historical survey. *Journal of Communication, 34*(3), 148–163.

Slater, M. D. (2003). Alienation, aggression, and sensation seeking as predictors of adolescent use of violent film, computer, and website content. *Journal of Communication, 53*, 105–121.

Slater, M. D., Hayes, A. F., Reineke, J. B., Long, M., & Bettinghaus, E. P. (2009). Newspaper coverage of cancer prevention: Multilevel evidence for knowledge-gap effects. *Journal of Communication, 59*, 514–533.

Smith, E. R. (1990). Reply to commentaries. In T. K. Srull & R. S. Wyer, Jr. (Eds.), *Advances in social cognition: Vol. III. Content and process specificity in the effects of prior experiences* (pp. 181–202). Hillsdale, NJ: Lawrence Erlbaum Associates.

Smith, R. (1986). Television addiction. In J. Bryant & D. Zillmann (Eds.), *Perspectives on media effects* (pp. 109–128). Hillsdale, NJ: Lawrence Erlbaum Associates.

Smith, S. L., & Granados, A. D. (2009). Content patterns and effects surrounding sex-role stereotyping on television and film. In J. Bryant & M. B. Oliver (Eds.), *Media effects: Advances in theory and research*. New York: Routledge.

Smith, S. L., Lachlan, K., Pieper, K. M., Boyson, A. R., Wilson, B. J., Tamborini, R., & Weber, R. (2004). Brandishing guns in American media: Two studies examining how often and in what context firearms appear on television and in popular video games. *Journal of Broadcasting & Electronic Media, 48*, 584–606.

Smith, S. L., Nathanson, A. I., & Wilson, B. J. (2002). Prime-time television: Assessing violence during the most popular viewing hours. *Journal of Communication, 52*, 84–111.

Smolak, L., Murnen, S. K., & Thompson, J. K. (2005). Sociocultural influences and muscle building in adolescent boys. *Psychology of men and masculinity, 6*, 227–239.

Snyder, L. B., Milici, F. F., Slater, M., Sun, H., & Strizhakova, Y. (2006). Effects of alcohol advertising exposure on drinking among youth. *Archives of Pediatrics & Adolescent Medicine, 160*(1), 18–24.

Sohn, D. (1982). On Eron on television violence and aggression. *American Psychologist, 37*, 1292–1293.

Sood, R., Stockdale, G., & Rogers, E. M. (1987). How the news media operate in natural disasters. *Journal of Communication, 37*(3), 27–41.

Southern Poverty Law Center. (n.d.).*Hate and Extremism*. Retrieved from: http://www.splcenter.org/what-we-do/hate-and-extremism.

Sparks, G. G., & Cantor, J. (1986). Development differences in fright responses to a television program depicting a character transformation. *Journal of Broadcasting & Electronic Media, 30,* 309–322.

Spence, P. R., Westerman, D., Skalski, P. D., Seeger, M., Sellnow, T. L., & Ulmer, R. R. (2006). Gender and age effects on information seeking after 9/11. *Communication Research Reports, 23,* 217–223.

Spigel, L. (2004). Entertainment wars: Television culture after 9/11. *American Quarterly, 56,* 235–270.

Squire, L. R., & Slater, P. C. (1975). Forgetting in very long-term memory as assessed by an improved questionnaire technique. *Journal of Experimental Psychology: Human Learning and Memory, 1,* 50–54.

Stacy, A. W., Zogg, J. B., Unger, J. B., & Dent, C. W. (2004). Exposure to televised alcohol ads and subsequent adolescent alcohol use. *American Journal of Health Behavior, 28*(6), 498–509.

Stanley, A. (Jan. 16, 2010). Broadcast coverage: Compassion and self-congratulation. *New York Times,* A10.

Starbird, K., Maddock, J., Orand, M., Achterman, P., & Mason, R. M. (2014). Rumors, false flags, and digital vigilantes: Misinformation on Twitter after the 2013 Boston Marathon bombing. In M. Kindling & E. Greifeneder (Eds.), Conference 2014 Proceedings (pp. 654–662). Retrieved from: https://www.ideals.illinois.edu/handle/2142/47257.

Stauffer, J., Frost, R., & Rybolt, W. (1983). The attention factor in recalling network television news. *Journal of Communication, 33*(1), 29–37.

Stein, A. H., & Friedrich, L. K. (1975). Impact of television on children and youth. In E. M. Hetherington (Ed.), *Review of child development research* (Vol. 5, pp. 183–256). Chicago, University of Chicago Press.

Steinhauer, J. (2011, January 9). Shooting casts a spotlight on Arizona's unique politics. *New York Times.* Retrieved from: http://www.nytimes.com/2011/01/10/us/10arizona.html.

Stempel, C., Hargrove, T., & Stempel, G. H. (2007). Media use, social structure, and belief in 9/11 conspiracy theories. *Journalism & Mass Communication Quarterly, 84,* 353–372.

Stempel, G. H. (2010). Hurricane Katrina: Flooding, muck, and human misery. In R. Izard & J. Perkins (Eds.), *Covering disaster: Lessons from media coverage of Katrina and Rita* (pp. 19–29). New Brunswick, NJ: Transaction.

Stempel, G. H., & Windhauser, J. W. (1989). Coverage by the prestige press of the 1988 presidential campaign. *Journalism Quarterly, 66,* 894–896, 919.

Stephen, W. G., & Brigham, J. C., eds. (1985). Intergroup contact [Special issue]. *Journal of Social Issues, 41*(3).

Stephenson, W. (1988). *The play theory of mass communication.* New Brunswick, NJ: Transaction Books.

Stice, E. (1998). Modeling of eating pathology and social reinforcement of the thin-ideal predict onset of bulimic symptoms. *Behaviour Research & Therapy, 36,* 931–944.

Stiff, J. B. (1986). Cognitive processing of persuasive message cues: A meta-analytic review of the effects of supporting information on attitudes. *Communication Monographs, 53,* 75–89.

Stiff, J. B., & Boster, F. J. (1987). Cognitive processing: Additional thoughts and a reply to Petty, Kasmer, Haughtvedt, and Cacioppo. *Communication Monographs, 54,* 250–256.

Stokes, L. C., & Pankowski, M. L. (1988). Incidental learning of aging adults via television. *Adult Education Quarterly, 38,* 88–100.

Strasburger, V. C. (Feb. 2004). Children, adolescents, and the media. *Current Problems in Pediatric Adolescent Health Care, 34,* 54–113.

Strasburger, V. C. (2012). Children, adolescents, drugs and the media. In D. G. Singer & J. L. Singer (Eds.), *Handbook of children and the media* (2nd edn.). Los Angeles: SAGE.

Strasburger, V. C., Wilson, B. J., & Jordan, A. B. (2009). *Children, adolescents, and the media.* Los Angeles: SAGE.

Stroman, C. A. (1986). Television viewing and self-concept among black children. *Journal of Broadcasting & Electronic Media, 30,* 87–93.

Sudman, S. (1986). Do exit polls influence voting behavior? *Public Opinion Quarterly, 50,* 331–339.

Suellentrop, C. (2010, February). Game changers: How videogames trained a generation of athletes. *Wired,* 88–93.

Sundar, S. S., & Marathe, S. S. (2010). Personalization versus customization: The importance of agency, privacy, and power usage. *Human Communication Research, 36,* 298–322.

Sundar, S., Nurayan, S., Obregon, R., & Uppal, C. (1998). Does web advertising work: Memory for print vs. online media. *Journalism & Mass Communication Quarterly, 75,* 822–835.

Sunstein, C. (2007). *Republic.com 2.0.* Princeton, NJ: Princeton University Press.

Surette, R. (1998). *Media, crime, and criminal justice: Images and realities* (2nd edn.). Belmont, CA: West/Wadsworth.

Surgeon General's Scientific Advisory Committee on Television and Social Behavior. (1972). *Television and growing up: The impact of televised violence.* Washington, DC: U.S. Government Printing Office.

Sweller, J. (2005). Implications of cognitive load theory for multimedia learning. In R. E. Mayer (Ed.), *The Cambridge handbook on multimedia learning.* New York: Cambridge University Press.

Tamborini, R. (2003). Enjoyment and social functions of horror. In J. Bryant, D. Roskos-Ewoldsen, & J. Cantor (Eds.), *Communication and emotion: Essays in honor of Dolf Zillmann* (pp. 417–443). Mahwah, NJ: Lawrence Erlbaum Associates.

Tamborini, R., Zillmann, D., & Bryant, J. (1984). Fear and victimization: Exposure to television and perceptions of crime and fear. In R. N. Bostom (Ed.), *Communication Yearbook 8* (pp. 492–513). Beverly Hills, CA: SAGE.

Tan, A. S. (1979). TV beauty ads and role expectations of adolescent female viewers. *Journalism Quarterly, 56,* 283–288.

Tan, Z. C. W. (1988). Media publicity and insurgent terrorism: A twenty-year balance sheet. *Gazette, 42,* 2–32.

Tankard, J. W. (2001). The empirical approach to the study of framing. In S. D. Reese, O. H. Gandy, & A. E. Grant (Eds.), *Framing public life: Perspectives on media and our understanding of the social world.* Mahwah, NJ: Lawrence Erlbaum Associates.

Tannenbaum, P. H. (1986). Policy options for early election projections. In J. Bryant & D. Zillmann (Eds.), *Perspectives on media effects* (pp. 189–302). Hillsdale, NJ: Lawrence Erlbaum Associates.

Tannenbaum, P. H., & Zillmann, D. (1975). Emotional arousal in the facilitation of aggression through communication. In L. Berkowitz (Ed.), *Advances in experimental social psychology* (Vol. 8, pp. 149–192). New York: Academic Press.

Tavris, C. (1988). Beyond cartoon killings: Comments on two overlooked effects of television. In S. Oskamp (Ed.), *Applied social psychology annual. Vol. 8: Television as a social issue* (pp. 189–197). Newbury Park, CA: SAGE.

Taylor, L.D. (2005). All for him: Articles about sex in American lad magazines. *Sex Roles, 52*(3/4), 153–163.

Taylor, S.E. (1975). On inferring one's attitudes from one's behavior: Some delimiting conditions. *Journal of Personality and Social Psychology, 31,* 126–131.

Taylor, S.E., & Crocker, J. (1981). Schematic bases of social information processing. In E.T. Higgins, C.P. Herman, & M.P. Zanna (Eds.), *Social cognition: The Ontario Symposium* (Vol. 1, pp. 89–134). Hillsdale, NJ: Lawrence Erlbaum Associates.

Television Information Office. (1985). *A broadcasting primer with notes on the new technologies.* New York: Author.

Tewksbury, D., Weaver, A.J., & Maddex, B.D. (2001). Accidentally informed: Incidental news exposure on the World Wide Web. *Journalism & Mass Communication Quarterly, 78*(3), 533–554.

Thomas, M.H., & Drabman, R.S. (1975). Toleration of real life aggression as a function of exposure to televised violence and age of subject. *Merrill-Palmer Quarterly, 21,* 227–232.

Thomas, M.H., Horton, R.W., Lippincott, E.C., & Drabman, R.S. (1977). Desensitization to portrayals of real-life aggression as a function of exposure to television violence. *Journal of Personality and Social Psychology, 35,* 450–458.

Thompson, K.M., & Haninger, K. (2001). Violence in E-rated video games. *The Journal of the American Medical Association, 286,* 591–598.

Thorson, E., & Lang, A. (1992). The effects of television video graphics and lecture familiarity on adult cardiac orienting responses and memory. *Communication Research, 19,* 346–369.

Tian, Y., & Robinson, J.D. (2009). Incidental health information use on the Internet. *Health Communication, 24,* 41–49.

Tibken, S. (2012, November 2). Twitter: Over 20M tweets sent about Hurricane Sandy. *Cnet.* Retrieved from: http://news.cnet.com/8301–1023_3-57544487–93/twitter-over-20m-tweets-sent-about-hurricane-sandy/.

Tichenor, P.J., Donohue, G.A., & Olien, C.N. (1970). Mass media flow and the differential growth in knowledge. *Public Opinion Quarterly, 34,* 159–170.

Tiedens, L.Z., & Linton, S. (2001). Judgment under emotional certainty and uncertainty: The effects of specific emotions on information processing. *Journal of Personality and Social Psychology, 81*(6), 973–988.

Tierney, K., Bevc, C., & Kuligowski, E. (2006). Metaphors matter: Disaster myths, media frames, and their consequences in Hurricane Katrina. *The Annals of the American Academy of Political and Social Science, 604,* 57–81.

Titus-Ernstoff, L., Dalton, M.A., Adachi-Mejia, A.M., Longacre, M.R., & Beach, M.L. (2008). Longitudinal study of viewing smoking in movies and initiation of smoking by children. *Pediatrics, 121,* 15–21.

Toch, H., & Klofas, J. (1984). Pluralistic ignorance, revisited. In G.M. Stephenson & J.H. David (Eds.), *Progress in applied social psychology* (Vol. 2, pp. 129–159). New York: Wiley.

Tönnies, F. (1957). *Community and society* (C.P. Loomis, Trans.). East Lansing: Michigan State University Press.

Traugott, M.W. (1992). The impact of media polls on the public. In T.E. Mann & G.R. Orren (Eds.), *Media polls in American politics* (pp. 125–149). Washington, DC: Brookings Institution.

Treisman, A. (1979). The psychological reality of level of processing. In L.S. Cermak & F.I.M. Craik (Eds.), *Levels of processing in human memory* (pp. 301–330). Hillsdale, NJ: Lawrence Erlbaum Associates.

Tuchman, G. (1978). *Making news: A study in the construction of reality.* New York: Free Press.

Tuchman, S., & Coffin, T. E. (1971). The influence of election night television broadcasts in a close election. *Public Opinion Quarterly*, *35*, 315–326.

Turner, C. W., & Berkowitz, L. (1972). Identification with film aggressor (covert role taking) and reactions to film violence. *Journal of Personality and Social Psychology*, *21*, 256–264.

Turner, J. R. (1993). Interpersonal and psychological predictors of parasocial interaction with different television performers. *Communication Quarterly*, *41*, 443–453.

Turner, J. S. (2005). An examination of sexual content in music videos. Unpublished Master's thesis. University of Delaware, Newark, DE. Retrieved from: http://www.udel.edu/communication/web/thesisfiles/jaketurnerthesis.pdf.

Tversky, A., & Kahneman, D. (1973). Availability: A heuristic for judging frequency and probability. *Cognitive psychology*, *5*, 207–232.

Urista, M. A., Dong, Q., & Day, K. D. (2009). Explaining why young adults use MySpace and Facebook through uses and gratifications theory. *Human Communication*, *12*, 215–229.

U.S. Department of Health and Human Services. (2012). *Preventing tobacco use among youth and young adults: A report to the Surgeon General*. Atlanta, GA: U.S. Department of Health and Human Services, Centers for Disease Control and Prevention, National Center for Chronic Disease Prevention and Health Promotion, Office on Smoking and Health.

U.S. Department of Justice, Federal Bureau of Investigation. (1999, October 17). Crime in the United States, 1998. Retrieved: https://www.fbi.gov/about-us/cjis/ucr/crime-in-the-u.s/1999/toc99.pdf.

Valente, T. W., Murphy, S., Huang, G., Gusek, J., Greene, J., & Beck, V. (2007). Evaluating a minor storyline on *ER* about teen obesity, hypertension, and 5 a day. *Journal of Health Communication*, *12*, 551–566.

Valkenburg, P. M., & Calvert, S. L. (2012). Media and the child's developing imagination. Chapter 8 in D. G. Singer & J. L. Singer (Eds.), *Handbook of children and the media* (2nd edn.). Los Angeles: SAGE.

Valkenburg, P. M., & Peter, J. (2013). The differential susceptibility to media effects model. *Journal of Communication*, *63*, 221–243.

Valkenburg, P. M., Semetko, H. A., & De Vresse, C. H. (1999). The effects of news frames on readers' thoughts and recall. *Communication Research*, *26*, 550–569.

Van Evra, J. (2004). *Television and child development* (3rd edn.). New York: Routledge.

Vancil, D. L., & Pendell, S. D. (1987). The myth of viewer listener disagreement in the first Kennedy–Nixon debate. *Central State Speech Journal*, *38*, 16–27.

Vidmar, N., & Rokeach, M. (1974). Archie Bunker's bigotry: A study in selective perception and exposure. *Journal of Communication*, *24*(1), 36–47.

Viswanath, K., & Finnegan, J. R., Jr. (1996). The knowledge gap hypothesis: Twenty-five years later. *Communication yearbook* (Vol. 19, pp. 187–227). Thousand Oaks, CA: SAGE.

Viswanath, K., Kahn, E., Finnegan, J. R., Jr., Hertog, J., & Potter, J. D. (1993). Motivation and the knowledge gap: Effects of a campaign to reduce diet-related cancer risk. *Communication Research*, *20*, 546–563.

Vorderer, P. (2000). Interactive entertainment and beyond. In D. Zillmann & P. Vorderer (Eds.), *Media entertainment: The psychology of its appeal* (pp. 21–36). Mahwah, NJ: Lawrence Erlbaum Associates.

Vossekuil, B., Fein, R. A., Reddy, M., Borum, R., & Modzeleski, W. (2002). *The final report and findings of the safe school initiative: Implications for the prevention of school attacks in the United States*. Washington, DC: United States Secret Service and United States Department of Education.

Walker, C. E. (1971). *Erotic stimuli and the aggressive sexual offender. Technical report of the Commission on Obscenity and Pornography* (Vol. 7, pp. 91–147). Washington, DC: U.S. Government Printing Office.

Walker, J. (2010, Oct. 30). Elder stereotypes in media & popular culture. *Aging Watch*. Retrieved from: http://www.agingwatch.com/?p=439.

Walker, J. R., & Bellamy, R. V., Jr. (1991). The gratifications of grazing: An exploratory study of remote control use. *Journalism Quarterly, 68*, 422–431.

Walma van der Molen, J. H., & Van der Voort, T. H. A. (2000). Children's and adults' recall of television and print news in children's and adult news formats. *Communication Research, 27*, 132–160.

Walsh-Childers, K., & Brown, J. D. (2009).Effects of media on personal and public health. In J. Bryant & M. B. Oliver (Eds.), *Media effects: Advances in theory and research*. New York: Routledge.

Walsh-Childers, K., Gotthoffer, A., & Lepre, C. R. (2001). From "just the facts" to "downright salacious": Teen's and women's magazine coverage of sex and sexual health. In J. D. Brown, J. R. Steele, & K. Walsh-Childers (Eds.), *Sexual teens, sexual media: Investigating media's influence on adolescent sexuality*. New York: Routledge.

Walters, R. H., & Parke, R. D. (1964). Influence of response consequences to a social model on resistance to deviation. *Journal of Experimental Child Psychology, 1*, 269–280.

Walton, G. M., & Cohen, G. L. (2007). A question of belonging: Race, social fit, and achievement. *Journal of Personality and Social Psychology, 92*, 82–96.

Wanta, W. (1997). *The public and the national agenda: How people learn about important issues*. Mahwah, NJ: Lawrence Erlbaum Associates.

Wanta, W., & Ghanem, S. (2007). Effects of agenda setting. In R. W. Preiss, B. M. Gayle, N. Burrell, M. Allen, & J. Bryant (Eds.), *Mass media effects research: Advances through meta-analysis* (pp. 37–51). Mahwah, NJ: Erlbaum.

Wartella, E., Heintz, K. E., Aidman, A. J., & Mazzarella, S. R. (1990). Television and beyond: Children's video media in one community. *Communication Research, 17*, 45–64.

Wartella, E., & Reeves, B. (1985). Historical trends in research on children and the media: 1900–1960. *Journal of Communication, 35*(2), 118–133.

Wasylkiw, L., Emms, A. A., Meuse, R., & Poirier, K. F. (2009). Are all models created equal? A content analysis of women in advertisements of fitness versus fashion magazines. *Body Image, 6*, 137–140.

Watt, J. H., Jr. (1979). Television form, content attributes, and viewer behavior. In M. J. Voight & G. J. Hanneman (Eds.), *Progress in communication sciences* (Vol. 1, pp. 51–89). Norwood, NJ: Ablex.

Watt, J. H., & Krull, R. (1977). An examination of three models of television viewing and aggression. *Human Communication Research, 3*, 99–112.

Watt, J. H., Mazza, M., & Snyder, L. (1993). Agenda-setting effects of television news coverage and the effects decay curve. *Communication Research, 20*, 408–435.

Waxman, J. J. (1973). Local broadcast gatekeeping during natural disaster. *Journalism Quarterly, 50*, 751–758.

Weaver, A. J. (2011). A meta-analytical review of selective exposure to and the enjoyment of media violence. *Journal of Broadcasting & Electronic Media, 55*, 232–250.

Weaver, D. H. (2007). Thoughts on agenda setting, framing and priming. *Journal of Communication, 57*(1), 142–147.

Weaver, D. H., Graber, D. A., McCombs, M. E., & Eyal, C. H. (1981). *Media agenda-setting in a presidential election: Issues, images and interest*. New York: Praeger.

Weaver, J., & Wakshlag, J. (1986). Perceived vulnerability to crime, criminal victimization experience, and television viewing. *Journal of Broadcasting & Electronic Media, 30,* 141–158.

Weaver, J.B., III. (1987). Effects of portrayals of female sexuality and violence against women on perceptions of women. Doctoral dissertation, University of Indiana. Dissertation Abstracts International, 48, 2482-A.

Weaver, J.B., III (1991a). Are "slasher" horror films sexually violent? A content analysis. *Journal of Broadcasting & Electronic Media, 35,* 385–392.

Weaver, J.B., III. (1991b). Exploring the links between personality and media preferences. *Personality and Individual Differences, 12,* 1293–1299.

Weaver, J.B., III. (1991c). The impact of exposure to horror film violence on perceptions of women: Is it the violence or an artifact? In B.A. Austin (Ed.), *Current research in film: Audiences, economics, and law* (Vol. 5, pp. 1–18). Norwood, NJ: Ablex.

Weaver, J.B., III. (1991d). Responding to erotica: Perceptual processes and dispositional implications. In J. Bryant & D. Zillmann (Eds.), *Responding to the screen: Reception and reaction processes* (pp. 329–354). Hillsdale, NJ: Lawrence Erlbaum Associates.

Weaver, J.B., III, Brosius, H., & Mundorf, N. (1993). Personality and movie preferences: A comparison of American and German audiences. *Personality and Individual Differences, 14,* 307–315.

Weaver, J.B., III, Masland, J.L., & Zillmann, D. (1984). Effect of erotica on young men's aesthetic perception of their female partners. *Perceptual and Motor Skills, 58,* 929–930.

Weaver, J., & Wakshlag, J. (1986). Perceived vulnerability to crime, criminal victimization experience, and television viewing. *Journal of Broadcasting & Electronic Media, 30,* 141–158.

Weaver-Lariscy, R.A., Sweeney, B., & Steinfatt, T. (1984). Communication during assassination attempts: Diffusion of information in attacks on President Reagan and the Pope. *Southern Speech Communication Journal, 49,* 258–276.

Webster, J.G. (1983). The impact of cable and pay cable television on local station audiences. *Journal of Broadcasting, 27,* 119–126.

Webster, J.G., & Phalen, P.F. (1997). *The mass audience: Rediscovering the dominant model.* Mahwah, NJ: Lawrence Erlbaum Associates.

Webster, J.G., & Wakshlag, J. (1985). Measuring exposure to television. In D. Zillmann & J. Bryant (Eds.), *Selective exposure to communication* (pp. 35–62). Hillsdale, NJ: Lawrence Erlbaum Associates.

Wei, R., Chia, S.C., & Lo, V.-H. (2011). Third person effect and hostile media perception influences on voter attitudes toward polls in the 2008 U.S. Presidential election. *International Journal of Public Opinion Research, 23*(2), 169–190.

Weibull, L., Lindahl, R., & Rosengren, K.E. (1987). News diffusion in Sweden: The role of the media. *European Journal of Communication, 2,* 143–170.

Weimann, G. (1983). The theater of terror: Effects of press coverage. *Journal of Communication, 33*(1), 38–45.

Weimann, G. (1987). Media events: The case of international terrorism. *Journal of Broadcasting & Electronic Media, 31,* 21–39.

Weimann, G., & Winn, C. (1994). *The theater of terror: Mass media and international terrorism.* New York: Longman.

Welch A.J., & Watt, J.H., Jr. (1982). Visual complexity and young children's learning from television. *Human Communication Research, 8,* 133–145.

Wellman, R.J., Sugarman, D.B., DiFranza, J.R., & Winickoff, J.P. (2006). The extent to which tobacco marketing and tobacco use in films contribute to children's use of tobacco. *Archives of Pediatrics & Adolescent Medicine, 160*(12), 1285–1296.

Welly, K., (2009, October). Media surveys shed new light and confirm old suspicions. *EContent*. Retrieved from: http://www.econtentmag.com/Articles/News/News-Feature/Media-Surveys-Shed-New-Light-and-Confirm-Old-Suspicions-56417.htm.

Wenger, D.E. (1980). A few empirical observations concerning the relationship between the mass media and disaster knowledge: A research report. In *Disasters and the mass media: Proceedings of the Committee on Disasters and the Mass Media Workshop* (pp. 241–266). Washington, DC: National Academy of Sciences.

Westerman, D., Spence, P.R., & Lachlan, K.A. (2009). Telepresence and the exemplification effects of disaster news. *Communication Studies, 60,* 542–557.

White, H.A. (1997). Considering interacting factors in the third-person effect: Argument strength and social distance. *Journalism and Mass Communication Quarterly, 74,* 557–564.

Williams, D., Martins, N., Consalvo, M., & Ivory, J.D. (2009). The virtual census: Representations of gender, race and age in video games. *New Media & Society, 11*(5), 815–834.

Williams, F., Rice, R.E., & Rogers, E.M. (1988). *Research methods and the new media.* New York: Free Press.

Williams, K.D. (2009). The effects of frustration, violence, and trait hostility after playing a video game. *Mass Communication and Society, 12,* 291–310.

Williams, T.M. (1986). Summary, conclusions, and implications. In T.M. Williams (Ed.), *The impact of television: A natural experiment in three communities* (pp. 395–430). Orlando, FL: Academic Press.

Williams, W. (1985). Agenda setting research. In J.R. Dominick & J.E. Fletcher (Eds.), *Broadcasting research methods* (pp. 189–201). Boston: Allyn & Bacon.

Willnat, L., Lee, W., & Detenber, B.H. (2002). Individual-level predictors of public outspokenness: A test of the spiral of silence theory in Singapore. *International Journal of Public Opinion Research, 14*(4), 391–412.

Wilson, B.J., Kunkel, D., Linz, D., Potter, J., Donnerstein, E., Smith, S.L., Blumenthal, E., & Gray, T. (1997). *National television violence Study: Volume 1.* Thousand Oaks, CA: SAGE Publications.

Wilson, B.J., Linz, D., Donnerstein, E., & Stipp, H. (1992). The impact of social issue television programming on attitudes toward rape. *Human Communication Research, 19,* 179–208.

Wilson, W.C. (1978). Can pornography contribute to the prevention of sexual problems? In C.B. Qualls, J.P. Wincze, & D.H. Barlow (Eds.), *The prevention of sexual disorders: Issues and approaches* (pp. 159–179). New York: Plenum.

Wimmer, R.D., & Dominick, J.R. (2000). *Mass media research: An introduction* (6th edn.). Belmont, CA: Wadsworth.

Winick, C. (1971). *A study of consumers of explicitly sexual materials: Some function served by adult movies. Technical report of the Commission on Obscenity and Pornography* (Vol. 4, pp. 245–262). Washington, DC: U.S. Government Printing Office.

Winslow, G. (2012, October 30). Sandy blasts record digital traffic. *Broadcasting & Cable*. Retrieved from: http://www.broadcastingcable.com/article/490163-Sandy_Blasts_Record_Digital_Traffic.php.

Wober, J.M. (1978). Televised violence and paranoid perception: The view from Great Britain. *Public Opinion Quarterly, 42,* 315–321.

Wober, J.M., & Gunter, B. (1986). Television audience research at Britain's Independent Broadcasting Authority, 1974–1984. *Journal of Broadcasting & Electronic Media, 30,* 15–31.

Wong, K.C. (2006). The making of the USA PATRIOT Act II: Public sentiments, legislative climate, political gamesmanship, media patriotism. *International Journal of the Sociology of Law, 34,* 105–140.

Wood, J. V. (1989). Theory and research concerning social comparisons of personal attribute. *Psychological Bulletin*, *106*, 231–248.

Wood, W., Wong, F. Y., & Chachere, J. G. (1991). Effects of media violence on viewers' aggression in unconstrained social interaction. *Psychological Bulletin*, *109*, 371–383.

Woodward, G. C. (1993). The rules of the game: The military and the press in the Persian Gulf War. In R. E. Denton, Jr. (Ed.), *The media and the Persian Gulf War* (pp. 1–26). Westport, CT: Praeger.

Wosnitzer, R., & Bridges, A. (2007, May). Aggression and sexual behavior in best-selling pornography: A content analysis update. Paper presented at the International Communication Association annual convention, San Francisco, CA.

Wright, C. R. (1986). *Mass communication: A sociological perspective* (3rd edn.). New York: Random House.

Wright, P. J., Malamuth, N. M., & Donnerstein, E. (2012). Research on sex in the media: What do we know about effects on children and adolescents?. In D. G. Singer & J. L. Singer (Eds.), *Handbook of children and the media* (2nd edn.). Los Angeles: SAGE.

Wright, P. J. (2009). Sexual socialization messages in mainstream entertainment mass media: A review and synthesis. *Sexuality & Culture*, *13*, 181–200.

Wright, P. L. (1974). Analyzing media effects on advertising responses. *Public Opinion Quarterly*, *38*, 192–205.

Wright, P. L. (1981). Cognitive responses to mass media advocacy. In R. E. Petty, T. M. Ostrom, & T. C. Brock (Eds.), *Cognitive responses to persuasion* (pp. 263–282). Hillsdale, NJ: Lawrence Erlbaum Associates.

Wu, W., & Koo, S. H. (2001). Perceived effects of sexually explicit internet content: The third-person effect in Singapore. *Journalism & Mass Communication Quarterly*, *78*, 260–274.

Wurtzel, A., & Lometti, G. (1987). Researching television violence. In A. A. Berger (Ed.)., *Television in society* (pp. 117–132). New Brunswick, NJ: Transaction.

Wyer, R. S., Jr., & Srull, T. K. (1986). Human cognition in its social context. *Psychological Review*, *93*, 322–359.

Xenos, M. A., & Becker, A. B. (2009). Moments of zen: Effects of *The Daily Show* on information seeking and political learning. *Political Communication*, *26*, 317–332.

Yaffe, M. (1982). Therapeutic uses of sexually explicit material. In M. Yaffe & E. C. Nelson (Eds.), *The influence of pornography on behavior* (pp. 119–150). London, Academic Press.

Yang, J. A., & Grabe, M. E. (2011). Knowledge acquisition gaps: A comparison of print versus online news sources. *New Media & Society*, *13*(8), 1211–1227.

Yang, M. (2013, May 11). Watch: Chris Christie's fleece jacket parody. *Time*. Retrieved from: http://newsfeed.time.com/2013/05/11/watch-chris-christies-fleece-jacket-parody/.

Ybema, J. F., & Buunk, B. P. (1993). Aiming at the top? Upward social comparison of abilities after failure. *European Journal of Social Psychology*, *23*, 627–645.

Yee, N., & Bailenson, J. (2007). The Proteus Effect: The effect of transformed self-representation on behavior. *Human Communication Research*, *33*, 271–290.

Yi, R. H. P., & Dearfield, C. T. (2012). *The status of women in the U.S. media 2012.* New York: Women's Media Center. Retrieved from: http://wmc.3cdn.net/a6b2 dc282c824e903a_arm6b0hk8.pdf.

Yokota, F., & Thompson, K. M. (2000). Violence in G-rated animated films. *Journal of the American Medical Association*, *283*, 2716–2720.

Youn, S., Faber, R. J., & Shah, D. V. (2000). Restricting gambling advertising and the third-person effect. *Psychology & Marketing*, *17*, 633–649.

Young, D. G. (2008). The privileged role of the late-night joke: Exploring humor's role in disrupting argument scrutiny. *Media Psychology*, *11*, 119–142.

Young, D.G. (2012, August). Laughter, Learning, or Enlightenment? Viewing and avoidance motivations behind *The Daily Show* and *The Colbert Report*. Paper presented at the American Political Science Association annual meeting in New Orleans.

Young, D.G., & Tisinger, R.M. (2006). Dispelling late-night myths: News consumption among late-night comedy viewers and the predictors of exposure to various late-night shows. *The International Journal of Press/Politics, 11*, 113–134.

Young, J.T. (1923). *The new American government and its work*. New York: Macmillan.

Yum, Y., & Schenck-Hamlin, W. (2005). Reactions to 9/11 as a function of terror management and perspective taking. *Journal of Social Psychology, 145*, 265–286.

Zaller, J. (1996). The myth of mass media impact revived. In D.C. Mutz, P.M. Sniderman, & R.A. Brody (Eds.), *Political persuasion and attitude change* (pp. 17–78). Ann Arbor: University of Michigan Press.

Zeng, L. (2011). More than audio on the go: Uses and gratifications of mp3 players. *Communication Research Reports, 28*, 97–108.

Zettl, H. (1973). *Sight sound motion: Applied media aesthetics*. Belmont, CA: Wadsworth.

Zettl, H. (2008). *Sight, sound, motion: Applied media aesthetics* (5th edn.). Boston, MA: Wadsworth Cengage.

Zhang, Y., Miller, L.E., & Harrison, K. (2008). The relationship between exposure to sexual music videos and young adults' sexual attitudes. *Journal of Broadcasting & Electronic Media, 52*, 368–386.

Zhao, X., & Cai, X. (2008). From self-enhancement to supporting censorship: The third-person effect process in the case of internet pornography. *Mass Communication & Society, 11*(4), 437–462.

Zillmann, D. (1971). Excitation-transfer in communication-mediated aggressive behavior. *Journal of Experimental Social Psychology, 7*, 419–434.

Zillmann, D. (1980). Anatomy of suspense. In P.H. Tannenbaum (Ed.), *The entertainment functions of television* (pp. 133–163). Hillsdale, NJ: Lawrence Erlbaum Associates.

Zillmann, D. (1982). Television viewing and arousal. In D. Pearl, L. Bouthilet, & J. Lazar (Eds.), *Television and behavior: Ten years of scientific progress and implications for the eighties* (DHHS Publication No. ADM 82–1196, pp. 53–67). Washington, DC: U.S. Government Printing Office.

Zillmann, D. (1989). Effects of prolonged consumption of pornography. In D. Zillmann & J. Bryant (Eds.), *Pornography: Research advances & policy considerations* (pp. 127–157). Hillsdale, NJ: Lawrence Erlbaum Associates.

Zillmann, D. (1991a). The logic of suspense and mystery. In J. Bryant & D. Zillmann (Eds.), *Responding to the screen: Reception and reaction processes* (pp. 281–303). Hillsdale, NJ: Lawrence Erlbaum Associates.

Zillmann, D. (1991b). Television viewing and arousal. In J. Bryant & D. Zillmann (Eds.), *Responding to the screen: Reception and reaction processes* (pp. 103–133). Hillsdale, NJ: Lawrence Erlbaum Associates.

Zillmann, D. (1998). The psychology of the appeal of portrayals of violence. In J H. Goldstein (Ed.), *Why we watch: The attractions of violent entertainment* (pp. 170–211). New York: Oxford.

Zillmann, D. (2000). The coming of media entertainment. In D. Zillmann & P. Vorderer (Eds.), *Media entertainment: The psychology of its appeal* (pp. 1–20). Mahwah, NJ: Lawrence Erlbaum Associates.

Zillmann, D. (2010). Excitation transfer theory. In W. Donsbach (Ed.), *The international encyclopedia of communication*. Boston, MA: Blackwell Publishing.

Zillmann, D., & Bryant, J. (1974). Effect of residual excitation on the emotional response to provocation and delayed aggressive behavior. *Journal of Personality and Social Psychology, 30*, 782–791.

Zillmann, D., & Bryant, J. (1982). Pornography, sexual callousness, and the trivialization of rape. *Journal of Communication, 32*(4), 10–21.

Zillmann, D., & Bryant, J. (1984). Effects of massive exposure to pornography. In N. M. Malamuth & E. Donnerstein (Eds.), Pornography and sexual aggression (pp. 115–138). New York: Academic Press.

Zillmann, D., & Bryant, J. (1985). Affect, mood, and emotion as determinants of selective exposure. In D. Zillmann & J. Bryant (Eds.), *Selective exposure to communication* (pp. 157–190). Hillsdale, NJ: Lawrence Erlbaum Associates.

Zillmann, D., & Bryant, J. (1986a). A response. *Journal of Communication, 36*(1), 184–188.

Zillmann, D., & Bryant, J. (1986b). Shifting preferences in pornography consumption. *Communication Research, 13*, 560–578.

Zillmann, D., & Bryant, J. (1987). A reply. *Journal of Communication, 37*(3), 189–192.

Zillmann, D., & Bryant, J. (1988). Pornography's impact on sexual satisfaction. *Journal of Applied Social Psychology, 18*, 438–453.

Zillmann, D., Bryant, J., Comisky, P. W., & Medoff, N. J. (1981). Excitation and hedonic valence in the effect of erotica on motivated intermale aggression. *European Journal of Social Psychology, 11*, 233–252.

Zillmann, D., Bryant, J., & Sapolsky, B. S. (1989). Enjoyment from sports spectatorship. In J. H. Goldstein (Ed.), *Sports, games, and play: Social and psychological viewpoints* (2nd edn., pp. 241–278). Hillsdale, NJ: Lawrence Erlbaum Associates.

Zillmann, D., & Cantor, J. (1972). Directionality of transitory dominance as a communication variable affecting humor appreciation. *Journal of Personality and Social Psychology, 24*, 191–198.

Zillmann, D., & Cantor, J. (1977). Affective responses to the emotions of a protagonist. *Journal of Experimental Social Psychology, 13*, 155–165.

Zillmann, D., & Gibson, R. (1996). Evolution of the horror genre. In J. B. Weaver, III and R. Taborini (Eds.), *Horror films: Current research on audience preferences and reactions* (pp. 15–31). Mahwah, NJ: Erlbaum.

Zillmann, D., Hay, T. A., & Bryant, J. (1975). The effect of suspense and its resolution on the appreciation of dramatic presentations. *Journal of Research in Personality, 9*, 307–323.

Zillmann, D., Hezel, R. T., & Medoff, N. J. (1980). The effect of affective states on selective exposure to televised entertainment fare. *Journal of Applied Social Psychology, 10*, 323–339.

Zillmann, D., & Weaver, J. B. (1989). Pornography and men's sexual callousness toward women. In D. Zillmann & J. Bryant (Eds.), *Pornography: Research advances & policy considerations* (pp. 95–125). Hillsdale, NJ: Lawrence Erlbaum Associates.

Zillmann, D. & Weaver, III, J. B. (1996). Gender-socialization theory of reactions to horror. In J. B. Weaver, III and R. Taborini (Eds.), *Horror films: Current research on audience preferences and reactions* (pp. 81–101). Mahwah, NJ: Erlbaum.

Zillmann, D., Weaver, J., Mundorf, N., & Aust, C. (1986). Effects of an opposite-gender companion's affect to horror on distress, delight, and attraction. *Journal of Personality and Social Psychology, 51*, 586–594.

Zimmerman, F. J., & Bell, J. F. (2010). Association of television content type and obesity in children. *American Journal of Public Health, 100*(2), 334–340.

Zimmerman, F. J., & Christakis, D. A. (2007). Associations between content types of early media exposure and subsequent attentional problems. *Pediatrics, 120*(5), 986–992.

Zucker, H. G. (1978). The variable nature of news influence. In B. D. Ruben (Ed.), *Communication yearbook* (Vol. 2, pp. 225–240). New Brunswick, NJ: Transaction.

Zuckerman, M. (1994). *Behavioral expressions of biosocial bases of sensation seeking.* Cambridge: Cambridge University Press.

Zuckerman, M. (1996). Sensation seeking and the taste for vicarious horror. In J. B. Weaver, III, & R. Tamborini (Eds.), *Horror films: Current research on audience preferences and reactions* (pp. 147–160). Mahwah, NJ: Lawrence Erlbaum Associates.

Zuckerman, M., & Litle, P. (1986). Personality and curiosity about morbid and sexual events. *Personality and Individual Differences*, 7, 49–56.

Zurbriggen, E. L., & Morgan, E. M. (2006). Who wants to marry a millionaire? Reality dating television programs, attitudes toward sex, and sexual behaviors. *Sex Roles*, 54(1/2), 1–17.

INDEX

theories 202–5; political attitudes effects 237; realism of 32–3; reducing impact of 220–1; sexually violent content 212–19; strength of effect 8, 9; theories of null effects 206–9
Virginia earthquake 2012 69
visual content 139–40
voluntary attention 130–1
voter turnout 119–21
voting decisions 4, 13, 28, 30, 48, 49, 113, 238; effect of public opinion polls 117–19

war reporting 80–1, 82
web-based media *see* internet
women: character stereotypes 159–60; gender-stereotyped television

commercials 48; representation in media 158–60; tv program preferences in pregnancy 41–2; violence against 213, 215, 217, 218; *see also* gender differences
Women, Action, & the Media (WAM!) 167–8
World Trade Centre attack (9/11) 56–7, 62, 64, 65; absence of critical reporting 80; disruption of media 71; misreporting 73; news diffusion 70; social impact of reporting 77

"yellow ribbon" stories 61, 80, 81
Yom Kippur War 58, 61